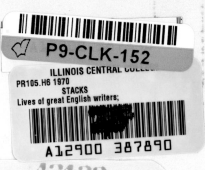

LIVES OF
GREAT ENGLISH WRITERS

FROM CHAUCER TO BROWNING

GEOFFREY CHAUCER

LIVES OF
GREAT ENGLISH WRITERS

FROM CHAUCER TO BROWNING

BY

WALTER S. HINCHMAN

AND

FRANCIS B. GUMMERE

Essay Index Reprint Series

 BOOKS FOR LIBRARIES PRESS
FREEPORT, NEW YORK

PR
105
.H6
1970

INTERNATIONAL STANDARD BOOK NUMBER:
0-8369-1930-0

LIBRARY OF CONGRESS CATALOG CARD NUMBER:
74-106409

PRINTED IN THE UNITED STATES OF AMERICA

INTRODUCTION

Not long ago, Mr. Walter S. Hinchman, who had been teaching English at Groton School for five years, called my attention to the need of a book which should give in succinct but comprehensive form the lives of the great English authors. Both for the student, who is required to show his real knowledge of these authors in examination, and for the general reader, who wishes to come at the heart of their work with as little hampering as possible from books about books, the main object should be first-hand acquaintance with good literature. But this first-hand acquaintance is too often delayed, clouded, endangered, by the preliminary courses in literary history, with their third-hand comments on æsthetical and critical questions, and their efforts, by phrases and formulas, often hopelessly mixed in the reader's memory, to impress literary values on minds that have not yet encountered literature. Some sort of preparation is needed; no one doubts that; but the preparation should be direct, inciting, practical. To prepare the student or the general reader for the various works which he is to undertake, to give him a perspective of them, and to rouse his interest in the men who wrote them, as well as to save actual time for this first-hand reading of them, he needs, not barren formulas and catchwords about æsthetic values, but a series of biographies of the great writers, shorn of all literary criticism save that which serves to characterize the writers and give them their due places. These biographies must present the author as he lived, note his surroundings, and give the pertinent facts of his life. Short transitional chapters should supply the connections of group with group, and create the proper impression of continuity in the course of English literature. A brief bibliography, a chronological table, and a literary map are obvious adjuncts to the plan.

So much for the general purpose of this volume as Mr. Hinchman conceived it. As for details of execution, to include in one volume the Great Writers of English Literature, one must exercise a choice that will not always go unchallenged. Fielding, greatest of our novelists, will be noted at once as an omission; but Fielding concerns the student less than many an inferior writer, and to make genius and literary prominence the sole test would have drawn in Ben Jonson, Marlowe, Herrick, and others, who would have stretched the volume to an impossible bulk. On the other hand, Ralegh, included as a typical Elizabethan, would yield to the superior literary claims of many who are not to be found in the list. The selection is intended to be representative.

Mr. Hinchman's ideas, derived from actual experience in preparatory English work, seemed sound; and it was determined that they should be embodied in the present book. He is responsible not only for the whole plan and purpose, but for most of the actual work. My own contributions are the lives of Chaucer, Spenser, Bacon, Shakespeare, Dryden, Johnson, Tennyson, Thackeray, and Matthew Arnold.

FRANCIS B. GUMMERE.

HAVERFORD, January, 1908.

CONTENTS

ILLUSTRATIONS

GREAT ENGLISH WRITERS

GEOFFREY CHAUCER

GEOFFREY CHAUCER is rightly called the father of
English poetry. There were English poets before him,
but the language which they spoke and wrote needs to
be studied by their descendants of to-day as if it were
a foreign tongue. The great chasm of the Conquest
sunders these Old English or Anglo-Saxon poets from
Chaucer's time; except in scattered dialects English literature had ceased as a national institution. The period
covered by Chaucer's life witnessed the birth of a new
English nation and a new English language. Of this
new nation Chaucer is a worthy representative, and indeed by the last years of his century he was the greatest
poet in Europe; by writing in English, moreover, he
established the traditions of our standard or literary
speech, which has been, with few changes, the dialect of
London and the Thames valley. By his persistent use
of English Chaucer showed his profound appreciation
of the forces which were at work about him. In 1300
French had been deliberately chosen as the language
which the people at large would best understand; in
1362, when the poet was barely twenty years of age, a
famous statute provided that all pleas in the courts
should be carried on in English, because French was
no longer known by the average client. By 1385, says
a chronicler of the time, even the gentry were neglecting
to teach their children French. Once more, too, national

feeling was English, and the wars with France served
to weld the nation into patriotic unity. The common
people asserted themselves more and more; Parliament
acquired new power and significance; and in many ways
the England of modern times may be said to date from
this fourteenth century.

Chaucer was born in London, perhaps on Thames
Street, about the year 1340. The name indicates Norman extraction, but the family had evidently been settled in England for some time. John Chaucer, the father,
was a vintner, a wine merchant; but this calling, like
that of the great English brewer of modern times, was
not regarded as a bar to aristocratic pretensions. Indeed, the merchant class generally had pushed to the
front, and were of great importance in English life.
While we have no exact information about Chaucer's
father, we may rightly assume what his station and
privileges were from the case of another vintner, Lewis
Johan, a Welshman who acquired the rights of a London
citizen and whom Professor Kittredge has recently established as a city-friend of the poet himself. It was at
supper in his house that Henry Scogan read the *Moral
Balade*, against foolish waste of time and in praise of
virtue and godliness, to the Prince of Wales, Shakespeare's Prince Hal, and his three brothers, Clarence,
Bedford, and Gloucester, sons of Henry IV. Professor
Kittredge infers that Lewis Johan was a vintner, "and
that he kept a restaurant, a fourteenth-century Sherry's,
at which young men of the highest rank were accustomed to dine." We find Johan, along with others,
presenting a large bill for wine furnished to the King;
moreover, like the goldsmiths, wealthy vintners were
engaged in banking; and in 1414 Johan obtained for

three years exclusive privileges of issuing bills of exchange for the Court of Rome, the Republic of Venice, and elsewhere. In 1422 he " asked to be relieved of the office of Master of the Coinage in the tower of London." Such a combination of city and court interests we may assume for Chaucer's father, accounting thus for the poet's range of sympathies.

Thus Chaucer himself, though not on a footing with nobility, was early received at court. It is true that he became the aristocratic poet of his time and country, leaving to a wandering priest like Langland the task of speaking for the common man, the ploughman and laborer ; but he was not spoiled by his associations ; he was interested in all classes of society, and, like Tennyson, he warned his readers that to be " descended out of old richesse " is not enough for " gentil " men. " Whoso," he says, " tries most —

> To do the gentil dedes that he kan,
> Taak hym for the grettest gentil man."

Allowing for the objective and conventional in these lines, one must nevertheless credit Chaucer with their sentiment, just as in dealing with the Church he sunders so rigorously the hypocrites and time-servers from the followers of Christ. On the whole, Chaucer's attitude, while distinctly sympathetic with the higher classes, is not that of a man who is fettered by the prejudices of his birth.

The poet's career followed the traditions of his family. His grandfather, Robert le Chaucer, had been a collector of the Port of London in 1310, and left an estate in lands. The father, besides inheriting this property and carrying on his business as a vintner, is

twice recorded as discharging public duties, now in
connection with the corporation of wine-merchants,
and now in affairs of the Court. He is said to have
accompanied Edward III to the Continent. Geoffrey
began with what we should call domestic service in a
royal household. The accounts of Elizabeth, wife of
Prince Lionel, son of Edward III, show that in April,
1357, an entire suit of clothes, cloak, " red and black
breeches, and shoes," were bought for Geoffrey Chaucer, and cost seven shillings, — say about twenty-five
dollars of our money. From the same source a gift of
two shillings and sixpence — say about ten dollars —
was bestowed upon him the next winter in Yorkshire
" for necessaries at Christmas."

How or where he was educated is not a matter of
record. He was probably taught to translate Latin into
French, and doubtless learned to use the former language as a living tongue. That he could make mistakes in reading it, several passages in his works bear
witness, notably in the *House of Fame*, where " per-
nicibus alis " is translated by " partridge's wings." His
knowledge of science, as science was then understood,
was fairly extensive, and is best shown by his treatise
on the Astrolabe, written in 1391 for " his little son
Lowis." Works like this, of course, could be translated
in bulk, but there are many scattered references which
testify to his general reading. While he took on faith
much that to us seems absurd, he could make fun
both of scholastic philosophy and of such a treatise
as Vinesauf's *Poetria*, a manual of practical poetics.
Attempts to connect him, now with Oxford, now with
Cambridge, are idle; like Shakespeare, he probably
got his best education from the busy life in which he

shared, the men of talent and achievement whom he met, and, unlike Shakespeare, from his wide and frequent travels. Records of this busy life have been found in abundance, and new discoveries are not out of the question.

Like all young men of his rank, Chaucer took part in the war with France, and was made prisoner there about the age of nineteen. The King paid a large sum toward his ransom. By 1367 he received a yearly pension for life, as one of the yeomen of the King's chamber. At first he may be supposed to have held torches and carried messages, and he is even credited with making the King's bed. But he soon rose to more dignified service with the rank of squire. All these experiences, his stay in France, his taste of war, his association with the King, did more for his own literary work than anything he may have read. War itself was at that time as romantic as war can well be, and, so far as the knights and upper classes were concerned, was carried on with extraordinary courtesy. Edward III was a pattern of the virtues of chivalry, and other monarchs of the day were not to be outdone, — when the Prince of France escaped from his prison in London, the old French King thought it incumbent on himself to cross the channel and take the fugitive's place. Even the humbler men-at-arms caught the infection, and one would like to think that some ballad of the Cheviot fight, or of Otterburne, reached the ears of Chaucer. His two knights, Palamon and Arcite, who fight each other for their lady-love, are not to be outdone in generous and chivalric conduct by the Percy and the Douglas themselves. Arcite, fully armed, finds his rival helpless and without weapon, but will not take

this foul advantage, promising instead to bring fighting
gear for battle on the morrow, and bidding his opponent to " choose the best, and leave the worst for me."
It was doubtless some humble singer of Chaucer's own
day who made the stanza about Percy's noble sorrow:

> " The Persë leanyde on his brande,
>   And sawe the Duglas de ;
> He tooke the dede mane by the hande,
>   And sayd, ' Wo ys me for the ! ' "

It is well to remember that Chaucer could breathe this
spirit in English air under Edward III, and to think
how different his inspiration would have been from the
brutal and degenerate times of Edward IV, a century
later. The gallery of portraits in the Prologue to the
Canterbury Tales not only affords a view of the actual
life which Chaucer led, and of the men and women
whom he daily met, but gives us some insight into the
tastes and preferences of the poet himself. The knight is
Chaucer's ideal man in high place; he loves "chivalrie,

> " trouthe and honour, fredom and courteisie."

He fights in far-off lands, now for some worthy master
and now for the Christian faith. He is kind and considerate to lowly folk as well as to his peers, and in his bearing " meek as a maid." His horse and weapons must
be of the best, but his dress is plain. To this pattern of
virtue the poet bows with unalloyed respect, and pays
compliments as sincere, if more familiar, to the squire.
The yeoman is praised as a good archer and forester ;
the prioress comes in for a little harmless satire, but
holds her own in courtesy and refinement. The monk,
another aristocrat, has to feel the real sting of the lash,
and so has the begging friar. Towards the merchant

Chaucer is somewhat too curt, if not contemptuous, forgetting his name. The lawyer and the doctor are lightly touched ; the shipman is called a good fellow and shown to be a pirate. The Oxford scholar gets Chaucer's sincerest and finest tribute of praise. The franklin, or country squire, is treated as an epicure ; the parson and his humble brother the ploughman are nobly portrayed in his most sympathetic vein. He finds vulgarity interesting in the Wife of Bath and in the miller, and shows more actual dislike, sturdy Englishman as he is, for the summoner and for the pardoner, tools for the meanest functions of the Church, than for any one else. Amid these various touches of reverence, sympathy, tolerance, disdain, nothing is more striking than Chaucer's appreciation of humble life. Thus in one of the Tales we find the description of a carter, first swearing at his horses as they pull in vain at their load, and then praising them for the final and triumphant struggle.

After serving as page and soldier, Chaucer seems to have been employed mainly in court affairs, and when he was over thirty he was intrusted with diplomatic errands. Beginning with missions to neighboring countries like Flanders, he was at last sent to Italy. Here he came in contact with the best learning and the noblest literature of the time. Whether he met Petrarch and Boccaccio cannot now be known, though it was entirely possible for Chaucer to have met them both ; and as the English poet had already made some reputation on the Continent, there is no reason why one should not fancy the great humanist Petrarch conversing with his far-come visitor at Padua in 1373. Chaucer's tribute to Petrarch at the beginning of the *Clerk's Tale* is couched in terms of the highest eulogy, but neither implies nor disavows the assumption of personal friendship. His stay in Italy was not long; but he made more than one visit, and came to be master of the language. He learned to admire and use the poems of Dante, whose influence is to be traced in the *House of Fame* and elsewhere, and especially of Boccaccio, from whom he paraphrased and adapted some of his longest and best poems.

Chaucer was an adherent of John of Gaunt, Duke of Lancaster, ambitious younger son of Edward III, and there seems to be good ground for assuming closer relations between the two. As early as 1366 the poet was probably married to one Philippa, a lady of the Queen's chamber, who then received a pension for life. It seems fairly certain that she was the sister of Katharine Swinford, who had been governess to John of Gaunt's daughters, and whom the Duke finally married as his third wife. In any case Chaucer was bound by no ordinary ties to this prince, and the connection must explain many of the favors he received from the court as well as the renewal of bounty which came to him so promptly with the accession of Henry IV, the Duke of Lancaster's son. One of the earliest poems which Chaucer wrote, *The Dethe of Blaunche the Duchesse*, is an elegy on the Duke's first wife, who died in 1369. It shows careful study of French models, but is not without its own force and beauty, though there is no sign of the qualities developed in Chaucer's later work. Another poem, written about this time, *The Compleynt unto Pite*, which passes as the poet's first original work, and is written in the so-called Chaucerian stanza, is regarded by many scholars as an expression of unrequited love, and is supposed to be " founded on fact." However this may be, Chaucer was certainly married and was certainly of the party of John of Gaunt. In our own day such work as he did on the Duke's behalf would be called political, and we are not surprised to find that the poet's fortunes rose and fell with his chief. Like modern politicians, too, Chaucer received important appointments besides his diplomatic work. He was Comptroller of the Customs, and for a long time worked hard at this and other duties. In one of the passages in his poems which count as autobiographical he tells how strenuous was his official life, how tired the evening found him, and how little leisure he had to devote to his favorite books. He is so busy, says the eagle in the *House of Fame* to the poet, —

> " That ther no tydyng cometh to thee,
> But of thy verray neyghebores,
> That dwellen almost at thy dores,
> Thou herest neither that ne this ;
> For when thy labour doon al is,
> And hast y-maad thy rekenynges,
> In stede of reste and newè thynges,
> Thou gost hoom to thy hous anoon,
> And, also domb as any stoon,
> Thou sittest at another boke,
> Til fully daswed [1] is thy looke,
> And lyvest thus as an heremyte,[2]
> Although thyn abstynence is lyte." [3]

In other words, he was an industrious official and a diligent student, — for it must be remembered that poetry and learning were nearer neighbors then than now, — and he was fond of good living. We shall see that he describes himself elsewhere as distinctly corpulent. He could not complain, however, of any lack of compensation. From the King he had the grant of a

---

[1] Dazed.   [2] Hermit.   [3] Little.

pitcher of wine daily ; after three years of this bounty
he contrived to have it exchanged for a second pension.
In 1374 another pension came to him from John of
Gaunt, and in the next year he was made guardian of
the estates of two minors, a profitable office at that
time. Later he was again engaged in diplomatic missions abroad, in Flanders, in France, and in Italy. This
brings him to his fortieth year, and for six years more
his prosperity continued, although there is no record
of foreign travel. He obtained another appointment as
Comptroller, and was allowed to have his work done by
deputy in both offices. Moreover he seems to have employed an amanuensis for his literary work ; but this
luxury was not without its drawbacks. The scribe made
frequent mistakes in taking down the master's words :

> " Adam Scriveyn, if ever it thee bifalle
> Boece or Troylus for to writen newe,
> Under thy long lokkes thou most have the scalle [1]
> But [2] after my making [3] thou write more trewe.
> So oft a day I mot thy werk renewe,
> Hit to correcte and eek to rubbe and scrape ;
> And al is through thy negligence and rape." [4]

The *Boece* to which the poet refers is his translation of the *Consolation of Philosophy*, by Boethius,
perhaps the most popular book of the Middle Ages.
Before Chaucer King Alfred had translated it into
Anglo-Saxon. Chaucer's knowledge of Latin was not
profound enough to make him free of a French translation already published, or to save him from some bad
mistakes. The *Troilus* we shall presently consider.

Through all these years of prosperity, which cul-
minated in 1386, when the poet was made member

---

[1] Scab.   [2] Unless.
[3] According to my composition.   [4] Hurry.

of Parliament for Kent, Chaucer lived in lodgings granted him by the city in the tower over Aldgate, and here he must have written some of his best known works. In his younger days his poetry seems to have been nearer those French models which were still the favorite literature of the court and higher classes generally in England. He had translated that great mediæval allegory, the *Romaunt of the Rose*, and had written poems like the *Boke of the Duchesse*. While it is perhaps too much to speak of an Italian period, it is certain that Italian poetry exercised a great influence on his more mature work. The *House of Fame* owes much to Dante, and *Troilus and Criseyde*, though full of vital original work, is taken from Boccaccio's *Filostrato*. In some respects this is Chaucer's masterpiece. In any case it combines the best traditions and culture of Italy with the more serious standards of the new English life.

The last twenty years of Chaucer's life seem to have been spent mainly in England; and again, though it is hardly fair to speak of an English period as contrasted with the Italian and the French, it is certain that Chaucer now planned his *Canterbury Tales* and wrote that prologue which gives him his best claim upon our remembrance. This is wholly English in its character and conception. Boccaccio gathered his ladies and gentlemen together in the Florentine villa and let them tell their charming tales; but there is neither character in the description of the group nor fitness in the relation between the tale and its teller. The pilgrims, twenty-nine in number, not only represent all sorts and conditions of English life at the time, but stand out in sharpest outline as individuals, and the tale in each case fits its narrator. The prologue was composed in Chaucer's later life, perhaps about the year 1387. Some of the actual tales were doubtless written with the Canterbury idea in mind, but it is certain that others were older poems which the author revised for the purpose. The plan was not half carried out; there *were* to be two tales for each pilgrim on the way to Becket's shrine at Canterbury, and two on the return. But for such tales as we have and for the glimpses at that pilgrim company, now in the Tabard Inn and now riding by Rochester and Sittingbourne, or by the mysterious Bob-up-and-Down, under Blee forest, we may be thankful enough. So fresh and bright are these glimpses that one feels sure Chaucer must have made the journey himself.

Another considerable poem of this period is the unfinished *Legende of Good Women*, in which he professes to atone for some of his satire against the sex. The prologue to this poem exists in two versions and contains passages which have been repeatedly quoted as autobiographical. Nothing, says the writer, can take him from his books, save only when the month of May comes with its birds and flowers. Then —

> " Farewel my boke and my devocion! "

He goes on to speak of his worship of the daisy. Probably the passage just quoted is true enough for Chaucer's case; but the praise of the daisy, along with other parts of this prologue, is taken directly from the French.

In spite of Chaucer's official duties and the studious habits which he professed, he must have taken part in the pursuits and diversions of his class. What some of these diversions were may be gathered from the numerous allusions to the contest for excellence between the

Flower and the Leaf; indeed a later poem under that
title was long attributed to Chaucer himself. The poet,
in the Prologue to the *Legende of Good Women*, says
that he has not undertaken to write poetry on behalf of
the Leaf against the Flower or for the Flower against
the Leaf; but it is certain that "English court society,
in the time of Richard II, entertained itself by divid-
ing into two amorous orders — the Leaf and the Flower
— and by discussing, no doubt with an abundance of
allegorical imagery, the comparative excellence of those
two emblems or of the qualities they typified." It is
supposed "that the two orders sometimes appeared in
force, each member bedecked with the symbol to which
he or she had sworn allegiance." One of the French
poets, Deschamps, in a charming little poem, names
Philippa of Lancaster as heading the faction of the
Flower. Another poem by the same writer, sent along
with certain of his works to the English poet, not only
praises Chaucer as the great translator but mentions
an Englishman, " presumably a friend of both poets,"
about whom much is known and whose story throws
considerable light on the ways of Chaucer himself.[1] If
this friendship be established, there is great probability
that Chaucer must have taken his side in a far more
serious contest, and supported, along with John of
Gaunt, the followers of Wyclif against the orthodox
party of Rome. It is usual to accept Chaucer as a good
churchman, in spite of his satire, and to reject the insin-
uation that he was a Lollard; and if his works alone
decided the question, there would be no quarrel with
this conclusion. But John of Gaunt was an ardent

[1] These facts are taken from an interesting paper by Professor Kittredge, " Chaucer and Some of his Friends," *Modern Philology*, I, 1.

defender of Wyclif; Chaucer was of the Duke's party; and the life of Chaucer's supposed friend Clifford adds weight to this evidence for the poet's sympathy with reform. It seems probable that he was Sir Lewis Clifford, somewhat older than Chaucer and a member of the household of the Black Prince. Like the Duke, he was a patron and protector of the Lollards. Froissart praises him as a valiant knight for his jousting in a tournament near Calais; and besides this he was active in diplomatic and domestic affairs. Very interesting is his repentance and the recanting of the Wyclif heresy. In his death-bed will he calls himself God's traitor, and wishes to be buried in the farthest corner of the church-yard. The story of Chaucer's own death-bed repentance, told by Thomas Gascoigne, should not be rejected, thinks Professor Kittredge, without some consideration of "this unquestionably authentic document, which expresses the last wishes of a very gallant and accomplished gentleman." It is further suggested that Chaucer's son, "litell Lowis," was named after this Sir Lewis Clifford. Such are the fleeting glimpses that may be obtained of Chaucer's amusements as well as of the friendships and sterner duties to which his position called him.

In much clearer light stand Chaucer's literary friends and the disciples who carried on his poetic work when he was gone. The moral Gower, who composed poetry in three languages, a man of wealth and position, was chosen by Chaucer as one of his two representatives while he was abroad on diplomatic service in 1378. To him and to the "philosophical Strode," another friend distinguished for his learning, Chaucer dedicates the *Troilus*. Gower, who outlived Chaucer eight years, pays a compliment in the *Confessio Amantis*, his long

English poem, to Chaucer as the disciple and poet of Venus herself, for whose sake he has made "dittees" and "songes glade," with which the whole land is filled. Thomas Hoccleve, who, with John Lydgate, tried to continue Chaucer's work, must have been about thirty years old when his master died. His well-known lament is in a singularly affectionate as well as reverent vein. To this disciple the dead poet is not only "flower of eloquence," "universal father in science," "this land's very treasure and *richesse*," Tully for rhetoric, Aristotle for philosophy, and Virgil in poetry, but also the friend and the patron.

> "Alasse ! my fadir fro the worlde is goo,
>   My worthi maister Chaucer, hym I mene !
>   Be thou advoket for hym, Hevenes Quene ! "

Chaucer had good need of friends in the latter part of his life, not to praise his poetry, but to prop his tottering fortunes. 1386 has been noted as the time when his prosperity was at its height; but his party soon went out of power, and he began to lose his appointments. He gave up his house, and sold two of his pensions for ready money. To crown his misfortunes, in 1390 he was twice the victim of highwaymen, who robbed him of the King's money. The kind of friend in need for him was a friend at court; and such was Henry Scogan, who, as we have already seen, was in favor under Henry IV and deemed worthy to read a moral ballad to the young princes; at this earlier date he is asked to say a good word to Richard II : —

> "Scogan, that knelest at the stremes hede
>   Of grace, of alle honour, and worthynesse !
>   In th' ende of which stream I am dull as dede,

Forgete [1] in solitarie wildernesse ;
Yet, Scogan, thenke on Tullius kyndenesse;
Mynne [2] thy friend ther it may fructifye."

This must have been in 1393 ; the " end of the stream "
means Chaucer's enforced residence near Woolwich,
while the " stream's head " is the court at Windsor.
Another poem of this kind, and probably the last that
we have of Chaucer's composition, was addressed to
the friendship of royalty itself. Henry IV, who took
the kingdom from his cousin Richard in 1399, was the
son of Chaucer's old patron John of Gaunt. To him
the poet sends *The Compleynt of Chaucer to his Purse.*
This purse Chaucer calls his dear lady, is sorry that it
is so light, and unless it be once more heavy, he must
die. He yearns to hear the blissful clink within and to
see again the gorgeous yellow of the coin. He is shaved,
he says, as close as a friar. With this last flicker of his
humor goes a very pathetic envoy to the king, whom he
calls Conqueror of Albion and Ruler both by his descent
and free election. The answer seems to have been
prompt, for a new pension was assigned to him in October, 1399. He leased a house in the garden of St.
Mary's chapel at Westminster, and for a scant year
enjoyed his new prosperity. On October 25, 1400, he
died and was buried in Westminster Abbey, first of the
long line who have made the Poets' Corner famous.

As for his personal appearance, we have not only his
humorous description of himself when his turn comes
to narrate in the Canterbury Pilgrim throng, but the
portrait which Hoccleve had painted in the manuscript
of that poem from which we have already quoted lines of
eulogy and affection. Dr. Furnivall describes the face as

---

[1] Forgotten.   [2] Make mention of.

"wise and tender, full of a sweet and kindly sadness at first sight, but with much *bonhomie* in it on a further look, and with deep-set far-looking gray eyes." The moustache is gray, the hair shows white under the black hood; "two tufts of white beard are on the chin." In the *Tales* Chaucer is described by Harry Bailey the host as shaped in the waist like himself, that is, a very fat man; the poet, moreover, "semeth elvyssh by his contenaunce," in other words, is shy, or like a stranger, in his general bearing, and abstains from familiar talk with the other pilgrims. Portrait and description agree with the character which Chaucer has impressed upon his poetic work. He is above all an observer of men and their ways, an interested, if reticent, spectator of the life about him. He is quite contented with the spectacle and has no mind to peer beyond it into those mysteries in which poets like Milton delight. He takes his stories, his ideas, from the stock of mediæval literature, borrowing at will, as was the custom in those days. But his shrewd observations of human nature, his kindly tolerance, and above all his humor, are his own. In a very garrulous age, when long-winded romances and interminable descriptions were the fashion, he contrives to be terse and to the point. No English poet has held so closely to the language of common life.

Chaucer combines the modern and the mediæval in what seems to be a startling contrast, until one reflects upon the peculiar conditions of his time. All the traditions of his day were of the Middle Ages, but new ideas and new ideals were in the air. Like Petrarch, he could say of himself that he was set like a sentinel on the confines of two ages and looked both forward and back. He died on the eve of a long and wasting civil war, in which the

literary life in England sank to its lowest ebb; and for
a century he remained a pattern to be imitated indeed,
but in a hopelessly distant and inferior way. Father of
English poetry he remained, no less to Spenser and to
Dryden than to Hoccleve himself. To the last-named he
was " the first fyndere of our faire langage ; " to Spenser
he was " Dan Chaucer, well of English undefiled ; " to
Dryden he was " God's Plenty ; " and so great a poet
as Keats was content to " stammer where old Chaucer
used to sing."

CHAUCER TO RALEGH

THE fourteenth century in English literature means for most readers Chaucer and Chaucer alone. It was, however, marked by great productivity, and by poetic achievements which remain unknown to modern times, mainly because they were confined, as regards expression, to remote dialects or, as regards their subject, to themes in which there is scant interest to-day. One of the best of English romances was written in the North of England in Chaucer's time, and can be matched by an allegorical poem, the *Pearl*, striking for its pathos and beautiful in its style. Other religious poetry could be cited of a power seldom rivaled in the whole reach of our literature. Popular verse, too, must have flourished in notable degree; no better narrative can be found anywhere than in the Robin Hood cycle, which came to perfection in the fourteenth century. Lyric, again, was in full flower; but to all this richness and poetic activity we are wont to shut our eyes and consider Chaucer alone. It is true that with his death, in 1400, there is an abrupt decline, so far as those literary traditions are concerned which were formed in London and Oxford and have continued down to the present time as national literature in contrast to the literature of the various dialects. Chaucer's own disciples were ridiculously inadequate; and before three decades of the new century had elapsed the Wars of the Roses, with their resulting barbarism, drove poetry from court and palace into the fields. The real succession of English literature for this time must be sought in Scotland, and it was not until the comparative quiet under Henry VIII that the old traditions asserted themselves on English soil.

Meanwhile the fifteenth century is not without its poetry, though we must go afield to find it. Mr. Pollard has pointed out that English poetry could not be dead in times that produced deep and sincere religious verse, " such a dramatic lyric " as the *Nut-Brown Maid*, such Christmas carols as are found in a manuscript at Balliol College, and some of the miracle plays and moralities. Morever, two events of supreme importance mark this period of transition, — the English Bible is advancing on its sure way to the hearts of the people, and the printing-press is beginning its career. Add to these innovations such tremendous changes as the Reformation, the New Learning, the discovery of America, — above all the new attitude of men's minds toward life itself, and one sees that " transition" is a word powerless to express the change from the time of Chaucer to the time of Ralegh. Separated from Chaucer by an interval of time not much greater than that which separates us from Dr. Johnson, the men of Ralegh's day looked back on Chaucer through changes in language, changes in thought, and still more in the habit of thought, which baffled any attempt at connection. For us, Dr. Johnson lived but yesterday ; for the Elizabethan, Chaucer was a dim and venerable, only half understood, figure of the remote literary past. Spenser, as we shall see, affected to follow him, but this was very much as Virgil followed Homer. To all intents and purposes, therefore, we begin English literature anew with the poets at the court of Henry VIII ;

and *Tottel's Miscellany*, which contained the "Songs and Sonnets by Henry Howard, Earl of Surrey, Sir Thomas Wyatt the elder, Nicholas Grimald, and uncertain authors," appearing in its first edition in June, 1557, may be taken as the first milestone on the new road.

WALTER RALEGH

As a martyr Ralegh was popular with the immediately
succeeding generation; but the romantic glamor which
has grown about his name in more modern times is
perhaps chiefly due to his adventurous spirit; he is
Ralegh the sea-captain and explorer. Even in the
sixteenth century there must have been a fine atmosphere of romance about those fearless Elizabethan
sea-dogs, Ralegh, Drake, Hawkins, Grenville, and the
Gilberts. Pirates they were for the most part, but
courageous loyal Englishmen too, with honor for good
Queen Bess and unquenchable hatred for Popery and
Spain; and they deserve a conspicuous place in the
annals of their vigorous age, for more than anything
they typify its daring spirit, its lust for gain, its un-
conquerable energy, and its splendid achievements.

Yet these brave sea-captains, however typical, present a very small feature of a myriad-sided age. Ralegh
was of them, but he was more than they. He represents in his brilliant, kaleidoscopic existence, more completely than any of his contemporaries, the versatility
of his time. As a statesman he rivaled Cecil; as a
courtier, Leicester and Essex; he commanded successfully on land and sea, and was sometimes called the
" scourge of Spain;" he was an expert on naval warfare, seaport fortifications, and ship-building; he organ-
ized, financed, and conducted colonization; he sat in
Parliament for seventeen years; he erected splendid
establishments; he studied and practiced chemistry and

WALTER RALEGH

From the Zucchero portrait in the National Portrait Gallery

agriculture ; with a careless mastery he wrote poetry
surpassed only by a few ; his moral reflections are pale
only beside Bacon's; his *History of the World* was
the inspiration of a century ; in his trial he showed an
intimate knowledge of the law ; in his death he was
calm and heroic ; and his memory was a guiding star
to Eliot, Hampden, and Pym.   Defeat and despair he
knew not ; he could conceive and execute the exploits
of a dozen men, — in his own words, he could "toil
terribly."

His versatility, in fact, was his ruin.   Men feared
his indomitable will and hated him for his ability and
easy success.   He was unable, moreover, so to give
himself up to a single project that he achieved final
results in any one thing.   In his many purposes it is
indeed hard to find a paramount interest, but there
seems on the whole to have burned most deeply and
lasted longest in his heart a consuming hatred of Spain
and a passion to secure English dominion in the New
World.   He was litérally an Elizabethan ; from the
moment of James's accession he ceased to thrive.

The date of Ralegh's birth is uncertain.   It has long
been supposed 1552, but if the age given on various
portraits be correct, it may have been 1553 or 1554.
He was born in his father's farmhouse, Hayes Barton, in the parish of East Budleigh, Devon.   Ralegh's
father, also Walter Ralegh, although of the gentleman
class and a landholder, was by no means a conspicuous
figure.   The mother, however, was a notable person.
A Champernoun by birth, the third wife of Walter
Ralegh senior, she had previously been the wife of Otho
Gilbert and the mother of those stalwart sons, John,
Humphrey, and Adrian.

Very little is known of the first twenty-five years
of Ralegh's life. It is a fair conjecture that the ardent
Protestantism of his father, together with a boyhood in
Mary's reign, did much to inspire that hatred for Popery which characterized the son's life. His mother, a
Catholic, Foxe tells in his *Book of Martyrs*, had one
time visited Exeter Gaol to comfort and convert the
prisoners ; but she returned convinced of the spiritual
fortitude of the poor creatures, especially of one Agnes
Prest, much to the delight of her husband. Such incidents make indelible impressions on listening children.

Ralegh is known to have attended Oriel College,
Oxford, where he became, says Anthony à Wood, "the
ornament of the juniors, and was worthily esteemed a
proficient in oratory and philosophy." This was probably before 1569, for it is known that he was abroad
most of that year : in his *History* he speaks of himself
as one of the hundred volunteers to help the French
Huguenots and as an eye-witness at the retreat after
Moncontour. On the rolls of the Middle Temple, London, there is an entry, dated February 27, 1575, which
leaves no doubt that Ralegh intended to study law. To
Gascoigne's *Steele Glasse* (1576), moreover, there
are prefixed some verses by "Walter Rawely of the
Middle Temple." Yet it is just possible that from 1575
to 1578 he was in the Low Countries with Sir John
Norris's force under the Prince of Orange. In 1578 he
took a command in his half-brother Sir Humphrey
Gilbert's expedition to discover a northwest passage ;
there is some doubt whether he actually went, but it is
certain that he was fired with the spirit of the enterprise
and was already interested in schemes of exploration.

During the next two years Ralegh is known to have

been about court. Here, it is fair to assume, he learned
all sides of the courtier's trade. He was well acquainted,
for instance, with such important persons as Leicester
and Burleigh; and he was committed, as another instance, to Fleet Prison for six days for brawling with
Sir Thomas Perrot. Another story of these days tells
how in a tavern he sealed up the mouth of Charles
Chester, a noisy fellow, by tying the moustache and
beard together. " For there is a great laugh in Ralegh's
heart," comments Charles Kingsley, " a genial contempt
of asses ; and one that will make him enemies hereafter : perhaps shorten his days."

But Ralegh's career really began in 1580. He then
accepted the captaincy of one hundred foot to fight the
insurgents of Munster, in Ireland. In the prosecution
of his duty he was relentlessly cruel. When Limerick
capitulated, he and Macworth put to the sword, it is
said, four hundred Spaniards and Italians, — a " great
slaughter," comments John Hooker. All the Irish men
and some Irish women were hanged. In a letter to
Walsingham he complained of the mildness of his
superior's rule. " I would to God," he says, " that
he looked more to the service of Sir Humphrey Gilbert." What that service was may be guessed from
a letter of Sir Humphrey's to Sir Henry Sidney, in
which he says if a castle or fort " would not presently
yield it, I would not thereafter take it of their gift, but
won it perforce . . . putting man, woman, and child of
them to the sword." This brutality finds some explanation in the fact that the Irish were conventionally
treated as pagans or as Catholics in league with Spain.
Ireland, Ralegh said with an Elizabethan flourish, was
" a common woe, rather than a commonweal."

There are many tales of Ralegh's brilliant, daring feats as an officer in Ireland. Once he risked his life to save a wounded soldier crossing a ford; with pistols and quarterstaff he fought one against twenty until the injured man had escaped. Finally he was given, with Morgan and Piers, the lieutenancy of Munster; but in December, 1581, his company was paid and disbanded, and he returned to England.

Soon after this Ralegh came into royal favor. It is not known just how: perhaps by the famous cloak incident, when he spread a garment, the story runs, for Elizabeth to tread on in crossing a muddy place. But Queen Elizabeth, for all her vanity, was too shrewd a person in 1582 to bestow great favor on a mere gallant. What is much more likely is that a man of Ralegh's parts must have stood head and shoulders above the other courtiers. Yet in spite of his polish and wit, he still retained with some pride his broad Devon accent — as indeed he did through life. He is described as being at this time tall, with thick curly hair, beard, and moustache, bluish-gray eyes, high forehead, and long face.

Court favor with Ralegh at first meant constant duty on various commissions — such as Irish investigations and estimates for the repair of Porstmouth fortifications — rather than official positions. In 1584, however, he was elected to Parliament as a member for Devon; and early the same year he was knighted. The following year he succeeded the Earl of Bedford as Warden of the Stannaries, or tin-mines, in the West. By virtue of this position he commanded the Cornish militia and had a claim to the same power in Devon; and soon after, he received the lieutenancy of Cornwall and vice-admiralship of the two counties. In 1586, however, came a more signal honor, the captaincy of the yeomen of the guard. During these years of royal favor, moreover, Ralegh acquired by grants many confiscated lands in England and Ireland, as well as control of wine licensing,[1] all very lucrative perquisites. As he was a true Elizabethan in all things, he now began to vie with his favored contemporaries in magnificent living; he spent lavishly on gardens, building, pictures, books, and splendid, jeweled clothes. All the while, moreover, he kept up his wide interest in study, particularly in medicine, chemistry, and letters. He hired Hariot, the astronomer mathematician, to teach him, and amanuenses to copy scarce and interesting manuscripts. He is found, too, taking the part of the oppressed. There is a story of one of his gallant replies: how, upon the queen's asking him when he would " cease to be a beggar," he answered, " When your Majesty ceases to be a benefactor." He had, furthermore, some scheme for an " office of address," which both Evelyn and Southey take to have been the beginning of the Royal Society.

The most striking of all Sir Walter's activities during these twenty odd years of prosperity were, however, his interest in colonization and his warfare against Spain. He has been found a prime mover in Sir Humphrey Gilbert's expedition of 1578. In March, 1584, be obtained a patent to hold by homage " remote heathen and barbarous lands " which he might discover within the next six years. In April, therefore, he sent out two captains who landed on the North Carolina coast.

---

[1] By this patent each vintner was bound to pay Ralegh one pound annually.

A year later he dispatched Governor Ralph Lane with
a colony of 107 under his cousin Sir Richard Grenville.
But the colonists, losing courage, were taken home a
year later by Sir Francis Drake, and passed unwittingly Ralegh's third expedition, again under Grenville.
In 1587 still another colony was sent out. Ralegh spent
on the plantation, which he had named Virginia in honor
of the Queen, altogether about £40,000. All four attempts, however, were failures; and when twenty
years later the Jamestown settlement was established,
no trace of Sir Walter's settlers was visible. Yet he
had never given up hope. He continued to aid in other
expeditions, and, whatever the actual results, his zeal
was the chief cause of English dominion on the North
American coast. " I shall yet live," he said in 1603,
" to see it an English nation."

Ralegh had been forbidden by the Queen to conduct
the Virginia voyages in person. In 1587, however, the
rise of the Earl of Essex, Leicester's ingratiating stepson, brought Ralegh into sufficient disfavor to make
the court less attractive and thus actually to promote
more various activities. In the summer of 1588 he was
given a prominent part in the defense of the southwest
coast against the Spanish Armada, and during the
fight he captained a ship. The next year he accompanied as a volunteer the expedition against Portugal.

On his return Ralegh found the star of Essex still
in the ascendant. He accordingly retired to Ireland,
to look after his Munster estates. During this rustica-
tion he became familiar with Spenser, secretary to
Lord Deputy Grey. Spenser showed him parts of the
Faerie Queen, and dedicated to him the poem *Colin
Clout's Come Home Again*. At this time, too, Ralegh's

long poem to Elizabeth, whom he addressed as "Cynthia," was at least conceived and in part written. Of this work, said to have contained fifteen thousand lines, the merest fragment is preserved. Many shorter poems, some of doubtful authorship, are ascribed to his pen at this period, such poems as "The Silent Lover," "The Nymph's Reply to the Passionate Shepherd" (printed in Walton's *Compleat Angler*), "The Lie," "The Passionate Man's Pilgrimage," and an "Epitaph on Sir Philip Sidney." Yet he was careless of poetic fame; in fact the only poem he really claimed as his is the famous "Farewell to the Court." The significant thing, however, is that he was treated by his contemporaries as a poet and that his immediate posterity was quite ready to attribute to him, on the slightest evidence, some of the best anonymous verse of Elizabeth's time.

But such an active spirit could not remain long piping ditties in Ireland. He gladly accepted in September, 1591, a commission as vice-admiral of a fleet, under Lord Thomas Howard, to intercept the Spanish plate fleet at the Azores. At the last minute his cousin, Sir Richard Grenville, was substituted for him. Ralegh's heart must have ached at missing the glorious fight that followed; for the Spaniard, getting wind of the plan, sent fifty-three towering galleons with their "battle-thunder and flame," and Sir Richard fought them single-handed in the little Revenge. The following November Ralegh published anonymously his *Report of the Truth of the Fight about the Isles of the Azores*, reprinted under his name in the Hakluyt of 1599. Besides praising the valor and skill of Sir Richard and his crew, and exonerating Lord Howard for his escape,

Ralegh took particular occasion to rouse England to an anti-Spanish policy. Spain was soon to learn that Sir Richard Grenville's cousin too could fight.

In May, 1592, Ralegh started in command of an expedition against the Spanish in Panama. In support he gave ships and a large part of his wealth. He was soon overtaken, however, by Sir Martin Frobisher and recalled on account of an affair with Elizabeth Throckmorton, one of the Queen's maids of honor. That Elizabeth Throckmorton, a person of as rare mettle as Sir Walter himself, became his devoted wife is true; it is also true that such irregular affairs were common enough in those days of the strange confusion of great virtue and great vice. Still, the " Virgin Queen " was in this instance, perhaps properly if inconsistently, incensed, and Sir Walter was forthwith put in the Brick Tower from June to September. He was finally released because he was considered the best man in all England to arrange the partition of spoil of the Madre de Dios, the "Great Carack" brought into Dartmouth by Sir John Burgh of the Panama fleet. Other spoilsmen, however, were at work, and Ralegh barely cleared expenses in the end; but, better than this, he achieved his ransom from prison. He acquired, moreover, by the Queen's help, the Sherborne estate, in Dorset, where he now lived in semi-banishment from court. He maintained as well several London residences, but Sherborne was his favorite retreat, and there he studied and planted, and planned future voyages.

Ralegh's unpopularity, however, is not to be wondered at. The courtiers, fearful of his extraordinary powers and whipped by his sharp tongue, had baited the more flexible Essex against him. Towards the common people, except his own tried servants, he was haughty, — "damnably proud," says Aubrey ; and Henry Howard wrote to Cecil of "Rawlie, that in pride exceedeth all men alive." His speeches in Parliament, moreover, where he sat off and on from 1584 to 1602, were too keen and arrogant for the more plodding legislators ; as Mr. John Buchan puts it, "he was a firebrand in any council-chamber." Self-seeker like the rest of them, he was a dreaded antagonist in the feverish race for success.

It is in his exploits on the high seas, then, or in his long imprisonment under James, when he escaped the petty jealousies of the moment, that Ralegh appears at his best. A half-conscious sense of this fact, as well as his ceaseless activity and his inborn Devon love of the open sea and sky, no doubt kept him so persistently at his pursuit of exploration. For after a couple of years at Sherborne he was off again on the high seas, this time bound for Guiana.

He first sent out in 1594 an expedition under Captain Whiddon, was satisfied of the possibilities in the adventure, and himself set sail on February 6, 1595. In Guiana he fought the Spaniards, made friends with the Indians, and pushed far up the Orinoco. Floods forced him to return before he reached the fabled city of gold, Manoa, but he was confident of its existence and of his future success. The next year he published his interesting *Discovery of Guiana*, crowded with information of all kinds, — the names and customs of various tribes, the fruits and resources of the country, minute details of topography and geology, and strange experiences in equatorial waters. England might share, he fully believed, the success of Pizarro and Cortez. In

1596 he sent out another expedition under Captain Keymis, but the Spaniards, who had taken possession of San Thome, the town near the mouth of the Orinoco, resisted every step.

The Guiana expedition, though it did not arouse Elizabeth's direct sympathy and support, brought Ralegh again into prominence. He urged offense rather than defense in the competition with Spain, and accordingly on June 1, 1596, a proud armament of ninety-six English and twenty-four Dutch sail set out from Plymouth under Essex and Lord Admiral Howard. Ralegh, who commanded twenty-two ships, was one of the war-council of five to advise the chiefs. In the attack on Cadiz there was some hesitation about beginning the fight and much manœuvring for precedence among the leaders. Ralegh took the bit in his teeth, forged ahead in the Warspright, " resolved to be revenged for the Revenge or second her with his own life," captured two of the biggest galleons, the St. Matthew and St. Andrew, and forced the St. Philip and St. Thomas to set fire to themselves. " If any man," he afterward wrote, " had a desire to see hell itself, it was there most lively figured." A wound kept him from going ashore in the sack of Cadiz, but the chief glory of the fight was his, as well as the envy of his rival commanders. Again his share of the spoil was slight, but again he gained a more valuable prize, complete restoration to favor at court.

The next adventure was the islands voyage, with the purpose of seizing the Indian treasure ships at the Azores. It was agreed first to attack Fayal. Ralegh arrived before the others, saw preparations for resistance going on, grew impatient, and, after four days of waiting, attacked and won with a handful of marines. Essex, soon coming up, was jealous and very wroth at Ralegh's presumptuous action, but the affair resulted only in a reprimand. Though some prizes were taken, the expedition was chiefly a failure.

Sir Walter's voyages were now over except for the last fatal Guiana expedition, twenty years later. Just at present he was very active at home: in Parliament, in valued counsel to the ministers, in court duties, and in his numerous private interests, — study, planting, collecting, subsidizing semi-piratical enterprises, and living splendidly. In 1600 he found a new activity in the governorship of Jersey. He had made his potatoes grow in Ireland, he had brought mahogany from Guiana, he had introduced oranges and tobacco. The last-named commodity recalls the well-known story of his immersion in spiced ale by a servant who fancied his master on fire within.

The execution of Essex in February, 1601, for a conspiracy against the crown, brought Ralegh popular dislike at the same time that it added royal favor. He had not at first wished the execution of Essex; in fact, he had contrived to get along very well with so natural an enemy. Towards the end, however, Essex's extravagant sayings and doings only increased the ill feeling between them, and Ralegh came to look on him as an inveterate foe. The public, whose idol was the easy-going earl, liked to tell many stories of Sir Walter's cold-blooded indifference, how, for instance, he smoked a pipe as he looked out of the window at Essex's execution.

At court, however, matters were different. For the next two years, with no Essex in the way and Robert Cecil, Burleigh's son, on friendly terms, Ralegh stood

higher than ever in the Queen's graces. During these
last days of Elizabeth he was in constant consultation
at court, he entertained foreign embassies, and he flourished as a patron of letters. If his institution of the
fellowship of rare wits presided over by Ben Jonson at
the Mermaid Tavern be a fact, it must have taken place
about this time. Ralegh would have been one of the
choicest in such a gathering. And some, wishing to believe that the master-mind and the master-hand of the
age came together, have fancied that there he knew
Shakespeare. This period of his life Mr. Stebbing has
fitly characterized as the " zenith," for with Elizabeth's
death and the accession of James in 1603, Ralegh lost
forever his position at court.

When James came down from Scotland, a swarm of
sycophants buzzed north to gain his ear. Ralegh was
among them, but he found the rough Scotsman already
prejudiced against him. If a story the not over trustworthy Aubrey tells be a fact, Sir Walter lost ground
steadily. On the King's asserting that he should have
been able to win the English crown had the nobles
not accepted him, Ralegh replied, according to Aubrey,
" Would God that had been put to the trial! " " Why? "
asked James. " Because then," answered the other, " you
would have known your friends from your foes."

What precipitated the trouble between James and
Ralegh was the latter's estrangement from Cecil, and his
association with Henry Brooke, Lord Cobham. As the
succession of James approached, Cecil, who mistrusted
the growing rivalry of Ralegh, had been easily led by
Henry Howard into treating Sir Walter as an enemy,
politically at least. Howard, a malignant intriguer, had
written to James of Ralegh and Cobham, " Hell did never

vomit up such a couple," and Cecil's letters to the King had been almost as vituperative. To James, however, such vilifications were hardly necessary ; he was, as Mr. Stebbing puts it, "already incurably prejudiced" against Ralegh.

Sir Walter's association with Cobham added to the suspicions of the King and his ministers. The conspiracy of Cobham, a conceited, cowardly spoilsman, was, briefly, to establish by intrigue with Spain, through one Count Arenberg, minister of the Low Countries, the claim of Arabella Stuart to the English throne. Spite against James, hope of favor from the new régime, and a cancerous love of intrigue were undoubtedly Cobham's motives. Of these Ralegh must have shared his dissatisfaction, with something of his love for intrigue, but it is ludicrous to think of him, "the Scourge of Spain," sincerely connected with Spanish machinations. Yet Cobham hoped to use his friend's sharp wits, talked freely to Ralegh of his purposes, and offered him bribes. There is, however, not one single piece of direct evidence that Ralegh accepted pay or was actively engaged in the plot.

The association with Cobham, nevertheless, was suspicious-looking to Cecil, sufficient for the unscrupulous Howard, and convincing to the prejudiced James. Accordingly in July, 1603, Ralegh was put under guard in his own house. He had already been stripped of his office of wine licenser and his captaincy of the Guard ; now he lost his control of the Stannaries and the Jersey governorship. Soon Cobham himself turned in his trial on Ralegh, and in an abject attempt to save himself actually asserted that Sir Walter had instigated the dealings with Arenberg. Most of the evi-

dence in confirmation of this was irrelevant and third
or fourth hand, but Ralegh was thereupon put into the
Tower.

At first the prisoner acted as if convicted before
tried and foolishly attempted suicide. Here again,
said his enemies, was confession of guilt. Ralegh later
repented the rash attempt, which was made, he asserted,
not from fear, as some alleged, but from a desire to
deprive his enemies of the unjust confiscation of his
estates; he wished to save Sherborne for his wife and
son. His impulse, whatever else it shows, proves that
Ralegh had a very correct estimate of the outcome of
his trial.

Cobham's feeble attempts to retract his accusations
were for the most part suppressed. The mass of worthless evidence was marshaled, and on November 17
Ralegh was brought to trial. In the proceedings,
which he justly stigmatized as a disgrace to an English court of justice, nothing conclusive of guilt was
produced. His one false action, so far as proof goes,
was to deny having written a letter telling Cobham to
hold his tongue. This was very significant to his judges;
they were incapable of seeing that the letter might have
been founded on a desire to save Cobham, and the de-
nial based on a later impulse to save himself when the
garrulous Cobham had lost all chance.

The really interesting features of the trial are Ralegh's calm bearing and his encounter with Sir Edward
Coke, then attorney-general, — a man, Cecil himself
said, " more peremptory than honest." Coke, in default
of evidence, resorted to vituperation. Speaking of
Cobham, he cried, " All he did was by thy instigation,
thou viper; for I *thou* thee, thou traitor ! " " You may

call me traitor at your pleasure," replied the prisoner
calmly, " yet it becomes not a man of virtue or quality
to do so. But I take comfort in it; it is all that you
can do; for I do not yet hear that you charge me with
any treason." When Coke later quibbled on a point
of law, Sir Walter answered, " It is a toy to tell me
of law; I defy law. I stand on the facts." Another
time, when Ralegh had objected to the use of evidence
derived from " hellish spiders," Coke roared, " Thou
hast a Spanish heart, and art thyself a spider of hell! "

Yet the jury contrived, after a quarter of an hour's
debate, to find Ralegh guilty of high treason. He was
sentenced to be hanged, drawn, and quartered; but at
the last moment, when the condemned was already
on the scaffold, James, with a childish passion for a
dramatic scene of which he should be the central figure,
came down with a reprieve, and Ralegh was removed
to the Tower. The truth was that the king feared on
such slight evidence to put Ralegh to death. The man's
bearing during his trial and the absurdity of the proceedings had turned popular feeling. A moment before,
Ralegh had been the best hated man in the kingdom;
now he was all but a martyr.

The prisoner was at first so ill in the Tower that he
was allowed to remove to a little garden-house, where
he kept a still for the study of his chemistry. Lady
Ralegh and their son Walter, now ten years old, were
permitted to live with him ; and in the Tower a second
son, Carew, was born, in 1604. Most of Ralegh's confinement was in the " Bloody" Tower. There he had
a gallery which looked down on the busy wharves, and
crowds are said to have gathered to catch a glimpse of
the great man — the jeweled captive of the king.

For years attempts were made to establish more
clearly the prisoner's guilt; he was suspected of connection with the Gunpowder Plot in 1605, — in fact,
of complicity in every new conspiracy. He was indeed
a man still to be reckoned with. He soon gained the ear
and support of Anne, James's queen, and of Henry,
Prince of Wales. "Who but my father," cried Henry,
"would keep such a bird in a cage!" The death of
the prince in 1612 unfortunately put an end to Ralegh's
chances of a pardon. Yet he never despaired. An irrepressible confidence in the work he had yet to do made
him cling tenaciously to life and hope.

This spirit kept him active. Besides his work in
chemistry, he wrote a great deal. He had ever been a
large reader; in fact, he was accustomed to take many
books on his voyages. Now, in the Tower, he found
plenty of leisure for further study and a mature judgment for assorting the omnivorous learning of fifty
years. Naturally his writings were on a multitude of
subjects. A mere list of the chief treatises is aston-
ishing in its variety and scope: *The Prerogative of
Parliaments*, *The Savoy Marriage*, *The Discourse of
the Invention of Ships*, *The Maxims of State*, *A Dia-
logue between a Jesuit and a Recusant*, *The Sceptic*,
A Treatise on the Soul, *A Discourse on Tenures
which were before the Conquest*, and the *History of
the World*.

The *History of the World* — entered on the Register of the Stationers' Company April 15, 1611, and
first printed in 1614 — is of all these prose writings
incontestably the greatest. Only an Elizabethan could
have conceived and dared such a heroic undertaking;
and the achievement is nothing short of marvelous

when it is remembered that this particular Elizabethan
was old, in poor health, defeated, in prison. He could
still " toil terribly." It is said that Ralegh was helped
by others in the writing, but at least the conception,
the supervision, and the best part of the work were his.
Of course it was not finished, but it is a monumental
fragment. In it Ralegh is most consistently at his best ;
the littlenesses of daily intrigue have fallen away ; for
pages he speaks with the oracular mastery that few
have ever genuinely attained. The *History* would live
indeed, if for nothing else, for its closing lines, the
famous apostrophe to Death. Ralegh had run the complete gamut of mortal experience ; he had enjoyed all
the " farre-stretched greatnesse " of which he speaks ;
he had fought for bare existence against a poisoned
court ; and he pronounces these last words with something of the tragic intimacy, the deep personal experience that Milton had of a lost paradise. More than
any one he knew life ; and he had veritably seen death
face to face. " O eloquent, just, and mighty death ! "
he says, " whom none could advise, thou hast per-
swaded ; what none hath dared, thou hast done ; and
whom all the world hath flattered, thou only hast cast
out of the world and despised : thou hast drawne together all the farre-stretched greatnesse, all the pride,
crueltie, and ambition of man, and covered it all over
with these two narrow words, *Hic jacet*."

Ralegh's release from prison came finally in March,
1616. Secretary Winwood, who thought well of him
and who secretly preferred a French to a Spanish alliance, did much to bring about the King's permission.
James, who was now strongly inclined to the Spanish
marriage of his son Charles, saw an excellent chance.

Spain still feared Ralegh alive — even in prison. So did James. Popular opinion had made it increasingly difficult to keep the prisoner quietly immured. Here, then, was a solution: another trip to Guiana meant conflict with the Spanish; Ralegh, who had been urging such an expedition, should be sent, with instructions not to break the peace with Spain, and the court at Madrid, forewarned of the adventure, should make the carrying out of such instructions impossible.

Just before Ralegh's departure French complications developed. He had received permission, if not a commission, from the French Admiralty to land Spanish prizes in French ports. A letter of his to a French councillor of state regarding coöperation in the Guiana work was obtained by James; and the whole packet — plans of the voyage, French letter, and explanations from the King — was sent via Madrid to the Spanish governor of Guiana. The cue of the Spaniard was of course to resist Ralegh's advance to the mine; then Sir Walter, with his hands tied, must fight or fail. To fight would be against the Crown's orders; to fail would prove his scheme a hoax and revive the old popular dislike.

Ralegh, who was ignorant of the fact that San Thome was moved so that a conflict would be inevitable, set out in hopeful spirits from Plymouth on June 12, 1617. Ill luck beset the expedition from the start; added to this, the crews were mutinous and incompetent. Arriving off Cape Oyapoco, he sent a party under his son Walter, with Keymis as guide, in search of the gold mine. He himself stayed at the mouth of the river in his flagship, the Destiny, partly to guard against Spanish attack, partly on account of ill health.

In his instructions to those setting out he said : "You shall find me at Puncto Gallo, dead or alive. And if you find not my ships there, you shall find their ashes. For I will fire, with the galleons, if it come to extremity ; run will I never." The mine expedition fared badly. Young Walter fell fighting gallantly in the capture of San Thome, where the Spaniards forced a fight ; the others turned back disheartened without reaching the mine ; and Keymis, overcome by Ralegh's reproof, committed suicide. Any chance of a second attempt or of piratical attacks on the Mexican fleet was lost by the desertion of some of the captains. The forlorn hope had failed. Ralegh returned, broken in health and spirit, to a satisfied King and a condemning people.

On arriving again at Plymouth, Sir Walter was immediately taken into custody. With all the world before him and French ports open to him, he had not taken the chance to escape. Now, persuaded by his wife and a Captain King, he foolishly attempted flight to France. Once in the boat, however, he ordered return and gave himself up again. But his tenacious eagerness for life soon returned. At Salisbury he feigned madness and sickness for a week, that he might gain time to write his *Apology for the Voyage to Guiana*. At London he made another attempt to escape, but was taken by his keeper, Sir Thomas Stukely, who accepted bribes and pretended assistance.

Once more Ralegh stood before the King's Bench. The judges, however, were again unable to find sufficient evidence. The Mexican plate fleet had not been attacked, the Spaniards had offered the first resistance at San Thome, and the French complication could not be proved treasonous. Pardon, however, was another matter. Winwood was dead, and Ralegh found few influential friends. James, moreover, had promised the King of Spain a public execution, either in Madrid or in London; it was clear that Ralegh must be a peace-offering to Spain. The old charges of 1603 were renewed; Ralegh was found guilty of high treason as before, and on October 29, 1618, was executed in Palace Yard.

In his death Ralegh was exalted into the same nobleness that is so pervasive in his great *History*. This is a significant characteristic in his life; it is always found breaking out in great crises, — in Guiana, at Cadiz, in his trial, in prison, on the scaffold; it, in fact, is what gives him the right, when the skillfully versatile courtier and daring buccaneer seem inadequate, to represent most truly of all men the "spacious" times of Elizabeth. He must have been in this spirit the night before his execution, when he wrote those famous lines : —

> "Even such is time, that takes in trust
> Our youth, our joys, our all we have,
> And pays us but with earth and dust ;
> Who, in the dark and silent grave,
> When we have wandered all our ways,
> Shuts up the story of our days.
> But from this earth, this grave, this dust,
> My God shall raise me up, I trust."

"He made no more of his death," said Dean Tounson, who administered him the sacrament, "than if it had been to take a journey." When he was asked whether he would lay his head toward the east, he answered, "So the heart be right, it is no matter which way the head lies." To the executioner's offer to blindfold him, he replied, "Think you I fear the shadow of the axe, when I fear not itself?" And when the headsman hesitated to strike, " What dost thou fear?" cried Ralegh. " Strike man, strike!"

Immediately he had become a martyr. James found it necessary, in fact, to issue an apology. Bacon, then lord chancellor, was appointed to the task, and though he had always been a friend and admirer of Ralegh, he accepted his ungenerous duty and wrote the *Declaration*. But neither Bacon nor James could quell the popular enthusiasm. The patriot, Sir John Eliot, who witnessed Ralegh's execution, spoke of "the fortitude of *our* Ralegh," and Hampden, Pym, and Cromwell believed they were bearing the same burden as he.

EDMUND SPENSER

SPENSER has been called the poets' poet, partly because of the unbounded praise which men like Milton have bestowed upon him, and partly because the qualities of his poetry appeal rather to the admiration of the artist than to the interest of the reader. Yet his *Faerie Queen*, like *Pilgrim's Progress*, is an allegory filled not only with adventures of every kind but with characters who are in many cases the counterparts of those who still absorb the attention of young and old in the career of Bunyan's hero. The difficulty for the modern reader lies in Spenser's complication of the allegory, and in a certain unreal quality not unlike that which we see in Shelley. About Mr. Worldly Wiseman there is no doubt, and the man himself is still with us; but we have to be told that Artegall represents not only justice but also Spenser's patron, Lord Grey of Wilton. A few readers, to be sure, enjoy the *Faerie Queen* as a story without reference to its moral or meaning; this meaning, however, played a great part in Spenser's own time. Milton speaks of " our sage and serious Poet *Spenser*, whom I dare be known to think a better teacher than *Scotus* or *Aquinas;* " and according to Dryden "acknowledged . . . that Spenser was his original." Still, what the poets love in Spenser is not so much his moral as his poetry. Of all men who have written English verse, to none has verse been such a natural and unforced expression as to Spenser.

Edmund Spenser was born in London not far from

the year 1552, son of John Spenser, who belonged to
the gentle Lancashire family of that name, but had become a clothmaker in the City. In his *Prothalamion*
the poet speaks of —

> " Merry London, my most kindly nurse,
>   That to me gave this life's first native source,
>   Though from another place I take my name,
>   A house of ancient fame."

In other words, humble as his condition was, he was connected with the Spencers of Althorpe, who made alli-
ances with some of the most powerful nobles of that day,
and are represented in our own time among the front
ranks of the peerage. The poet was educated in the
Merchant Taylors' School, and was most fortunate in
his lot. Richard Mulcaster, who presided over this newly
founded grammar school, was not only a great teacher,
but one of the first educational writers who insisted on
English "as a medium of education and a vehicle for all
kinds of learning." Although these views of Mulcaster's
were not published until 1581, we may assume that his
teaching reflected them from the start; and they must
have strengthened the poet not only in the love and knowledge of his native tongue, but in that finer sense of its
poetic genius which made him reject in practice the
theory of classical imitations to which he gave for a
while half-hearted allegiance. He seems to have been an
excellent scholar, and as such received from a wealthy
Londoner pecuniary help both while a pupil at the
school and as sizar at Pembroke Hall in the University
of Cambridge. As head of the school, moreover, he
probably attracted the notice of the Bishop of London,
Grindal, whom he afterwards praised in the *Shepheard's
Calendar* under the name of Algrind. At the age of

seventeen he had composed verse, not an unusual performance; the unusual fact was the publication of this
verse and the quality of it. Dean Church points out
that in these translations are to be found a grace and
an ease of style due entirely to the young poet himself.
There was no master in English from whom he could
copy.

At Cambridge Spenser lived on terms of intimate
friendship with Edward Kirke, the E. K. of the *Shepheard's Calendar*, and with Gabriel Harvey, whose pedantry and vanity afterwards received such a scoring at
the hands of clever pamphleteers like Tom Nashe, that
his sound scholarship and love of learning have been
overlooked. With these friends Spenser studied eagerly
the classics and the new learning of the Renaissance,
as well as the poets of France and Italy, and presumably what he regarded as masterpieces in his own tongue,
the works of Chaucer. He left Cambridge, a Master of
Arts, in 1576. After spending some time in the North
of England, the original home of his family, losing his
heart meanwhile to a certain Rosalind, who seems to
have appreciated the poet in Spenser but refused him
as a husband, he appeared in London. By the autumn
of 1579 he is writing thence to Gabriel Harvey. He is
already on fairly intimate terms with Sidney and nobles
of the court. Harvey has introduced his friend to the
Earl of Leicester, and by 1578 Spenser is living at the
latter's house in the Strand. He has had an audience
of the Queen, and is leading, as far as his means allow,
the life of a man of fashion. The letters to Harvey tell
only of his literary life, along with a few flirtations.
He signs himself "Immerito," and with his correspondent's full sympathy outlines the plan of the "Areopa-

gus," a club whose members were to unite in driving
out the tyrant Rhyme from English poetry, and substi-
tuting for it the unrhymed measures of classical verse.
All of them made experiments in these new metres; it
is enough to say that if Spenser had written nothing
better than the iambics which he sends to Harvey, he
would neither have won a name in English poetry nor
even achieved a success in the club. His instinct was
better than his belief. At this very time he was writing
the smooth rhymed verses of his *Shepheard's Calendar*,
which appeared in December, 1579, as the work of
"Immerito," with notes and a commentary by "E. K."
Despite these disguises the public knew it for Spenser's work, and he was everywhere hailed as the " new
poet." This poem, a series of twelve pastorals in the
Italian style, with an allegory centred in the humble life
of shepherds, instead of the world of knights and fan-
tastic adventure chosen for the *Faerie Queen*, includes
the poet himself, who is called "Colin Clout," and "Hob-
binol," or Gabriel Harvey, and fair "Elisa," the Queen,
and even her mother, Anne Boleyn. Besides this, Spenser
had tried his hand at other kinds of poetry, even the
drama. Nine comedies in the Italian style had been
read by Harvey and preferred to a specimen which
Spenser had shown him from the *Faerie Queen*. But
though these were real plays, they were never published
and have not been preserved. Another lost work of
Spenser's, written about this time, was entitled "The
English Poet." It would be interesting if we could read
the New Poet's prose about his art. After all, it was
in the *Shepheard's Calendar* that Spenser revived the
best traditions of English poetry, and it is not in vain
that "E. K." places him, next to Chaucer, "the load-

star of our language." Spenser himself, in the June
eclogue, names Chaucer as his master.

> " The God of Shepheards, Tityrus, is dead,
> Who taught me homely, as I can, to make." . . .

His two years in London brought him no real favor
at court. He made friends among the courtiers, but
envy and even hatred were already astir, and what he
mourned later was doubtless revealed to him in this
first experience : —

> " discontent of my long fruitlesse stay
> In Princes Court, and expectation vaine
> Of idle hopes, which still doe fly away."

In outright satire, too, he gives advice about the way to
succeed at court, when one "must learn to laugh, to lie,
to forge, to scoffe, to company, to crouch, to please, to
be a beetle-stock of thy great Master's will, to scorn
or mock." The whole of the *Mother Hubberd's Tale*,
closely imitating Chaucer's style, is a satire on the times,
and contains moreover a fine passage describing the
"rightful courtier," the ideal gentleman, as the poet
conceived him, in service to a noble prince. Whether or
not the fox in this fable is the great man at court
who baffled Spenser himself is not clear ; but the following famous passage is autobiographical, and the poet
says it was "composed in youth."

> " Full little knowest thou, that hast not tride,
> What hell it is in suing long to bide ;
> To loose good dayes, that might be better spent;
> To wast long nights in pensive discontent ;
> To speed to-day, to be put back to-morrow ;
> To feed on hope, to pine with tears and sorrow;
> To have thy Princes grace, yet want her Peeres ;
> To have thy asking, yet waite manie yeeres ;

To fret thy soul with crosses and with cares ;
To eate thy heart through comfortlesse dispaires."

It is said that Burleigh blocked the poet's advancement. In any case, the best that Lord Leicester could do for him was to persuade Lord Grey of Wilton, just appointed Lord Deputy of Ireland, to take Spenser with him as his private secretary. This was in 1580 ; and for eighteen years, almost to his death, the poet spent nearly all his time in the exile of a turbulent and dangerous province. It was surely no fit place for such a man as Spenser ; war, when it deserved the name, was carried on without regard to the simplest claims of justice and mercy, but as a rule desperate outbreaks of the natives alternated with bloody reprisals on the part of the conquerors. Laws slept ; murder and arson were the rule ; and those to whom lands were given in the rebellious districts lived as if over a volcano. Towards the end of his stay Spenser wrote in prose *A View of the Present State of Ireland*, in which he sets forth the desperate condition of affairs, yet not without recognition of the claims which Ireland might well urge upon English justice and common sense.

He held various official posts in Ireland, and besides his pay secured large gifts in land, and in 1588 settled as one of the new planters or, as they were called, " undertakers," at Kilcolman Castle, in the county of Cork, on an estate of about three thousand acres granted him two years before. This exile, embittered by quarrels, had its bright side in the neighborhood of Sir Walter Ralegh. In 1589, after he had shown his friend three books of the *Faerie Queen* in manuscript, and aroused unbounded enthusiasm for its beauty, Spenser took Ralegh's advice and with him repaired to London in

order to see the Queen and if possible secure some post
at home. Doubtless as means to this end, though literary
ambition must also have played its part, Spenser published the three books of the *Faerie Queen*, dedicating
them to Elizabeth and explaining in an introduction
addressed to Ralegh what was to be done in the twelve
books of the whole poem. This, as "a continued Allegory, or darke conceit," must have its general intention clearly set forth: it is "to fashion a gentleman or
noble person in vertuous and gentle discipline." Such a
moral, the poet goes on, should be "coloured with an
historicall fiction, the which the most part of men delight
to read, rather for variety of matter then for profite
of the ensample." The fiction which he chose was the
"historye of King Arthure." The Faerie Queen herself,
he explains, in the general sense is glory, for which the
true knight should strive; but in particular is "the most
excellent and glorious person of our Soveraine;" and
then follows an analysis of part of the intended poem.
That such an undertaking flattered the vanity of Elizabeth and filled what modern slang terms "a long-felt
want" among the splendid and adventurous nobles as
well as the gentry of England, is evident enough. Moreover, the moral part of Spenser's plan, springing
from certain Puritan proclivities which seem to have
remained alive in him despite his courtier's career,
appealed not only to spirits akin to his own, but to that
large class of men who made the ideal, no matter in
what sordid mixture, a part of their lives. Ralegh himself is a case in point, but thousands of his countrymen
were inspired by these glittering dreams. Men sought
a fountain of youth, a land of gold, a Northwest
Passage; in brief, the old knightly quest seemed close

enough to reality for Elizabethan minds. Hence the large appeal of Spenser's poem and the instant favor which it received. The stingy Queen granted him a goodly pension which Burleigh is said to have cut down to fifty pounds. The court was enthusiastic and made this new poem a kind of gentleman's handbook; and its author, already famous as the New Poet, received in that great decade of our literature what may fairly be called the homage of his fellow poets. In a poem which Spenser composed after his return to Ireland, — for his quest had been in vain so far as English preferment was concerned, — he wrote, under the title of *Colin Clout's Come Home Again*, a pastoral addressed to his friend Ralegh from Kilcolman in December, 1591, in which many of the English poets are named. The stanza,

> "And then, though last not least, is Ætion,
> A gentler shepheard may no where be found;
> Whose Muse, full of high thoughts invention,
> Doth like himselfe Heroically sound," . . .

of which the last line would fit Shakespeare, is probably though not certainly a genuine allusion to the greater poet.

Although this poem was not published for some years, the publisher of the *Faerie Queen* put forth a volume of Spenser's minor poems in 1591. In the *Ruines of Time* Spenser bewails the deaths of his friend Sidney [1] and of his patron Leicester; but in *Mother Hubberd's Tale*, quoted above for its satire on the court, as well as in the *Teares of the Muses*, with its lament for the decadence of poetry, there was opportunity for offense in high places. Tradition has it that offense was taken.

---

[1] Of the elegies on Sidney, published in 1595 with *Colin Clout*, only the *Astrophel* belongs to Spenser.

In June, 1594, the poet married Elizabeth, daughter
of James Boyle. Eighty-eight sonnets and an epithala-
mion, the latter a most exquisite poem, record his courtship and marriage. In one of the sonnets he praises the
name of his bride as belonging to his own mother and
to his Sovereign Queen, tells what they have done for
him, and cries, —

> " Ye three Elizabeths! for ever live,
> That three such graces did unto me give."

In the marriage lay he tells us that the time of year is
" when the Sunne is in his chiefest hight," that is, the
middle of June ; and thus pictures his bride : —

> "Behold, whiles she before the altar stands,
> Hearing the holy priest that to her speakes,
> And blesseth her with his two happy hands,
> How the red roses flush up in her cheekes." . . .

By his wife Spenser had three sons and a daughter ;
descendants of the eldest son are still living.

Late in 1595 Spenser journeyed again to London,
taking with him three more books of the *Faerie Queen*.
The King of Scotland, afterwards James I of England,
complained through the English ambassador of the calumny thrown upon his mother, Queen Mary, who appears
in no attractive guise as Duessa in the fourth book
of the poem. " False Duessa" she is called, and is recorded as guilty of the worst crimes conceivable. In
fact, she is foil to the perfectly virtuous Elizabeth, who
is represented by both Gloriana and Belphœbe. This
protest, though it failed to bring about the punishment
of the poet, is good proof of the wide circulation and
the popularity of the book. Spenser, moreover, had
a powerful protector in the Earl of Essex, at whose
house he was for some time a guest ; and it was proba-

bly to show his usefulness as an official, his loyalty,
and his claims for promotion to more congenial service,
that he wrote the above-mentioned *View of the Present
State of Ireland*, licensed in 1598, but not printed until
after his death. But as in Swift's case, there was to be
no return from Spenser's Irish exile. It was after a year
of unavailing endeavors that he wrote, in his *Prothalamion*, a wedding lay for two daughters of the Earl of
Worcester, those lines about his " long fruitless stay in
Princes Court and expectation vain," which we have
quoted above. Early in 1597 Spenser returned to Ireland; nor could his appointment in September, 1598,
as sheriff of Cork, a high and dignified office, console
him for his failure. It was no sinecure. In October thousands of rebels, under the Earl of Desmond, swarmed
through this part of Ireland, and Kilcolman Castle was
burned to the ground. Spenser escaped to Cork with
his wife and children; it was reported on the authority
of Ben Jonson, though the fact needs better proof, that
one of the children was burned to death. In December
Spenser was sent to England with official dispatches
about the war; but he seems to have been a dying man,
and survived his arrival in London little over a month.
Ben Jonson told Drummond, in the famous Conversations, that the poet " died for lack of bread, in King
Street, and refused twenty pieces sent to him by my
Lord of Essex, saying that he had no time to spend
them." Other writers of the time refer to his poverty
and the misery of his death, and the general fact must
be accepted as true ; on the other hand, starvation seems
an almost impossible assumption. His friends were numerous ; he was a kind of royal messenger, and could
have been neither neglected nor utterly destitute. What

seems most likely is that a broken-hearted man, with mortal illness upon him, fresh from the overwhelming tragedy of Kilcolman, crept into those obscure lodgings in Westminster and called for " easeful death."

Biographers quote Aubrey's statement on the authority of an old actor that Spenser was " a little man, wore short hair, little bands, and little cuffs." As a writer he has been placed among the foremost English poets. In his own day he was not popular in the ordinary sense, but he was the favorite of the aristocracy and of the leading men of letters. As the people of Queen Anne's age saw themselves depicted in *Gulliver's Travels*, the Elizabethan gentleman saw in the *Faerie Queen*, though by a very different method and with praise and abuse substituted for satire, the great characters of his time in transparent disguise. He saw his enemies attacked, his friends and his sovereign praised to heart's desire. He could recognize Ireland in the scenery of the *Faerie Queen*, and the revival of chivalry and knightly deeds could blind him to the horrors of actual Irish war. All these elements of interest are now stripped from Spenser's verse, and what remains is poetry pure and simple. Spenser wrote his poetry with consummate ease, and we may be sure that, like Shakespeare, he " never blotted." But he differs from Shakespeare, he differs from his own master Chaucer, in shunning the real. His feet are almost never on the ground. Lovers of poetry for poetry's sake, however, will always turn to him ; and he gave England its first great poem in its greatest age.

FRANCIS BACON

POPE's famous line about Bacon, "the wisest, brightest, meanest of mankind," has been denounced by recent writers as inadequate and false. Bacon was not the meanest of mankind; in one sense he was not mean at all. But in another sense the line is true, expressing the greatest possible contradiction between Bacon's greatness of intellect, the sweep and range of his ideas, his plans for the increase of human knowledge and the advance of human achievement, and that pitiable and recurrent weakness in his conduct of life. Weakness is not the only charge against him; after making all allowances for the ways of his time, there remains nothing but a very ugly word for ingratitude to his patron and treachery to his friend, in the case of the Earl of Essex. But we cannot judge character by the weakest link in the chain. Bacon's enemies, foremost among them Coke, the greatest English lawyer, brought about his downfall, and have, in a manner, written the verdict passed upon Bacon by history; his friends, however (and there are great names among them), bear witness to qualities and general disposition the reverse of mean. Above all, his works give Bacon the stamp of greatness. He cannot be summed up in a few words. There must have been something in his make-up which rendered him unable to stand the test of action, and inspired practical men with distrust of his splendid powers. Queen Elizabeth never put any real responsibility upon him or intrusted him with any important office, though a keen intellect like Bacon's was the kind which she loved to employ in her service. And if he rose to eminence under James, it was because he consented to be the tool of one of the weakest of English kings and of the most despicable of royal favorites.

Bacon began life with great advantages. Born in London January 22, 1561 (new style), the son of Sir Nicholas Bacon, Lord Keeper, and of the highly accomplished daughter of Sir Antony Cook, a woman well versed in Greek and Latin, deeply religious and zealous for the best interests of her children, Bacon could ask nothing better on the score of family inheritance and influences. His uncle by marriage was Elizabeth's great minister, William Cecil, Lord Burleigh, and the men who frequented his father's house were leaders of the nation which was now beginning to lead Protestant Europe. Bacon literally grew up along with the greatness of Elizabethan England. His religious training was on the stricter lines of the reforming party, and although he took little part in the religious disputes of his time, there can be no doubt that these early influences had their part in the greatest reform that philosophy and science have ever known. He was the great reformer, not of men's belief, but of men's thought.

He went to the University of Cambridge at the age of twelve. This feat, now impossible, was not then an uncommon thing for boys of birth and ability. Lord Herbert of Cherbury, Waller the poet, are in this list, and many other names could be added. At sixteen, already a member of Gray's Inn in London, he was sent to France to complete his education abroad with the English ambassador, and remained there for two years. So far things had gone rapidly and well for Bacon ; but

when he was eighteen the death of his father called him
back, a younger son, to a career dependent upon his
own exertions, — long and fruitless so far as the favor
of the court was concerned, and hindered, it would
seem, rather than helped, by powerful relatives, Lord
Burleigh and his son Robert Cecil, whose ministry
lasted well into the days of King James. He devoted
himself to the law, lived at Gray's Inn, and seems to
have divided his time between the study of his profession and vain appeals for employment. In our modern phrase, he kept himself before the public, writing
papers on matters of national interest. These were
circulated in manuscripts, but, as Dean Church says,
" In our day they would have been pamphlets or magazine articles." His health, particularly his digestion,
during these early years, was by no means satisfactory;
but it does not seem to have interfered with his powers of continuous and concentrated literary toil. Even
after his disgrace and downfall, a ruined man, upwards
of sixty, so ill that he could not leave his house, his
power of production was unabated, and he accomplished
some of his most brilliant work. When twenty-four he
became member of Parliament, and four years later
he began to figure as one of its most active members.
With the reign of James I Bacon became one of the
leaders of the House, and was active both in the business of legislation and in debate. Ben Jonson praises
his powers as an orator and pleader in the highest terms:
" His hearers could not cough or look aside from him
without loss." In conversation he was equally brilliant,
though he seems to have been somewhat too fond of his
jest. Meanwhile he tried his hand at the flatteries of a
courtier, and composed toward the close of Elizabeth's

reign several pieces for the entertainment of the Queen. But in spite of all his efforts, legal, literary, social, in spite of all his appeals to a powerful relative, he found himself at thirty, an age then regarded as we regard middle life, still obscure and without prospects. He now writes the famous letter to Lord Burleigh, " from my lodgings at Gray's Inn," which sets forth the plan of his life, the scope of his ambition, and his pressing lack of means.

" I wax now somewhat ancient; one and thirty years is a great deal of sand in the hour-glass. My health, I thank God, I find confirmed; and I do not fear that action shall impair it, because I account my ordinary course of study and meditation to be more painful than most parts of action are." Then comes the great profession: " Lastly, I confess that I have as vast contemplative ends as I have moderate civil ends; *for I have taken all knowledge to be my province;* and if I could purge it of two sorts of rovers, whereof the one with frivolous disputations, confutations, and verbosities, the other with blind experiments and auricular traditions and impostures, hath committed so many spoils, I hope I should bring in industrious observations, grounded conclusions, and profitable inventions and discoveries." . . .

In short, Bacon asks his uncle for some means by which he can live in state befitting his rank, and devote an abundant leisure to the reform of human knowledge. This letter, however, brought him nothing but promises, and he went on living as he could and using his enforced spare time for literary ends. In 1597 he appeared in print with the first edition of his essays. Though the style of these essays places them among the great

achievements of English prose, it is characteristic of
him, the man who "took all knowledge to be his province," and made his appeal to mankind at large, that
he caused them to be put into Latin. The modern languages, he wrote to a friend, would at some time "play
the bankrupt with books;" though it must be added that
these same essays were translated into Italian.

Meanwhile Bacon had been making a short-lived
friendship and a life-long enmity. The Earl of Essex,
prime favorite of the Queen, a man of great parts and
endowed with all the qualities that make for success
save prudence, was one of the few who appreciated
Bacon's real greatness. The two were on terms of intimate friendship; and Essex threw himself into the
cause of his friend's advancement with characteristic
zeal, urging his appointment as Attorney-General. The
Queen, like her advisers, the two Cecils, father and son,
wished to appoint Coke to this place; and after a long
delay, which only served to deepen the great lawyer's
hostility to Bacon, the efforts of Essex came to an ignominious end, and Coke secured the prize. It was supposed that Bacon could have the post of Solicitor, which
had been suggested as a compromise during the struggle
with Coke, but even this favor was now refused. Bacon
was thoroughly disgusted, and seems to have thought
of retiring to Cambridge to devote himself entirely to
his studies. This course was recommended not simply
by the disappointment but also by Bacon's financial
embarrassment; twice he was arrested for debt. In this
latter respect, however, Essex could be helpful without
leave of minister or Queen, and gave Bacon lands worth
£1800 in the money of those days. He also tried to
make a rich marriage for his friend; but again the

hard-headed and implacable Coke carried off the prize,
the wealthy widow of Sir Christopher Hatton.

In what was left of the ill-fated Earl's career Bacon
seems to have played the part of a wise and consistent
friend, barring of course the last and tragic scene, the
trial for high treason, in which Bacon, as special counsel
along with the Attorney-General, directed the examination, selected the evidence, and pressed the dangerous
charges against his friend. There seems to be no doubt
that the trial might have resulted differently but for
Bacon's conduct of the case. Excuses have been offered
in his behalf, but they are of little weight. It is said
that he could not refuse to do the bidding of the Queen,
but there have been many men who would at least have
offered passive resistance in the interests of so bountiful
a patron and so close a friend. After the Queen's death
Bacon himself wrote an *Apology* for this affair, claiming
the part of one who tried to reconcile his sovereign and
the Earl. The exact truth will never be revealed; but a
guess may be hazarded that in private Bacon served
Essex to the extent of his powers both by advice and
by attempts before the actual trial to mitigate the severity of the charge. The correspondence of the two
shows Bacon's earlier efforts to dissuade Essex from
schemes and deeds which his enemies were only too glad
to forward. But in the conduct of the case the learned
counsel played his part as prosecutor only too well. As
in Bacon's other misfortunes, it was the public part
which attracted attention and passed into history, while
the underground stream remains largely a matter of
surmise.

Even this sacrifice of friendship to interest failed of
its full reward. He was forty-one years of age and

badly in need of funds, but only his pittance was given him. Coke was forever blocking his way, and in open court the two came to words which Bacon himself has reported. " Mr. Bacon," said the lawyer, " if you have any tooth against me pluck it out; for it will do you more hurt than all the teeth in your head will do you good." Bacon " answered coldly in these very words : ' Mr. Attorney, I respect you ; I fear you not ; and the less you speak of your own greatness, the more I will think of it.' " After further insult from Coke, Bacon " said no more but this: ' Mr. Attorney, do not depress me so far; for I have been your better, and may be again, when it please the Queen.' " It never did please the Queen ; but, under James, Bacon, if only for a time, carried out his threat against Coke. He was knighted by the new King, not alone, as he wished, for the sake of the distinction, but, as he feared, " gregarious in a troop " with three hundred others.

About this time, he says, he had " found out an alderman's daughter, an handsome maiden, to his liking," and nearly three years later he married her in a splendid fashion described in a letter of the time. " He was clad from top to toe in purple, and hath made himself and his wife such store of raiments of cloth of silver and gold that it draws deep into her portion." These three years had been full of activity. The first of them was largely devoted to preparation for his great work " for the service of mankind." He wrote in Latin a sort of introduction to a treatise on the interpretation of nature, and describes himself in the following words : —

" For myself, I found that I was fitted for nothing so well as for the study of Truth ; as having a mind

nimble and versatile enough to catch the resemblances
of things (which is the chief point) and at the same
time steady enough to fix and distinguish their subtler
differences ; as being gifted by nature with desire to
seek, patience to doubt, fondness to meditate, slowness
to assert, readiness to reconsider, carefulness to dispose
and set in order ; and as being a man that neither
affects what is new nor admires what is old, and that
hates every kind of imposture. So I thought my nature
had a kind of familiarity and relationship with Truth."

But this quest of truth was soon broken. As member of
Parliament, Bacon contrived both to gain the confidence
of the House of Commons, to direct its affairs, and at
the same time to win the favor of the King, obtaining
for him terms of compromise that ended a very serious
dispute between the monarch and his first Parliament.
It must not be forgotten that Bacon also did useful work
in reforming ancient abuses. Between the Parliament
of 1604 and that of 1605 he wrote and published another English book on *The Advancement of Knowledge*. In 1607, almost in sight of his fiftieth year,
Bacon was at last appointed Solicitor-General. A year
later, he wrote down a remarkable account of his present standing, his plans, and his prospects, and called it
Commentarius Solutus, "A Book of Loose Notes," as
Spedding interprets it. Barring those endless and often
morbid journals which have lately come into fashion,
such as the Journal of Amiel or of Marie Bashkirt-
seff, it would be hard to find such a revelation of self.
It contains a detailed statement of Bacon's physique,
rules for the care of his health, household matters,
rules for his own conduct and speech in public, notes
on persons with whom he had to deal, and, above all,

outlines of his great scheme for the reform of human
thought. But unlike the journals above mentioned, it
does not seem to have been meant even remotely for
the public eye. Some of his ideas are surprisingly modern, and on the whole this document, on the personal
and intellectual side, matches Defoe's equally wonderful
anticipation of public and practical progress in his *Essay on Projects*. Another book now appeared on *The
Wisdom of the Ancients*, in which Bacon interprets
mythology as a series of allegories dealing with the most
intricate problems of human life. It is absurd enough
to us, who know that the old myths spring from the
earliest and rudest stages of man's development, but in
the author's time was widely read; indeed it was "one
of the most popular of his works."

The death of Robert Cecil, Lord Salisbury, in May,
1612, removed the last restraint upon Bacon's progress,
as well as upon the King's folly. Indeed the two now
went hand in hand. Though baffled at first in his appeals for office, Bacon in 1613 persuaded the king to
make Coke Chief Justice of the King's Bench, and give
one Hobart Coke's place at the Common Pleas. This
was his first victory over Coke, who wept both at the
cause of his own promotion and at the consequent loss
in salary. Thus in October the way was made for
Bacon to gain the office of Attorney-General, which
had been refused to him twenty years before.

Bacon's activity in his new post left nothing to be
desired; but while he did many good and useful things,
aiming at the reform of abuses and the surer and
swifter course of the law, he was forced to carry out
the disgraceful schemes of his masters. He wished to
revise the laws, and drew up a plan to this end, but to

no purpose. With all his excellent ideas, his clear insight, and his designs for impartial administration of the law, Bacon the Attorney-General is rightly regarded by history as the tool and creature of the Duke of Buckingham. For a short time the new official tasted the sweets of revenge upon his old enemy Coke, who mainly through Bacon's agency was removed from his post as Chief Justice in 1616. He aided the King in his struggle for absolute rule; but it must be remembered that if Bacon could have had Buckingham's influence, that rule would have been just and beneficent. But this was not the case. He continued to do the bidding of the favorite, and was rewarded early in 1617 with the great post of Lord Chancellor, receiving, however, the full title not until a year later. Honors were now crowded upon him. He was made Baron Verulam in 1618 and somewhat later Viscount St. Albans. Thus at the age of sixty Bacon had reached the highest honors of his profession. More than this, he had just published, in however fragmentary shape, his great scheme for the Reform of Human Thought, the *Novum Organum*, a work which by general consent marks the new era in philosophy and the beginning of the modern scientific spirit.

From this height, seemingly without any warning, Bacon fell to the depths of disgrace. That he was sacrificed to popular indignation, which had been growing steadily under the pressure of misgovernment and abuse of the king's prerogative, is clear enough; but why he fell so unresistingly, so suddenly, and so far, can be explained only by that fatal weakness in his character which has been noticed before. He had been an able Lord Chancellor; but he was after all

the creature of Buckingham, and when the storm broke,
popular indignation, heedless of the exact merits of the
case, swept him away. Most important of all, his old
enemy Coke was now directing that very storm. Bacon
was charged by the House of Commons with corruption
in office; witnesses alleged that he had taken gifts
from suitors in his court. He had accepted bribes, they
said, as high as one thousand pounds. Writing to the
King, Bacon defended himself, and maintained that he
had not perverted justice. To the public he seemed
to put a sufficiently bold face on the matter, but in
private he had already given up the fight. He made
his will, and in a prayer which curiously reminds one
of a man opposite to Bacon in every way, the sturdy
old Dr. Johnson, confessed his weakness, while in a
manner justifying his course: " The state and bread of
the poor and oppressed have been precious in mine eyes:
I have hated all cruelty and hardness of heart: I
have (though in a despised weed) procured the good
of all men." Why, we are forced to ask, could not
Bacon have faced his accusers with words like these,
and dared them to produce their facts and to prove
the credibility of their witnesses? Instead of this, he
appeals to the good offices of the King. But his enemies pressed him the harder. He offered to resign the
Great Seal and so escape further condemnation; and
towards the end of April, 1621, a full statement of the
charges against him was brought forward. Without
protest of innocence, without the least attempt to fight
his case, he threw himself upon the mercy of the
House of Lords, his judges, with the general plea of
guilty. To a committee of this house, which demanded
that he should confess all the separate abuses in the

charge, he yielded with what seems to us pitiful haste,
and asked them to be " merciful to a broken reed." He
was summoned to the bar of the House of Lords to receive sentence, but illness kept him at home. This sentence was severe enough, though some peers wished it
even harder, and Coke hinted at the penalty of death.
He was fined £40,000, an enormous sum for those
days, was sent to the Tower during the King's pleasure,
court and Parliament were closed to him, and he was
never to hold office of any kind.

Never in history has so great a man suffered such a
great disgrace ; it can be accounted for, if at all, by two
considerations. By the practice of those times Bacon's
attitude was by no means as culpable as it would seem
now ; he was no vulgar and persistent taker of bribes,
and probably rendered decisions according to the law ;
but he did take gifts from successful suitors. Moreover, he was continuing a system of court influence on
the large scale, and shaping certain decisions to suit
the purposes of his masters. With this system the
public had become thoroughly enraged, and Bacon was
the scapegoat whom they drove into the wilderness of
disgrace. In the second place, Bacon's natural protec-
tors, the King and Buckingham, lacked even the elementary gratitude to defend so able and so willing a
servant, though the Duke cast the solitary vote against
the sentence of the House of Lords ; while Bacon himself had nothing of that courage, even in a bad cause,
which ennobled a later victim of the Stuart ingratitude, and made Strafford's watchword " Thorough " as
conspicuous in adversity as in success. Still a third
excuse has been urged in Bacon's behalf : he knew
well that resistance was useless.

Bacon's confinement in the Tower was cut short, after a few days, by the King. His fine was practically forgiven, and in spite of opposition he received a partial pardon. Nothing, however, could remove his disgrace, nor could he play any further part in public life, and he was dependent on the King's bounty. Yet it is a great mistake to think that Bacon was overwhelmed by his misfortunes and that he died of a broken heart. He fell back on that greater service to which he had devoted his leisure and to which he ought to have devoted his life. In the same year that saw his fall he wrote his admirable *History of Henry the Seventh.* He never gave up the hope of a full pardon and renewal of his public service. But neither of these came to him. All the more room was left for his greater work. To the last he was busied with his system for the new sciences, corresponding with learned men abroad, revising and translating his earlier writings. His service to philosophy was rather that of a pioneer than that of a colonist. He gives the idea and plans the system, leaving other men to do the work. It is a mistake to suppose that he accomplished something practical in the so-called natural sciences, although his death, as every one knows, was due to a scientific experiment. But everywhere he stimulated, reformed, and showed the way to better things. This is true even of his English style. Few books have a fresher appeal than Bacon's essays. In an era of ponderous and periodic prose it is refreshing to meet such sentences as that which opens the essay on Death: " Men fear death as children fear to go in the dark." No one has ever packed so much into so small a compass without prejudice to simplicity and clearness of style. His ideas, too, are almost invariably sound ; for example, the essay on *Plantations* might be taken as a forecast of England's best colonial policy.

Bacon was an extravagant man, never free from debt even in the days of his largest income. This state of things may be explained partly by his amazing fondness for display. His married life seems to have been no great success, as may be gathered from his will : " To my wife, a box of rings." Indeed, the chief interests of this document, like Bacon's whole life, lean to the advancement of science, for which purpose he left funds to the two universities. He died April 9, 1626. His fatal illness was due to an experiment which he had made of the antiseptic properties of cold, stopping his carriage while he stuffed a chicken with snow from the wayside. In a famous passage of his will, he leaves his name " to the next ages and to foreign nations." Posterity and the world at large have responded nobly to his wish, and general opinion assigns him a rank equaled by no man in the world's history save Aristotle for eagerness and breadth of mind.

WILLIAM SHAKESPEARE

It is a mistake to suppose that we know little concerning the life of Shakespeare. More is known about him than about other poets of his time, such as Fletcher and Chapman. It is because his works are so well and so widely appreciated that the facts of his life seem scant and unsatisfactory ; moreover, absurd suppositions — Baconian and other heresies — about the authorship of the plays have tended to make Shakespeare a far more obscure figure than he really is. And much as we know of his life, it is impossible to express him in a phrase. What Dryden said in satire of George Duke of Buckingham could be said of Shakespeare in earnest: —

> " A man so various that he seemed to be
> Not one, but all mankind's epitome."

Byron may be called explosive, Shelley visionary, but for Shakespeare no single expression has been found.

The name Shakespeare [1] was early discovered in Yorkshire and Cumberland, but is met more often in Warwickshire, where there were many of that name. Both spellings seem to have been used by the dramatist himself.

He was born at Stratford-on-Avon, April 22 or 23, 1564. One must not ignore the importance both of the time and the place of his birth. For the time, it is enough to recall the great names and the quickening national life of Elizabethan England. Warwickshire,

---

[1] *Shakspere* has the sanction of the New Shakspere Society. *Shakespeare* is the prevailing literary form.

often called the Heart of England, was not only beautiful in landscape but rich in folk-lore, while its nearness to London put Shakespeare in the line of purely English literary traditions. North of the Tweed he would have been almost an alien to them. But the Thames valley from the time of Chaucer was the home of the literary language.

During the poet's earliest boyhood his father, who came of a good yeoman stock, must have been one of the chief men of the town. He was successively " ale-taster, constable, affeeror, chamberlain, alderman ; lastly . . . Justice of the Peace and High Bailiff of the Town." But he was incurably fond of lawsuits, sanguine, and given to undertaking tasks beyond his means of performance. He fell into difficulties of many kinds, and it was probably only through his son's success that he subsisted comfortably in later life. The attitude of Shakespeare in his plays towards old men in general, and fathers in particular, has been traced to recollections of his own experience. The elder man has been conceived as " fervent, unsteady, and irrepressible . . . excitable, sententious, and dogmatic; " and Dickens's portraiture of his father as Mr. Micawber is suggested as a parallel case. However this may be, there can be no doubt that Shakespeare's mother, Mary Arden, who inherited considerable money and lands from her father, was of gentle blood. To her and her ancestors biographers trace the undoubted sympathy which the poet shows in all his works for the gentler strain and for those modes of life and thought which can flourish only along with the traditions of the better classes.

In trying to reproduce, however, the boyhood of Shakespeare, we must by no means think of him as an

WILLIAM SHAKESPEARE

From the Droeshout portrait, used as the frontispiece of the First Folio Edition, 1623

aristocrat. The lad, who by a tradition which Aubrey has handed down on fairly good authority, was after· wards apprenticed to a butcher, stood at no remove from the other children of the town. At the Stratford Grammar School he went through the usual course of education for boys of his degree. Latin in those days was still taught to some extent as a living language ; Shakespeare probably learned it to better purpose than schoolboys of our own day. Nevertheless, he seems as an author to have preferred translations to originals ; he took from Ovid much of his mythology and classical references, and from North's Plutarch direct material for plots and characters. Every one knows Ben Jonson's account of the poet's " small Latin and less Greek." But when discussing Shakespeare's education we must remember that its importance lay in what it did for him as a reader and not as a scholar. His library has been noted, but we must not assume that all the references in his plays, traced to certain books, are based on reading. Conversation and a retentive memory will account for many a phrase and many an allusion ; especially after his arrival in London, when the most important part of his education was achieved, we must lay stress upon this source for so much of his varied and catholic information. We may compare the oral power of Athenian life, where the spoken word was so prevalent, and cite the conversation in *Hamlet* where Marcellus asks, " Who is 't that can inform me ? " and Horatio says, —

> " That can I ;
> At least, the whisper goes so. Our last king
>
> .   .   .   .
>
> Was, as you know, by Fortinbras of Norway,
> Thereto pricked on by a most emulate pride,
> Dared to the combat ; "

and gives a short account of the development of hostilities between Norway and Denmark.

Before Shakespeare went up to London, about the year 1585, by the evidence of certain facts and fairly trustworthy traditions, he was a wild and undisciplined but by no means vicious youth. The fact of his forced marriage with Ann Hathaway, in November, 1582, when he was but eighteen years of age, stands beyond reasonable dispute. That he was a confirmed poacher tradition asserts so vigorously that modern biographers are inclined to accept the main fact. In 1583 a daughter Susanna was born, and in 1585 Hamnet and Judith, the twins. Of these children his only son Hamnet died in 1596. Susanna, the oldest daughter, was married in 1607 to Dr. John Hall, and lived in Stratford until her death in 1649; while Judith, who married Thomas Quiney, a wine merchant, just before her father's death, lived until 1662. The best traditions about Shakespeare, collected, as Professor Raleigh remarks, by people who had no case to prove or theory to defend, passed upon record soon after the death of this younger daughter, were quite local in origin, and therefore, if not worthy of implicit belief, are to be accepted in the main as true.

According to a conversation held in 1693 with a Stratford man who was born before Shakespeare died, the latter " ran from his master " — the butcher — " to London, and there was received in the playhouse as a servitor." Another tradition which there is no reason to discredit makes his flight to London the result of his poaching and the consequent hostility of the main sufferer, Sir Thomas Lucy. According to Rowe, Shakespeare made a ballad upon the knight, so bitter that the prosecution was renewed, and the budding poet fled to London. Davies says that Shakespeare "was much given to all unluckiness in stealing venison and rabbits, particularly from Sir Thomas Lucy, who had him oft whipt and sometimes imprisoned, and at last made him fly his native county to his own advancement." Moreover, there is little doubt that Sir Thomas has been hung in Shakespeare's gallery, not of rogues, but of imbeciles, in the person of Justice Shallow, a foolish country squire who appears most entertainingly in the second part of *Henry IV* and at the beginning of the *Merry Wives.*[1]

Whatever the energies of Shakespeare may have done to make him the hero of such exploits as these, it is certain that he found no literary expression of his powers until his arrival in London; and although the only works which he published himself, his poems, appeared early in his career, one may be sure that his ambitions as a poet resulted from his work upon and for the stage. The flight to London, therefore, as in so many other lives of eminent men, was the prime factor in his career as an artist.

London, as Shakespeare saw it, was a far brighter and lustier town than the modern city of perpetual smoke. As Professor Baker points out, the city proper had a population of one hundred thousand. In the neighboring villages and on the Bankside across the river were perhaps as many more. Strangers gathered in the inns of the last-named place, and there too were built the theatres known as the Swan, the Hope, the Rose, and the Globe. In 1590, however, London had but two playhouses, the Theatre and the Curtain, "built near

---

[1] The Lucys had three luces in their coat-of-arms, and Shakespeare with a malicious pun refers to the "dozen white luces" on Shallow's "old coat."

together in Shoreditch, just outside the city limits." The
plays were also given in the inn-yards. Besides licensed
companies of players there were the choir-boys of St.
Paul's, who acted, as Professor Baker thinks, in the
yard of the Convocation House. From all ground within
the city, controlled by the council, mainly a Puritan
body, plays and players were jealously excluded. The
early theatres were crude affairs. The pit was uncov-
ered, though a sort of hood projected over the stage ;
the stage itself was double, with an upper and a lower
division, and there was a rude mechanism for stage effects. The play began early in the afternoon and lasted
less than three hours. Patrons of the theatre, so far as
the better class was concerned, were courtiers, members
of the nobility and their adherents, and such persons as
barristers and students in the inns of court. Add to
these the floating population of the taverns, and the
more or less disreputable folk of the kind that frequent
a modern race-track, and we have the audience to which
playwrights of Shakespeare's time made their appeal.

The career which Shakespeare chose, or which may
have been forced upon him, had the disadvantage of
ill repute. That he felt at times the shame which attached to the calling of the actor, a shame derived not
only from edicts of the Church but from one long line
of tradition, through the Middle Ages, of the old Roman contempt for the *mimus*, is probable enough, and
one of his sonnets may express the actor's bitterness.
He would chide fortune —

> " That did not better for my life provide
> Than public means which public manners breeds.
> Thence comes it that my name receives a brand,
> And almost thence my nature is subdued
> To what it works in, like the dyer's hand."

But a rapidly growing profession offered great possibilities and promise. The theatre when Shakespeare left it was very different from the theatre when he began, and it is clear that he played no small part in this progress. Companies of players, often made up of noblemen's servants, and at first strolling about the country but afterwards settling near the city, had really founded this new trade. Its profits rose enormously. Plays improved with the fortunes of the player ; rude and uneven, they served originally as mere occasion and vehicle for the popular actor. The clown or jester, as we know from Shakespeare's own complaint, had the prominent place. Rough action predominated. Then came that group of university-bred men who really created Elizabethan drama, — Lyly, Greene, Peele, and above all, Marlowe. Plays of real worth, even of genius, had now appeared ; and it was at this supremely favorable time that Shakespeare began his work. Identified with the players by his lack of academic training and by his early efforts as an actor, perhaps even as a servitor, according to one tradition, he knew how to profit by the example of the academic group, and learned his most important lessons as a playwright from Marlowe. He revised old plays for new uses ; and the first recorded notice of him is the denunciation in Greene's *Groat's-worth of Wit*, the famous death-bed confession, written in 1592. The writer warns his friends of the university group not to trust the players : " For there is an upstart Crow, beautified with our feathers, that with his *Tigers heart wrapt in a Players' hide*, supposes he is as well able to bumbast out a blank verse as the best of you ; and being an absolute *Johannes factotum*, is in his own conceit the only Shakescene in the country."

The verse in italics is paraphrased from *Henry VI*, and the Shakescene himself must be its author. The whole quotation has more meaning than appears on its surface. Up to this time the players, so to speak, had bought a new kind of drama from its inventors and makers, but now the prosperous companies, handling, as we should say, an increasing business, began to manufacture their own goods, using and improving the pattern of their old purchases, and driving the first makers out of the market. That Shakespeare nevertheless contrived to put himself on good terms with the academic school is certain evidence of his genial character. These men, like the Johnsons and Goldsmiths of a later day, were men of letters simply, living by their wits and selling their brains to the players as the later men sold their work to the publisher. Shakespeare's attitude was altogether different. Authorship with him began as part of his larger business. Revision and adaptation revealed to him his own powers of independent production. He could make as well as re-make; genius took the place of talent; and thus what Hallam calls the "Shakespeare of Heaven" grew out of the "Shakespeare of Earth," and the poet asserted himself apart from his trade.

By his poems, however, *Venus and Adonis* and *The Rape of Lucrece*, which were published and read under his own name, he became favorably known to the world of letters, and gained a distinction which his plays would never have given him. The sonnets also, circulated for some time in manuscript before their publication, contributed to this result. Dramatists were hardly ranked as poets until the publication of the works of Ben Jonson, in folio, about the time of Shakespeare's death. So he was lifted out of the ordinary run of play-wrights. These poems, dedicated as they were to a peer conspicuous for his patronage of letters, opened to Shakespeare the door of noble and even of royal favors; and the acquaintance, reacting on his work as a play-wright, procured him a welcome at court. He was commanded to produce his pieces before the Queen; and tradition has it that he wrote the *Merry Wives* to oblige Elizabeth, just as his *Macbeth*, in subject and allusion, was a compliment to King James. He praises the Queen in certain well-known lines in the *Midsummer Night's Dream*. The favors of his noble friends seem often to have been substantial; the Earl of Southampton is re-ported to have given him £1000,—equivalent to eight times that amount in modern money. The custom of the day warrants us in supposing other gifts from other friends. But this intercourse brought him something far better than money. Patrons of letters, traveled, versed in all the arts and accomplishments of the day, and in Italian and French literature, gave to Shakespeare his best education, and may go far to account for those characters in his plays which bring before us so vividly the soldiers, courtiers, and great men of former time.

The difficulty which many have found in accepting this Stratford yeoman's son as author of the plays that go under his name, and which they base on the contrast between Stratford schooling on the one hand and on the other the wealth of knowledge, experience, and observa-tion displayed in the dramas, vanishes when one thinks what an education the best society of London could give to a man as keen and vigorous as Shakespeare. If it be objected that the despised actor had no entry into this world of refinement, two answers are obvious. Then, as now, a man of parts, who could entertain by his wit and please by his fancy, was made welcome in the houses of the great. Then, as now, money and property were keys to open almost any door. Actors made money. In a very different way, and to a different purpose, it was the life of London which educated Dickens. Like Goethe, Shakespeare must have been sensitive to the influence of noble women and to their charm; and we cannot think that his splendid gallery of Portias, Rosalinds, and Imogens was without counterparts in the real life which he saw and shared.

Greater difficulties are met in the discussion of the plays themselves. His London life has actually been reconstructed from the spirit and subject of his dramatic works in their probable order of production. The facts are these: after his early comedies, *Love's Labour's Lost*, *The Two Gentlemen of Verona*, and the *Comedy of Errors*, and his early tragedy, *Romeo and Juliet*, which reflect the single-hearted gayety and single-hearted sorrow of youth, Shakespeare produced his plays at an average rate of two every year, with increasing mastery of his art. Thirty-seven titles are included in the whole list. By 1594, the end of his first or experimental period, he had written, besides the plays just named, the bloody and repulsive *Titus Andronicus*, *Henry VI* in its three parts (where, however, he was only collaborator and reviser), *Richard III*, and *Richard II*. In *Henry VI* he had worked with Marlowe; in the other two plays he imitated him. His beautiful tribute, —

"Dead Shepherd! Now I find thy saw of might :
Who ever loved that loved not at first sight ?" —

more than makes up for the parody of Marlowe's style

which he introduced into his *Henry IV*. To the year
1594 belong his *King John* and *The Merchant of Venice* in its earlier, unrevised version. The playwright's
reputation was now assured, and between this date and
the turn of the century appeared *Midsummer Night's
Dream*, *All 's Well*, *Taming of the Shrew*, *Henry IV*
(with its popular figure of Falstaff), *The Merry Wives*,
Henry V, and three perfect comedies, *Much Ado*, *As
You Like It*, and *Twelfth Night*. The turn of the century was marked by the building of the new theatres as
well as by the new prosperity of the players themselves;
but this change is not reflected in the spirit of Shakespeare's dramatic work. His comedy, once so gay and
lately so serene, becomes intricate and cloudy; in *Measure for Measure* it trembles on the verge of tragedy.
This drama is placed about 1604, midway in that
splendid procession of tragedies which began in 1601
with *Julius Cæsar*, and proceeded with *Hamlet*, *Troilus and Cressida*, *Othello*, *Macbeth*, and *King Lear*,
till 1608, when in *Timon of Athens* tragedy almost
turns to outright pessimism. This was followed by
Shakespeare's part of *Pericles* and by the two Roman
plays, *Antony and Cleopatra* and *Coriolanus*. The
final group of plays is of an entirely different stamp.
In *Cymbeline*, the *Winter's Tale*, and *The Tempest*,
strong threatening of tragedy is averted, a domestic
complication — in two cases the parting of husband
and wife, in a third the hostility of two brothers — is
reconciled by a woman's influence, and there is a happy
if not a merry ending. There is no doubt that these
plays were written at the time when Shakespeare's visits
to Stratford grew more frequent, and his final retirement there was close at hand. One biographer suggests

that they were written at Stratford in the summers, to be acted later at the Globe Theatre in London, and suggests that Judith Shakespeare served as model to her father for the charming figures of Perdita and Miranda.

How far now we can reconstruct Shakespeare's London life, about which absolutely nothing is known in detail, from the sequence and character of his dramatic work and more particularly from his personal lyric in the sonnets, is no easy question. The " sugred sonnets," which according to Francis Meres were circulated as early as 1598 among the poet's private friends, were published for sixpence in quarto in the year 1609 by one Thomas Thorpe, a bookseller. The dedication to " Mr. W. H." has occasioned a vast amount of controversy ; but we are now concerned with the sonnets themselves. There is great variety of opinion. Wordsworth says that " with this key Shakespeare unlocked his heart," and the majority of critics and biographers incline to accept the sonnets as a transcript from his actual life. Mr. Sidney Lee, on the other hand, noting in how many cases the English sonnets of that day proved to have been paraphrases or translations from foreign models, Italian or French, refuses to give to these anything but an artistic value. They reveal, he says, nothing of the poet's actual life, only the perfection of his art.

In viewing the dramas extremes must be avoided. On the one hand there is no doubt that the plays stand for themselves and are to be explained, now on business grounds, — being totally objective and outside Shakespeare's life, as in the historical plays which were demanded by the rising patriotism of England, — now on artistic grounds, where the poet flung himself into creative work out of interest in his subject and from no similar experience of his own. Moreover, the sequence of mood and subject, noted above, corresponds not so much to the development of Shakespeare the individual as to the maturing powers in any artist and the course of most human lives. Another factor to be considered is the old community of ownership in literary goods. Not only could several men unite, as now, to make a play, but one could take older plays and modify them at will. In Chaucer's time translating and paraphrasing were as creditable as authorship. But it must be remembered that while Shakespeare borrowed the material of his plays, he selected it; and his work is anything but that of a copyist. Of his spontaneity of production there can be no doubt. The players told Ben Jonson that the poet " never blotted out a line " of what he had penned; and his editors Heming and Condell said that " what he thought he uttered with that easiness that we have scarce received from him a blot in his papers." It is clear that he did not require great influences on his own life to force expression, nor need one see life tragedy in theatre tragedy. Undoubtedly he was a good man of business, and his plays were put on the stage as commercial ventures, yet Pope overstates the case when he says that Shakespeare —

> " For gain, not glory, winged his roving flight,
> And grew immortal in his own despite."

There is evidence that he did care for glory and intended his works to be collected in a final shape. He took some steps in this direction; and there is all the evidence in the world that he wrote with that deep feeling and conviction without which there can be no poetry.

To sum up, we can tell nothing of Shakespeare's life or opinions directly from his plays, while in the sonnets, although nothing is to be taken literally, there is sure testimony of his serious views and a picture of his inner, if not of his outer, life.

Something can also be learned of the great dramatist's career in London from the friends with whom he lived. Apart from his noble patrons already named, there were the playwrights with whom he worked and the comrades with whom he passed his leisure hours. Among the former were Marlowe and perhaps others of that early group of university-bred men, brilliant, dissolute, lacking Shakespeare's splendid self-command. The Stratford yeoman's son seems to have won respect and esteem on all sides, was praised for his " civil demeanor," and came to be one of the leading men of letters in the city. He is probably the " Ætion " in Spenser's list of contemporary poets. While in his early days he had served as factotum on the stage, taking this or that part at need, he soon became not only a leading playwright but a person of the highest authority in dramatic affairs generally. It was due to him that Ben Jonson's first comedy, *Every Man in his Humour*, was performed in 1598 against the decision of the manager of the company, and Shakespeare himself took the part of Old Knowell in this play. Furthermore, unscrupulous publishers tried to get readers for inferior or valueless plays by printing them as Shakespeare's own. At the Mermaid Tavern in Bread Street he met Jonson and other men of letters in those wit-combats recorded by Beaumont's verse and Fuller's prose. No amount of literary inference can supplant these famous descriptions of the life in which he actually shared. Jonson was " like a Spanish great gal-

leon ; . . . Shakespear, with the English man-of-war,
lesser in bulk but lighter in sailing, could turn with all
tides, tack about, and take advantage of all winds by
the quickness of his wit and invention."

Shakespeare was keen in business as well as in wit,
like some other poets of his nation. Such records of his
career as have been discovered point to business activities. He invested money in London and purchased
houses and lands. In 1597 he bought the largest house
in Stratford, and there are records of his building and
plantings. While he did not settle here until 1611,
we may fancy him a frequent visitor. In the same year
that he bought New Place a lawsuit was begun by his
father and mother for the possession of their mortgaged
estate. Three letters, written during 1598 from Stratford, are quoted by the poet's biographers to show his
reputation "for wealth and influence." Mr. Lee calculates that his income up to this time, due mainly to
his pay as actor on the stage and in noblemen's houses,
would average about $5000 a year of our money.
With such additional gifts as his patrons made him,
he might well seem a rich man to his Warwickshire
friends. After 1599 his fortunes rapidly increased.
Documents are quoted which describe the Globe Theatre,
built in 1598, as managed by "those deserving men,
Shakespeare, Heming, Condell, Philips and others,"
who shared in its receipts. This was a large theatre,
and we may conclude that Shakespeare's income from
such a source must have resulted in making him one
of the prosperous business men of London. He was
also a shareholder, with smaller profits, in the Black-
friars Theatre. He had still other sources of income,
and the diary of the Rev. John Ward, vicar of Strat-

ford from 1662 to 1668, records that Shakespeare in his last years spent at the rate of a thousand pounds a year. The poet figured, moreover, in numerous lawsuits, mainly for the recovery of debts.

We know, then, that Shakespeare was a keen man of business, and that he grew rich. More than this, he aspired to the rank and privileges of a gentleman. His purchase of land in Stratford points this way, and it was surely in his interests that the father, John Shakespeare, applied for a coat-of-arms. This was obtained in 1599, and the poet, though his business was in London, was henceforth described as "of Stratford-on-Avon, gentleman."

The first decade of the seventeenth century perhaps saw the end of Shakespeare's London career. He sold his shares in the two theatres, probably about 1611, and retired to his native town. There is no reason to believe that he undertook any independent dramatic or poetical work after this time, although his interests in theatrical affairs were maintained by his friendship with Ben Jonson and other playwrights, by his visits to London, and perhaps by the revision of his plays with a view to the publication which they finally secured through the good offices of his friends Heming and Condell. The rest of his life must be imagined on the basis of his general character: such incidental matters as are recorded — his function as god-father, his relations with the corporation of Stratford, his entertainment of a Puritan preacher, — throw no real light on the situation.

In November, 1614, he paid his supposedly last visit to London; his will was prepared in January, 1616, but was not signed until March. The diary of Ward, already cited, says that Drayton and Ben Jonson visited the poet about this time and "had a merry meeting." Another and later legend makes Shakespeare the hero of a carouse at Bidford, a village in the neighborhood of Stratford. But the parson adds that they drank too hard and that Shakespeare "died of a fever there contracted." The poet's character, however, so tolerant, so temperate, so averse from extremes, forbids us to accept without better authority the notion that he shared the fate of a Robert Greene. He died on the 23d of April, 1616, a date which is generally regarded as his birthday.

As for his personal appearance, both tradition, as reported by Aubrey, and the portraits make him "a handsome, well-shaped man." These portraits have been much discussed, but critics now agree that the bust in the Stratford church and the engraved portrait prefixed to the first folio edition (1623) of the poet's works — with certificate to the likeness in Ben Jonson's "Lines to the Reader" — are the only portraits of Shakespeare which admit no doubt of genuineness. It is probable, though not certain, that the so-called Flower portrait, now hanging in the Memorial Gallery at Stratford, is the original painting from which this engraving for the first folio was made. The bust, whitewashed in 1793 by order of Malone, the great Shakespeare editor, was cleaned in 1861, revealing the eyes as "light hazel" in color and "the hair and beard auburn." Even allowing for clumsy reproduction in both cases, one cannot suppose the face to have been of the highly intellectual and impressive type. In looks, as in manner and in character, the over-worked adjective "genial" will probably best describe him. "We feel sure," says Professor Raleigh, "children did not stop their talk when he came near them, but continued, in the happy assurance that it was only Master Shakespeare." He is rightly called the prince of poets because in his poetry men have found a wider range and a closer grasp of humanity itself than in the works of any other man. His poetry has defects, and he himself had limitations obvious enough to those who compare him with such a poet as Milton. He was neither a great moralist nor, to use Matthew Arnold's phrase, "a friend and aider to those who would live in the spirit." But in the power to interpret human life, in the sweep of imagination, and in the beauty and melody of poetic speech, he stands without a peer.

THE PURITAN AGE

THE period covered by the reign of James I (1603–25) has been often called the Decadence. After 1610 the Elizabethan flower was overblown, writers became consciously artificial, men sought new and elaborate forms of expression, and literature, lacking a fresh impulse, naturally went through a process of disintegration. Much of the literature of the time, especially the drama, became very coarse. As far as form went, the drama and the lyric reached great excellence, but they lacked the old freshness and genuineness. It was in such an atmosphere that the masque, an elaborate court entertainment, reached its height.

This literature of coarseness, skillful technique, and little vital energy was the expression of its time, the so-called Jacobean Age. Against it grew up the great protest of *Puritanism*. Puritanism, in its beginnings, back in Elizabeth's reign, was merely an emphasis on individual purity. Though later associated with Presbyterianism and the cause of Parliament against the King and the Church of England, it was properly an attitude of mind, not a religious sect. It did come in course of time, however, to be a more or less clearly defined body, embracing the severe doctrines of Calvinism. These, roughly speaking, were that man was by Adam's fall doomed to eternal punishment, but that God in his infinite mercy had "elected" a few to salvation. The whole concern of the Puritan, therefore, was the salvation of his individual soul; it behooved him to watch and fast and pray, lest he lose his one chance of redemption or by his frivolity destroy the chances of his descendants. Earthly things became mere fleeting joys or sorrows, of no account when one's mind dwelt continually on an eternity of joy or of suffering. The Puritan thus grew into a severe and steadfast man, insensible to danger and fatigue. The period of dominant Puritan influence was from 1625, the accession of Charles I, to 1660, the Restoration of Charles II.

The effect of such a body of men on literature was withering; by 1640 " Merrie England " was irrevocably buried in the past. The theatres were closed in 1642; dancing, games, and all singing but psalm singing were reprobated. The rich, sonorous service of the Church of England was considered an idle, wicked vanity. England, as Green says, became a nation of one book, the Bible. Puritan literature, therefore, with two striking exceptions, was given over to controversial pamphlets and sermons, both of which died for the most part in a few years. The two exceptions, of course, were Milton, who retained the artistic Elizabethan impulse, who was, as Dr. Neilson has put it, " the lasting proof of the possibility of the combination of Puritanism and culture," and Bunyan, who had a message for a whole nation.

Puritanism, however, did not absorb every one. Indeed, probably less than half of the population of England were avowedly Puritans. There still remained many of the King's followers, " Cavaliers " as they were called, who were writing incomparable lyrics. Besides them, moreover, were many excellent persons, touched with the emphasis on personal purity, but repelled by

the harsh manner, solemn garb, and sanctimonious
speech of the extreme Puritans. These remained in the
Church and, along with a few poetical Puritans, composed many religious lyrics.

JOHN MILTON

IN a letter to his friend Charles Diodati, in 1637,
Milton wrote : " He (God) has instilled into me, if into
any one, a vehement love of the beautiful." And in
Paradise Regained, writing of his youth, he says : —

> " When I was yet a child, no childish play
> To me was pleasing : all my mind was set
> Serious to learn and know, and thence to do,
> What might be public good ; myself I thought
> Born to that end, born to promote all truth,
> All righteous things. "

These two quotations illustrate the two chief elements
in Milton's nature, — a passionate love of the beautiful, and a not less passionate service of duty. He was
brought up in an atmosphere of art and music, and
chose the vocation of poet; but when his conscience
called he gave up his poetic delights and wrote himself
blind in defense of his country; yet when his years of service were over he retired in solitude to sing the greatest
poem of his time. As Shakespeare's work was the consummation of the Elizabethan Renaissance, so Milton's
struck the highest note of what has been aptly called
the Puritan Renaissance. No two centuries are of greater
importance in English history than the sixteenth and
seventeenth, and no two periods have had such magnificent expression.

Milton's birth took place in an epoch-making period.
Queen Elizabeth had been dead five years, and with
James a new character began to stamp itself on the
English people. Shakespeare had by this time written

most of his great tragedies; Ben Jonson was rising to fame; Ralegh and Bacon had already attained renown; and Oliver Cromwell, who was to be the genius of the Commonwealth, was a boy of nine years. When Milton was three, the King James Bible was published; and nine years later the Pilgrim Fathers set sail for the New World.

The life of Milton is commonly divided for convenience into three periods: his education, life at Horton, and travels (1608–1639); civil life (1640–1660); retirement(1660–1674)

Part I (1608–1639)

The exact date of the poet's birth was December 8, 1608. His father was John Milton, born probably in 1563, the son of Richard Milton of Oxfordshire, a Romanist. His mother, it seems, was a Sara Jeffrey (1573–1637) of Essex. The elder John Milton, disinherited on account of Protestant beliefs, was in London about 1585, though nothing is known of his trade until about ten years later, when he started as a scrivener's apprentice. In five years, two less than the regular period of apprenticeship, he was admitted to the full power of scrivener, at that time a trade consisting chiefly in the drawing up of deeds, wills, and contracts. Milton's father seems to have been moderately successful, for he soon married and settled in a comfortable house in Bread Street. This house, in a day when many houses were named like inns, was called "The Spread Eagle." Besides three who died in infancy, John and Sara Milton had three children: Anne (born between 1602 and 1607), John (1608), and Christopher (1615).

Milton's boyhood was passed in the heart of London. Hard by "The Spread Eagle" was the Mermaid Tavern, famous as the haunt of great dramatists. A little way down Bread Street, towards the north, one came to Cheapside, the great shopping street which ran down to St. Paul's Cathedral, and not far beyond St. Paul's was Smithfield. On the south, only a few minutes' walk away, ran the Thames, with just a fringe of buildings on the now populous Surrey side; and to the east rose London Tower.

Milton received a good training from his earliest youth. His father was a skillful musician and a composer of some fame, and from him the boy early acquired a taste for music. In 1618, when he was ten, a Mr. Thomas Young began giving him private lessons in school work, which were continued till 1622, probably after Milton had begun attending St. Paul's School. He was at St. Paul's probably from 1620 till 1625. There he studied Latin and Greek, and possibly French, Italian, and Hebrew. From the first he showed skill at his books and tireless application — "serious to learn and know." "From the twelfth year of my age," he says in the *Defensio Secunda*, "I scarcely ever went from my lessons to bed before midnight." Among his school-fellows should be remembered Charles Diodati, with whom he formed a very beautiful and lasting friendship.

On February 12, 1625, Milton was admitted a Lesser Pensioner to Christ's College, Cambridge. In his second year he had a little quarrel with his tutor, Chappell. He was perhaps whipped, and probably rusticated for a short time; at all events, he was absent from the University for a few weeks in 1626, and in a Latin poem to his friend Diodati speaks of Cambridge, " where my

forbidden cell causes me little regret." He soon returned
to favor, however, and was transferred to a Mr. Tovey's
tutelage. His high character and his scholarly excellence won him friendship and renown, and he was often
called upon to take part in college and university exercises. In 1629 he received the degree of B. A. and three
years later was admitted to that of M. A. It is interesting to note, in connection with his future Puritanism,
that to receive his degree Milton had to subscribe to
the Articles of Royal Supremacy, Church Liturgy, and
Doctrinal Standards of the Church of England. In 1635
Oxford bestowed upon him an M. A. as an honorary
degree.

To follow Milton's literary career we must go back
a few years. Until his graduation most of his work was
in Latin, but he had already in 1632 written English
poems, some of great promise. *Paraphrases of Psalms
CXIV and CXXXVI*, written about the time of his
leaving St. Paul's, were his first efforts. *On the Death
of a Fair Infant Dying of a Cough* (probably his
niece) was written in 1626. In 1629 he wrote his *Ode
on the Morning of Christ's Nativity*, his first really
great poem, which admitted him, only twenty-one, to
a high rank among poets. In 1630 came *The Passion*
(a fragment), and in 1632 his *Epitaph on Shakespeare*, published among the verses prefixed to the
Shakespeare Folio of that year. In 1631 he wrote two
poems on Hobson, the famous university carrier, who
had driven his coach to London when Shakespeare was
a boy. They were meant to be humorous, but humor
was not Milton's affair. To the same year belong his
Epitaph on the Marchioness of Winchester and, far
more significant, his Sonnet *On Having Arrived at*

the Age of Twenty-three, in which he dedicates himself
to the public service already hinted at. Of his many
Latin epistles, elegies, and dissertations, the seven
Prolusiones Oratoriae (Oratorical Exercises), not published till 1674, are the most famous. About the time
of his leaving Cambridge he wrote a Latin poem, *Ad
Patrem*, in which he explains to his father his choice
of poetry as a vocation.

Milton is described as being at this time (1632)
under middle height, with a fair complexion, dark gray
eyes, and auburn hair. His personal appearance, coupled
with the purity of his character, had won him the
nick-name of " Lady of Christ's." Yet it must not be
thought from this that he was of a soft, yielding disposition. Gentle he undoubtedly was, in the better sense
of the term, but no man was more fearless in expression of his opinions, no man resented more openly inter-
ference with intellectual freedom. He had, moreover, a
confidence in his calling, a consciousness of his high
task ; "from the first," says Lowell, " he looked upon
himself as a man dedicated and set apart." In speaking
of his youth, Milton says : " Only this my mind gave
me, that every free and gentle spirit, without that oath,
ought to be born a knight, nor needed to expect the
gilt spur or the laying of a sword upon his shoulder to
stir him up both by his counsel and his arms, to secure
and protect the weakness of any attempted chastity."
And in the same account : " I was confirmed in this
opinion, that he who would not be frustrate of his hope to
write well hereafter in laudable things, ought himself
to be a true poem ; that is, a composition and pattern
of the honourablest things ; not presuming to sing high
praises of heroic men, or famous cities, unless he have

in himself the experience and the practice of all that
which is praiseworthy." Such was the lofty standard
that the young poet set himself, and such the " high
seriousness " with which he judged of his qualification.
" He had an ambition," says Professor Masson, " to be
not merely a *poeta*, but a *vates.*"

Milton had been destined, as were most young men
of his scholarly attainments, for the Church, but a letter
written about 1632 shows that he felt unprepared
for the work ; though he says nothing of objection to
doctrines, he yet prefers to wait. By 1637 *Lycidas,*
in the picture of the corrupted clergy, gives a more
positive attitude ; and in 1641 his words in *The Reason
of Church-Government* leave no doubt. "Perceiving,"
he says, " what tyranny had invaded the Church, — that
he who would take orders must subscribe slave, and take
an oath withal, which unless he took with a conscience
that would retch, he must either straight perjure or
split his faith, — I thought it better to prefer a blame-
less silence before the sacred office of speaking bought
and begun with servitude and forswearing."

So, instead of taking orders, Milton went to live
with his father, who, comfortably successful, had retired
about 1632 to a country place at Horton, in Buckinghamshire. The country there is mostly flat pasture-land,
with full-flowing streams and many little runnels,
branches of the river Colne. On the west rise the towers
of Windsor Castle. At Horton, in reading and study,
Milton passed most of the following five years. Here
he lived the lives of his own *Allegro* and *Penseroso,* developing his sympathy with nature and increasing his vast store of classical knowledge. Occasionally
he made short trips to London, chiefly, he says, to study

mathematics and music. There he met Henry Lawes, the great musician, who was soon to play an important part in his life.

While at Horton Milton composed most of the so-called *Minor Poems* (published together in 1646). In 1632 *L'Allegro* and *Il Penseroso* were written. In the following year came the *Song on a May Morning*, the *Sonnet on a Nightingale*, and *At a Solemn Music*, and in 1634 the two poems, *On Time* and *Upon the Circumcision*.

Arcades and *Comus*, the masques, have a special significance. The masque was a musical dramatic performance given privately in honor of some great or noble person, and it is important to realize that Milton, the well-to-do scrivener's son, had come into sufficient acquaintanceship with such people to be asked to take part in composing their masques. *Arcades*, conducted chiefly by Lawes, in honor of the Countess of Derby, a lady praised in verse ever since Elizabethan days, contains a small literary part which Lawes asked Milton to write. The date was probably 1633 or 1634. *Comus*, a much longer and more famous piece, was acted in 1634 at Ludlow Castle, in honor of the stepson of the Countess of Derby, the Earl of Bridgewater, who had recently been nominated Lord President of Wales. Possibly Milton was present at the performance, in which case he must have actually seen the western part of England, with which he shows so much familiarity. In 1637 Lawes, who had written the music for *Comus*, published the whole piece.

In the same year as the publication of *Comus*, three important pieces of writing came from Milton's pen,— two letters to his friend Diodati, and his famous elegy

Lycidas, in memory of his college friend Edward King, " unfortunately drown'd in his passage from Chester on the Irish Seas." Both the letters and *Lyci-das* are interesting in connection with the poet's bio-graphy. In the letter of September 23 he says : "And what am I doing? Growing my wings and meditating flight; but as yet our Pegasus raises himself on very tender pinions. Let us be lowly wise." At the same time that these words show Milton's faith in his calling they indicate a characteristic modesty, a conviction that he had not as yet struck his true note, that he must " scorn delights and live laborious days " to prepare him-self for a flight of song truly " above th' Aonian Mount." Indeed, he had intended to cease writing poetry till he had trained himself to pursue " Things unattempted yet in prose or rhyme." Hence it is that *Lycidas* begins with an apology for once more taking to verse. His friend's death, he felt, justified the step.

The most important autobiographical passages in *Lycidas,* however, as well as in *Comus,* are those in-terpreting Milton's character in the growing austerity of the times. In *Comus* the Enchanter has no real power over the lost Lady because she is fortified by innocence and purity ; and the moral of the poem is :

" Love Virtue, she alone is free."

In *Lycidas* the two digressions are significant. The first, on Fame, might have occurred to any serious, high-minded person ; at this time Milton's Puritanism found expression in personal purity rather than in op-position to government. Little by little, however, he was drawing away from the pleasure-loving Cavaliers ; the ways had parted ; ahead he saw a life of serious

toil. In the digression on the Church he is more outspoken. There may be "prophetic strain" in his assurance at the end, whether he means the axe of the
gospel, or the two houses of Parliament, or what, that

> " That two-handed engine at the door
> Stands ready to smite once, and smite no more."

Lycidas is the clearly marked conclusion of Milton's
earlier work; his middle and later life were in truth
in " pastures new."

That Milton, with such conjectured forebodings of
future strife, should have gone to Italy indicates at
least how strongly the Elizabethan artist survived in
him. Italy, with its storehouses of antiquity, with its
long roll of illustrious painters and poets, was a Mecca
to a man of his natûre. In the spring of 1638, therefore, when nothing very definite called at home, he
started on his tour. One's imagination is not likely to
overestimate the deep impression that Italy and the
men there made on the young scholar. Armed with
many letters, — particularly from Sir Henry Wotton
and his friend Lawes, — he found no difficulty in gaining entrance into the highest circles, whether of society
or learning, and his scholarship and personality won
him many complimentary letters and poems.

Milton went first to Paris, where he met the great
Hugo Grotius, Dutch philosopher and theologian, at
that time banished from his own country and serving
as ambassador for Sweden. From Paris the poet traveled via Genoa and Pisa, in August, 1638, to Florence.
After two months at Florence, in which he met Galileo,
the old blind astronomer, now a captive in his own
villa "for thinking in astronomy otherwise than the
Franciscan and Dominican licensers thought," Milton

journeyed to Rome, where he stayed about two months
and heard Leonora Baroni sing. Arriving in Naples
late in November, 1638, he made there a warm friendship with Manso, the munificent patron of letters.
Milton had intended to proceed thence to Sicily and
Greece, but on receiving news of the war between the
Scotch Covenanters and Charles I he gave up these
projects; " for I considered it base," he says, " that,
while my countrymen were fighting at home for liberty,
I should be traveling abroad at ease for intellectual
culture." Yet he did not hurry straight home. Warned
against a second visit to Rome, on account of the danger his outspoken Protestantism had already brought
him, he went willfully thither and expressed freely his
views. Luckily he escaped the " grim wolf " of Rome,
and arrived about March, 1639, in Florence. There he
remained till the end of April, renewing his old acquaintances and taking part in the exercises of the
many *Accademie*. Then, hurrying through Bologna
and Ferrara, he arrived at Venice early in May. His
five Italian sonnets and one *canzone* were perhaps written at this time, for they show a familiarity with the
region about Bologna, though the brief visit to that
town and our ignorance of the lady, if she was a real
person, to whom they were addressed, makes this only
conjecture. From Venice Milton traveled home *via*
Geneva, the home of Diodati's relatives, and Paris,
reaching England about August 1, 1639. To his own
account of the journey, given in the *Defensio Secunda*,
he adds : " I again take God to witness that in all
those places, where so many things are considered lawful, I lived sound and untouched from all profligacy
and vice, having the thought perpetually with me that,

though I might escape the eyes of men, I certainly could not escape the eyes of God."

On reaching England, Milton was at first busied with thoughts of his dearest friend, Charles Diodati, who had died in August, 1638, and probably late in the autumn of 1639 he wrote the famous Latin elegy, *Epitaphium Damonis*. In this poem Milton refers to his own literary projects, particularly a long epic on the story of King Arthur. His notes made at this time reveal, moreover, numerous schemes ; they include plans for a dramatic form of *Paradise Lost*, sixty-one subjects taken from the Bible, thirty-three from English history, and five from Scottish.

Part II (1640–1660)

To follow the turn which Milton's life now takes it is necessary to keep in mind the main developments in Church and State. It is essential to remember, above all, that Puritanism grew first out of an emphasis on purity, that many early Puritans remained in the Church of England, — witness Milton's father, — and that it was only after the gradual assimilation of Calvinism and after the political developments between Charles I, who thought himself the "deputy elected by the Lord," and Parliament, which found its rights openly violated, that the great body of Puritans opposed themselves to the English Church. Then, indeed, matters hastened to strife ; for the Puritans, who disliked idle shows and much ritual, were especially provoked by Archbishop William Laud, a man who, Macaulay says, had "a childish passion for mummeries." At the same time Thomas Wentworth, Earl of Strafford, developed his policy of "Thorough." Charles dismissed Parliament; rules of doctrine and conformity were published; taxes were increased; emigration to America was forbidden. From March, 1629, to April, 1640, the King's Ministry and Privy Council, with its Star-Chamber and Court of High Commission, was the sole legislative body. Finally the King, with an untrained and discontented army, with no Parliament to fall back on, and with the well-trained Scots marching against him in battle, was compelled to call the Long Parliament. To his dismay it at once set about the trial of his creatures who had shared with him the spoils of eleven years. Matters got beyond his control; Wentworth was brought to the block in 1641, and Laud to the Tower, and in 1642 civil war broke out.

When the civil war began all England and Scotland were involved, and it hence became necessary for every one to take sides. The King, who was at first successful, numbered among his followers many of the best men of the day. It is as unfair to judge of the Royalists by the profligate rabble, which did nevertheless belong to them, as it is to judge of the Puritans by their extreme fanatics. The Royalists were thoroughly in earnest; they believed, as Professor Wendell has pointed out, in the *royal right* no less than the Parliamentarians in their *inalienable rights*. With them stood courtesy, chivalry, and the traditions of their fathers. The Parliamentarians, on the other hand, inspired by the ideals of liberty and justice, were impelled for the most part by religious zeal. Cromwell and his " God-fearing " men, rolling their battle-hymn " strong and great against the sky," were invincible foes.

It was not unnatural, moreover, that the Church, with its increased respect for forms and traditions,

should have become one with the Royalists, and that
the Puritans, with their zeal for religious liberty, should
have joined the Parliamentarians. Among these Puritans were many Independents, men unwilling to accept
Presbyterianism as the only alternative to Prelacy.
Roughly speaking, however, all the parties may be resolved into two great divisions, — King and Church
against Parliament and Puritanism. The one was made
a fact by Charles' Star-Chamber and Laud's Court of
High Commission; the other, expressing at once the
protest of Independent and Presbyterian, was made a
fact in 1643 by the *Solemn League and Covenant between England and Scotland.*

Milton's position, if the tendencies of his youth are
kept in mind, should now be clear. He was brought
up as an old-time Puritan in the Established Church
and had a deep veneration for the beauties of music,
art, and literature. But he could never bow down before
such things; and when Laud and his Prelates seemed to
be doing so, Milton, it will be remembered, did not see
his way clear to taking orders; he was, in his own words,
" Church-outed by the Prelates." It was above all the
sacred principle of liberty which chiefly drove him to
his choice of sides. He lingered fondly with the bright
splendors of his youth; he held back from the ugly,
extravagant harshness of the later Puritanism. When,
however, a choice was necessary, when he saw that liberty was the cause of Parliament against the tyranny
of Church and King, he did not hesitate a moment.
Throwing aside all the artistic delights which must have
tugged so strongly at his heartstrings, he nobly chose for
Parliament. In so doing he allied himself with all the
harsher forms of Puritanism and with Presbyterianism.

But he did not become a Presbyterian. At first, to be sure, as is shown in his early pamphlets, he looked on Presbyterianism as the only alternative, but that he soon saw the futility of his hope is clear from his poem *On the New Forcers of Conscience* (1647), in which he says : " New *Presbyter* is but old *Priest* writ large." Yet to be effective it was necessary to take sides, and so John Milton cast in his lot with the Presbyterians. " He fought their perilous battle," says Macaulay, " but he turned away with disdain from their insolent triumph." *Purity* and *Liberty* were, in short, the tenets of his creed ; he was a Puritan of the elder time and an Independent ; " in the ordinary sense of that much-abused term," says Dr. Garnett, " no Puritan, but a most free and independent thinker, the vast sweep of whose thought happened to coincide for a while with the narrow orbit of so-called Puritanism."

On returning to England in 1639, Milton did not at once take active part in the struggle, but, renting lodgings in St. Bride's Churchyard, began a small school, in which he taught his two nephews and one or two other pupils. Dr. Johnson has hence charged him with " great promises and small performances." It is perhaps fairer to remember Wordsworth's words, —

" Thy heart
The lowliest duties on herself did lay."

The time was not yet ripe. His was not a fight with the sword, and his pen generally demanded some immediate impulse. This soon came, however, and produced the long line of prose writings, Latin and English, in which he steadily upheld the cause of liberty. He had moved about 1640 from St. Bride's Churchyard to a " pretty garden-house " in Aldersgate Street, and here in 1641 and 1642 he wrote the five pamphlets setting forth his views on church government.

The next series of pamphlets had a very real impulse in his own marriage. In June, 1643, he married Mary Powell, a girl of seventeen, daughter of an Oxfordshire squire who was a debtor of Milton's father. A month after a visit to Oxfordshire, perhaps to collect interest, Milton returned with his bride. His wife, however, being " used to a great house, and much company and joviality," did not take kindly to the austere Puritan household in Aldersgate Street, and before a month was out returned to her parents. By letter she obtained permission to remain away till the following Michaelmas. Michaelmas come, however, she did not return, and Milton, says his nephew Phillips, " thought it would be dishonorable ever to receive her again." Whereupon, Phillips adds, Milton wrote his first treatise on *Divorce*—that is, after Michaelmas. But Professor Masson has fixed the date of this pamphlet as early as August 1, 1643. Pattison suggests that Milton may have been " occupying himself with an argument in favor of divorce for incompatibility of temper, during the honeymoon." The pamphlet was written hurriedly, however, as we know Milton did write when the impulse was on him, and it is probable that he wrote it, in bitter disappointment, right after the separation, which took place some time in July. During the next two years he added three pamphlets on the same subject.

Concerning all Milton's relations to his first wife we are unfortunately in possession only of facts unpleasantly suggestive. In the summer of 1645 he was paying his addresses to one of Dr. Davis's daughters, and yet late the same summer he was reconciled to his wife. That great happiness ever entered the household is unlikely, though there is no knowledge of a second quarrel. Milton's ideal of marriage, like his ideal of education, was too lofty and unpractical to be realized in any but a Utopian state. "He for God only, she for God in him" explains his attitude better than pages of comment. Mistress Milton died in 1653, having given birth to a son who died in childhood and to three daughters, Anne, Mary, and Deborah.

In 1643 Milton's aged father came to live with him, and in September, 1645, after the reconciliation with his wife, the growing family moved to a more commodious dwelling in the Barbican, just off Aldersgate Street. To this period (1643–45) belong his pamphlet on *Education*, adressed as a letter to Samuel Hartlib, a German-Pole, and his most famous pamphlet, the *Areopagitica ; a Speech for the Liberty of Unlicensed Printing*. "God intended to prove me," he says boldly, "whether I durst take up alone a rightful cause against a world of disesteem, and found I durst." Itself unlicensed, the *Areopagitica* put Milton for some time in danger of the law. It was about the same time that he collected and brought out the so-called 1645 edition of his poems (not actually published till January 2, 1646, N. S.), including *L'Allegro, Il Penseroso, Comus, Arcades, Lycidas*, his first ten sonnets, and most of his Latin poems.

It is again necessary to revert to public events. Though the Royalists had been at first successful, they were completely routed in the battles of Marston Moor and Naseby, and Parliament held control. In 1645 Laud was executed, and in 1646 Charles surrendered himself

to the Scots, who promptly sold him to the English for
£400,000. But the Parliament, now that the King was
secured, found itself confronted by the difficulty of
governing many contending parties. For several years
England was without any real executive. The Westminster Assembly, filled with zealous Presbyterians,
imposed a régime in many ways as distasteful as that
of the old Prelacy. The army, however, was the strongest party; in 1647 it seized Charles, and on January
30, 1649, put him to death.

It is necessary only to remind the reader of events
from this time on, — how Parliament was reduced to
the "Rump;" how Cromwell, the man of the hour, mas-
terfully imposed on disunited England a severe military despotism, expelled the Rump, was made Lord
Protector (in 1653), and raised his country to the first
rank among great nations; and how — soon after his
death — England slipped back to easy ways and rejoi-
cingly called King Charles II to the throne.

On February 13, 1649, just two weeks after the
execution of Charles, Milton published *The Tenure of
Kings and Magistrates, proving that it is lawful . . .
for any who have the power to call to account a tyrant
or wicked King, and after due conviction to depose and
put him to death.* Dr. Garnett points out that this is
to hand over the law to Judge Lynch; in its unpractical
idealism it is very characteristic of Milton. It is significant, however, that the author of the pamphlet was [1]
sufficiently known to be made on March 15, 1649, Secretary for Foreign Tongues. While Milton's influence

---

[1] Space does not permit an adequate description of the Commonwealth. The student should read at least the account in Green's *Shorter
History of England* and Macaulay's arraignment of Charles in the *Essay on Milton.*

in the Commonwealth has often been greatly over-estimated, he was nevertheless, as an able controversialist and one of the best Latin scholars in England, a man much desired by the Commonwealth. His duties were the preparation of addresses, the writing of letters to foreign states, and the defense by pamphlet of the Commonwealth.

Milton's public position under these conditions again needs justification. There has been much shaking of heads over the support given by the champion of liberty to a despotism so complete as Cromwell's. But his choice lay, as Macaulay has well expressed it, " not between Cromwell and liberty, but between Cromwell and the Stuarts." With the certainty of losing his fast-failing sight in the work, he accepted the position; and it is fair to believe that the ideal of service prompted him more than pride of place. Indeed, his private choice had been " some still removéd place," — perhaps back at Horton, hidden " from day's garish eye."

Milton was soon called upon to defend the Commonwealth. To the *Eikon Basilike* he replied, October, 1649, in *Eikonoklastes*. Soon after appeared *Defensio Regia pro Carolo I*, from the pen of a Frenchman, Claudius Salmasius, one of the chief knights of the controversial field. Milton, per order, met and routed his opponent with his *Defensio pro Populo Anglicano* (1651). Salmasius died while writing his reply, but the contest was continued by one Morus (or More), a Scotchman living in France, who brought out Peter Dumoulin's defense of the Frenchman. Milton, though he had totally lost his sight in March, 1652, replied in his *Defensio Secunda* (May, 1654). This pamphlet is especially interesting because, in defending his own character, Milton gives a fairly complete account of his own youth.

Since the Barbican days Milton's changes of residence had been frequent. In 1647 he moved to High Holborn, and before entering his official appartments in Whitehall, in 1649, for some months after his appointment as Secretary he lived at Charing Cross. In December, 1651, he made another change on account of his health, this time to Petty France, Westminster. Here he remained till he lost his position, in April, 1660.

In November, 1656, Milton married his second wife, Katharine Woodcock. Fifteen months later she and her child died. In Sonnet XXIII, picturing a dream, he says : —

> "Methought I saw my late espousèd saint
> Brought to me like Alcestis from the grave."

It is pleasant to think that the brief happiness of this second union may have made up in part for the disappointments of the first.

Throughout the period of the Commonwealth Milton's prose work continued. In 1655 came another reply to Morus, in 1659 two more pamphlets on church matters, and, in March, 1660, only two months before the bells rang in Charles II, the *Ready and Easy Way to Establish a Free Commonwealth*. Altogether he wrote twenty-five pamphlets, of which four are in Latin. The only English outlet for his poetic feeling during this time of service was in his *Sonnets*, all of which, twenty-three in number, had been written by 1658. These, aside from their high literary merit, are important as showing the poet's political and religious views. Nowhere else does the large-minded Independent stand out so clear. " Avenge, O Lord," he cries in the sonnet *On the Late Massacre in Piedmont* (1655), —

> " Avenge, O Lord, thy slaughter'd saints, whose bones
> Lie scatter'd on the Alpine mountains cold."

He attacks, too, the " New Forcers of Conscience ; " addresses the Lord General Fairfax, —

> " Whose name in arms through Europe rings ; "

and reminds Cromwell, " our chief of men," that —

> " Peace hath her victories
> No less renown'd than War."

Among these sonnets, also, are found some of his most personal poems, such as that *On His Blindness*, with its great conclusion, —

> "They also serve who only stand and wait."

Part III (1660–1674)

Unspeakably sad is the picture of the defeated champion of liberty, now surrounded by the shallow mockeries of the Restoration. Yet for him the conflict had been infinitely significant; it produced *Paradise Lost.* He was no longer the accomplished, scholarly poet who had written *Comus* and *Lycidas.* He had passed through twenty years of toil and trial, civil and domestic ; he had run the race, he had fought the good fight — and, what is more, he had kept the faith. Those were big times in which Milton had lived, when a whole nation was stirred to its uttermost depths, when to live was to fight ; and the old blind poet was scarred deep with the fierceness of the onset. To string together pretty verses about King Arthur had now been almost blasphemous ; after his deep experience and in his infinite sorrow there was only one theme suited to his pen ;

he of all men in England was best prepared and tried for the high task, — to sing "Of man's first disobedience," and "To justify the ways of God to men."

The first few months of the Restoration were spent by Milton, who was in danger of the proscriptions against supporters of the Commonwealth, in hiding in Bartholomew Close. On June 16 his writings against Charles I were ordered to be burned, but he himself, whether from pity for his blindness and reverence for his position as poet, or from his comparative insignificance politically, escaped proscription, though he was arrested, charged exorbitant fees, and detained by the Sergeant-at-Arms till the Commons ordered his release on December 15. From then on he was a free man, but forced to live, especially at first, in considerable obscurity. His fortunes had been reduced to about £1500. He accordingly took a little house in Holborn, near Red Lion Fields, but moved in 1661 to Jewin Street. In 1664 he moved again, to Artillery Walk, Bunhill Fields. Here he lived until his death, except for the year 1665, when to escape the plague he took a cottage in Chalfont St. Giles, Buckinghamshire, and a few weeks in 1670, when he stayed at the house of the bookseller Millington, in Little Britain.

In February, 1663, Milton married for the third time. His wife, Elizabeth Minshull, whom he never saw, was recommended by a friend, Dr. Paget. She, it seems, appreciated the old man's needs and was content with the position of housekeeper. Living in the house with them were Milton's three daughters, whom he considered very undutiful children. Though he had never properly educated them, he expected them to enjoy taking down his dictation and reading five or six hours a day in languages which they could not understand. Still, exacting as he was, one can conceive of no nobler duty for a sympathetic child than a share in the work of a blind father's genius. But they chose rather to bring sorrow on his gray hairs and to win the reproaches of posterity. They connived with the maidservant "to cheat him in her marketings;" they even sold some of his books to ragwomen; and when one of them heard of his prospective marriage she replied she had sooner heard of his death.

In 1667 *Paradise Lost* was published. It had been planned much earlier, as we have seen, in dramatic form. The main work was probably begun, however, about 1658, and the manuscript was practically complete in 1663. The poem was published first in ten books, but by a rearrangement it assumed in the edition of 1674 its final form of twelve books. Milton's dictation was spasmodic. He told his nephew Phillips " that his vein never happily flowed but from the autumnal equinoctial to the vernal." When he was in the vein, he " would dictate ten, twenty, or thirty lines at a time to any one that was near and could write." When he dictated " he sat leaning backward obliquely in an easy chair, with his leg flung over the elbow of it." At times the song came upon him " with a certain *impetus* and *œstro*," when, " at what hour soever, he rung for his daughter to secure what came." Thomas Ellwood, a young Quaker, was a frequent visitor and was in the habit of reading to Milton and of taking down his dictation, with more eagerness than the undutiful daughters.

Among the many incidents connected with the contemporary fame of *Paradise Lost* was Milton's remark to Dryden, when the latter asked permission to bring out a rhymed dramatic version of the poem. " Ay," he said, " tag my verses if you will." Thomas Ellwood, the Quaker, on seeing the completed form of the poem, asked, " What hast thou to say of Paradise Found?" And in 1771 *Paradise Regained*, the sequel to *Paradise Lost*, came out. It is, however, not so great as the epic of man's fall; sin, error, and defeat had burned more strongly than redemption into Milton's Puritan mind; *Paradise Lost* was more elementally, more vitally a part of his own experience than *Paradise Regained*.

During these last years Milton's mind was remarkably active. A Latin Grammar (1669) ; a *History of Britain*, from the earliest time to the Norman Conquest, famous especially for the Faithorne portrait of the author (1670) ; *Paradise Regained* and *Samson Agonistes, A Dramatic Poem* (1671) ; a Latin treatise on the *Art of Logic* (1672) ; a second edition of his poems, and a pamphlet on *True Religion, Hæresie, Schism, and Toleration* (1673) ; a second edition of *Paradise Lost* (1674), — these are the publications of his last five years, though *Paradise Lost*, of course, as well as two thirds of the *History*, had been written before 1669. He approaches nearest to the level of his great epic in *Samson Agonistes*, a subject peculiarly appropriate to the last sad years of the old Independent. In 1682 was published a *Brief History of Muscovia*, written by him probably in the first years of his secretaryship. Not till 1823 was his Latin treatise, *De Doctrina Christiana*, discovered. It is one of his most important prose works, revealing his faith towards the end in the Bible and the Inner Spirit.

Of the last years of Milton, at his house in Bunhill Fields, we have many accounts. One Dr. Wright, says Richardson, found him in a room "hung with rusty green," "sitting in an elbow chair, black clothes, and neat enough, pale but not cadaverous, his hands and fingers gouty and with chalk-stones." In sunny weather he sat in a gray coarse cloth coat at the door, and "received the visits of people of distinguished parts, as well as quality." At eight o'clock he took supper, "which was usually olives or some light thing; and after supper he smoked his pipe and drank a glass of water, and went to bed." Particularly did he enjoy music in his last days. In religion he held aloof from all sects, partly on account of his blindness, partly from a disgust for their formalities.

In 1674 Milton's gout grew worse, and on the 8th of November he died, "with so little pain that the time of his expiring was not perceived by those in the room." He was buried beside his father, in the parish church of St. Giles, Cripplegate.

Milton the man impresses us perhaps as much as Milton the poet. His intensity of emotion and his passionate earnestness were no doubt characteristic of the age, but the great scope of his thought and the unwavering nobility of his purpose set him apart from and above all the men about him except Cromwell. Yet by the unpractical idealism of everything he thought or wrote he was precluded from very great effectiveness among his contemporaries. He was only a "Puritan by the accident of his times," says Dr. Garnett, "whose true affinities were with Mill and Shelley and Rousseau." From his childhood he saw the clear light of duty before him, and with an uncompromising earnestness he performed that duty. Yet he was a poet, too, with " a vehement love of the beautiful," and he turned in his old age to complete the great work of his life. Great dramas there have been, but few tragedies more sublime or elemental than that of the life of John Milton, written across the page of history. And in the closing lines of *Samson Agonistes*, his last great poem, he sets down for us the abiding moral of his own tragedy : —

> " His servants He, with new acquist
> Of true experience from this great event,
> With peace and consolation hath dismissed,
> And calm of mind, all passion spent."

JOHN BUNYAN

Pilgrim's Progress, one of the few books that
successive generations and whole nations read, is written, the title-page says, "in the similitude of a dream."
Every man has visions and spiritual conflicts in some
degree, even in the most frivolous, worldly times. Few
ages, however, have been so wholly given over to religious dreams and aspirations as was the Puritan Age
of the seventeenth century; and of all the earnest
struggles for salvation in that time of zeal, despair,
and ecstasy, few were so real as Bunyan's, few visions
were so clear as his, no book expressed so forcibly as his
the sincere effort of the soul. His "dream" became at
once the true record and the satisfying answer for half a
nation. For to Bunyan and the Puritans salvation was
literally and absolutely the only concern of this world,
a matter of terrible moment.

Bunyan's book, then, the record of his struggle and
victory, must interest all who realize that in it they
can see how the man was made. He himself, like Christian, had escaped from the specious advice of Mr.
Worldly Wiseman; he had been deserted by Pliable
at the Slough of Dispond; he had descended into the
Valley of Humiliation and wrestled with the monster
Apollyon; he had passed safely through the alluring
shows of Vanity Fair; he had known just such judges
as those who condemned Faithful; he had met, too,
with Hopeful, through whose aid he endured the dun-
geon of Doubting Castle; and he had come through,

scarred and victorious, to the "pleasant land of Beulah," whence the Two Shining Ones were soon to conduct him across the River of Death to the Holy City.

John Bunyan was born in a cottage just outside of the hamlet of Elstow, in Bedfordshire, late in the year 1628. His father, Thomas Bunyan, was a tinker in very poor circumstances, and his mother, Margaret Bentley, was of as low an estate. Nothing is known of John's education, though it is supposed, since he could read and write, that he went for a time to the village school. His book learning, however, was very slight; even in later life his reading was confined almost wholly to the Bible and Foxe's *Book of Martyrs*. While he was still a boy he began to help his father, whose trade he followed throughout his life.

Bunyan, in his *Grace Abounding*, the most autobiographical of his works, says that he was a hopeless sinner as a boy, — "filled with unrighteousness," with "but few equals both for cursing, swearing, lying, and blaspheming the holy name of God," "the very ringleader in all manner of vice and ungodliness." It was hence for some time the fashion to suppose that the author of *Pilgrim's Progress* was a converted reprobate, — a particular example of God's grace. Later biographers, however, have realized that Bunyan's condemnation of his youthful practices as unpardonable was the result of a morbid conscience. He was not the first godly person, in his "awakening," to consider himself the most miserable of sinners. At all events, "The four chief sins of which he was guilty," says Macaulay, "were dancing, ringing the bells of the parish church, playing at tipcat, and reading the history of Sir Bevis of Southampton." Such, the same author

says in another place, " would have passed for virtues
with Archbishop Laud."

When he was a boy of about seventeen Bunyan
served as a soldier. It has been said that he was at the
siege of Leicester and on the side of Parliament, but
he himself says another was sent in his place, and
there is only probability in favor of his having been in
Cromwell's army. There is, indeed, no knowledge that
he saw actual fighting. When the armies were disbanded in 1646 he returned to his father's trade at
Elstow.

Besides the mere incidents of his life, there is really
only one thing to tell about Bunyan — the story of his
conversion and its results. His spiritual conflict, beginning when he was about twenty and lasting for about
seven years, brought forth a new man ; thence grew his
influential ministry, his imprisonment for conscience'
sake, and his great book.

The struggle seems to have begun in earnest shortly
after his marriage, about 1648. He had been troubled
as a boy by religious visions, "fearful dreams," he says,
" apprehensions of devils and wicked spirits ; " but his
unremitting contest with evil really dates from his
marriage. Nothing is known of his first wife except that
she was a " godly person " and brought as dowry two
religious books which he fell to reading. From the
parish church, which he had begun to attend, he went
home one Sunday with a " great burden " on him. But
by afternoon he had forgotten the sermon and was off
to the village green, where he led the lads of Elstow in
the innocuous sport of " tip-cat " or " sly." Just as he
was going to give the " cat " a second blow, however, he
heard a voice from heaven asking whether " he would

leave his sins and go to heaven, or keep his sins and go
to hell." This only shook him a little ; he soon resolved
that he was " past pardon" and that he might as well
sin to his heart's content. But his heart was far from
content ; the leaven was at work. Rebuked by a woman
for " the ungodliest fellow for swearing that she ever
heard," he managed to leave off swearing, to his " great
wonder." Soon he began to read the Bible in earnest.

The regeneration was not, however, of even growth.
At times he relapsed into what he later considered his
hopeless depravity. The Bible filled him with hopes and
fears and terrible visions. Sometimes he felt the
devil pulling at his back when he tried to pray. If he
had faith, the Bible told him, he could work miracles.
Once, when " the temptation came hot " upon him to try
this promise, he was about to say to the puddles in the
road, " Be dry," and to the dry places, " Be ye puddles;"
but he was saved by the thought that it might be better
to go under the hedge and pray to God to help him.
While he was praying, he saw that his failure to work miracles would not so much prove the falseness of the Bible
as his lack of faith, so he did not put the promise to the
test. Little by little, moreover, he found strength to renounce worldly pleasures. Chief among these for him
were dancing and bell-ringing. To give up the latter
was not an easy task. He first abandoned pulling the
rope, but continued to stand in the doorway, where he
might hear the sweet sound of the bells. But after a
time the fear that these with the tower might fall on
him for his sins led him to move farther away, and at
last the conviction that he was trifling caused him to
depart wholly.

Thus the progress continued, with the pilgrim's pas-

sionate yearning for salvation, his chaotic despair and
ecstasy. At times the evils of his youth haunted him;
in his own eyes he was " more loathsome . . . than
a toad." Once he took much comfort from Luther's
Commentary on the Galatians. " Now I found, as I
thought, that I loved Christ dearly. . . . I felt love to
Him hot as fire." But thereupon came a voice saying,
" Sell Him, sell Him, sell Him." For a time he resisted,
but one morning as he lay in bed in spiritual torment
he gave up. " Let Him go if He will," he said. Alas!
Now all was truly lost; the Devil had won; Judas was
poor Bunyan's only peer in sin.

The vividness of the man's visions, the terrible reality
of his torment, — these are the striking things about his
struggle. It is hard for us, for any age indeed, to understand how much the outcome mattered to him. He lived
in a time when men went into battle singing hymns,
when Cromwell himself wept " hysterical tears," and
when commanders of the Parliamentary forces bore
such names as " Captain Hew-Agag-in-pieces-before-the-
Lord." Nothing in all Puritanism was so vitally important as this struggle of the human soul for salvation,
this agony so vividly pictured in the life of Bunyan.

At last, too, he did come, like Christian, to a land
of spiritual rest. For a while the conflict had broken
his health, but with new faith and hope, which gained
slowly upon him, he grew strong again. The texts of
the Bible now " looked not so grimly as before; " " now
remained only the hinder part of the tempest." About
the year 1653 he was publicly baptized in the Ouse,
by Mr. Gifford, pastor of a congregation in Bedford.
For a few years he suffered set-backs and periods of
despair, but by 1655 he had attained a spiritual calm

and fortitude which never deserted him. In that year
he moved to a house in Bedford, and was made a dea-
con of the congregation. From then till his death he
was unceasing in good works.

If there is very little known about Bunyan's youth,
there is not a great deal known about his maturity.
His own statements about himself are exasperatingly
few except in spiritual matters. Thus, the name of his
first wife and the date of their marriage are unknown ;
the time of the composition of his greatest work is conjecture, and many of the stories of his life in prison
are mere fiction. His second wife, Elizabeth, who survived him, was married probably in 1655, the first
year of his ministry. It is known that he had six children, all of whom except his blind daughter, Mary,
outlived him.

There is, however, plenty of evidence of Bunyan's
success as a preacher. " Hundreds," it was said, came
in " to hear the word." Yet his head was not turned.
" What, thought I," he says, " shall I be proud because
I am a sounding brass? Is it so much to be a fiddle?"
He did not hold back, however, when he felt sure of
his true mission ; he had a story to tell, and there were
thousands eager to hear it. He spoke straight from the
heart in plain English ; he felt, he says, " as if an angel
of God had stood at my back." There is a story that
once a listener remarked what a sweet sermon he had
delivered, to which Bunyan replied, " Ay, you have no
need to tell me that, for the devil whispered it to me
before I was well out of the pulpit."

Very soon after taking to the ministry, Bunyan began to write. In 1656 he published his first volume,
Some Gospel Truths Opened. He was answered by

a young Quaker, Edward Burrough, and shortly after
had ready a reply, *A Vindication of Gospel Truths
Opened* (1657). From then on till his death, except
for a few years during his imprisonment, he turned
out controversial books, religious allegories, and exhor-
tations with the fertility of a Scott or a Defoe. Of
the long list of writings mainly read the most famous
are: *The Holy City* (1665), *Grace Abounding to the
Chief of Sinners* (1666), *Saved by Grace* (1675),
The Strait Gate (1676), *The Pilgrim's Progress,
Part the First* (1678), *Life and Death of Mr. Bad-
man* (1680), *The Holy War* (1682), *The Pilgrim's
Progress, Part the Second* (1684).

But Bunyan had not been long preaching and writing
before he came into conflict with the law. For soon
after May, 1660, when the bells were rung for King
Charles II to " come to his own again," there began a
zealous prosecution of non-conformist ministers. Men
were forbidden to call people together for unauthorized
religious services in private houses or barns. Bunyan
was taken in the act, and was therefore legally guilty.
He was not, however, treated with peculiar severity;
quite the contrary, when it was discovered that his simple flock had none of the violent, rebellious purposes
of Fifth Monarchy men, he was given a chance to escape
punishment if he would give his word that he would re-
frain in the future. But when Bunyan replied, " If I
was let out of prison to-day I would preach the gospel
again to-morrow by the help of God," his committal to
prison was, as the law stood, a just sentence. Some of
his judges, to be sure, especially one Sir John Keeling,
who was still smarting from Puritan ungentleness during the Rebellion, were unnecessarily harsh in manner.

Keeling received his reward, however, by being sent down to fame as Lord Hategood in *Pilgrim's Progress*.

Bunyan's flock did not give up their pastor without a fight. Nothing, however, could be done unless he would promise to stop preaching, and this he quietly but firmly refused to do. Mr. Cobb, Clerk of the Peace, spent much time reasoning with him in jail; Bunyan thankèd him for "his civil and meek discoursing," but would not change. Soon after, on the King's coronation, when prisoners had, according to ancient custom, the permission to sue for pardon, Bunyan's wife, Elizabeth, traveled three times up to London with a petition to the House of Lords. But she met with no success, and Bunyan therefore remained in prison, except for a short release in 1666, during the next twelve years.

Tradition has ascribed the place of imprisonment to the picturesque little jail which used to perch on the bridge over the Ouse. Careful investigation, however, has proved nearly conclusively that both this imprisonment and the later one, in 1675, were in the Bedford county jail. Almost all prisons at that time were unfit for long habitation, but Bedford prison, though the weak did "rot" there, as the saying goes, was probably not so foul as Bunyan partisans have pictured it. Certainly Bunyan was not badly treated, nor did he suffer greatly from the physical confinement. He was depressed, however, by the thought of the separation from his work and from his needy family, especially from his blind daughter, Mary, of whom he often speaks with tender affection. "Oh, the thoughts of the hardships my blind one might go under would break my heart to pieces!"

Yet the prisoner was by no means wholly cut off from his work. In the first place, he had some liberty between the Autumn Assizes of 1661 and the Spring Assizes of 1662, and again for a short period in 1666. At these times he preached frequently, in the face of the law. Besides, in prison he found a little group who were ready to take comfort from his teaching. Then, too, he had his Bible to read, and, most of all, his recent spiritual experiences to think out. He spent much time, moreover, in writing, especially at first. Of the last six years of his confinement, during which he wrote nothing authenticated, very little is known. There are some grounds for supposing that he was less strictly guarded than before, that he enjoyed indeed occasional liberty and was sometimes allowed to preach.

By the King's Declaration of Indulgence in 1672 Bunyan was made a free man. On May 9 he was granted a license to preach in a barn in Josias Roughead's orchard in Bedford. This in 1707 was replaced by a meeting-house, itself followed in 1849 by the present chapel, one of the chief, though not most beautiful, places of Bunyan interest in Bedford.

Bunyan's second imprisonment has received special notice because during it he is supposed to have begun *Pilgrim's Progress*. The Declaration of Indulgence was withdrawn in 1673, the Test Act, which required strict conformity to the Church of England, was passed, and the Bedford preacher was therefore again in danger. Dr. William Foster, one of his chief accusers in 1660, procured a warrant with the signatures of thirteen magistrates, dated March 4, 1675, and Bunyan, guilty as before, was again imprisoned. But after six months the intervention of Dr. Owen and of Barlow, the Bishop of Lincoln, brought Bunyan a release and practical security against future imprisonment. His great book, not published till 1678, must have been begun, it is now generally conceded, in this second durance, if in either; for Bunyan usually published hot from the pen, and it is unlikely that he should have kept the manuscript unprinted for six years.

Pilgrim's Progress at first did not find great favor among scholars, but it was popular enough to go through ten editions during the author's lifetime. In the eighteenth century Cowper feared he should be laughed at for admiring it, but early in the nineteenth century it was recognized by the ablest judges as the book which, along with *Paradise Lost*, stands out as the most typical, the most genuine work of Puritan England. Men no longer look to it as the one volume besides the Bible wherein may be found the only solution of their troubles; but it now holds its place by its literary merit, irrespective of its religious value. The best evidence of its widespread popularity is the fact that it has been translated into over seventy-five languages and dialects.

Towards the end of his life the tinker's celebrity as a preacher became very great. Charles Doe, who knew him, says that " when Mr. Bunyan preached in London, if there were but one day's notice given, there would be more people come together than the meeting-house could hold. I have seen by my computation, about twelve hundred at a morning lecture by seven o'clock on a working day, in the dark winter time." When Charles II wondered how the great Dr. Owen could " sit and listen to an illiterate tinker," Owen answered,

" I would gladly give up all my learning if I could preach like that tinker."

In all this fame, however, Bunyan preserved his humility. He refused to be more than a visitor to London, and from his release to his death lived in a simple cottage in the parish of St. Cuthbert's, Bedford. A. M. Bagford, curious to see the study of so great a man, one day visited the tinker. To his surprise he found a small room, the contents of which, says Canon Venables, one of Bunyan's best biographers, were " hardly larger than those of his prison cell. They were limited to a Bible, and copies of *The Pilgrim's Progress* and a few other books — chiefly his own works."

There is little to add to Bunyan's story except the incident which hastened his death. He often left Bedford to preach in neighboring towns, to comfort the afflicted, and to settle foolish disputes. In the summer of 1688 he rode to Reading for the purpose of mending a quarrel between a father and a son. He was successful, but in the subsequent ride through a driving rain to London, where he was to preach the next Sunday, caught a severe cold. He managed to preach on the Sunday, August 19, but on the following Tuesday he fell seriously sick and a few days later, August 31, he died. He was buried in Bunhill Fields cemetery.

In spite of rather meagre facts, the figure of the great Puritan preacher stands out very clear. There are one or two striking descriptions of him. Charles Doe says, " He was tall of stature, strong-boned, though not corpulent ; somewhat of a ruddy face, with sparkling eyes, wearing his hair on his upper lip after the old British fashion. His hair reddish, but in his later days time had sprinkled it with grey. His nose well

set, but not declining or bending. His mouth moderately large, his forehead something high, and his habit
always plain and modest." A more vigilant, active man,
one would say, than the well-fed laborer so often depicted on the frontispiece of his books. Canon Venables adds the testimony of John Nelson, who knew
Bunyan in prison: " His countenance was grave and
sedate, and did so to the life discover the inward frame
of his heart, that it was convincing to the beholders and
did strike something of awe into them that had nothing
of the fear of God." As regards Bunyan's creed, we
have his own words: " I would be, as I hope I am, a
Christian. But for those factious titles of Anabaptist,
Independent, Presbyterian, and the like, I conclude that
they come neither from Jerusalem nor from Antioch,
but from Hell or from Babylon."

The one important point of Bunyan's life, after all,
is his conversion and its results ; above all, the chief
result, *Pilgrim's Progress.* How he went up into the
pulpit at a time when people strained by day and by
night to hear the story of the Bible ; how he, fresh from
his tinker's trade and speaking the simple, homely English of the great Book, stirred their hearts ; how true
to the eager listeners the story of the Carpenter's Son of
Nazareth sounded from his lips, — of this we to-day get
only a faint impression. Bunyan the preacher may indeed be forgotten, but Bunyan the author of *Pilgrim's
Progress* has taken a permanent place in history. In
the tinker's book is revealed the best type of Puritan,
— the man too big to be lost in the unessential disputes
of sects, the man whose single, absorbing interest was
the salvation of the soul. Cromwell and Milton were the
only other Puritans who combined his intensity of re-

ligious zeal with his breadth of mind and power over men. The lives of these three, warrior, poet, and preacher, best explain why Puritanism set such an indelible stamp on the English nation.

JOHN DRYDEN

JOHN DRYDEN has been called a lock, by which the waters of English poetry were let down from the mountains of Shakespeare and Milton to the plain of Pope. By his admirers and followers he was regarded as the man who redeemed our poetry from its wildness and barbarism and taught it to be elegant and refined. By general consent he is now considered a master of smooth and energetic verse, the best satirist and one of the most judicious critics in the history of our literature. He was among the first to write that easy and vigorous prose which was almost unknown in the time of our great poetry. More than this, he was a kind of literary dictator in his day, though his rule was not without frequent dispute; too often, however, he is found ministering to the degraded taste of his contemporaries when he ought to have been maintaining the best traditions of a literature which he comprehended and valued so well. He cannot be absolved from the charge of pandering to the vices of the Restoration period. Maturing slowly, for he was doing his best work at the end of his life upon the verge of threescore and ten, Dryden was just ready for his poetic task with the accession of Charles II in 1660. At once he became the favored dramatist of the court, and the representative poet for these new times.

What these times were must be briefly recorded by way of explanation of the poet's career. To Milton and his friends of the lost cause it seemed that the "sons of Belial, flown with insolence and wine," were in full control of the situation. To the restored cavaliers it merely seemed that sour rebellion was at last put down, Astræa had returned, and the King was come to his own. Extreme repression had quite naturally yielded to recklessness just as extreme. Where in Puritan times men were constrained to assume a virtue they did not begin to feel, and where many a man went about as a kind of compulsory Roundhead, so here in the reaction against that excess of piety Englishmen exaggerated their own profession of license and even vice, and many a man was constrained to pretend the immorality which at heart he really loathed. Hypocrisy now became the cardinal sin, and to be self-contained, orderly, and moral seemed to the world clear evidence of double dealing. Hence a general spirit of indulgence and freedom from moral restraint, with the Merry Monarch setting a brave example to his people.

To the call of this new spirit in English life Dryden responded only too well. Vigorous, earnest, and, while no Puritan, a naturally clean-minded man, he nevertheless produced comedies so indecent that even the boundless license of his public was overstepped. And after its third night the worst of them had to be called in, condemned for grossness which even now, considerably reduced in print, offends the most indulgent reader. Yet this is not the only instance when Dryden seems to float passive upon the current of his time; nor was immorality the only method by which he did violence to his literary conscience. He had, for his generation, a profound knowledge of older English literature, and reverence for its best traditions. He was, moreover, among the fit audience, though few, who understood the greatness of *Paradise Lost.* "This man," he is reported

to have said, "cuts us out, and the ancients too;" and
tradition has it that he went to Milton and asked leave
to put *Paradise Lost* into rhyme. Whatever was
Milton's reply, it is certain that Dryden carried out
his purpose and published in 1669 the *State of Innocence*, an opera based on the epic. Here, however, is the
contradiction in point. Dryden regards Milton's poem
as "one of the greatest, most noble, and sublime;" yet
he makes an opera of it, and turns the blank verse,
which is its chief glory, into rhyme. So with his plays.
English traditions required tragedy to be written in
blank verse; but King and court were for the French
models, and Dryden wrote his tragedies, after French
precedent, in rhymed couplets. One tragedy indeed,
All for Love, he composed in blank verse, the only
one, it is said, which he wrote to please himself. It is
in these contradictions, this knowing of the better and
following of the worse, that the character of Dryden
must be explained. But neither contradiction nor duplicity will serve as the explanation itself. It is true
that he preferred the old English masters to the new
French models, and recognized the greatness of Milton;
but it is also true that he saw the need for regularity,
constraint, and elegance in English letters. It is true
that in his heart he despised the immorality that he
forced into his plays; but it is also true that, like
Fielding after him, he believed in the spirited, hearty,
and open life, and hated whatever smacked of the hypocrite. Part of his revolt against the Puritans, then, and·
part of his critical and literary reform were genuine;
to a great degree he must be regarded as an honest
representative of his time.

John Dryden was born in August, 1631, at Aldwinkle

All Saints, in Northamptonshire, to that happy condition which passes in England under the name of country gentleman. His grandfather was a baronet, Sir Erasmus Dryden, whose third son, bearing the same name, married Mary, daughter of the Rev. Henry Pickering. It is interesting to note that on both sides the ancestors of this royalist poet had espoused the Puritan cause. Indeed, Dryden's own heroic stanzas on the death of Oliver Cromwell, September, 1658, are thoroughly Puritan in their tone. We know little about his boyhood, although the tradition remains that he was always very fond of fishing. He had a scholarship at Westminster School in London, under the famous headmaster Dr. Busby; and again secured a scholarship at Trinity College, Cambridge, which he entered in 1650, at the age of nineteen, another proof of the slowness with which Dryden's mind matured. He took his bachelor's degree in January, 1654, and must have employed his time in serious and extended studies. However that may be, he got no fellowship, and probably felt no call to the academic profession. In the same year he inherited a small landed estate from his father, but his tastes were not for country life, and his permanent residence was in London. He wrote, as we have seen, a eulogy upon Cromwell, but greeted the Restoration of Charles with two poems of almost fulsome praise. Still, it is fair to say that his heart was in this poem of welcome, and praise in those times had to be fulsome if it was to count for praise at all. In 1663 Dryden married Lady Elizabeth, sister of his friend Sir Robert Howard and daughter of the Earl of Berkshire. It was by no means an ideal marriage. The wife was neither beautiful nor intelligent, and her conduct may not have been all that was desired. Dryden was hardly a model husband. Yet there is good evidence that they were fond of their children. He sent his two older boys to Westminster School, under the same Busby whose floggings were so renowned and had quickened the somewhat sluggish temperament of the poet. If we are to take seriously the various allusions to matrimony scattered through Dryden's works, we may well agree with Sir Walter Scott that they speak " an inward consciousness of domestic misery ;" but marriage, always a target for wit, was never more so, or with better reason, than under Charles the Second. Certain it is that Dryden's marriage brought him no solid advantages of preferment ; and the liberal income which he earned during the next succeeding years was due to his efforts as a playwright and as the favored dramatist of the court.

With the restoration of Charles English drama came out of its long seclusion, due to the closing of the theatres by Puritan command. Dryden's first play, *The Wild Gallant*, 1663, was unsuccessful ; but *The Rival Ladies* was well received. He helped his brother-in-law Howard in *The Indian Queen* and wrote his own *Indian Emperor* for successful performance in 1665. Dryden was now one of the recognized leaders among literary men in London, and was a conspicuous figure at those coffee-houses which served as a kind of literary exchange. Typically English in the slow but persistent maturing of his powers, he now showed in his *Annus Mirabilis* a sureness and vigor in poetic composition best noted in his vivid description of the great London Fire. This poem, appearing in 1667 and frequently reprinted, contains an account of the memorable events of the preceding year. It is Dryden's first long poem, and was his last, until, thirteen years later, he turned from drama to satire. Scattered through his plays, however, are many songs and lyrics, some of great charm, which have been too often neglected by the critic. About the same time as the *Annus Mirabilis* he wrote his prose *Essay on Dramatic Poesy*, defending his use of rhyme in tragic plays. Meanwhile his dramatic work went on triumphantly. He made a contract with the King's Theatre to write them three plays a year; and while this undertaking was not strictly carried out, his profits from the arrangement were consistently large. In 1670 he was made Poet Laureate, and also Historiographer; and we are told that for his work in both capacities he had "a salary of two hundred pounds a year, and a butt of Canary Wine." Of his various plays little is to be said except that they followed with painful obsequiousness what their author took to be the popular demand. They deserve no notice apart from those "heroic tragedies" in which the famous Nell Gwyn took a conspicuous part, and from that play which he wrote to please himself and in imitation of Shakespeare, *All for Love, or The World Well Lost*. This was in 1678; its success was instant; the author's profits were considerable; and with his more national conception of dramatic poetry it seemed as if Dryden was destined for greater honors in this field. Fortunately for him and for English literature, his dramatic career was rudely interrupted, and his long course of prosperity came to an abrupt end. Drawn into a quarrel between the Earl of Rochester, witty, profligate, and cowardly, and Lord Mulgrave, Dryden was assaulted, December 18, 1679, by ruffians in Rochester's pay; that night he was "severely beaten as he passed

through Rose Street, Covent Garden, returning from
Will's Coffee-House to his own house in Gerard Street."
Eight years earlier Dryden had been wittily ridiculed
under the name of Bayes, in the *Rehearsal*. In 1673
his enemies had set up as his rival in poetry and drama
an absolutely worthless rhymester named Elkanah Settle. Finally it was hinted that the poet was concerned in
certain satires directed against the King. These hints,
however, came to nothing when Dryden published, in
1681, his great political satire, *Absalom and Achitophel*.

This is a conspicuous point in the career of Dryden.
When most men look back, he was beginning to look
forward, and was finding his real vocation as a poet.
He was now fifty years of age; his varied dramatic experiments in verse, always vigorous but uneven and often
deficient in elegance, were now exchanged for that political and personal satire in which his ripe experience
of life, his keen observation, his remorseless wit, and his
inexhaustible energy of phrase made him master of the
field. Nor did the public fail to respond. Large editions
of *Absalom and Achitophel* were sold ; it struck the very
bull's eye of popular agitation. The Earl of Shaftesbury,
with a considerable following, was in opposition to the
King, and he was pressing the claims of the Duke of
Monmouth against the unpopular and "papistical"
Duke of York, heir to the throne. Shaftesbury was
committed to the Tower on a charge of high treason,
and it was in the exciting days between the imprisonment and the decision of the Grand Jury that Dryden's
poem appeared. Although the Biblical story had been
used before, with Monmouth as Absalom and Shaftesbury as Achitophel, the genius of Dryden, particularly
the consummate skill with which he characterized the

leaders of the faction, rendered ridiculous all charges of plagiarism. Among the memorable personal sketches are those of Shaftesbury himself, whose crime as traitor was thrown, in the second edition of the poem, into even sharper relief by the praise of his purity as a judge ; of Dryden's old enemy, the Duke of Buckingham, satirized under the name of Zimri, —

> " Stiff in opinions, always in the wrong,
> Was everything by starts and nothing long,
> But in the course of one revolving moon
> Was chymist, fiddler, statesman, and buffoon; "

and also of certain friends of the King, such as Ormond, Mulgrave, and Halifax. Shaftesbury, however, was set free ; the Grand Jury refused to find a bill of high treason against him, and a medal was struck by his friends in honor of the event. By command of the King, who appreciated Dryden's merits, the poet published, in March, 1682, another poem called *The Medal*, *a Satire against Sedition*. In October of the same year appeared *MacFlecknoe*, said to have been the model of Pope's *Dunciad*, a literary satire directed against a poet of the opposite faction named Shadwell. Many who know neither this poem nor its occasion can quote the lines where " Shadwell never deviates into sense ; " it is a masterpiece of its kind, and the author is credited with thinking it the best of his poems. A continuation of *Absalom and Achitophel*, published in the autumn of this same busy year, 1682, is only in part the work of Dryden ; the bulk of it is by Nahum Tate.

Risen to renown and literary sovereignty, Dryden had suffered a corresponding fall in his fortunes. Cut off from the regular profits of a playwright in public favor, he depended on the good offices of the court and on his earnings as a writer of translations, dedications, and the prologue or epilogue of another man's play. So great was his authority that his words of commendation in this latter form were eagerly sought by the dramatists who put new pieces upon the boards, and Dr. Johnson tells how he " raised his price " from two guineas to three. In addition to his salary as laureate, the King had given him a pension of one hundred pounds ; payments, however, were often uncertain, and the poet fell frequently into pecuniary distress. He had a family to support and sons to educate. It is clear that he looked to the court for constant assistance, and that the court looked to him for the powerful aid of his pen. For the one case may be noted his appointment as collector of customs late in 1683 ; for the other his attitude towards the religion secretly acknowledged by Charles and openly professed by James. With the accession of the latter, Dryden changed his faith. In the Layman's Creed, *Religio Laici*, he had not long before defended the Church of England ; now he was impelled to defend his new belief as well as to aid the unpopular cause of the King. He entered into prose controversy with some of the ablest writers on the side of the national Church, and in an allegorical poem, *The Hind and the Panther*, in which the various sects are represented by animals (the Quaker, for instance, by the hare), he makes a vigorous plea for the traditions of Rome. In this change of faith, far more than in his earlier political change, Dryden laid himself open to the charge of time-serving and insincerity. With almost any other man this charge would be strictly true, but Dryden's temperament, a strange mixture of energy and good sense with personal shyness and a kind of mental timidity, goes far to explain his act. Moreover, in his own eyes the change of attitude from that strong desire, which he shows in his *Religio Laici*, for settled and final authority in religious affairs, to his recognition of papal supremacy in *The Hind and the Panther*, was not such a momentous step. It is said that after his conversion, as before, he cordially disliked the priests. Finally, he had at least the courage of his second convictions. The Revolution of 1688, which secured Protestantism in England and stripped Dryden of all his official income, failed to influence his new faith and made the last twelve years of his life a period in which his character appears at its best.

Cut off from all hope of assistance from the court, Dryden now labored sturdily and well as the leading man of letters in England. He undertook every kind of literary work. He wrote plays, and succeeded both in tragedy and in comedy, but came to wreck with his last play in 1694. In 1698, two years before his death, Dryden had to endure a not undeserved drubbing from the cudgel of Jeremy Collier, who attacked " the immorality and profaneness of the English stage." In the preface to his *Fables*, one of his most attractive writings, Dryden, with great simplicity and manliness, acknowledged that in the main the parson's attack was just. He had written no plays after the failure of his *Love Triumphant*, and in a poem addressed to the rising dramatist Congreve he commits the care of the drama to his junior, and adds in pathetic conclusion : —

> " Already I am worn with cares and age,
> And just abandoning the ungrateful stage,
> Unprofitably kept at Heaven's expense,
> I live a rent-charge on His providence.

But you, whom every Muse and grace adorn,
Whom I foresee to better fortune born,
Be kind to my remains ; and oh, defend,
Against your judgment, your departed friend !
Let not the insulting foe my fame pursue,
But shade those laurels which descend to you ;
And take for tribute, what these lines express ;
You merit more, nor could my love do less."

Yet he worked on. Age, poverty, disease, and cares could not daunt his sturdy heart or stay his hands. His last work was his best; and almost on the threshold of death he could make his famous assertion that thoughts crowded in so fast upon him that his only difficulty was " to choose or to reject, to run them into verse, or to give them the other harmony of prose." He translated Juvenal and Persius, and published by subscription his famous translation of Virgil, gaining, it is said, some twelve hundred pounds by the performance. He made versions of stories from Ovid, from Chaucer, and from Boccaccio. He wrote for the second time an ode for St. Cecilia's Day, 1697, commonly known as *Alexander's Feast*, one of the most musical and spirited English odes. These latter years, moreover, form the period about which are gathered the anecdotes and traditions of Dryden as the dictator of English letters. To his many friends and disciples he was the arbiter of their poetic destiny. For his use there was a chair by the fire in winter and by the window in summer, at Will's Coffee-House ; and hither flocked the younger men of letters, who found in the offer of a pinch of snuff from his box the assurance of literary success. Not all were thus favored, though it is to be hoped that Swift's contempt for Dryden is not to be explained by his kinsman's remark upon

verses submitted for his approval, " Cousin Swift, you
will never be a poet." In the spring of 1700 he had
a fatal attack of gout, and died on the first of May
at his London home, and was buried in Westminster
Abbey.

The personal appearance of Dryden was far from
striking; his face was fat and without particular expression. He is said to have borne the nickname of
" Poet Squat." His character seems to have been generous and confiding ; nor should his biting satire lead
us to think of him as what is called a " good hater "
in actual life. As a poet he is the herald and in many
respects the hero of the Augustan age, surpassing his
great scholar Pope in energy and originality, but surpassed by Pope in a certain urbanity and finish. Unlike Pope, he leaves the impression of sturdiness, manliness, sincerity, — qualities which séem, it is true, to
be contradicted by the shifts, evasions, flatteries, and
inconsistencies of his life, but which, nevertheless, per-
sist in the reader's mind as somehow essential to the
character of " glorious old John."

THE EIGHTEENTH CENTURY

DRYDEN bridges the space between the Puritans and the eighteenth century. The period from his death, 1700, to the publication of the " Lyrical Ballads," 1798, is sometimes divided into the Age of Pope and the Age of Johnson, but the same general literary tradition held throughout the century, and the whole time may therefore, for want of an exact and comprehensive term, fitly be called *The Eighteenth Century*. Its great characteristic was its sane, unimaginative reasoning, and its great contribution was its development of English prose.

The chief interests of men during this century, more particularly during the first part, were in the city. All important English life centred around London. Newspapers were started,[1] and great advances in commercial prosperity were made. Yet this life was for the most part a very superficial, frivolous one, and the card-table, the sedan-chair, the patch and the periwig, the coffee-house and the levee figure largely in the interests of the day. Following a model of etiquette and elegance, but not of profound thought, men, generally speaking, ceased to think greatly for themselves. No burning questions of " God, immortality, freedom " consumed them. If they looked within, they found reflected there only the shallowness of the life about them. Each one thought his first duty was to cut an elegant figure in this world; a display of violent emotion or fresh ingenuousness was

---

[1] There had been newspapers a few years before the turn of the century, but their real development belongs to the time of Queen Anne.

a sign of a lack of polish. There was, to be sure, beneath this superficial refinement, something of the coarseness and rudeness of Restoration England. To a Frenchman the Englishman of Queen Anne's day was still largely a boor, beaf-eating, hard-drinking, profane, violent. Nor was London a model of cleanliness and well-ordered beauty. Though there had been vast improvements since the great fire, most of the streets were crooked and without light by night; the sewage was discharged down a gutter in the middle of the street; there were no sidewalks, and the posts which protected the pedestrian from being knocked down did not shelter him from a shower of mud on a wet day. At night the single wayfarer ran a good chance of being beaten and robbed by city highwaymen or by a band of disorderly youths who dubbed themselves Mohawks. In no other age, nevertheless, has restraint and formality so got the better of the English nation. There was, in spite of much fundamental rudeness, an unmistakable grace and urbanity about the city gentlemen of two hundred years ago.

As men followed rules and correctness in social matters, as they too often considered form of greater importance than substance, so in their literature they tended towards lifeless conformity. Dryden, as has been seen, gave to literature the new direction, after the French model, along the lines of correctness and polish at the expense of naturalness. But what in Dryden was only tendency became, in the writers of the eighteenth century, a confirmed habit, and mere skill and deftness passed frequently for poetic genius. Poetry was made, to a great extent, after a geometrical pattern — like the trim gardens at Versailles. Only one poet, in fact, was conspicuously great. He, however, exercised a sway over English verse which rivaled the influence of Chaucer. In his hands the heroic couplet reached perfection, and for fifty years after him it was the chief form of poetic expression. The Queen Anne Age, however, was distinctly an age of prose and reason. In the *essay* lies its special fame. In fact, prose, tentative until Dryden, first began to hold its own with poetry under Addison and Swift. And satire, it must not be forgotten, whether in verse or prose, was by far most successfully handled in the early eighteenth century.

In the second half of the century, under the Georges, life became again more openly vulgar ; the veneer of delicacy was worn thin. Literature, however, with the exception that it lost some of its terseness and sparkle, carried on the tradition set by Addison and Pope. The chief interest, of course, centres around Dr. Johnson, with whose name are grouped those of such powerful writers as Goldsmith, Gibbon, and Burke ; but the real contribution of the second half of the century was the *novel*, which had never reached any considerable maturity before the work of Richardson and Fielding.

This century, more particularly the earlier part, has often been called " The Augustan Age," because of its almost pathetic attempt to copy the " Golden Age " of Virgil and Horace. On account of such imitative work the epithet " pseudo-classic " has been not inappropriately applied to the literature of the day. Yet it must not be forgotten that it had a worth of its own, borrowed from no other people or time ; the prose of the century stands on its own merits.

DANIEL DEFOE

THE life of Defoe is full of contradictions. In the first place, nothing could have been more characteristic of the Augustan Age in which he lived than his political pamphleteering and clever satire. Yet nothing could have been more un-Augustan than his carelessness of form and his great versatility. Again, he was in most of his writings a moralist, sometimes obtrusively so. Yet no writer of distinction has ever descended to greater trickery. Furthermore, he made a business of politics and succeeded in spite of many difficult, unexpected situations. Yet in all his business pursuits he was a theorizer and sooner or later a financial failure.

Defoe's fame to-day rests, of course, on his great novel, *Robinson Crusoe;* but novel-writing was only one side of a very active life. He conducted magazines and wrote for them, he made poetry, composed treatises, and all through his life poured out a large stream of political pamphlets. Added to this, he was very closely involved in politics for twenty years, and he tried his hand at many forms of business. He had the versatility of an Elizabethan, but none of the splendor. He was a kind of squalid, calculating Ralegh in an age when large designs and noble deeds were rare. Defoe's duplicity, however, is not always easy to detect; indeed one often feels he did not always detect himself. He soon learned, without reliable friends and with a half-

unconscious selfishness, to manage cleverly for himself;
as Mr. Minto has put it, he was a man of "incomparable plausibility."

Very little is known of Defoe's earlier years. He
was born in 1661, in the parish of St. Giles, Cripplegate. His father, James Foe, was a butcher. The son
was sent to Mr. Morton's Academy in Newington Green,
with the intention that he should prepare for the dis-
senting ministry. How much learning he got there is
altogether conjectural, for the thousand and one bits
of knowledge which he later so ingeniously turned to
account might have been picked up anywhere by so
active a mind. University men taunted him with ignorance, and Swift referred to him as "an illiterate fellow,
whose name I forget." In 1705 he challenged John
Tutchin "to translate with him any Latin, French, or
Italian author, and after that to retranslate them
crosswise for twenty pounds each book." That Tutchin
declined the challenge is not so significant of Defoe's
scholarship as of Defoe's readiness to meet an issue. Some
years later he cleverly defended his learning in *Applebee's Journal*. "For, *said I*, here's a man speaks five
Languages and reads the Sixth, is a master of Astronomy, Geography, History, and abundance of other useful Knowledge (which I do not mention, that you may
not guess at the Man, who is too modest to desire it),
and yet, they say *this Man is no Scholar*."

After five years at Newington, the young Dissenter
left the academy without entering the ministry. He
followed for a while the trade of hosier — evidently as
a kind of middle-man — and acted as a commission
merchant in other matters, some of which probably took
him to Spain. About 1692 he failed completely and took

refuge in Bristol. There he was known as the "Sunday Gentleman," on account of his appearing only on the day when there was no fear of arrest. He managed somehow to appease his creditors, though he did not clear himself wholly of debt. Soon after, he started a pantile factory at Tilbury, in Essex, but that, too, brought him heavy debt.

Before his business catastrophe Defoe had already begun a political career. In spite of his assertion to the contrary, he probably began to write pamphlets as early as 1683. He is known to have taken part in the Duke of Monmouth's rebellion in 1685 ; and soon after 1688 he is found currying favor with William of Orange. Although he afterwards declared that he had been the King's intimate adviser, it is probable that William knew little of him until just before the accession of Anne. Defoe wrote numerous pamphlets in favor of the King, the first of which, in 1691, a verse pamphlet entitled *A New Discovery of an Old Intrigue, a Satire levelled at Treachery and Ambition*, is the first publication certainly his. As a result of his services, Defoe was appointed, "without the least application" on his part, Accountant to the Commissioners of the Glass Duty. This position he held from 1694 to 1699. Throughout William's reign he showed great loyalty to the King, — a more consistent loyalty than he ever showed before or after, — and defended the royal cause with a vigorous pen. His crowning work of this kind was the *True-born Englishman,* 1701, a poem which pointed out that William had as good a right to the throne as any " heterogeneous Englishman."

Besides his business and politics, Defoe found time for other work. In 1697 he published his *Essay on*

Projects, a long work in which banks, highways, friendly societies, a pension-office, wagering, fools, bankrupts, academies, seamen, and other matters are discussed with mathematical accuracy. About this time, too, he changed his name from " Foe " to " Defoe."

In 1702 came out his *Shortest Way with the Dissenters*, a pamphlet aimed at the " High Fliers," or Tories and High Churchmen. The satire, however, was so blunt that the Dissenters themselves misunderstood it; they took Defoe's conclusion, " Now let us crucify the thieves ! " in dead earnest. And the worst of it was that the government party, the " High Fliers," understood and resented. In February, 1703, Defoe was found guilty of seditious libel, fined 200 marks, sentenced to stand three times in the pillory, to be imprisoned during the Queen's pleasure, and was bound over to keep the peace for seven years.

Before his trial Defoe went into hiding, and it was then that the only authentic description of him appeared. The *Gazette*, in advertising a reward for his capture, described him as " a middle-aged, spare man, about forty years old, of a brown complexion, and dark-brown coloured hair, but wears a wig ; a hooked nose, a sharp chin, grey eyes, and a large mole near his mouth."

The author of the *True-born Englishman*, however, was greeted with acclamation in the pillory, with flowers instead of offal. Pope's line in the *Dunciad*, —

" Earless on high stood unabashed Defoe,"

is wholly false. His ears were not clipped and he had done nothing of which to be ashamed. He was clever enough, moreover, to turn the incident to account. His

Hymn to the Pillory was scattered broadcast about London.

> " Hail hieroglyphic state machine,
> Contrived to punish fancy in,"

it began, and it closed with the lines, —

> " Tell them the men that placed him here
> Are friends unto the times;
> But at a loss to find his guilt,
> They can't commit his crimes."

After one day Defoe's enemies saw that he was making popularity in the pillory faster than he ever made tiles at Tilbury, so they quickly removed him to prison.

Defoe was in prison just above a year. It was at this time that he started his *Review of the Affairs of France*, which he kept up, writing most of it with his own hand, until 1713. While in prison, too, he wrote his *History of the Great Storm*, which he described with the minuteness of an eyewitness, though of course he did not see it. In the summer of 1704 Harley, Lord Oxford, who had recognized Defoe's power as a pamphleteer, secured his release, and Defoe the Whig thus became, with remarkably easy grace, the friend of a Tory government. He was sent at this time on some sort of mission to Scotland, probably to find out the strength of the Pretender and his party there. He asserted that he went as a private gentleman, sometimes out of personal interest, sometimes (so far did he descend) to flee his creditors, but there is little doubt that the government was backing him. In the *Review* Defoe appeared as the apostle of peace and advocated, in a series of brilliant articles, the union of Scotland and England.

By 1708, however, the Whigs were again in power. Harley realized that Defoe's success depended on government favor and generously gave the pamphleteer permission to seek work from Godolphin and the Whigs. Defoe did not hesitate; he had ever been a Whig at heart, he asserted.

A more difficult manœuvre was necessary in 1710. Dr. Sacheverell, a "High Flier," whose "bloody flag" had inspired the *Shortest Way with the Dissenters*, was now brought to trial by Godolphin for his seditious, High-Church sermons. At first Defoe counseled moderation. "You should use him," he said, "as we do a hot horse. When he first frets and pulls, keep a stiff rein and hold him in if you can; but if he grows mad and furious, slack your hand, clap your heels to him, and let him go. Give him his belly full of it. Away goes the beast like a fury over hedge and ditch, till he runs himself off his mettle; perhaps bogs himself, and then he grows quiet of course." But Defoe could not hold back the indignant Whigs. As he had foreseen, Sacheverell's sentence turned popular opinion against the government, — it raised all the dogs of the parish, as he put it. Immediately further fault was found with the Whig policy; very suddenly not one but all of them were dismissed; and the Tories came in for their most successful period of government.

Defoe's position was difficult. He had often called himself a Whig; he had supported the Whig cause for two years; he was an enemy of the Tory, Sacheverell. To change colors now would seem impossible. Yet he did manage with his usual shrewdness to slip out on the winning side. "One hardly knows which to admire most," comments Mr. Minto, "the loyalty with which he stuck to the falling house till the moment of its collapse, or the adroitness with which he escaped from the ruins." He now maintained that his duty was to the Queen, irrespective of party prejudice, that her policy was at bottom a Whig policy, and that he could therefore easily subscribe to the new government.

But the Whigs, who knew that Queen Anne's policy was what certain intimate advisers wished and that Defoe's policy was what he himself wished, did not altogether believe his protestations that he had not really deserted them. They therefore brought him to trial for libels against the House of Hanover, but he managed to secure a pardon from the Queen. On the accession of George I, in 1714, however, the Whigs came definitely into power, and in 1715 brought new charges of libelous writings against him. This time he was found guilty, but he got the sentence deferred, and the wily politician finally made peace with the Whig government. This was his last change of party. He had steered a rather uncertain and hazardous course since his first service under the Whigs of William III. He was more of a Whig than a Tory — though he was not so much so as he liked to believe. The only man to whom he was genuinely loyal was William.

Defoe's pen was by no means idle during these active years. Besides the *Review* and a swarm of pamphlets, he wrote in 1706 his famous little *Apparition of Mrs. Veal*. In 1709 came his *History of the Union* (of Scotland and England) ; in 1713 he started, as a successor to the *Review*, the *Mercator*, which ran for one year; in 1714–15 he wrote *The Secret History of One Year* (the year after William's accession), *An Appeal to Honour and Justice*, *The Family Instructor*, and *A History, by a Scots Gentleman, in the Swedish Service, of the Wars of Charles XII.* This list does not include, moreover, numerous pamphlets, many of which were certainly from his pen.

Defoe's magazine activities did not cease, as was once supposed, with the death of the *Mercator,* in 1714. He used his pen actively in political writings until, about 1730, old age, gout, and apoplexy forced him to give in. His most important work of this kind was with a Jacobite paper, Mist's *Journal.* The discovery of certain papers by Mr. William Lee in 1864 has revealed the until then well-guarded secret. The government, it seems, was looking about for a man who, apparently aiding Mist, should in reality check him. Defoe, who had already been suspected of Jacobite conspiracies in Ireland, was just the man ; for the government, knowing the secret, could run no danger, and Mist, believing in Defoe's sympathy and rejoicing in a friend not altogether the enemy of the government, readily accepted his coöperation. " *The Weekly Journal* and *Dormer's Letter,* as also *The Mercurius Politicus,*" Defoe reported to the government, " . . . will be always kept (mistakes excepted) to pass as Tory papers, and yet be disabled and enervated, so as to do no mischief or give any offence." For eight years he kept up the deception and reported to his employers. Finally Mist discovered the secret and attempted to murder Defoe, much to that gentleman's astonishment at such ingratitude ! The *Mercurius Politicus* ran for four years (1716–1720), and *Dormer's News-Letter* for two (1716–1718). Defoe also wrote for many other periodicals, chief among them *Applebee's Journal,* during the years 1720–1726.

The climax of Defoe's literary work, however, was in the novel. He was about sixty years old when *Robinson Crusoe* was written, and he had not written much fiction as such until then. He had had, nevertheless, abundant practice in the use of effective details; he had learned, in the journalistic sense, to make a good " story," so that novel-writing was really not ·a new step for him. As early as 1706, in the *Apparition of Mrs. Veal*, he had shown himself able to write excellent fiction. The first part of *Robinson Crusoe* appeared in 1719, the second and third parts in 1720. Defoe asserted that the story, really based on the adventures of Alexander Selkirk, was written as early as 1708 from his own experiences, thus cleverly putting the date just one year ahead of Selkirk's appearance in London. The significant thing is that the tale is so real that the author might as well have been Selkirk himself. That was Defoe's greatest art; by it only did he play so successfully the various games, political and literary, which he attempted.

During the years 1720 and 1722 Defoe turned his hand to the writing of fiction with an energy since equaled only by Scott. In 1720 appeared *Captain Singleton*, *Duncan Campbell*, and *Memoirs of a Cavalier*. In 1722 were brought out *Moll Flanders*, *Colonel Jack*, and the *Journal of the Plague Year*, as credible as if Defoe had actually undergone the experiences he describes. *Roxana*, of the same type as *Moll Flanders*, was written in 1724. Defoe was indefatigable. The *Tour through the Whole Island of Great Britain* belongs to 1724–26; the *Complete English Tradesman* to 1725–27; *Everybody's Business is Nobody's Business* to 1725; the

History of the Devil to 1726; and *Captain Carleton* (possibly not his) to 1728.

This ceaseless publication, together with salary from the government, put him for a time in considerable comfort. He built a large house at Stoke Newington, kept a coach, continued his schemes of business, and worked several plantations. Towards the end, however, financial ruin again beset him. His last years are clouded in strange obscurity. Mist seems to have kept his creditors busy. At all events, the old man went into hiding in September, 1729. From his hiding-place he addressed in 1730 a pathetic, querulous appeal to a rather shrewd and unsympathetic son-in-law, Baker. The only redeeming feature of these last years, in fact, is his eagerness to provide for his family. He died finally on the 26th of April, 1731, in Ropemaker's Alley, Moorfields, then a more respectable quarter than now.

Pausing to contemplate the life of Defoe one is filled with various emotions, — pity for his infirmities, disgust at his trickery, and complete wonder at his vitality and versatility. Perhaps one of the most striking things about him is his loneliness, his lack of friends. The gay wits and great writers of Queen Anne's day knew one another; they gathered often at the coffee-houses, for both jest and quarrel. Even spiteful Mr. Pope was there, and the calm Mr. Addison. But the face of the "Sunday Gentleman" never looked in on their gatherings. He never jested with them, never even quarreled frankly and openly in society. In closing his account of him Mr. Minto says, "Sometimes pure knave seems to be uppermost, sometimes pure patriot; but the mixture is so complex, and the energy of the man so restless, that it almost passes human skill to unravel the two elements." Yet, whatever, good or bad, may be said of Defoe's life, posterity will never forget the author of *Robinson Crusoe*. Mankind will always be interested in the man who wrote a book which has taken so strong a hold on two centuries of readers.

JONATHAN SWIFT

JONATHAN SWIFT, the great Dean of St. Patrick's, the famous author of Gulliver, the fiercest satirist of English literature, stands alone in the age of Queen Anne. Addison had his little coterie, Pope had his bright circle of wits, Steele was the cheerful friend of all; Congreve, Gay, and Prior may be thought of in their groups. True, Swift had many friends, notably Pope, Gay, Arbuthnot, but, in the deeper sense, he was a solitary figure, — solitary by the sad circumstances of his life and by the might of his intellect. Even when dictator of London letters and politics, the centre of all eyes, he was alone. He needed friends, needed them bitterly. Yet no one could completely satisfy his demand; had one given all, Swift would have asked more. And so, when Stella, the one for whom he cared more than for any other, was gone out of his life, his strong intellect turned savagely on itself and broke him on his own wheel. Once his had been the keenest intellect in the whole kingdom, but towards the end, as his mind weakened, he grew violent. Unlike his polished contemporaries, he strove earnestly to speak "the plain truth," and was consistently misunderstood. Nothing is more illustrative of the comparative shallowness of the Augustan Age than Swift's solitariness in it.

There has been, however, especially in the shorter biographies of Swift, a great deal of injustice done the man. Those that have not been misled by a phrase or two or by the unfairness of Irish biographers, who knew Swift only in his decline, or of Dr. Johnson, who had a strong prejudice against him, have frequently used too glaring colors for the sake of effect. It makes a very pretty story and gives excellent opportunity for striking paradox to believe that Swift was benevolent yet ungrateful, loving yet brutally resentful, eager for renown yet indifferent to praise. Thackeray, whose knowledge of Vanity Fair should have saved him his blunders, mars his account, in many ways the most sympathetic, by hasty inferences and play to the gallery. The author of *Vanity Fair* and *The Newcomes*, whose Life of Swift will continue to be read long after more accurate accounts by unknown hands, should have been particularly careful and moderate. To take one example, Thackeray speaks of "the guilty, lonely wretch, shuddering over the grave of his victim" — a remark which the reader must interpret as applied to a man who, though refusing to marry openly one woman, Esther Johnson, had yet kept her in subjugated exile, and who, after openly refusing to marry another woman, Hester Vanhomrigh, had treated her so brutally that he killed her. Professor A. S. Hill, in the *North American Review* for 1868, was one of the first to give Swift fair play. He showed that Thackeray's opinion in this instance was the result of hasty inference, that there was no direct evidence to prove the calumnious reports, in the case either of Miss Johnson or of Miss Vanhomrigh, and that, on excellent testimony, Swift, instead of being the cruel hater of womankind, as Thackeray asserts, was, quite the opposite, the one man of his time who strove to exalt the position of woman in an age of loose principles and superficial decency. It is undoubtedly true that Swift's realism was often brutal, that his pride was insatiable, that he did

not know how to forgive and forget. It is nevertheless important to remember, when his faults have been
summed up and his strikingly brutal satire has made us
wince, that such men as Addison, Oxford, and Bolingbroke found him, in his most characteristic moments,
of a sweet and loving disposition. Addison says he was
" the most agreeable companion, the truest friend, and
the greatest genius of his times." It is misleading to
judge Swift by occasional sentences which, though said
with great gravity, may very well have been "excellent
fooling," could we recall all the exact circumstances that
attended their utterance. Taken alone, they sound brutal
enough, to be sure. Of some malice it is certainly impossible to acquit him. Still, these sharp sayings are for the
most part more picturesque than significant; on their
account it is unjust to call Swift a "hangman," as does
Taine, or a "Yahoo," as does Thackeray. It is, furthermore, wholly unfair to judge him by the last fifteen
years of his life, when he was sunk in bitterness and
insanity.

Jonathan Swift, the son of Jonathan and Abigail,
was born in Dublin on the 30th of November, 1667.
His parents were English; and the Dean always resented the imputation that he was an Irishman, though
he finally took up the Irish cause with patriotic zeal.
Dr. Johnson characteristically dismisses the subject
with: "Whatever was his birth, his education was
Irish." Thackeray gives a much truer estimate. "Goldsmith," he says, "was an Irishman, and always an Irishman; Steele was an Irishman, and always an Irishman;
Swift's heart was English and in England, his habits
English, his logic eminently English; his statement is
elaborately simple; he shuns tropes and metaphors, and

uses ideas and words with a wise thrift and economy, as he used his money."

A strange sort of loneliness beset Swift at the outset. His father died before the boy was born, and his mother, failing in health, removed in his early childhood to her native Leicester. Jonathan was thus left for his education to his uncle Godwin, who sent him to Kilkenny school, the Eton of Ireland, where he made friends with Congreve. Swift later remarked that his uncle had given him " the education of a dog," to which he received the reply, it is said, that he then had not " the gratitude of a dog." From most accounts he showed in school and college no signs of future greatness, though he says that he could read any chapter of the Bible when he was three years old, so well was he taught by an old nurse, who kidnapped him and carried him off to Whitehaven for over two years. In 1682 he entered Trinity College, Dublin, where, after many visits to Irish inns and an exhibition of general waywardness and dullness, he finally received, in February, 1685, by " special grace " the degree of B. A. His Physics was registered as done " badly ; " his Greek and Latin " well ; " and his Theme " negligently." It is fair to add that the dullest sort of antiquated logic was the chief diet of university education in the reigns of Charles II and James II ; and it is hence not remarkable that Swift, whose keen mind demanded real nourishment, took little interest in scholastic success. He continued to study in Dublin for a few years, but, on the outbreak of the war in which William routed the army of James at the Boyne, he left for England. There it was necessary to find work, for he had as yet no money and no reputation. A desire for independence, which had already taught him rigid economy, had, moreover, taken complete possession of him.

Swift's presence at this time was probably not very striking, though later it was commanding. Scott says the young Irishman was " tall, strong, and well-made, of a dark complexion, but with blue eyes . . . and features which remarkably expressed the stern, haughty, and dauntless turn of his mind. He was never known to laugh." Pope, who could see very little bad in Swift, says the Dean's " eyes were as azure as the heavens and had an unusual expression of acuteness." Dr. Johnson, on the other hand, who could see very little good in him, asserts that " he had a kind of muddy complexion " and " a countenance sour and severe." Like all the Augustan wits, save Pope, he was portly. In his personal habits he was clean, " with oriental scrupulosity," says Dr. Johnson. He was fond of exercise, especially of walking. Every year of his stay at Moor Park, in Surrey, he walked to Leicester to visit his mother. He seems to have had a belief that much walking would rid him of a tendency to deafness, giddiness, and scrofula — a malady caused, he thought, by a surfeit of apples at Moor Park, a theory dismissed by Dr. Johnson with " Almost every boy eats as much fruit as he can get, without any great inconvenience." There is no doubt, however, that this malady, from whatever cause, hastened Swift's insanity in later life.

When he first came to England, in 1689, Swift received an appointment under Sir William Temple, an accomplished scholar, rhetorician, and diplomatist of the Restoration, a man of considerable fame, who had retired in his old age to Moor Park. Swift's position was that of an under-secretary. He ate in the kitchen, wrote for his master when desired, and had the use of Sir William's well-stocked library. The position was sufficiently dependent, however, to gall Swift's independent spirit. He never could endure an inferior position. At Moor Park he craved recognition and appreciation; later, in London, where the great wits and lords thronged about him, he had grown bitter and insulted the admiration which he craved.

It must not be supposed, however, that Sir William Temple was an unkind patron. Indeed, Swift so rose in his esteem that he was recommended by Temple to King William. But Swift on his part was impatient: In 1694 he quarreled with his patron and left for Ireland. Soon, however, he returned to seek Temple's recommendation for his ordination in the ministry. The old courtier, with the large view of a man accustomed to granting favors, generously responded. In 1695 Swift was ordained priest and given the Prebend of Kilroot, worth about £100 a year. Soon tiring, however, of life in a remote country district, and finding a young married clergyman who needed the help of a living, he resigned Kilroot and returned in 1696 to Moor Park.

Just before leaving his Irish parish, Swift wrote to the sister of a college friend, to a Miss Jane Waring, whom he affectionately addressed as " Varina." He solemnly offered " to forego all [that is, chances of English preferment] for her sake." Varina, however, did not agree, and her action may have accounted to a great extent for his readiness to return to Moor Park and dependence. For some years she resisted his entreaties, on the ground of her own ill-health and his want of fortune. In 1700, however, when he had advanced in the world, she considered the difficulty removed. Swift replied in a brutal letter. He reproaches her with the company in which she lives, including her mother; and he says that, though he doubts her improved health, if she will " submit to be educated so as to be capable of entertaining him," he will take her, " without inquiring into her looks or her income." Swift's treatment of Varina was of course unpardonable, however much she deserved snubbing; it is not, nevertheless, as some like to believe, a fair indication of his general attitude towards women.

To return to Swift at Moor Park. Two great things he gained there, — the use of Sir William Temple's excellent library and the undying friendship of Esther Johnson, the adopted child of his patron. As a result of the first his literary style blossomed and bore fruit, for the manuscripts of his two great satires, *A Tale of a Tub* and *The Battle of the Books*, were finished by 1698, though they were not published till 1704. So great are they that Dr. Johnson doubted whether Swift wrote them, and Swift himself was heard to mutter in later years, as he turned the pages of *A Tale of a Tub*, " Good God, what a genius I had when I wrote that book ! "

The name of Esther Johnson, the well-known " Stella," the girl who made Moor Park more than tolerable for Swift, is inseparably linked with his; it runs like a ray of sunshine through the gloom of his life. When he was at the zenith of his power, dictating even to Harley, the Prime Minister, and St. John, the Secretary of State, his greatest pleasure was in his letters to her; she should know all that went on in London. Again, when the chance of even deferred preferment was gone, when

Swift " fired his pistols into the air " and returned to
Ireland, to " die like a rat in a hole," his one comfort was in the friendship of Stella. And when she died,
love passed out of his life, and he dragged out fifteen
years of despair and insanity.

The death of Sir William Temple in 1699 cast Swift
almost penniless on the world. Already the stream of
his life had set one way. A morbid desire for praise and
contempt for those who gave it, growing distrust of mankind, insatiable pride, a mind too keen to find complete
sympathy, — these qualities made up the sad equipment
with which he stepped, already isolated, into the new
century. This period is marked by certain resolutions.
One particularly is remarkable : " Not to be fond of
children, or let them come near me hardly." This
strange man, thinking perhaps of Stella at the moment
he wrote, was fortifying himself against those he loved.

After Temple's death Swift got a position as secretary
to Lord Berkeley, but he lost it soon after arriving at
Dublin. He then (1700) received a living at Laracor,
a village about twenty miles from Dublin, with a salary
of £230 a year and a congregation that did not often
exceed fifteen in number. Though Swift did much to
improve the living, he felt the meanness of the position
as keenly as the dependence at Moor Park. While small
men were rising rung on rung, here was he, the keenest
mind in the kingdom, unknown in a country parish. It
is told that one stormy day when only the sexton, one
Roger, attended worship, Swift in all gravity began the
service : " Dearly beloved *Roger*, the scripture moveth
thee and *me*." Whether the story is true or not, it is
very characteristic of the author of *A Tale of a Tub*.

One pleasant feature of the life at Laracor was the

coming of Esther Johnson. She, with Mrs. Dingley, an old retainer of Sir William Temple's, took a house in the neighborhood. The monotony of the period, moreover, was broken by frequent visits to London ; at least four years between 1700 and 1710 were spent in the capital. The *Tale of a Tub* and the *Bickerstaff Almanac*, a satirical pamphlet in which Swift dealt the deathblow to charlatan astrologers, brought him into literary prominence.[1] In London he met the great wits and for the most part despised them, though he always had a word of praise for the great Mr. Addison, and later for Pope and Gay. But Swift was too outspoken to curry favor ; while others slipped into easy berths, he remained the incumbent of Laracor. The issue in 1708 was largely on church matters, and the New-Church Whigs were in the ascendency. Swift, past forty years of age, saw bishoprics and foreign embassies slip through his fingers. For though he supported the Revolution of 1688 and disapproved heartily of the Stuart principles of government, he remained a stanch Tory and High-Churchman to the end. In 1710, however, Marlborough, the hero of Blenheim, and his followers were turned out in favor of Harley and St. John, the Tories. This brought Swift to England once more, and for the next three years he enjoyed his greatest power. The Tory leaders at once recognized the influence of his pen, at a time when the pamphlet, now supplanted by newspaper reports of parliamentary speeches, was the chief political weapon ; and Swift, without any actual position, rose for a brief time to a veritable dictatorship.

[1] The *Bickerstaff Almanac* was particularly directed against one Partridge. Swift had predicted, among other things, Partridge's death, and, when the date came round, published a verification. Partridge, despite his protestations of existence, could no longer gain an audience.

It is well to consider a moment, before noticing the arrogance of Swift at this time. In the first place, he was already forty-three in 1710 ; his habits and manners were formed. In the formation of those manners, in the next place, he had not gone through a political apprenticeship. Quite the contrary, he had struggled through half a lifetime, unfriended for the most part when he needed friends bitterly, dependent when he craved independence, as a poor student, an amanuensis, and a "hedge-parson." Since he was a young man he had possessed a desire to dominate those whom the world pointed out as his superiors ; and twenty years is a long time for an impatient man to wait for recognition. When, then, by the skill of his pen he suddenly jumped into political prominence, his arrogance and his contempt for the ruling classes were strongly developed. It is worth remembering that, however violently he came to despise mankind in the abstract, he was always a friend and a hero among the poor. He was arrogant only towards that class which he had learned to suspect of arrogance. And by the time he entered its ranks his habits of thought were irrevocably fixed.

No man in England was more feared or honored than Swift between 1710 and 1713. Once a week he dined with Harley and St. John. Harley called that day his "whipping day," and we may be sure the political sycophants were well scourged, for Swift had a sharp tongue and spoke "the plain truth." When Harley had sent him fifty pounds, in payment for literary services, Swift refused the money, demanded an apology, received one, and then wrote to Stella : "I have taken Mr. Harley into favor again." And of St. John he says : "One thing I warned him of, never to appear cold to me, for

I would not be treated like a schoolboy." The famous
General Webb, who had fought so well at Oudenarde,
hobbled up two flights of stairs to congratulate Swift and
invite him to dinner. Swift accepted and then an hour
later changed his mind. In such manner did he treat
the great, the rich, and the powerful. " I will never beg
for myself," he said, "though I often do it for others."

There are many stories about the great satirist during
his brief dictatorship. It is said that when dining with
the Earl of Burlington, he remarked to the mistress of
the house : "Lady Burlington, I hear you can sing ; sing
me a song." Upon her refusing this unceremonious
request, he replied that she should sing or he would
make her. " Why, madam, I suppose you take me for
one of your poor English hedge-parsons ; sing when I
bid you." Lady Burlington retired in tears. When Swift
next saw her the first thing he is said to have remarked
was : " Pray, madam, are you as proud and ill-natured
as when I saw you last ? " Were such things merely
pleasantries on the part of the gruff satirist? Through
all his writings there runs a dry humor, grim enough at
times, which might account, if the whole situations could
be reproduced, for many of his blunt sayings. Were they
the result of ill-timed humor, or of boorishness (for
Swift was nearly forty before he saw much of fashionable life), or of natural, uncontrolled brutality? Biographers have been rather headlong in deciding for the
third quality ; there was very reasonably a large mixture of the three. It is significant that Swift thought
so little of the mere delights of higher social circles that
he never went to a coffee-house, the rendezvous of the
élite, except for a letter ; and the step from indifference
to hate was but a short one.

Swift has been accused, however, of a like brutality to servants. Dr. Johnson, in commenting upon his " perpetual tyrannick peevishness," relates how Swift, when dining with the Earl of Orrery, said of one of the servants, " That man has, since we sat at table, committed fifteen faults." But Swift, who always prided himself on exact discipline in his own household, was at the time of this remark near enough insanity to take a childish delight in his accurate observation. His own servants, like the poor of his parish, loved him as they feared him ; and they willingly put up with his little foibles, such as calling them back, in one instance, from a journey already begun, to " please to close the door." A good instance of the sly humor with which he reproved and corrected them is the story that he once sent out some overdone meat with orders that it should be done a little less. " But how can I?" asked the cook. " Then be careful next time," said Swift, " to commit a fault which can be remedied."

For a time, then, Swift was in great favor with the Tory leaders. In 1710–11 he ran the *Examiner*, a political sheet, strong because he saw what was on every one's lips and said it clearly and concisely. In 1713, however, the Tories went out of power. Swift, whose humor had always bordered on irony, became despondent, wrote more venomously, and resented bitterly personal attacks. From this time on his mockery of human ambitions grew more violent. He did not become a bishop ; his desire for complete power was never satisfied ; he felt defeated. The climax of his life had been reached, and the catastrophe hurried after. Finally, the Deanery of St. Patrick's, with a debt of £1000, was held out to him, and he accepted it, — not

as a just reward, but as a forlorn hope; not in the
spirit of enthusiasm, but in that of ingratitude and
despair. He returned to England in 1714, to try again,
but with no success; and with Anne's death all chances
of preferment for the Tory were at an end.

Such was the bright period of this man's life, —
bright only in contrast to the gloom of later years.
Soon after returning to Ireland he took up the cause
of the Irish with vigorous zeal. England was at fault,
— in his mind, wholly so. There was in him nothing
of the calm rebuke of Addison, nothing of the gentle
merriment of Steele, nothing of the spiteful ridicule
of Pope. Still speaking "the plain truth," he spoke
it with an irony sharper than plainness, — a bruising,
unrelenting irony. Among the Irish poor, however, he
was a great man, honored for his fearlessness, loved
for his generosity. When still a struggling parson he
gave a tithe of his income to charity; when Dean, he
gave a third, sometimes a half. His thrift was never
at the expense of his starving, down-trodden countrymen. So unhesitatingly did they believe in him, in
fact, that once when people had left their work on
account of a predicted eclipse, Swift had only to say,
in order to bring them back to work, that the eclipse
had been postponed by order of the Dean of St. Patrick's. Sir Robert Walpole, who threatened to arrest
Swift for his bold writings, was advised not to do it
"unless you have ten thousand men behind the warrant."

During one of Swift's visits to London in the days
of Laracor he met a young lady named Hester Vanhomrigh. There was no doubt a good deal of affection
on Swift's part, but it was largely that of a teacher to

a pupil, as he tried to show in his poem, *Cadenus and Vanessa*. But Vanessa took the matter much more seriously, wrote him many letters, and finally followed him to Ireland. There the question of Stella's relation to Swift arose. Vanessa wrote to Stella, who showed the letter to Swift. There is a story that he took the letter in a rage, threw it down on the table before Miss Vanhomrigh, and stalked out silently. Much has been made, too, of the romantic manner of Vanessa's death, which occurred soon afterwards, but it has been pointed out that both her brothers and her younger sister had died before her and that her own health had always been weak. It is unfair, spectacular, to accuse Swift of " killing " her by his brutality.

Before considering the much mooted question, Swift's relation to Stella, it is well to notice his general attitude towards women. There is plenty of evidence that he held strong theories against a man's marrying before his fortune was secure, that he had, in fact, a horror of it. He determined, moreover, never to marry unless he could marry young. The inconsistency of his addresses to Varina, when he was decidedly poor, is repeated often enough in the lives of poor young men to be in no sense remarkable. This theory of his in regard to marriage, furthermore, was backed up by his disgust at the neglect of women who had passed the limits of youth and beauty ; in an age when woman was too often treated as a mere commodity, he did much to exalt her position, to assert the necessity of her companionship, whether she was old or young, a wife or a friend. Such a view, at first glance, conflicts strangely with what often appears to be his brutal treatment of certain women, such as Lady Burlington or Vanessa; Thackeray calls him a " bully," " who made women cry and guests look foolish." But on examination it develops that he thought more highly of women than did most of his contemporaries, and that his occasional outbursts were accountable to his irony's momentarily getting the better of him or to his contempt for the amenities of society.

Swift's *Journal to Stella*, written chiefly in the years 1710–13, is full of playfully affectionate expressions. Here is an example: "I assure oo it im vely late now; but zis goes to-morrow; and I must have some time to converse with own deerichar MD. Nite de deer Sollahs." And again: " And now let us see what this saucy, dear letter of MD says. . . . What says Pdf to me, pray? says it. Come and let me answer to you for your ladies. Hold up your head, then, like a good letter." [1] It must be remembered that at Moor Park Stella had been a mere girl, Swift's pupil. What he writes is perhaps no more than playfulness — especially in Swift, whose great, lonely mind must have craved relief in a little " sublime foolishness." There is no proof, furthermore, that Stella ever lived alone with Swift. If she lived in the same house in Ireland — a thing highly improbable, for any length of time at least — Mrs. Dingley was there too. There is certainly nothing remarkable in the fact that two women — one old and the other no longer young — should live in great intimacy with a clergyman of middle age. When Vanessa asked Stella whether she was married to Swift, Stella said " Yes," but this can

---

[1] There are various hypothetical explanations of Swift's " little language." *MD* = *my dear*; *Sollahs* = *Sirrah*(?); *Pdf* (*Podefar*) = *Swift*, possibly *Poor*, *dear*, *foolish Rogue*.

hardly be taken as proof; it must be remembered that
the same Stella, when she heard that Swift had written
beautifully about Vanessa, remarked, "We all know
the Dean could write beautifully about a broom-stick." [1]
Swift himself, who nowhere intimates that they were
married, frequently emphasizes the platonic nature of
their friendship : —

> "Thou, Stella, wert no longer young
> When first for thee my harp I strung,
> Without one word of Cupid's darts,
> Of killing eyes or bleeding hearts;
> With *friendship and esteem* possess'd
> I *ne'er admitted love* a guest."

There are many witnesses on both sides. It looks as
if Swift, by the time Stella came to Ireland, had fully
made up his mind not to marry; or, if he did marry,
as if he wanted to keep the marriage a secret. Stella
was at all events not displeased with whatever arrangements were made. It is, moreover, wholly unfair to
suspect Swift of foul play. Few men in his day were
so scrupulously moral as he; so much did he detest
profligacy and uncleanness, indeed, that his mockery of
vice becomes a morbid interest.

Whatever his connection with Stella, then, Swift
was for thirty years devoted to her. What little sympathy crept into his lonely existence was from her;
and those who forget or ignore his long, unbroken
affection for the person who was his pupil and friend
miss wholly the tragedy of his life. On hearing of her
illness, while he was in London in 1726, he wrote to a
friend : " This was a person of my own rearing and
instructing from childhood, who excelled in every good

---

[1] Swift wrote for Lady Berkeley his *Meditations upon a Broom-Stick*,
published in 1704.

quality that can possibly accomplish a human creature.
. . . Dear Jim, pardon me, I know not what I am
saying; but believe me, that violent friendship is much
more lasting than violent love."

Swift's story is nearly told; for the sad end, which
dragged itself through thirty years, began with his
return to Ireland. Once again, when the fame of the
M. B. Drapier Letters (1724), which attacked savagely
the abortive scheme of Wood's halfpence, brought him
into prominence, he returned to England, seeking preferment. Failing here, he went back to Ireland, — a
" coal-pit," as he called it, " a wretched, dirty dog-hole
and prison," " a place good enough to die in."

On his trip to England, when he visited Pope at
Twickenham, he took with him *Gulliver's Travels*,
published the same year (1726). The first two parts,
the visits to the Lilliputians and Brobdingnags, begun some years earlier, are fascinating to both old and
young; even those who miss the satire delight in the
ingenious narrative. Towards the end of the book,
however, the satire, marking as it does Swift's declining intellect, grows savage and repulsive. " He becomes disgusting," says Leslie Stephen, " in the effort
to express his disgust." In the Houyhnhnms, a kind
of horses, social conditions far superior to those in
England are discovered, and the Yahoos, their bestial
servants, out-Caliban Caliban in hideous, half-human
ferocity. Swift had long been disgusted with the pettiness and coarseness of English society; he had, moreover, long had a grudge against the English nation;
and now, in his savage old age, his irony and brutal
satire get the better of him. Yet Taine, after a review
of the rottenness of English society during the reign

of George I, concludes " that the Yahoo whom he depicted he had seen, and that the Yahoo, whether naked or riding in his carriage, is not beautiful."

The death of Stella, in 1728, only aggravated Swift's despair and bitterness. The treatment of the Irish, moreover, had lashed him into madness ; and the gravity with which he spoke was more terrible than the explosion would have been if he had burst out in mania. In 1729 he came out solemnly with *A Modest Proposal for Preventing the Children of Poor People in Ireland from being a Burden to their Parents or Country.* And what was the Dean's *Modest Proposal*, made in such bitter gravity? Merely that five sixths of the Irish children should be fattened and eaten. " I rather recommend," he says calmly, " buying the children alive, than dressing them hot from the knife, as we do roasting pigs." Truly an awful, inverted way of calling attention to the extreme poverty of Ireland. But with Swift the thing had got beyond expostulation ; it had become a madman's jest.

Fortunately he soon passed the vigor of these brutal expressions. Years before, he had prophesied, on seeing an old ash tree, " I shall die as that tree, from the top down." He continued to write considerably until 1738, and in some of his work, notably *Polite Conversation* and *Directions to Servants*, showed his old satiric power. But by 1738 the malady which had threatened him ever since his youth took strong hold of him. Not long after he developed fits of mania, during which it was difficult for his attendants to restrain him from tearing out a suffering eye. By 1740 he sank into a kind of torpor, broken only by occasional bursts of savageness or pettiness. Once he was heard to mutter, " I am what I am ;

I am what I am." And he is said to have written the
following epigram while on a walk with his attendants : —

> "Behold a proof of Irish sense!
> Here Irish wit is seen!
> When nothing 's left that 's worth defense,
> They build a magazine."

Thus he lingered till the 19th of October, 1745, when,
after a night of great pain, he died quietly at three
in the afternoon. Most of his carefully saved fortune,
£12,000, he left to found St. Patrick's Hospital for
the insane — an awful legacy for an insane man to
comtemplate! Swift saw the Valley of the Shadow of
Death while yet a long way off, and must needs ride
alone down the strait road. On his grave is inscribed:

> "Ubi saeva indignatio
> Cor ulterius lacerare nequit."

The character of the great Dean is altogether too
complex to be summed up in a glib phrase. He was not
a "bully," a "footpad," or a "Yahoo;" yet it would
be presumptuous, on the other hand, to assert that his
savage style was a quite necessary rebuke to his times.
It is more fitting, in closing, to call attention to the
chief elements, however conflicting, that composed so
unhappy and so savage a nature.

Whoever holds the most partial brief for Swift must
admit that he early showed most of his weaker characteristics : false, insatiable pride, distrust of mankind,
instinctive cynicism, and misanthropy. There is no doubt,
on the other hand, of his genuine hatred of sham, his
sincerity; Bolingbroke called his character "hypocrisy
reversed." His savage style, moreover, at first a mannerism rather than a manner, was not the most character-

istic thing about him till he reached middle age. Then
his loneliness, partly the result of his intellectual un-
congeniality and superiority, partly the result of the
circumstances of his life, developed in him a bitterness
which towards the end passed all bounds of moderation.
He did finally become a scourge, a mad jester upon life.

Taine calls Swift the most unhappy genius in history.
Certainly the melancholy of such men as Byron seems
like childish pettishness beside the misery of Swift, a
misery as great, as inevitable, as inexorable as classic
Fate. "An immense genius," says Thackeray; "an
awful downfall and ruin. So great a man he seems to
me, that thinking of him is like thinking of an empire falling." And Taine concludes: "A philosopher
against all philosophy, he created a realistic poem,
a grave parody, deduced like geometry, absurd as a
dream, credible as a law report, attractive as a tale,
degrading as a dishclout placed like a crown on the
head of a divinity. These were his miseries and his
strength; we quit such a spectacle with a sad heart, but
full of admiration; and we say that a palace is beautiful even when it is on fire. Artists will add: especially
when it is on fire."

JOSEPH ADDISON

"It is no small thing to make morality fashionable. Addison did it, and it remained in fashion." These words by Taine sum up the greatness of Addison's genius. The task which was set before him was a delicate one; Swift, Steele, and Pope were all, for one or another reason, unqualified to perform it; and it was only through his own patience, his breadth of view, his quiet gentlemanliness, and his wit which left no sting that Addison was able to attain success. As a writer of poetry he rarely rises above the mediocrity of his contemporaries ; but as an essayist on his own ground he is unsurpassed in any age ; and as the most successful moralist, the man with an effective message to the people of his day, he towers above all.

Joseph Addison, the eldest son of Lancelot Addison and Jane Gulston, was born May 1, 1672, at Milston, in Wiltshire. His father, at the time of Joseph's birth rector of Milston, was a man of experience and accomplishment. He had been chaplain in Dunkirk and Tangier, in 1675 was made a prebendary of Salisbury Cathedral, and in 1683 was awarded the Deanery of Lichfield. As a writer he had considerable contemporary reputation, especially for his works on Mohammedanism and Judaism.

Thus young Joseph, perhaps as much as any English author of note, grew up in an atmosphere of refinement, scholarship, and piety. It has been pointed out, too, that his boyhood must have received a strong impres-

sion from the peaceful scenery of Wiltshire : the gently
rolling Salisbury plain, with the ancient fragments of
Stonehenge standing boldly on the treeless Downs,
the winding Avon, with its deep summer shade, and
Salisbury spire ever in the southern sky as he trudged
to school at Amesbury. This is no doubt more
than a fancy, for in later life, however little he
may have reveled Byron-wise in beetling crags and
the wild sea-wave, Addison preferred the natural
beauty of Fontainebleau to the precise formality of
Versailles. In a letter to Congreve he says: " I . . .
wou'd as soon see a River winding through woods and
meadows as when it is tossed up in such a variety of
figures at Versailles." And in the Spectator, No.
444 : " I do not know whether I am singular in my
Opinion, but for my part I would rather look upon a
Tree in all its Luxuriancy and Diffusion of Boughs and
Branches, than when it is thus cut and trimmed into
a Mathematical Figure." This is of especial interest,
because a delight in formality was, generally speaking,
the characteristic of the age. Addison was in most
senses thoroughly Augustan, but his lack of enthusiasm for the Alps has too often been magnified, by
reasoning from a possibility, into a profound horror for
natural beauty. It is precisely by such little differences as Addison's appreciation of Fontainebleau that
a man's individuality takes on a distinctive reality.

When Addison's father moved to Lichfield the boy
was sent to the town grammar school. There, Dr. Johnson tells us, Joseph planned and conducted a *barring-
out.* " The practice of barring-out," continues Dr. Johnson, " was a savage license, practiced in many schools
toward the end of the last [17th] century, by which the

boys, when the periodical vacation drew near, growing
petulant at the approach of liberty, some days before
the regular recess, took possession of the school, of
which they barred the doors, and bade their master defiance from the windows." The savage vigor of young
Joseph in this instance, in great contrast to his proverbial calmness and gentlemanly behavior, has been
much quoted and very likely magnified.

From Lichfield Addison passed to the Charter House
School, then in London, and long since famous for its
roll of illustrious students. There he gained a reputation for scholarship and wrote Latin verses, one of the
necessary accomplishments of an Augustan gentleman,
with fluency and conventional skill. In fact, intellectual success always came easily to him. At Charter
House he became a great friend of Dick Steele, an
impetuous Irish boy of his own age. Thackeray says
Steele fagged for Addison, in payment for assistance
in his work. This is hardly likely, for the boys were of
the same age; but there is no doubt that Steele showed
from the first for his gentlemanly scholar-friend an almost servile loyalty which easily found a place in his
affectionate nature.

With no reverses to check his advance, Addison went
in 1687 to Queen's College, Oxford. After two years
his Latin verses procured him a demyship — "a term,"
Johnson says, "by which that society denominates those
which are elsewhere called scholars" — in Magdalen
College, and in 1693 he received the Master's degree.
In 1697 he was elected Probationary Fellow and the
next year actual Fellow — a position which he retained
till 1711. At Oxford Addison's reputation for scholarship and good conduct increased. The shady avenue

of elms along the Cherwell, hard by the College, conjures up perhaps more vividly than anything the serenity and meditative study of his years at Oxford. It is now known as " Addison's Walk."

While at the University Addison wrote, in 1693, an *Account of the Greatest English Poets.* This poem is interesting chiefly because it is his first considerable composition in English. In it the Latin classics are too frequently an infallible standard, Dryden and Congreve are the chief representatives of the Drama, there is no mention of Shakespeare, and Cowley is considered a " mighty genius."

Addison, who was by nature exceedingly shy, — so much so, in fact, that his great gifts of conversation never appeared to advantage except when he was with one or two friends, — had little inclination to take orders, a step usually necessary to the retention of the fellowship. He was much influenced in his decision, moreover, by a pension of £300, granted him by the Crown in 1699 through the aid of his friend Charles Montagu, later known as Lord Halifax. The object of this pension was to allow Addison by foreign travel to prepare himself for state affairs. The value to the state of an able writer, in the days when telegraphy was unknown and the newspaper in its infancy, when the place of parliamentary speeches, now printed all over the world the same day they are delivered, was taken by the pamphlet, was incalculably great. Montagu and Lord Somers were quick to fix upon the young and accomplished Mr. Addison as their protégé, and Addison, who eagerly embraced the opportunity, started on his travels in 1699.

The period of his travels extended over four years.

After a short stay at Paris and visits to Versailles and Fontainebleau, he went direct to Blois, where he remained nearly eighteen months. Having at last acquired with considerable difficulty a knowledge of French, he returned to Paris, where, before starting for Italy, he met the great French critic Boileau, who, though' old and peculiarly sparing of compliment, praised Addison's Latin verses very highly. To-day no critic is looked up to as a final arbiter, so it is perhaps difficult for us to appreciate how much it meant to Addison to receive this praise from a man who had set the fashions in French literature as Louis XIV had set them in society.

In December, 1700, the traveler embarked at Marseilles for Genoa. Thence he visited nearly all the important towns and cities of Italy, as far south as Naples. In connection with his supposed aversion for the Alps, it is interesting that he mentions with pleasure the crossing of the Apennines. He is more orthodox, according to Augustan standards of art, in his inability to understand Gothic architecture. To the modern traveler, steeped in mediæval lore and filled with curiosity for the past, Addison's opinion of Siena Cathedral is almost amusing. " Nothing in the world," he says, " can make a prettier show to those who prefer false beauties and affected ornaments to a noble and majestic simplicity."

On the accession of Queen Anne in 1702, Halifax and the Whigs went out of power, and Addison's pension ceased. Though he was not forced to give up his travels immediately, his lack of resources probably hastened his return, which took place in 1703. For a short time he lived in London in a condition not much

better than that of the Grub Street "hack." Soon,
however, he was taken into the famous Kit-Kat Club,
a half political, half literary society founded by Jacob
Tonson, the bookseller. The club consisted of thirty-
nine leaders of the Whig party, who, seeing the necessity of making a strong front against the Tories and
the Queen, and appreciating the value of an able
writer, readily elected Addison. This membership,
though it did not at once relieve his poverty, put him
in a position to gain great fame. For Godolphin, then
Lord Treasurer, when Marlborough's successes had
partly restored the Whigs to power, asked Halifax to
suggest a poet who might celebrate the great victory of
Blenheim. Addison was named, and the result was *The
Campaign*. The poem acquired for Addison some literary renown, as well as a Commissionership of Appeal
in the Excise, and in 1706 the position of Under Secretary of State.

At thirty-four, then, Addison had acquired a thorough education, had traveled extensively on the Continent, and had reached a position of political importance. It was about this time that he began, in his
grave, gentlemanly fashion, to reign over the wits at
Button's Coffee-House. His classical learning, his talents for conversation and gentle wit, his good taste
and critical judgment, easily gained him the honored
position. Around him were grouped most of the great
men of the day. Lord Halifax was his patron and
friend; Pope, the young author of the *Pastorals*,
looked up to his calm judgment; Dick Steele, his companion at school and college and later Captain of the
Guard, was there too; even the great Dr. Swift, bitterly
jealous of fame, admired him and praised him in his

Journal to Stella. "Mr. Addison," he writes, "who goes over [to Ireland] First Secretary, is a most excellent person." Though his conversational powers were never shown to a crowd or to strangers, on account of his great shyness and reserve, yet if one or two friends stepped into Button's, Addison's discourse immediately charmed them. "There is no such thing," he said, "as real conversation but between two persons."

But though every one admired him, few loved him. There was a touch of cold reserve, of self-sufficient superiority — a little too much truth in Pope's line that describes him as assenting "with civil leer," for any one to approach beyond the footstool of the great man. One picture represents him sitting alone in a coffee-house meditatively smoking his pipe and reading a paper, while the more genial frequenters crowd to the opposite corner. There was something just a little forbidding about his serenity; as Thackeray puts it, he never saw any piece of writing but he felt he could do it better. And Pope says of him: "With any mixture of strangers, and sometimes with only one, he seemed to preserve his dignity much, with a stiff sort of silence." His bashfulness, combined with his self-sufficiency, held men at arm's length from him.

Yet one always feels that Addison was, next to Swift, the master mind of the age. As Swift was above others in keenness, Addison was above them in the scope of his intellect. He bore his greatness easily, as if it belonged to him. Indeed, his lack of ready sympathy may have been the result of a very real superiority to the men about him.

Meanwhile Addison gradually rose in political im-

portance. In 1708 he was elected to the House of
Commons,— a position acquired rather by the power
of his pen than by his ability as an orator. He
tried only once to speak and then failed dismally.
Towards the close of the same year he was appointed
Chief Secretary for Ireland. Though he lost this position in 1710, when the Tories came into power, he
regained it again in 1714, on the accession of George I,
but resigned it the following year for a seat on the
Board of Trade. In 1717 he reached his highest
political preferment, that of Secretary of State, under
Lord Sunderland's ministry, but was forced by failing
health to resign it in less than a year.

Hand in hand with his political advance rose Addison's literary fame. The *Campaign* was followed
by more pretentious literary effort, of which the two
most successful expressions were his drama *Cato*
and his essays in the *Spectator*. His other work, except for some of his contributions to periodicals, has
sunk into insignificance as far as the general reading
public goes. In 1706 his opera *Rosamund* was acted,
but failed, chiefly on account of inferior music. In
1715 he tried his hand at comedy in the *Drummer*,
but it, too, met with little enthusiasm, though after his
death, when the author's fame and name were known,
it was played with some success. *Cato*, on the other
hand, met with complete success, partly on account of
the generous assistance of Steele and the excellent
acting of Booth. It was not acted till 1713, though
most of the first four acts had been written while
Addison was on his travels in Italy. It was considered by some to be a great argument for the Whigs,
Cato struggling for the liberties of Rome being

compared to Halifax and Wharton. But the Tories claimed its sentiments as their own ; and Addison, of course, profited by the enthusiasm of both parties. Among Addison's contemporaries it was probably the chief cause of his fame.

It is in the *Spectator*, however, that Addison is truly great. The *Spectator* was the child of Steele's paper, the *Tatler*, to which Addison had contributed. The first number of the *Tatler* appeared April 12, 1709. Addison's first contribution was No. 18, and during the two years of the paper's publication he wrote 42 out of 271 numbers. The real author of the *Tatler*, then, was Steele, who wrote 188 numbers. Addison's share, however, was sufficient to give him the practice which resulted in the *Spectator*, a paper as characteristic of him as the *Tatler* is of Steele.

The *Spectator* began March 1, 1711, and ran through 555 issues before December 6, 1712, when its publication was stopped for a year and a half. Addison contributed 274 numbers, Steele 236. The paper met with unprecedented success, and on its collection into octavo volumes, which were sold for a guinea apiece, more than nine thousand copies, Steele writes in the last number, were sold off.

The general plan of the paper was probably conceived by Steele, and he also sketched the characters of Sir Andrew Freeport, Captain Sentry, the Templar, and the Clergyman, who stand as a background for the inimitable Sir Roger de Coverley and Will Honeycomb. For these two Addison is responsible, as well as for the character of the Spectator, which he probably drew largely from himself. Macaulay, in his essay on Addison, thus excellently gives us a picture of the two in one — Addison the Spectator: " The Spectator himself is a gentleman who, after passing a studious youth at the university, has bestowed much attention on curious points of antiquity. He has, on his return, fixed his residence in London, and has observed all the forms of life which are to be found in that great city, has daily listened to the wits of Will's, has smoked with the philosophers of the Grecian, and has mingled with the parsons at Child's, and with the politicians at the St. James's. In the morning he often listens to the hum of the Exchange; in the evening, his face is constantly to be seen in the pit of the Drury Lane Theatre. But an insurmountable bashfulness prevents him from opening his mouth, except in a small circle of intimate friends."

Though the *Spectator* would be very great had the Sir Roger de Coverley papers never been written, it is the story of the old knight and his friends that gives it its lasting fame. It is perhaps not too sweeping to say that no writer between Shakespeare and Fielding has portrayed so real or so delightful a character as Sir Roger. After we have been with the old knight to church, to the theatre, and to the coffee-house, or have wandered with him for a day on his estate, — when, in fact, we have grown to love his simple virtues, his courtly manners, and his immemorial prejudices, we no longer know the man in a book, as perishable as the paper on which he is printed, but see him before us in person.

The most significant feature of the *Spectator*, however, is its influence on the life of the Queen Anne Age. It was the best possible means of expression for Addison's message. Life during the Restoration had been notoriously, recklessly loose. There was, moreover, a kind of degenerate delight in guilt and folly; men were not even genuinely vigorous in their wickedness; a faded, jaded atmosphere, theatrical, make-believe, hung over society. The chief thought was for the pleasure of the moment, with no real relish for that pleasure. True, there was plenty of wit, but it was no wit for gentlemen, much less for ladies. To be witty and yet virtuous had become unthinkable. It was not only against the open indecency, furthermore, that Addison took a stand, but against the meaningless frivolity, the vanity of society. Steele, by his plays and the *Tatler*, in which people were given wholesome reading and shown genuine interest and sympathy, coupled with delightful wit, had done much to improve matters. It remained for Addison, however, to lead men little by little, by hints rather than by denunciations, by satire that left no sting, to a cleaner, more genuine life. In No. 10 of the *Spectator* he outlines his purpose. "Since I have raised to myself so great an Audience," he says, "I shall spare no Pains to make their Instruction agreeable and their Diversion useful. For which Reason I shall endeavor to enliven Morality with Wit, and to temper Wit with Morality. . . . And to the End that their Virtue and Discretion may not be short, transient, intermitting Starts of Thought, I have resolved to refresh their Memories from Day to Day till I have recovered them out of that desperate State of Vice and Folly into which the Age has fallen. . . . It was said of Socrates that he brought Philosophy down from Heaven to inhabit among Men; and I shall be ambitious to have it said of me that I have brought Philosophy out of Closets and Libraries, Schools and

Colleges, to dwell in Clubs and Assemblies, at Tea-tables and in Coffee-houses." A knowledge of the Spectator and of Sir Roger will tell us more than all the commentaries written thereon about the character and the work of Addison.

From time to time until near the close of his life Addison wrote for numerous periodicals. He contributed to the *Guardian*, which Steele had started as a successor to the *Spectator*; but when Steele, for political reasons, dropped the *Guardian* and began the *Englishman*, Addison, who was always a moderate Whig, refused to contribute. In 1714 he published alone an eighth volume of the *Spectator*, which ran through eighty numbers. "Nothing can be more striking," says Macaulay, "than the contrast between the *Englishman* and the eighth volume of the *Spectator*, between Steele without Addison and Addison without Steele." This criticism is no doubt too severe; it was probably Steele with violent political opinions as much as Steele without Addison that condemned the *Englishman*. During the general election in 1710 Addison published the *Whig Examiner*, in opposition to Swift's *Examiner*. "On no occasion," says Dr. Johnson, "was the genius of Addison more vigorously exerted." In 1715 he issued for a short time a political paper called the *Freeholder*. Steele naturally enough complained that it was too moderate, but his opposition paper, *Town Talk*, fell quite flat. The character of Lord Somers in the *Freeholder*, Nos. 22, 44, and 47, reflects the same master-hand that drew Sir Roger.

It is a tribute to Addison's generosity to remember that in his political and literary success he did not forget his friends. Tickell, Budgell, and Ambrose Phillipps

were all provided for, his friend Craggs succeeded him
as Secretary, and Steele, whose wild political views had
shut him out from preferment, was raised to knight-
hood. Even the Tory Swift, who had been Addison's
political antagonist, retained a high admiration for the
successful Whig. It may fairly be said, in fact, that
Addison quarreled with no one, though two quarreled
with him. His .manner of complacent superiority no
doubt aggravated the strife, but the quarrels were directly provoked, in the one case, by the trickery of Pope,
and in the other by the hot-headedness of Steele.

Addison's troubles with Pope began as early as 1713,
when one John Dennis, who had already an old score
with Pope, attacked Addison's play, *Cato*, for which
Pope had written a prologue. Pope replied in an abusive
pamphlet entitled the *Narrative of the Frenzy of
J. D.*[1] Addison, who had no wish to be implicated,
sent word, perhaps a little too coolly, that he was quite
capable of defending himself. Now Pope, who was a
very suspicious person, had for years considered Addison
a literary rival; he looked with no little jealousy on the
latter's successful reign over the wits at Button's. Thus
it was an easy step for Pope, when his revised *Rape
of the Lock* (1714), which Addison had urged him
not to recast, proved a huge success, to argue himself
little by little into the belief that Addison was jealous
of him, that the great essayist and Lord of Button's
did in fact fear the rivalry of a " brother near the
throne." As a result he changed to the offensive and
attacked violently the *Pastorals* of Ambrose Phillipps, one of Addison's friends, who waited for him with
a birch. Pope, who dared not risk a physical encounter,

[1] See chapter on Pope, p. 196.

shook his fist at Button's and laid up another grudge against King Addison.

The next incident precipitated the quarrel. In 1715 the first volume of Pope's *Homer* came out, and at the same time a version by Tickell, one of Addison's friends. To Pope, eagerly jealous, the case was plain : Tickell's version was much too good to be his alone — Addison must have helped him ; the same Addison, furthermore, had ungraciously declined his defense of *Cato*, and had advised him not to recast the *Rape of the Lock* ; Addison, it was clear, feared an able rival, even employed that birch-bearing bully, Phillipps ; Addison, it was certain, had written the rival translation of *Homer* and published it under Tickell's name, that the defeat of Pope might be the more ignominious.

The breach was now complete. Addison bore himself throughout the whole affair with gentlemanly calmness, tinged perhaps by just a little too much self-sufficiency, a withheld derision, a barely perceptible curl of the lip that was more intolerable than a scornful reply. Pope's behavior, as has been indicated, was spiteful, unfairly suspicious, and often vicious. He saw straight enough, however, to produce one of the cleverest satires in the language. It is perhaps overdone ; Addison's unusual generosity and fundamental sincerity are not given due credit. It is well to remember, on the other hand, that Pope credits Addison with many of his most characteristic virtues, —

> " One whose fires
> True genius kindles and fair fame inspires,
> Blest with each talent and each art to please,
> And born to write, converse, and live with ease " —

before he begins his terrible arraignment.[1] And
though Pope by no means draws the whole of Addison,
what he does draw is near enough to hit home. Did
not the great man "just hint a fault and hesitate dislike"? Was this not his power? Was he not perhaps sometimes "so obliging that he ne'er obliged"?
"I sent the verses to Mr. Addison," says Pope,[2] "and
he used me very civilly ever after." Thackeray adds:
"No wonder he did. It was shame very likely more
than fear that silenced him. . . . His great figure
looks out on us from the past — stainless but for that
— pale, calm, and beautiful ; it bleeds from that black
wound."

The quarrel with Steele, in no way so serious or
protracted as that with Pope, is of importance chiefly
because Addison and Dick Steele had been friends
since Charter House days. But once manhood was
reached, there was very little except the pen in common
between them. Addison developed by easy degrees into
political prominence and dignity ; Steele, impetuous,
rushing from one pursuit to another, found himself at
forty in no political prominence except a kind of notoriety that attached to rabid Whiggism. Addison was
too judicial in his nature for Steele ; Steele was too injudicious for Addison. It was hardly remarkable, then,
that two things should have precipitated the quarrel
between men who were drawing thus naturally apart.
Addison had frequently lent Steele money, and had
been, felt Sir Richard, who took little thought for the
morrow, just a suggestion cold-blooded and severe in
exacting payment. In the second place, Addison raised

[1] See an admirable essay by Mr. G. K. Chesterton on " Pope and the
Art of Satire," in *Varied Types*.
[2] The verses were not published till 1723.

Tickell, a young man of thirty, to the position of Under Secretary of State, while Steele, the friend of his boyhood, the editor of the *Tatler* and *Spectator*, and a Member of Parliament, was left in the cold. When the famous bill for limiting the number of peers was brought in, therefore, it was not unnatural that Steele should defend the Opposition against Addison and the Ministers. Steele's weapon was a paper called the *Plebeian;* Addison replied in the *Old Whig*. Macaulay has pointed out that Steele, however he blundered upon the truth, was illogical in his arguments, and that Addison, however unsound his premises, by logical argument and superior style easily defeated the *Plebeian*. There is no evidence that the friends of a lifetime, who thus quarreled almost at the grave, were ever reconciled.

In 1716 Addison, after a long courtship, married the Countess Dowager of Warwick. His married life, which lasted only three years, does not seem to have been particularly happy. Perhaps the most significant feature of the union was Addison's removal to the Countess' home, Holland House, " a house," says Macaulay, " which can boast of a greater number of inmates distinguished in political and literary history than any other private dwelling in England."

Soon after moving to Holland House, Addison was forced by recurring attacks of asthma to abandon his work, political and literary. He declined quietly from now on, and, with many unaccomplished literary projects before him, died, as serenely as he had lived, on June 17, 1719. He was buried in Westminster Abbey.

Addison's last hours were characteristic of his whole life. It is said that just before he died he sent to ask

Gay's pardon for some offense of which Gay knew not.
We regret that Pope and Steele could not also have been
summoned to that bedside, not only to receive his forgiveness, but also to hear his last remark to his dissolute stepson, the Earl of Warwick, " See how a Christian can die." Pope would probably have gone off and
written a satire on the words; and one does feel that
Addison was exasperatingly sure of himself even in
death: his unbroken successes, even his immortality,
came as easily to him as eating his dinner. At bottom,
however, he was a great and good man ; his faults grow
very little in the light of his learning, his refinement,
his sanity, his genuineness, and his generosity. He was
above party strife. He was the ablest prose writer of his
time ; he stands, in fact, preëminent with two or three
others in the whole history of English literature. Among
the intellects of the day he had only one peer — Swift.
Above all, he " reconciled wit and virtue," one of the
most important contributions to morality in the eighteenth century.

ALEXANDER POPE

POPE held a unique position in the age of Queen Anne. Most of the great writers at that time depended for their eminence as much on the favor of Church or State as on their literary merits. Addison, for instance, was Secretary for Ireland and later Secretary of State ; Swift was as much the Dean of St. Patrick's as the author of Gulliver ; Steele was a member of Parliament, Prior was an ambassador, and Gay depended on a patron. Much of this favor, it is true, was the reward of literary excellence ; the success and the preferment, however, went hand-in-hand. Pope, on the other hand, in the face of physical deformities and religious ostracism, fought his way purely by his pen to the first place among contemporary poets. He perfected the heroic couplet, and he gave serious dignity to letters as a calling. So great was he, in fact, that poets unquestioningly made him their model for a half century ; his influence extended into the very heart of the reaction against him and his school. His life will be found interesting as it touches the lives of his great contemporaries, as it develops a character that was a strange mixture of petty vanities and high purpose, of bitter jealousy and genuine tender-heartedness ; but it must be chiefly kept in mind that Pope was, from the age of twelve to his grave, peculiarly, professionally a man of letters.

Alexander Pope was born of Roman Catholic parents on May 21, 1688, in Lombard Street, London. His father, of the same Christian name, acquired as a linen merchant a fortune sufficiently great to enable him to retire, when Pope was still a small child, to Binfield, on the border of Windsor Forest. His mother, whose maiden name was Edith Turner, — of good Yorkshire stock, — lived to the great age of ninety-three. The lasting affection of the son for his mother is a refreshing contrast to the quarrels and petty deceits that checkered his whole life.

Two things withheld from Pope the education common to English boys. The "glorious Revolution" of 1688, in the first place, brought Catholics into disfavor, frequently into persecution. Besides this, Pope was deformed. It was only by patient nursing and constant attendance throughout his life that soul and body — his "crazy carcase," as Wycherley called it — were kept together. He did attend three schools, between the ages of eight and twelve, but most of his schooling came through the help of a family priest and his own eagerness to learn. He himself told Spence that he had taught himself "Latin, as well as French and Greek." The result was a very defective scholarship, but a useful familiarity with Homer, Virgil, Statius, Horace, and Ovid.

Pope has been considered, largely on his own suspicious testimony, one of the great examples of poetic precocity. On his own authority he versified almost from the cradle. Adopting the phrase from Ovid, he said : —

> "As yet a child, nor yet a fool to fame,
> I lisp'd in numbers, for the numbers came."

He submitted his verses for correction to his father, who, when not satisfied, returned them with the comment, "These are not good rhymes." But the young

ALEXANDER POPE
From the portrait by Jonathan Richardson in 1732

poet persevered. The *Ode on Solitude*, said to have been written at the age of twelve, does not merit the parent's criticism. Many other juvenile pieces — chiefly imitations or translations — developed the style of which Pope found himself master at twenty-three. His greatest youthful effort was an epic poem of about 4000 lines on Alcander, Prince of Rhodes. This long work was perhaps fortunately left uncompleted and was later burned by Pope himself.

Pope's boyhood, then, little as it saw of the pastimes and comradeship that go to the development of most Englishmen, prepared him peculiarly for his life-work. As he sat, book in hand, in Windsor Forest, or spent long afternoons fumbling the pages of Virgil or Horace, and sometimes Spenser and Milton, in his father's library, his life centred itself on the one thing he knew. He had few friends ; how he must have loved his books ! And as he translated and imitated, himself occasionally striking off a deathless phrase, how he must have warmed to his poetry, rejoiced in the feeling that day by day crept over him, — " I, too, am a poet ! "

This desire to write verse, moreover, was no idle fancy of youth, but a conviction borne out by the praise of great men. As early as 1706 William Walsh had advised him to make correctness his aim ; " we have had great poets," said Walsh, " but never one great poet that was correct." The *Pastorals*, though not published till 1709, were largely written when Pope was sixteen, and Wycherley, a writer of plays and relic of the Restoration, so admired them that he at once formed an intimate friendship with the young author. On their publication the *Pastorals* brought Pope great popularity. However artificial, they were " correct," and that to an Augustan meant much. It is significant that Pope, at the age of twenty-one, took his place among great wits like Addison, Steele, and Swift.

At the same time that he stepped into literary prominence Pope began his quarrels. He always moved in a bright circle of friends; but he seemed unable long to avoid falling out with so ne one. Hardly any of his long poems arose without jealous dispute; and the *Dunciad* — one of his latest works and really the consummation of his genius — rounded out a life of quarrels by paying off in keen satire the accumulated scores of years.

Much of Pope's irritability and petty wrangling may be traced directly to his deformity; he was the victim of both physical and mental disease. At times suffering was intense; he could work for only a few hours together. Dr. Johnson thus describes him : " When he rose, he was invested in a bodice made of stiff canvas, being scarcely able to hold himself erect till it was laced, and he then put on a flannel waistcoat. One side was contracted. His legs were so slender that he enlarged their bulk with three pair of stockings, which were drawn on and off by a maid." Dr. Johnson goes on, evidently with considerable fellow-feeling, to recount how Pope was " too indulgent to his appetite." " If he sat down to a variety of dishes he would oppress his stomach to repletion."

Closely connected with his physical weakness was a mental disease, probably fostered by his solitary youth. Pope was morbidly suspicious, often of his friends. He had so diligently hoarded and fingered his poetic store that he became bitterly jealous of rivalry, fearful of honest emulation. Under the influence of this malady he would stoop to almost any trick. By publishing concocted correspondence, by distorting facts, by spreading scandal, by slandering the innocent, he made in many ways a despicable figure among the great wits. He successively quarreled with Wycherley, Dennis, Addison, Tickell, Phillipps, Theobald, Cibber, and, finally, with Bolingbroke.

Yet—in remarkable contrast—Pope was a great man in a circle of great men. Thackeray thus enumerates his closest friends : " Garth, the accomplished and benevolent, whom Steele has described so charmingly, of whom Codrington said that his character was 'all beauty,' and whom Pope himself called the best of Christians without knowing it; Arbuthnot, one of the wisest, wittiest, most accomplished, gentlest of mankind; Bolingbroke, the Alcibiades of his age; the generous Oxford; the magnificent, the witty, the famous, and chivalrous Peterborough : these were the fast and faithful friends of Pope, the most brilliant company of friends, let us repeat, that the world has ever seen. The favorite recreation of his leisure hours was the society of painters, whose art he practiced. In his correspondence are letters between him and Jervas, whose pupil he loved to be— Richardson, a celebrated artist of his time. . . — and the wonderful Kneller, who bragged more, spelt worse, and painted better than any artist of his day." In this list should be added Dean Swift, who, as his letters show, was one of the poet's firmest friends and greatest admirers.

In spite of his deformity, Pope for a time longed to be a coffee-house swell. His first glimpse of the life was at an early age, when he was taken, in 1700, to see the great Mr. Dryden presiding over the wits at

Will's. Later, when the *Pastorals* had brought him
fame, he went up to London and tried for a few years
to live "about town." "For a brief space," says Thackeray, "upon coming up to town, Pope formed part of
King Joseph's [1] court, and was his rather too eager and
obsequious humble servant. Dick Steele, the editor of
the *Tatler*, Mr. Addison's man, and his own man too,
a person of no little figure in the world of letters,
patronized the young poet and set him a task or two.
Young Mr. Pope did the tasks very quickly and
smartly. . . . He thought it an honor to be admitted
into their company; to have the confidence of Mr.
Addison's friend, Captain Steele." But the coffee-house
life was soon too exacting for poor Pope's little body;
he fortunately had the good sense to retire from the
field, in favor of such vigorous trencher-men as Steele.

Pope's quarrels began in his boyhood. In a long correspondence with Wycherley he soon perceived that he
was wasting time "propping up an old rake," grew more
severe in the correction of his senior's verses, and finally
sent him certain insulting replies. A quarrel resulted.
Whether the two ever became friends again is uncertain.
Pope, as if to gain a quite unnecessary triumph, — for
the death of the old dramatist was forlorn enough, —
had the audacity to publish many years later an altered
correspondence. "The first man of letters of his day,"
says Mr. Leslie Stephen, "could not bear to reveal the
full degree in which he had fawned upon the decayed
dramatist, whose inferiority to himself was now plainly
acknowledged."

The next quarrel was with one John Dennis, a pon-

[1] King Joseph refers to Addison, who was the leader at Button's,
opposite Will's.

derous and somewhat vituperative writer of the old
school. In 1711 Pope published his *Essay on Criticism*, in which he attacked Dennis in the character of
Appius. Dennis had looked with disfavor, not unmixed
perhaps with jealousy, on the *Pastorals*. He was easily
enraged, then, by the following lines in the *Essay* : —

> " But Appius reddens at each word you speak,
> And stares, tremendous, with a threatening eye,
> Like some fierce tyrant in old tapestry."

His savage reply, though it does make some good points,
descends into personal abuse. After five not wholly unfair criticisms, he goes on to insinuate that Pope is a
" downright monkey " and a " hunch-backed toad." We
shall meet Dennis again ; Pope, we shall see, never forgot injuries.

Whatever his detractors had to say, the *Essay on
Criticism* landed Pope, at the age of twenty-three, in
the front ranks of living poets. The essay is, to be sure,
little more than a succession of detached sayings, taken
chiefly second-hand from the classics. Yet every one is
familiar with such lines as —

> " A little learning is a dangerous thing;
> Drink deep, or taste not the Pierian spring."

and —

> " Fools rush in where angels fear to tread,"

and —

> " To err is human, to forgive, divine."

The Rape of the Lock, in the following year, took
London by storm, and Pope's position as first poet was
secured.

In 1713 began Pope's quarrel with Addison, which
lasted over several years and dragged in many other

antagonists, whose names Pope duly remembered for entry in his last answer, the *Dunciad*. In the first place, Addison advised Pope not to recast *The Rape of the Lock*, which was, he said, "a delicious little thing," as it stood. Pope, however, did change the poem and met with a huge success. He immediately inferred that Addison had been prompted by some mean motive; he put himself on the defensive. The next step in the quarrel recalls the abusing and abused John Dennis. Pope had written a prologue for Addison's *Cato*. Dennis, in the spirit of blind revenge, attacked both play and prologue. Pope promptly replied anonymously in the *Narrative of the Frenzy of J. D.* — a satire as coarse and personal in style as Swift at his worst could have written. Addison, in his cold and irritatingly polished manner, disavowed all complicity, intimating to Pope that he was quite capable of fighting his own battles. Pope, feeling that he had gone too far, and making matters worse by vain attempts to hide past errors by new slander, changed to the offensive. About this time he attacked the *Pastorals* of one of Addison's friends, Ambrose Phillipps, "namby-pamby Phillipps," as Gay called him. Phillipps, who was a good swordsman, hung a birch behind the door of Button's Coffee-House, in readiness for Pope's appearance. Pope, who justly resented a physical test as a reference to his deformity, grew more enraged. Plotting underhand schemes, eyeing suspiciously anything connected with Addison, he continued the quarrel. It is not strange that Addison wrote to Lady Mary Wortley Montagu: "Leave Pope as soon as you can; he will certainly play you some devilish trick else." On the whole, Addison treated Pope with gentlemanly calmness, though he does seem just a little too serene, too exasperatingly self-righteous. Still his attitude shows most favorably in contrast to that of his snarling, spiteful antagonist.

Pope's translation of Homer brought forth new strife. Tickell, a friend of Addison's, published in the same year as Pope, 1715, a translation of the first book. Addison, who naturally wished to support a friend and fellow Oxonian, praised Tickell's version, perhaps gave him a few suggestions. But Pope suspected him of having written it and published under his friend's name — that a mortal might seem to bring down an Olympian. Fortunately for Tickell, Pope's translation was universally preferred. It was shortly after this that Pope sketched Addison in the well-known lines on *Atticus*. Though they were not published till 1723, Addison is said to have seen them, and to have generously complimented Pope on the characterization.

Pope's *Homer* brought him, in eleven years, nearly £9000, an almost unprecedented sum in those times. It has been praised by Addison, Swift, Gray, Gibbon, Dr. Johnson, and Byron. So popular was it throughout the century that Cowper's more accurate translation was barely recognized. Yet it has few Homeric qualities. Pope knew little Greek; and one may be sure that he was more familiar with the French Homers of La Valterie and Dacier and the English of Chapman, Hobbes, and Ogilby than with the original Greek. His mind was so wrapped up in himself that the poem, especially toward the end, grew more and more to be *Pope*, not *Homer*. As Bentley said to him, "It is a pretty poem, Mr. Pope, but you must not call it *Homer*."

With the money realized on his *Homer*, Pope moved, in 1718, to Twickenham, a small town on the Thames about half way between Windsor and London. Here he laid out his formal gardens, where —

"Grove nods at grove, each alley has a brother."

As at Versailles, the gardening was geometrical — like the heroic couplet, like the Augustan life. In his villa Pope, now the recognized master-poet, sat in easy retirement, gathered his friends about him, wrote at his leisure, and planned new subterfuges and literary schemes. For all this, Pope had no great reputation for hospitality; indeed, Swift says he entertained stingily. There is a story of how, when he had two guests, " he would set a single pint upon the table ; and, having himself taken two small glasses, would retire and say, ' Gentlemen, I leave you to your wine.' " Yet the great wits crowded around him at Twickenham, heard and praised his verses, and consulted his literary judgment. Bolingbroke, Bathurst, and Peterborough were among them. On the whole, it was the happiest time of Pope's life, and in it his best side is shown. There is an attractive old-world atmosphere about those days. The central point of the Augustan age is Pope, with his flavor of Horace and Virgil, in his villa at Twickenham, with its artificial grotto and trim Louis XV gardens.

So far only men have been spoken of in connection with Pope. Thackeray has pointed out how Pope was, like Addison and Swift, " a man's man." Besides his mother, only three women play any considerable part in the poet's life ; but his relations to them are so illustrative of certain characteristics that a short consideration is necessary. Before Pope had sought admittance to the

fashionable life of London he became acquainted with
the Misses Teresa and Martha Blount. His regard seems
to have been chiefly for the second sister, but to both
he showed throughout his life great friendship and un-
selfish devotion. There have been various scandals about
Pope's relations to these two ladies, but nothing has
been proved, and the deformed little creature in the
guise of a lover makes only a grotesque figure. The
significant point is that, so far as we know, Pope showed
no change in this affectionate regard. And to Martha
Blount he left the largest share of his personal property.
But as Pope's dealings with men showed two natures,
so his relations with the Blounts and his tender affection
for his mother stand out in contrast to his attitude
toward Lady Mary Wortley Montagu. This lady, one
of the most accomplished and wittiest conversationalists
and correspondents of the age, excited at first considerable admiration in Pope. She even allowed him to
address her in the manner of a lover in the correspondence between them when she was with her husband at
Constantinople. But Lady Mary was altogether too
energetic a person and Pope too jealous of success
to avoid occasional tiffs. These grew to quarrels, and
then to hatred. When the two dined at Lord Oxford's
table, one of them, it is said, frequently left the table in
a rage. Pope made some insulting remarks and Lady
Mary replied much too vigorously. The upshot was that
the satirist had one more name for caricature, and that
Lady Mary's phrase descriptive of Pope, the " wicked
wasp of Twickenham," became immortal.

Thackeray advises his readers to pass over Pope's
letters to women ; " in which there is a tone of not
pleasant gallantry, and, amidst a profusion of compli-

ments and politeness, a something which makes one
distrust the little pert, prurient bard. There is very
little indeed to say about his loves, and that little not
edifying. He wrote flames and raptures and elaborate
verse to Lady Mary Wortley Montagu; but that passion probably came to a climax in an impertinence and
was extinguished by a box on the ear, or some such
rebuff, and he began on a sudden to hate her with a
fervor much more genuine than that of his love had
been. It was a feeble puny grimace of love, and palter-
ing with passion. After Mr. Pope had sent off one of
his fine compositions to Lady Mary, he made a second
draft from the rough copy, and favored some other
friend with it. . . . A gentleman who writes letters *à
deux fins*, and after having poured out his heart to the
beloved, serves up the same dish *réchauffé*, to a friend,
is not very much in earnest about his loves, however
much he may be in his piques and vanities when his
impertinence gets its due."

It is refreshing to contemplate, after these bickerings
and disputes, the quiet life at Twickenham and the
enduring affection between mother and son. "When
Pope," as Thackeray says, "in a fever of victory, and
genius, and hope, and anger, was struggling through
the crowd of shouting friends and furious detractors
to his temple of Fame, his old mother writes from the
country, 'My deare . . . I hope to hear from you and
that you are well, which is my daily prayer; and this
with my blessing.' The triumph marches by, and the car
of the young conqueror, the hero of a hundred brilliant
victories: the fond mother sits in the quiet cottage at
home and says, 'I send you my daily prayers, and I
bless you, my deare.'" Pope's father having died in

1717, she came to Twickenham, where she lived almost as long as her son, being mourned by him in 1733 with genuine affection.

The life at Twickenham developed much of Pope's best work, the chief example of which is the *Essay on Man*. As early as 1723 he had become fast friends with Bolingbroke. Flattery was mutual, and between them one of the few works of Pope which did not arise from a quarrel was produced. In 1733–34 the *Essay* was published. Bolingbroke, who dabbled in philosophy, supplied most of the material, and Pope versified it. The *Essay* is in no way a sustained, coherent theory, but rather, like the poet's other work, a succession of clever maxims; it does not, as it professes —

> "Vindicate the ways of God to man."

But, though few read it, every one knows lines which have become familiar quotations, such as —

> "Hope springs eternal in the human breast;
> Man never is, but always to be, blest."

and —

> "Know then thyself, presume not God to scan;
> The proper study of mankind is man."

Although it began in friendship, the *Essay on Man* brought forth quarrel. It had now become difficult for Pope to speak without exciting detractors. The *Essay* was attacked on the score of pantheism and deism. Poor Pope, who had after all only very general ideas of philosophy, took refuge behind a burly divine, one William Warburton. Bolingbroke, who called the new champion " the most impudent man living," never quite forgave Pope; and though both Bolingbroke and Warburton mourned at his bedside, they fell to quarreling over his grave.

The work, however, which is most truly and comprehensively illustrative of Pope's character is the *Dunciad*. No poem so completely epitomizes the life of a man who " scarcely drank tea without a stratagem." It bears, one must admit, the marks of Swift's coarse wit and Warburton's " elephantine pleasantry." *The Rape of the Lock* is perhaps the ablest of Pope's poems; *Eloisa to Abelard* shows more genuine emotion than any other; the *Essay on Man* is more replete with quotable lines. But no poem so fitly as the *Dunciad* expresses the two sides of Pope's nature — the painfully nurtured grudge and the genuine scorn for petty Grub-Street wit.

The *Dunciad* has a long history. In the last years of Queen Anne, Pope belonged to Swift's " little Senate," of which the chief members, after Swift and Pope, were Atterbury, Arbuthnot, Gay, and Parnell. They projected, among other things, the " Scriblerus Club," in which the life and works of one Martinus Scriblerus, an imaginary person, were to form a satire on dullness. The Club never came into actual existence, but it inspired Swift, with his terrible crushing satire, and Pope, with his nimble execution, to begin the work. Ultimately Pope did most of the labor, but the revengeful spirit of Swift is ever at his elbow as he writes. Theobald, a mild and ponderous critic, who had found just fault with Pope's edition of Shakespeare, was made Chief Dunce. Around him were grouped the scribblers whom Pope hated as a class, and others against whom he bore private malice. Taine describes them thus vividly: " In fact, all the filth of literary life is here; and

heaven knows what it then was! In no age were hack
writers so beggarly and so vile. Poor fellows, like Richard Savage, who slept during one winter in the open
air on the cinders of a glass manufactory, lived on what
he received for a dedication, knew the inside of a prison,
rarely dined, and drank at the expense of his friends;
pamphleteers like Tutchin, who was soundly whipped;
plagiarists like Ward, exposed in the pillory and pelted
with rotten eggs and apples; courtesans like Eliza Heywood, notorious by the shamelessness of their public
confessions; bought journalists, hired slanderers, ven-
ders of scandal and insults, half rogues, complete roy-
sterers, and all the literary vermin which haunted the
gambling-houses, the stews, the gin-cellars, and at a signal stung honest folk for a crownpiece. These villanies,
this foul linen, the greasy coat six years old, the musty
pudding, and the rest, are to be found in Pope as in
Hogarth, with English coarseness and precision." In
the second book Dulness with her court descends —

> "To where Fleet Ditch with disemboguing streams
> Rolls the large tribute of dead dogs to Thames.
>
> . . . .
>
> Here strip, my children, here at once leap in,
> Here prove who best can dash through thick and thin."

The *Dunciad* first appeared in 1728, but a revised
and amplified edition came out in 1743. In this Theobald was dethroned and Colley Cibber, the poet-laureate,
was installed as Chief Dunce. To satisfy a grudge Pope
thus spoiled the congruity of the book; for Cibber,
however much a representative of vice and folly, was,
as Mr. Stephen points out, "as little of a dullard as
Pope himself." Cibber, it seems, had ridiculed Pope in
the *Rehearsal*, and, despite Pope's wrath, had protested,

in great good humor, his intention so to continue. In
the ensuing quarrel Cibber kept his temper irritatingly
well ; and Pope indeed pretended to take the offense
lightly. When the two Richardsons one day visited
him, they found him reading one of Cibber's pamphlets.
"These things are my diversion," he said ; but as he
read, they perceived his features "writhing with anguish." And when they left, the younger Richardson
told his father that he prayed he might be spared such
diversions as he had that day seen Pope enjoy.

The *Dunciad* brought forth a long succession of attacks and bitter pamphlets. Pope usually dodged the
issue or protected himself behind the portly person of
Warburton. The general effect of the book, however,
was a wholesome rebuke to the crowd of scribblers.
Most men have long forgotten the names of Pope's victims, and nearly all have ceased to read the coarse and
abusive language that makes the poem at once a terrible and a revolting invective; but in the final lines —
the genuine declaration of war against dullness and deceit, in a satirical apostrophe to Chaos — Pope reaches
a height nowhere else attained by him : —

> "Lo ! thy dread empire, Chaos, is restored,
> Light dies before thy uncreating word;
> Thy hand, great Anarch, lets the curtain fall,
> And universal darkness buries all."

When Dr. Johnson was told that Pope himself so much
admired these lines that his voice failed him in repeating them, he replied, "And well it might, sir, for they
are noble lines."

Pope lived only about a year after the final form of
the *Dunciad* appeared. It seems as if the last years of
a man who had gained such universal distinction might

have been spent more nobly than in bickering with
venal publishers. But Pope had become inextricably
entangled in his petty subterfuges; his only way out,
he thought, was to cover his tracks by new deceits. It
was in the years between 1730 and 1740, while the *Essay on Man* and the *Dunciad* were maturing, while
he was amusing himself with the *Epistles* and *Satires*,
that Pope undertook to publish his correspondence. In
it he appears in a very favorable light, and for some
time critics believed it to be an honest biography; but
it is now generally known that Pope not only falsified
by omission, but, far worse, by addition. The better to
cover his tracks, he induced one Curll, a piratical bookseller, to steal the altered correspondence with Wycherley from the library of Lord Oxford, where it had
been conspicuously placed. Then, however, Pope grew
uneasy until he could secure all outstanding correspondence which might incriminate him. Curll became suspicious, and published certain letters without Pope's
authority, as well as notes which Pope could not deny.
A scheme to publish most of the real correspondence,
a step which would have proclaimed Curll a humbug,
was then hit upon by Pope. To do this he descended
even to deceiving his old friend Swift, who was now
sinking into mental feebleness. Altogether, Pope made
a bad business of the whole affair, and at the same
time acquired, in the eyes of posterity, the name of an
habitual swindler.

In strange contrast to his wrangling with Curll,
Pope's last hours were comfortable and happy. As his
friends gathered about his bedside, his truer, gentler
nature rose; he forgot all the petty animosities of his
life. Once he cried, "What's that?" pointing to the

air, and then with a gentle smile added, " 'T was a vision." Bolingbroke said touchingly, " I have known him these thirty years, and value myself more for that man's love than — " and his voice broke down. In his last days Pope always had a kind word for his friends; in Spence's comment, " as if his humanity had outlasted his understanding." And it is pleasant to think that the man who was never known in his life to laugh smiled cheerfully on his deathbed. He died quietly on May 30, 1744.

In a concluding estimate of Pope one is confronted by the conflicting elements that made up his whole life. For at the same time that one feels contempt for his littlenesses, his deceit, his silly vanities, one's admiration is excited by his occasional genuineness, one's respect by the consecration of his life, in spite of almost over-whelming obstacles, to a literary ideal, and one's sympathy by the tender-hearted affection which, after all, was the deepest quality in his character. His love and hate, like his little crooked body, were frail, spasmodic. Where Addison had been displeased, and Swift com-pletely, crushingly angry, Pope would have been only peevish. And his love — a passing mood — lacked, by the same comparison, the serenity of Addison's and the consuming fire of Swift's. Yet for all this, Pope's is a permanent personality ; in no other man is the truest and most characteristic worth of the Augustan Age so completely revealed.

One must not fail, furthermore, always to think of Pope as a writer. No less a man than Dr. Johnson told Boswell that " a thousand years may elapse be-fore there shall appear another man with a power of versification equal to that of Pope." But, more than his technical skill, Pope did a lasting service to literature as an art. " The master passion in his breast," concludes A. W. Ward, in his preface to the Cambridge edition of Pope, " was not his vanity ; it was his veneration for what is great and noble in intellectual life, and his loathing for what is small and mean and noxious. He could not exterminate Grub Street; but as long as he lived and battled against it, it felt that it was only Grub Street, and the world around was conscious of the fact. He served literature neither for power, like Swift; nor, like nearly all his contemporaries, for place and pay ; not even for fame chiefly, but for her own sake."

SAMUEL JOHNSON, 1709–1784

No critic has been more alive to the importance of biography than Samuel Johnson; his *Lives of the Poets* show him at his best, and he always took pains to collect from competent authority details about the personality of the author with whom he was dealing. In return, Fate has given Johnson himself the best biography that ever was written. Moreover, this same biography has furnished the material and the inspiration for a life of Johnson which is unrivaled in its vivid descriptions of the man and of his times. Every schoolboy reads Macaulay and should look forward to the reading of Boswell.

Samuel Johnson as a representative man of letters is a supremely good example of character outlasting performance. Even more than in Macaulay's day his actual work as a writer has fallen into neglect. His dictionary has long been out of date; the moral essays of the *Rambler*, once so widely read and imitated, are unknown even to the most general reader. A few of his *Lives of the Poets* have been edited and praised, but they would probably not have been edited or praised save for a desire to rescue at least something of the great man's work from oblivion, and vindicate his place in the world of letters. The modern editor of Shakespeare sneers at Johnson's notes, and suppresses, often with injustice, Johnson's comments on character and plot. Even *Rasselas*, a piece of allegorical fiction once thought supremely good, is unread. But his personality, his actual sayings and doings, remain as fresh as ever, as well on account of the personality itself as of the vivid biography which describes it.

Johnson was born at Lichfield, a somewhat sleepy old market and cathedral town, on September 18, 1709. His father, Michael Johnson, a fair scholar and at one time a man of considerable means, who held the office of churchwarden and even of sheriff, though the close of his life was darkened by loss of property, was a book-seller and stationer. From him the son inherited not only a sturdy frame and a mind of unusual strength, but also "that vile melancholy" which colored his whole life, fostered his indolence, and by natural reaction drove him into the social habits of which he was so fond. Unwilling to write except under the pressure of necessity, Johnson was always ready to talk; but for this melan-choly which made him fear solitude, the world would have had more of his composition and less of his con-versation and would probably now know little or nothing about him. Johnson's mother was "a woman of distin-guished understanding," and it may well be that the piety which was so marked in Samuel was due to her precept and example. Tales of his childhood, partly from his own recollection and partly from that of his friends, are plentiful. He developed when very young extraor-dinary powers of memory, learning by heart a Collect from the Prayer-Book while his mother was going up one flight of stairs. He was taken to London, one of the last instances of a very old superstition, to be "touched" for the King's Evil, or scrofula; and he had "a sort of solemn recollection of a lady in diamonds and a long black hood," that is, of Queen Anne, whose touch unfortunately failed to effect a cure. In the dame

school he was the best scholar his teacher ever had.
Next he was under the master in English whom he afterwards called Tom Brown, author of a spelling-book
" dedicated to the Universe; " and then for two years
learned Latin with Mr. Hawkins, under-master of Lichfield school. The head-master, Mr. Hunter, made a bad
impression upon Johnson, using the rod on all occasions
and inspiring this characteristic comment : " Now, sir,
if a boy could answer every question, there would be
no need of a master to teach him." Yet on another
occasion Johnson accounted for his knowledge of Latin
by saying, " My master whipped me very well. Without
that, sir, I should have done nothing." He was a big
clumsy boy, best scholar in his school, but without capacity and liking for games of any kind. He was an
enormous reader. In 1763 he said to Boswell, " Sir,
in my early years I read very hard ; it is a sad reflection
but a true one that I knew almost as much at eighteen
as I do now."

At fifteen he was sent to a school in Worcestershire,
staying there a year, and then seems to have spent two
years at home in comparative idleness ; but his father's
bookshop was a school in itself. In an irregular manner, he says, he " looked into a great many books which
were not commonly known at the Universities." Even
a provincial collection such as Michael Johnson kept
for sale differed absolutely from the corresponding mass
of fiction and other popular reading with which we are
now familiar. Learned works of all kinds, translations
from the classics and foreign languages, essays and
treatises in theology, passed under his eyes in those
two years, and, thanks to his amazing memory, helped
to make him in after years one of the best-read men of

his time. In October, 1728, he went to Oxford. While
at college he translated Pope's *Messiah* into Latin
verse, which was printed in a miscellany published at
Oxford in 1731. During one of his vacations he suffered from a violent attack of melancholy and wrote
out in Latin for his physician a careful statement of
his case. About this time, too, he began, by his own
statement, to think in earnest of religion, largely impelled by the famous book, Law's *Serious Call to a
Holy Life;* for the rest of his days he was an unusually pious man. On the whole, his college life was
irregular and unsatisfactory. As Boswell says, he was
" depressed by poverty and irritated by disease." Popular with his fellow-students, he seemed to one of the
tutors " a gay and frolicsome fellow," but his comment
on this statement probably tells the truth, "Ah, sir,
I was mad and violent. It was bitterness which they
mistook for frolic. I was miserably poor, and I thought
to fight my way by my literature and wit; so I disre-
garded all power and all authority."

In the autumn of 1731 he ceased to be a member of
the college, leaving it without a degree; as a matter
of fact, he was in actual residence there for little over
a year. After December, 1729, he visited his University
several times, but was not in permanent residence. He
is reported to have told the tutor who fined him for
absence: " Sir, you have sconced me two pence for
non-attendance at a lecture not worth a penny." At
another time he excused himself by saying that he had
been sliding on the ice in Christ Church meadow. The
friend in whom he had trusted for support had deceived
him; he was in debt, and his father, already bankrupt,
died in December of the same year. Twenty pounds

was all that he received from the sale of his father's
effects, and he was forced to find immediate means of
support. He was employed as usher in a Leicestershire
school, but left it after a few months of very irksome
employment. Next he went to Birmingham and tried
for the first time that work as bookseller's hack to
which so much of his life was devoted. For five guineas
he translated a book of travels from the French, and
Boswell sees even in his translation that ponderous and
balanced style which is best known as Johnsonian. But
he was not yet to plunge into the struggles of Grub
Street. Matrimony and school-teaching were both in
his mind. He married, July 9, 1735, Mrs. Porter, a
woman nearly twice his age, with a grown daughter.
Miss Porter's picture of her new stepfather is striking
enough. . . . "Lean and lank," she says, an "immense
structure of bones, the scars of scrofula deeply visible."
She mentions, too, those "convulsive starts and odd
gesticulations" recorded so often of Johnson in his later
days. Miss Porter's account, however, should be offset
by a remark of Sir Joshua Reynolds and a description
by Mrs. Thrale, friends of his later life, the former
remarking that Johnson's limbs were well formed, and
the latter describing his features as "strongly marked,
and his countenance particularly rugged . . . his sight
was near, and otherwise imperfect; yet his eyes, though
of a light gray color, were so wild, so piercing, and at
times so fierce, that fear was, I believe, the first emotion in the hearts of all his beholders." Tetty, or Tetsy,
as Johnson called his wife, was described by Garrick,
Johnson's pupil at the private academy which he now
set up near Lichfield, probably with Mrs. Johnson's
money, as very fat, " with swelled cheeks of a florid red,

produced by thick painting and increased by the liberal
use of cordials; flaring and fantastick in her dress, and
affected both in her speech and her general behavior."

A year and a half exhausted the possibilities of the
school; and having written part of his tragedy, *Irene*,
he went up to London along with his pupil Garrick.
He lodged near the Strand, and, as he says, "dined very
well for eight-pence, with very good company, at the
Pine-Apple in New Street just by." He himself accounts
for the cheapness of this meal by the fact that he drank
no wine; and Dr. Hill, quoting Johnson's remark in
1778 that in early life he drank wine, for many years
drank none, then drank a great deal, had a severe illness, left it off and never began again, calculates that
he was an abstainer from about 1736 to 1757 and from
1765 to the end of his life. He described himself in
1757 as "a hardened and shameless tea-drinker." He was
not without acquaintances, and was often entertained
at the house of a gentleman named Hervey, of whom
he afterwards said: "He was a vicious man, but very
kind to me. If you call a dog Hervey, I shall love
him." Meanwhile, he wrote to his subsequent employer,
Mr. Cave, the publisher of the *Gentleman's Magazine*, proposing to translate a history of the Council of
Trent, and worked at his tragedy, finishing the latter
during a summer visit to his wife at Lichfield, and
returning with her to London in the autumn. Here he
attempted in vain to have this tragedy put on the stage,
but it was not accepted until Garrick, when manager
of the Drury Lane Theatre, undertook to produce it.
Steady employment, however, awaited him with Mr.
Cave, for whose famous magazine Johnson acted not
only as contributor, but as a kind of under-editor. He

corrected and improved the various articles, and prepared, often with the slenderest material, reports of the debates in both Houses of Parliament.

In May of 1738 appeared *London — a Poem in Imitation of the Third Satire of Juvenal.* This satire had been paraphrased before by Boileau for Paris and by Oldham for London, but the force and keenness of Johnson's work are unsurpassed. Some of its most successful lines come from the very heart of his experience, —

"Slow rises worth, by poverty depressed."

It was published by Dodsley without the author's name, and brought him but ten guineas. It made its way at once and reached a second edition within a week. Pope, on being told that the author's name was Johnson, an obscure man, remarked that he would soon be *deterré,* unearthed. He seems to have tried to put to practical account the praise which he received for this poem. Offers were made to set him at the head of a school if he could get the degree of Master of Arts ; and a friend applied, but in vain, for that favor from the University of Oxford. Pope recommended him to a nobleman for a degree from Dublin, but again without success. Johnson even thought of practicing as an advocate in civil law, but this attempt also failed, and he settled down to his work as the hack of Mr. Cave. This work was thoroughly miscellaneous, short essays, biographies such as lives of the admirals Blake and Drake, translations from various languages, criticisms, proposals, and the like, along with the Parliamentary Debates, which he wrote up for about two years. It must be remembered that the orations quoted in these debates were very largely of his own composition.

His private life during these days has been often described. His obscure lodgings, his precarious meals, not,
however, to be confused with the subsistence of a mere
tramp, eaten with voracious appetite and small regard
for the customs of society, his poor and ill-fitting clothes,
his friendship with genial vagabonds like Savage and
Psalmanazar, his sturdy independence of patronage from
the great, and his equally sturdy dealings with booksellers, have been set again and again in sharpest relief.
Always reasonable, indeed often far too moderate, in his
charges for literary work, Johnson brooked no insolence
in his employers, as in the case of Osborne. When Mrs.
Thrale asked him about his altercation, he replied
" There is nothing to tell, dearest lady, but that he
was insolent, and I beat him, and that he was a block-
head and told of it, which I should never have done.
. . . I have beat many a fellow, but the rest had
the wit to hold their tongues." To Boswell he was even
more laconic. " Sir, he was impertinent to me and I
beat him. But it was not in his shop ; it was in my own
chamber." Years afterwards, when Macpherson proclaimed that he would chastise Johnson for his attacks
on the authenticity of Ossian and the good faith of its
alleged translator, the old man procured an oak staff
and said he was ready. In 1744 he wrote the life of
Richard Savage, the remarkable adventurer who had
died a year before in Bristol Prison, and with whom
Johnson had often walked the streets of London in
strange intimacy. With regard to his speed in composition Johnson remarked that he wrote forty-eight octavo printed pages of this book at a sitting, " but then,"
he says, " I sat up all night." It was while praising,
and justly praising, this biography, that a guest of Mr.

Cave unwittingly delighted the anonymous author, who, too shabbily dressed to appear at the table, was eating his " plate of victuals " behind a screen.

Meanwhile Johnson had achieved a very solid reputation, not only for this journalistic work but for his learning ; and in 1747 sundry booksellers contracted with him to make a dictionary of the English language. The price was £1575, all of which and more had been paid to him by the time the work appeared. No one had ever before attempted to perform such a task alone; Johnson felt confident that he could do it in three years, but in the plan for his dictionary which he addressed to Lord Chesterfield the author confesses himself "frighted at its extent." He had six amanuenses and worked in a room " fitted up like a counting-house for the purpose." In 1749, while engaged on his large task, he published the *Vanity of Human Wishes*, imitated, like his *London*, from a satire of Juvenal. It had been written the preceding year at Mrs. Johnson's lodgings in the country. This poem, for all its satire, is less keen and piercing than *London*, and probably reflects the easier circumstances of the poet. Indeed, he was now realizing his old ambition, and the same year saw his tragedy of *Irene* put on the stage by David Garrick. It was not a great success, but it ran nine nights and is said to have brought its author something like £300. He appeared at the theatre on the first night of the play in the unwonted splendor of "a scarlet waistcoat, with rich gold lace, and a gold laced hat." He was no longer the mere bookseller's hack ; and in the next year, 1750, he began to publish his *Rambler*, a not altogether unworthy successor of the *Tatler*, *Spectator*, and *Guardian*, and in it he made good his claim as the foremost moral writer of his nation. No one, it is true, now reads these heavy philosophical disquisitions on the conduct of life ; but their authority and popularity in their own day and throughout the eighteenth century stand beyond dispute. It ran from the 20th of March, 1750, appearing every Tuesday and Friday, until March, 1752, and practically all the work was done by Johnson. But the real success of the *Rambler* was not as a periodical, but when revised and published in book form. The author himself " lived to see ten large editions of it in London alone." It was mainly through these essays that Johnson acquired his reputation as the chief upholder of sound old English morality as well as of revealed religion. What his writings did in this respect he fortified by his conversation ; and when Boswell once asked him if the roughness of his manner had been an advantage or not, Johnson defended himself as follows ; " No, sir ; I have done more good as I am ; obscenity and impiety have always been repressed in my company." At a time when the free-thinking, so-called, of France had become fashionable in certain English quarters, these vigorous and uncompromising utterances were doubly welcome to conservative England. Here, too Johnson's somewhat frigid style reached its most distinctive stage. One writer has hinted that as the making of the dictionary was going on while he wrote his *Rambler*, he was tempted to use many far-fetched words in his essays.

The practice of morality was as conspicuous in Johnson's life as its theory. An outspoken foe of Milton the republican, he not only did justice to Milton's genius as a writer, but did all he could to make successful the acting of *Comus* at Drury Lane Theatre for the benefit of Milton's granddaughter, composing a prologue which was spoken by Garrick, and, as we should say, writing it up in the newspapers. In a letter to one of these newspapers he speaks of " our incomparable Milton," and begs its readers "to lay out a trifle" for the benefit of Mrs. Elizabeth Foster.

Two years later Johnson had need in his own life for the sympathy of friends. On March 17, by the Old Style, or by the New, which went into effect in September of the same year, March 28, Mrs. Johnson died.[1] Before his wife's death, however, Johnson had not only formed his varied and notable circle of friends, but had begun to gather about him those objects of his charity who seemed so strange to friends as well as foes. Mrs. Williams, old, blind, and poor, was already dependent on him ; and Levet, an obscure physician, a taciturn and grotesque figure, could boast of Johnson's friendship as well as of his bounty. No more sincere or touching memorial verses exist in the English language than those which the great man wrote on Levet's death. Later came another poor lady, Mrs. Desmoulins, with her daughter, and yet one more inmate, Miss Carmichael. This menagerie, as Macaulay terms it, dependent on Johnson's charity, too often paid him with complaints and the racket of their own petty quarrels. Yet that charity was unwearied, and there is no finer trait in the testy and often bullying autocrat of letters and arbiter of morals than this tolerance in his own household of baitings which the best of philanthropists would have found unbearable. It is true that Johnson could

---

[1] " March 28, 1753. —I kept this day as the anniversary of my Tetty's death, with prayer and tears in the morning. In the evening I prayed for her conditionally, if it were lawful."

always escape from his housemates to his friends. These friends represented all phases of London life. There was Reynolds the painter, afterwards Sir Joshua, most lovable of men, Bennet Langton, a country gentleman whose learning and high moral character endeared him to his friend, and Topham Beauclerk, a dissipated but brilliant aristocrat, great-grandson of Charles II and Nell Gwyn. Instead of the earlier picture, Johnson and Savage, penniless both, pacing the streets of London all night for lack of a few pence to pay for lodging, one sees now Beauclerk and Langton knocking up Johnson at three in the morning in his chambers in the Temple. He appears in his shirt, a poker in his hand; but recognizing his visitors cries out: "What, is it you, you dogs? I 'll have a frisk with you!" And so they sally out into Covent Garden and thence repair to a neighboring tavern. With Garrick, too, he maintains the old friendship; in brief, it may be assumed that even now he knew most of the men who were worth knowing in the London of his day.

At last the great work, the Dictionary, was done. Lord Chesterfield expected that the work would be dedicated to him, and published some fine compliments to the author. These overtures were received with scarcely veiled contempt. " I have sailed," said Johnson to Garrick, " a long and painful voyage round the world of the English language ; and does he now send out two cock-boats to tow me into harbor ? " To the earl himself he wrote a letter which may pass as a kind of declaration of independence in English authorship. One sentence gives its purport: " Is not a Patron, my Lord, one who looks with unconcern on a man struggling for life in the water, and, when he has reached ground, encumbers

him with help?"[1] Not content with this sturdy rebuff,
Johnson made his celebrated epigram: "This man I
thought had been a Lord among wits; but I find he is
only a wit among Lords." Rejecting the favor of noble
patrons, the author of the Dictionary was nevertheless
glad to welcome the degree of Master of Arts to grace
its title-page, bestowed upon him by his own University of Oxford. The great work was published in two
folio volumes. Every one knows the anecdotes about
his various indiscretions and mistakes. "Why did you
define *pastern* as the 'knee of a horse'?" asked a lady.
"Ignorance, Madam," answered the lexicographer,
"pure ignorance." His definition of *net-work* should
be reversed, as the word is needed to define its own
definition. *Tory*, *Whig*, *pension*, *oats*, *excise*, are examples of his prejudice; and the last-named nearly led
to a lawsuit for libel from the Commissioner of Excise.
Humor plays about his definition of *lexicographer* as
"a writer of dictionaries, a harmless drudge." Defining
Lich as "a corpse," and *Lichfield* as the "City of the
Martyrs," he adds, "Salve magna parens" as a tribute
to the place of his birth.

From this time, though Johnson still had to work for
his bread, he shrank more and more from drudgery
of daily toil. He told Boswell that he always felt an
inclination to do nothing. His constitutional indolence
asserted itself, and necessity's sharp pinch was less keen
than before. He laid himself open to the charge of dis-
honor by issuing a proposal for a new edition of Shakespeare, to be finished in a short time. Though many

---

[1] This and the preceding quotation are capital examples respectively
of Johnson's style in his letters and conversation — essentially different from the labored and ponderous style of his formal writings.

subscriptions were paid in, Johnson failed to keep his
promise ; it was not till nine years later, in 1765, that
the edition appeared. Meanwhile many changes had occurred in his manner of life. He had issued a new series
of essays called the *Idler*, appearing every Saturday
in a weekly newspaper. These continued for two years,
and out of the 103 numbers only twelve were contributed
by Johnson's friends. During the course of these publications his mother had died, and to defray the expense
of the funeral as well as to pay off certain of her debts
he wrote his famous story *Rasselas*. He "told Sir
Joshua Reynolds that he composed it in the evenings of
one week, sent it to the press in portions as it was written,
and had never since read it over." The book was very
popular in England and was translated into most of the
modern languages. In 1762 George III, whose opening
reign was hailed on all sides with delight, bestowed on
Johnson "as a very learned and good man " a pension
of £300 per year. This sum meant far more then than
now, and it meant more to Johnson than to most men.
Apparently, too, it set the seal on his indolence. On the
other hand, it is urged that the rest so obtained was
absolutely needed, that his mind had been " strained
and over-labored," and that, in the words of Birkbeck
Hill, " without this pension he would not have lived to
write the second greatest of his works, the *Lives of the
Poets*." He let his definition of *pensioner* remain as
it stood, and his letter of thanks to the Earl of Bute
made this characteristic statement : " You have conferred your favors on a man who has neither alliance
nor interest, who has not merited them by services,
nor courted them by officiousness ; you have spared him
the shame of solicitation, and the anxiety of suspense."

From the date of his pension the great writer becomes the great talker, and by a happy stroke of fortune in the first year of his leisure he was introduced to Boswell and thus secured the keenest observer, the most attentive listener, and the most devoted admirer who ever penned a biography. From their first meeting Boswell records several of Johnson's sayings, for example, " Derrick may do very well, as long as he can outrun his character; but the moment his character gets up with him, it is all over."

Here is the Johnson whom the world knows and always will know, a man of pithy phrases, of blunt and often reckless but always telling criticism, of argument for argument's sake, and of opinions whose unvarying prejudice gives them a consistency better appreciated by present readers than by men of his own time. His reputation was of course tremendous; his circle of friends included the greatest actor and the greatest orator of English record — Garrick and Burke; men supreme in their own lines, like Reynolds and Gibbon; and men of fashion and of authority, hardly remembered now, but formidable in their day. Yet in the club where these men gathered Johnson was easily the first, and all were content to listen when he spoke. The literary club, as Boswell calls it, was proposed by Sir Joshua Reynolds, and founded in 1764. They met once a week. New members were taken in, and in 1792 there were thirty-five upon the list, including half a dozen peers. In Johnson's time, however, it was a group of men allied by commanding, if varied talent; and over these men the dictator of English letters held undisputed sway. No better illustration of his supremacy could be found than the famous Round Robin protesting against the use of Latin in the epitaph on their fellow-member, Dr. Goldsmith. Partly in jest, partly in earnest, this form of petition was used " so as not to let it be known who puts his name first or last to the paper." Burke framed the address and Sir Joshua carried it to Johnson, who " received it with much good humor, and desired Sir Joshua to tell the gentlemen, that he would alter the epitaph in any manner they pleased, as to the sense of it ; but *he would never consent to disgrace the walls of Westminster Abbey with an English inscription.*" Such was their awe of Johnson, and awe tempered by affection ruled even in their social meetings. Of these meetings Macaulay's description cannot be improved : —

" The club-room is before us, and the table on which stands the omelet for Nugent, and the lemons for Johnson. There are assembled those heads which live for ever on the canvas of Reynolds. There are the spectacles of Burke and the tall thin form of Langton, the courtly sneer of Beauclerk, and the beaming smile of Garrick, Gibbon tapping his snuff-box, and Sir Joshua with his trumpet in his ear. In the foreground is that strange figure which is as familiar to us as the figures of those among whom we have been brought up, the gigantic body, the huge massy face seamed with the scars of disease, the brown coat, the black worsted stockings, the gray wig with the scorched foretop, the dirty hands, the nails bitten and pared to the quick. We see the eyes and mouth moving with convulsive twitches ; we see the heavy form rolling ; we hear it puffing ; and then comes the ' Why, sir ! ' and the 'What then, sir? ' and the ' No, sir ! ' and the ' You don't see your way through the question, sir ! ' "

Besides this club life, of which Johnson was so fond,
there were other places where he was welcomed for his
talk and forgiven for his manners. His later life was
passed not only with this aristocracy of intellect, but to
a great extent in a house of wealth and refinement.
For more than a dozen years he lived on the most intimate terms with the household of Mr. Thrale, a
wealthy brewer, whose 'wife is described by the not
too enthusiastic Boswell as " a lady of lively talents,
improved by education." Indeed, Johnson came to call
their comfortable house his home. Mr. Thrale himself
had been educated at Oxford and not only appreciated
but instigated the brilliant conversations in which
the sage took part. Mrs. Thrale, in the anecdotes of
Johnson published after her second marriage, says that
" Dr. Johnson, commonly spending the week at our
house, kept his numerous family in Fleet Street upon
a settled allowance; but returned to them every Saturday to give them three good dinners and his company,
before he came back to us on the Monday night."
While it lasted, this friendship with the Thrales made
his life happy; the society of his other friends banished
his cares ; and from other quarters, too, honors came
thick and fast upon him. First Trinity College, Dublin,
and then his own University, granted him the advanced
degree. He was now indeed Doctor Johnson. The king
himself desired to meet his distinguished subject, and
the interview is carefully described by Boswell, from
the doctor's own account. The monarch's compliment
and Johnson's comment on it are well known. Johnson said he " had already done his part as a writer. ' I
should have thought so, too,' said the king, 'if you had
not written so well.' " Johnson remarked to his friends

that this was " decisive," and needed no reply. " When
the king had said it, it was to be so. It was not for
me to bandy civilities with my sovereign."

During these years of his life, happy in spite of the
melancholy and indolence with which he constantly reproaches himself in his meditation and prayers, he lived
either at the Thrales' or at his lodgings in London.
Here about twelve o'clock a visitor would find him "in
bed or declaiming over his tea . . . he generally had
a levee of morning visitors, chiefly men of letters . . .
and sometimes learned ladies . . . he declaimed all the
morning, then went to dinner at a tavern, where he
commonly stayed late, and then drank his tea at some
friend's house, over which he loitered a great while but
seldom took supper." Dr. Maxwell, who furnished this
account to Boswell, goes on to say that Johnson must
have read and written chiefly in the night; and quotes
Johnson's saying that Burton's *Anatomy of Melancholy* was the only book that ever took him out of bed
two hours sooner than he wished to rise.

As to his writing, his political pamphlets must have
cost him little labor, and done nothing for his reputation. That which he wrote against the Americans, *Taxation no Tyranny*, published in 1775, is weak in its
argument, and the vigor of its language fails to conceal
the author's blind and unreasoning prejudice against the
colonists. He revised his Dictionary and wrote small
articles on various subjects, including legal opinions for
Boswell. But conversation was his main employment
until the persistence of Boswell and the solicitations of
his old friends the booksellers led respectively to two of
his major works, the *Journey to the Western Islands
of Scotland*, published in 1775, and the *Lives of the*

English Poets, published as prefaces to the different
volumes of the collection, four volumes appearing in
1779 and the remaining six in 1781. Accompanied by
Boswell, whom he met in Edinburgh about the middle
of August, 1773, he crossed the Highland border and
visited the remote and untraveled but hospitable islands
of the Hebrides group, meeting there those feudal conditions of the clan and its chieftain which appealed so
powerfully to his Tory prejudices. The return was
made in November by way of Boswell's family place in
Ayrshire. "I believe," says his biographer, "ninety-
four days were never passed by any man in a more
vigorous exertion;" and Johnson was now sixty-four
years of age. Two years later he went with the Thrales
to France, and one must echo Boswell's regret that the
doctor did not write an account of his travels. A brief
and unfinished journal records his impressions. Fond
as he was of the city, he enjoyed traveling; even when
sixty-nine years old he spent a week with Langton in
the camp of the Lincolnshire militia.

It was in spite of the state of his health, however,
and not by reason of it, that Johnson made these expeditions. The concluding years of his life saw the vain
struggle of his powerful constitution against insidious
disease. The death of Mr. Thrale and the consequent
breaking up of that pleasant home at Streatham made
up a calamity which darkened in many ways the close
of Johnson's life. Mrs. Thrale's affection for the old
man weakened under the pressure of an attachment to
Piozzi, an Italian music-master, whom she finally married; and though Johnson was afterwards her guest at
Brighton, his parting prayer in the library at Streatham
was really his farewell. This was in October, 1782.

The two remaining years of his life were spent in a struggle with complicated bodily disorders, borne with fortitude but sharpened by that overwhelming dread of death which he never concealed. His mind meanwhile remained as vigorous as ever, and there was no difference in his powers of conversation except perhaps an increased severity of retort and epithet, due to physical irritation. Doubtless, however, his love of little children remained to the end, as well as his kindness to his servants and his fondness for animals, which made him go out and buy oysters for his cat Hodge. In June, 1783, he had a stroke of palsy and was deprived for a while of the powers of speech. It is interesting to note that in order to prove that his mind was spared he composed a prayer in Latin verse at the first onset of the attack. His recovery was prompt, and in December we find him forming a little dining club " to insure himself society in the evening for three days in the week." During this severe winter he was afflicted with dropsy, but continued to talk with his friends and to write his admirable letters. In February, 1784, he was very ill but again obtained partial relief. In May Boswell found him greatly recovered, and reports him as dining here and there " in fine spirits." Early in June he and Boswell visited Oxford, staying a fortnight and even visiting country places in the neighborhood.

He met his literary club for the last time on June 22. In July he visited friends in Staffordshire and Derbyshire, hoping that travel would bring him relief. He spent some time in his native city of Lichfield; though surrounded here by friends and conscious that death was no longer remote, he nevertheless yearned for the familiar ways of London, arriving there on

November 16, 1784. His pains were now violent, but he
beguiled his sleepless nights translating from Greek into
Latin verse. Physicians of the highest rank attended
him without fee, and friends like Burke and Langton
were constant at his bedside. Informed that death was
inevitable — " Then," said Johnson, " I will take no
physick, not even my opiates; for I have prayed that I
may render up my soul to God unclouded." He died on
the evening of Monday, the thirteenth of December,
and was buried a week later in Westminster Abbey.

OLIVER GOLDSMITH

IF singularity be a sign of genius, Goldsmith had his full share. His manners, his mirth, his vagabond ways, his tastes in dress — all were strikingly singular. He was, moreover, an important figure. He found his way, in spite of his odd manners and blundering speeches, into one of the most renowned literary circles of all time; he numbered among his friends such men as Burke, Reynolds, and Johnson; and it is no small thing that the great lexicographer should have pronounced after his death, " He was a very great man." The humor of his life is constantly bordering on pathos: in his squalor and incompetence and misfortune he figures in scene after scene that is almost wholly sad. Yet, like Garrick, one is frequently forced to laugh at his strange adventures and odd blunders. Still more, like Johnson, one is called to admire his genius.

Oliver Goldsmith was born on November 10, 1728, in the village of Pallas, County Longford, Ireland. His father, the Rev. Charles Goldsmith, of a stock, says Washington Irving, well-known for its " kindliness and incompetency," its " virtue and poverty," scarcely managed to keep a roof over his family of eight children. In the generous and guileless Dr. Primrose in *The Vicar of Wakefield* and in the village parson of the *Deserted Village* — " passing rich with forty pounds a year," whose " pity gave ere charity began " — Goldsmith had for models his own father and older brother Henry.

When Oliver was a small child his father, presented

with the living of Kilkenny West, worth about £200 a year, moved to a farm of seventy acres on the borders of the village of Lissoy, County Westmeath. This was the scene of Oliver's boyhood, the model in all probability for " Sweet Auburn, loveliest village of the plain ; " though, as Macaulay points out, only Auburn's decay is Irish ; its prosperity is altogether English.

Goldsmith's schooling was picturesque rather than thorough ; it gave him a poor foundation for the scientific work he later professed, but it fed his imagination with a rare collection of pictures. At six he passed from the dame-school of Mistress Elizabeth Delap to the charge of the village schoolmaster, Thomas Byrne, commonly known as Paddy, a retired quartermaster on half-pay. This man's knowledge of foreign lands, his stories of robbers and pirates and " the whole race of Irish rogues and rapparees," his ballad-making and his superstitious fairy-tales crowded out of his pupil most of the more prosaic knowledge generally acquired by boys ; under his influence young Oliver began to scribble verses ; and, whatever his inherited disposition to poverty and genius, the boy's love in later years of the "open road " was largely due to this ballad-making quartermaster, Paddy Byrne.

Goldsmith, after an attack of the small-pox, which disfigured him for life, was put under the care of the Rev. Mr. Griffin, a schoolmaster of Elphin, in Roscommon. From here he passed, through the generosity of his uncle, the Rev. Thomas Contarine, who wished Oliver to have a university education, to more pretentious schools, first to one at Athlone, and two years later to one at Edgeworthstown. From the latter he went up in June, 1745, to Trinity College, Dublin.

One famous anecdote of his school-days shows perhaps better than anything Oliver's youthful characteristics — his love of adventure, his thriftlessness, and his gullibility. On returning home from Edgeworthstown he stopped at Ardagh and, intent on making a fine display with the one guinea he possessed, asked for the best house in the town. A wag named Kelly directed him to the private residence of a Mr. Featherstone, and the guileless Goldsmith rode forthwith thither, ordered his horse stabled, and made himself at home in the mansion. Mr. Featherstone, who knew Goldsmith's father, had good humor enough to conceal the youth's blunder from him and played the part of landlord to perfection. Goldsmith ordered wine, swaggered about the house — and the next morning discovered his mistake. All who know *She Stoops to Conquer* will recognize in this incident the origin of the plot. When we add to this happy-go-lucky character Goldsmith's generosity and simplicity, and remember his pock-marked face, his short, ungainly figure, and his passion for fantastically colored garments, we have a very fair picture of the man as he entered college — a man not too well fitted to pursue scholarship, but admirably equipped to turn his picturesque poverty and odd experiences to literary account.

At college Goldsmith was at first forced, on account of his father's straitened circumstances, to take the position of a sizar, an office in which the student performs certain kitchen duties in payment for board and tuition. Soon, however, the distinctive gown and the contempt of the more fortunate stung the proud and sensitive Goldsmith to the quick; and after throwing a dish at one of the sneerers he was relieved of the menial task.

His whole college career, as may be guessed, was

picturesque rather than scholarly. His writings bear
witness to his intelligence, and he did no doubt pick up
much incidental knowledge by the academic way; but
his main path led to other things — boon companions
and considerable indolence. " I was a lover of mirth
from my childhood," he says. He was never vicious, —
indeed quite too guileless for that, — but he loved dearly
a good song at a tavern. It is not surprising, then, to
see him soon in disgrace and setting out for America —
half for the adventure, half to escape humiliation and
poverty at home. In the first place, he had always quarreled with his tutor, the Rev. Theaker Wilder, a stiff-
necked mathematician. In 1747 his father's death forced
him to depend wholly on his uncle Contarine. Added
to this was the disgrace of public admonition for complicity in the riot of one Gallows Walsh, who proposed
to break open the jail and free a fellow-student. He
partly redeemed himself by winning a college prize, but
while he was celebrating in his rooms with friends of
both sexes, in burst the Rev. Wilder and the guests
were turned incontinently forth. So, dreading the ridicule of his fellows and the severity of the authorities,
but above all loving a rare adventure, Goldsmith
straightway sold his books and started for Cork. It is
not remarkable that he spent all but a shilling before
he left Dublin. He was soon forced to return, and
through his brother Henry, a man held in esteem as
a scholar and clergyman, was reconciled to the college
authorities.

For two years longer Oliver continued at the University and did creditable work in the classics. Against
the mathematics he had a strong prejudice, born of
association with the Rev. Wilder and of a natural

inaptitude for anything exact. Yet even in the classics Goldsmith did not greatly shine, and of his college career such incidents as his expedition to Cork or his attempt to keep warm by covering himself with feathers from his bed, when he had given his blankets to a poor woman with five children, will be remembered longer than his academic achievements. He did, however, receive the degree of B. A. on the 27th of February, 1750.

He was now pressed by his uncle Contarine to prepare himself for the Church. This occupied another two years, spent, not altogether in clerical pursuits, sometimes with his brother Henry, who was living in the old house at Pallas in quiet parsonage beneficence, sometimes with his friend Robert Bryanton in a club of happy spirits at the inn of Ballymahon. His disinclination for orders was seconded by the bishop, possibly because of his lack of interest and evident unfitness, probably because of his appearing for ordination, so the story runs, in scarlet breeches.

Next he received a position as tutor in the house of a Mr. Flinn, but after a few weeks a quarrel at cards caused him to resign it. With his pay, however, he bought a horse, and, his pocket still being full of money, set off on his second expedition to see the world. He reached Cork, but the ship he had engaged passage on got away while he was gaming in a tavern, and finally, having lost his horse and most of his money, he returned home on a sorry nag called " Fiddleback." His friends and family thereupon, on some unthinkable hypothesis, decided he should go to London and study law. This time he got no farther than Dublin. His mother had scolded him for his Cork adventure, and now even the gentle Henry's patience began to weaken; the only welcome the poor vagabond received was from his steadfast uncle Contarine.

Depending on this man's benevolence, Goldsmith sallied forth once more, in the autumn of 1752 — this time to try medicine in Edinburgh. The Scotch capital was actually reached and some study was no doubt done there; but boon companions and gaming and unrestrained charity — all of which impoverish — were chiefly in evidence. "Has George Conway put up a sign yet; or John Binley left off drinking drams; or Tom Allen got a new wig?" he writes to his friend Bryanton, and a deal more of the fair ladies of Scotland and of protestations of friendship for Robert Bryanton, Esq., of Ballymahon, — but no word of midnight lamp "in some high lonely tower" and of realms conquered in the region of physic.

It must not be inferred from this that Goldsmith was either a dullard or a degenerate. His pranks never meant more than excessive mirthfulness, and his improvidence and indolence were brightened by his wit and by a very sensitive observation. He did, moreover, spend two winters at Edinburgh in something like study. Then he determined to polish off his medical education at the great Continental universities of Paris and Leyden.

As might be supposed, foreign manners interested Goldsmith more than studies. He did spend about a year at Leyden and some time at Paris, though there is some doubt whether he ever attended Padua, from which place he afterwards asserted he was graduated. Of course he was thrown into all sorts of adventures. His purchase of an expensive tulip, as a gift for his

uncle Contarine, was of a piece with his earlier extravagance, and he was consequently forced to teach English
to earn his bread. But the crowning touch to his picturesque existence was his setting forth for a tour of
the continent, early in 1756, with an equipment of one
shirt, a flute, and a guinea. At Geneva he got the position of traveling tutor to the son of a wealthy English
pawnbroker, but they got on poorly together and separated at Marseilles. In Italy, where his flute would not
earn him a lodging, — for, he says, "Every peasant was
a better musician than I," — he had recourse to what
he calls his "skill in disputation." "In all the foreign
universities and convents," he writes, "there are, upon
certain days, philosophical theses maintained against
every adventitious disputant, for which, if the champion
opposes with any dexterity, he can claim a gratuity in
money, a dinner, and a bed for one night." Goldsmith
was a better disputant than conversationalist, but the
picture of him standing up in his gay garments and
gravely opposing philosophical theses, his flute sticking
out of his pocket the while, is one altogether humorous
and picturesque.

Finally, on hearing of the illness of his uncle, he
turned towards home. On foot through France he was
carried along by his "magic flute." Of this life he gives
a picture in the *Traveller :* —

> "Gay, sprightly land of mirth and social ease,
>   Pleased with thyself, whom all the world can please,
>   How often have I led thy sportive choir
>   With tuneless pipe beside the murmuring Loire !
> .   .   .   .
>   Yet would the village praise my wondrous power,
>   And dance forgetful of the noontide hour."

An almost Orphean performance — to make a whole
French village forget its lunch!

Here comes properly a division in any account of
Goldsmith. Now begins his literary story: his poverty
and hack-writing in London, his meeting with Johnson,
his admittance into the " Club," his greatest literary
achievements, and his sudden popularity. It has been
necessary to dwell at some length on his early days, that
a fair idea of his character may be given. It is not to be
thought, however, that his picturesque adventures now
cease, — indeed, half of them would fill a volume, —
but the greater genius of the man begins, during these
London days, to break forth, and it must naturally claim
the chief attention.

At first he lived in abject poverty. He was rejected by
an apothecary and forced to take part in barn-theatri-
cals. " Poor houseless Goldsmith!" says Irving; " to
what shifts he must have been driven to find shelter
and sustenance for himself in this his first venture into
London! Many years afterwards, in the days of his
social elevation, he startled a polite circle at Sir Joshua
Reynolds' by humorously dating an anecdote about the
time he 'lived among the beggars of Axe Lane.'" For
a short time he endured the position of usher in a school,
but the laughter of the boys at his manners and dress,
and the discomfort of sleeping in the same bed with a
pomatum-scented French teacher, led him hastily to
abandon the situation. Again he tried medicine, and
set up in a small way in Bankside, attiring himself inappropriately in a second-hand suit of green and gold.

The opening wedge to his literary career, however,
was his acquaintance with Samuel Richardson, the
author of *Clarissa Harlowe*. Richardson's printer was

Goldsmith's patient, and through him work was procured at Richardson's press in Salisbury Court. He began, too, to make other acquaintances — notably Dr. Edward Young, the famous author of *Night Thoughts*. Finally, through a Dr. Milner, the father of an Edinburgh friend, whose school he took charge of during Dr. Milner's illness, Goldsmith met Griffiths, editor of the *Monthly Review*. For Griffiths he did Grub Street work at small pay, but after five months quarreled with his " illiterate, bookselling " editor.

Indeed, the way to literary recognition was yet long and perilous. After spending some time more in hackwork for various publishers, Goldsmith jumped at Dr. Milner's promise to use his influence to get him a medical appointment in India. Goldsmith, in anticipation of future splendor, left his garret for a first floor room, but the post, to his great discomfort, was given to another. Added to this humiliation was his rejection by the College of Surgeons at an examination in December, 1758. Poor Oliver must back to his garret and his debts.

No picture, from all accounts, of a dingy garret, with rat-riddled floor and dirty, broken window-panes, with meagre furniture and a bed that fairly protests against incumbrance, can exaggerate the squalor of Goldsmith's lodgings at No. 12, Green Arbor Court. Here at the top of " Breakneck Stairs " he scribbled at times literally for his life — cold as he was in scanty raiment and hungry for scanty fare. Below, the court rang with the cries of quarreling washerwomen and guttersnipes; alleys crowded with the victims of poverty, vice, and disease were his daily and nightly passages. It may have been well that he took little thought for the morrow; his

geniality perhaps saved him. At all events, he managed
somehow to endure a condition bordering on destitution.

Little by little, however, his ability asserted itself.
His *Inquiry into the State of Polite Learning in
Europe* at least attracted attention; and his contributions (later published as the *Citizen of the World*) in
1760 to Newbery's *Public Ledger*, and his writings
in the *Bee* relieved his circumstances sufficiently for
him to take good lodgings in Wine Office Court, hard by
the Cheshire Cheese, Fleet Street, an inn frequented by
Dr. Johnson and his friends. In his new lodgings Goldsmith was visited by men of some contemporary renown,
and on one memorable evening, the 31st of May, 1761,
he was the host of Dr. Johnson. Johnson had passed
through an apprenticeship hardly less severe than Goldsmith's, but now he was the " great lexicographer," the
defier of Lord Chesterfield, and the " Ursa Major " of
literary circles. His friendship, which rapidly grew in
warmth, proved invaluable to Goldsmith. Through him
the young Irishman became a visitor at Davies's bookshop and a guest at Mrs. Davies's tea-parties, where he
met Bennet Langton, the scholar, Dr. Percy, of ballad
fame, and Warburton, the burly divine and defender of
Pope.

It was through this friendship with Johnson, in fact,
that Goldsmith was taken as an original member into
the famous literary club, started in 1764. The sententious doctor was indisputably the chief, and his will pre-
vailed in spite of objections to Goldsmith's Grub-street
trade. No literary gathering, unless that with the " wit-
combats " at the Mermaid, has numbered such a rare
assemblage. They met weekly at the Turk's Head on
Gerard Street. Reynolds, the great painter, was there,

Burke, soon to startle Parliament with his oratory, Topham Beauclerk with his graceful sarcasm, Langton with his wisdom, Garrick with his sallies on Goldsmith, who, he said, —

"Wrote like an angel and talked like Poor Poll,"

Gibbon the historian, Jones the great linguist, Boswell with his note-book, and, above all, the disputatious doctor, thundering oracularly, prepared for any encounter, ever ready to support sincerity and to condemn hypocrisy and cant. Goldsmith was of course often the butt, but he usually found a sturdy champion in Johnson, and he was generally beloved for his geniality and generosity. He managed, too, to contribute his share of clever sayings, perhaps the best of which was his remark, when some one called Boswell a Scotch cur at Johnson's heels, that the Scotchman was not a cur; "he is only a bur," he said. "Tom Davies flung him at Johnson in sport, and he has the faculty of sticking."

It is not to be supposed, however, that Goldsmith was from now on financially at ease. The very year of his prosperity, 1764, news came to Johnson that his friend was in the direst straits and at the mercy of a relentless landlady. The doctor sent a guinea as earnest of succor and as soon as possible hurried himself to Wine Office Court. There he found Goldsmith, who had already converted the guinea into Madeira, entertaining the now more amenable landlady. By luck the doctor learned of the manuscript of *The Vicar*, saw at a glance its merit, and sold it to a bookseller for sixty pounds.

Newbery, to whom the book was sold, did not, how-

ever, publish it for two years, and meanwhile the work
which first brought Goldsmith an established reputation appeared. It was *The Traveller*, and was hailed
on all sides with admiration. At last Goldsmith had
achieved some sort of permanent success, and he never
again suffered greatly from lack of recognition. He continued to write voluminously and often worthlessly, for
he had the boldness to attempt, after marshaling a wide
but superficial knowledge, histories of England, Rome,
and Greece, and a Natural History. In the last-named
Goldsmith said that the cow sheds its horns at three
years old. Johnson had already remarked : "Goldsmith,
sir, will give us a very fine book upon the subject ; but
if he can distinguish a cow from a horse, that, I believe,
may be the extent of his knowledge of natural history."
Five of his works, however, have by their popularity
for a century and a half amply justified Johnson's admiration for his genius. In *The Traveller* (1764) and
The Deserted Village (1770) he took rank as a good
if not a great poet in an age of prose ; and he brought
to the heroic couplet a simplicity and a sincerity long
unknown. In *The Vicar of Wakefield* (1766) he wrote
one of the most famous novels of all time ; and in his
two plays, *The Good-Natured Man* (1767) and *She
Stoops to Conquer* (1773) he not only did much to
cure the silly sentimentality of the stage, but he wrote
in the latter a play that still acts astonishingly well.
These five works live for their gentle humor and genuine pathos. It is indeed a very great thing to have
written a novel which has contrived to keep its place on
the shelf beside such works as *The Pilgrim's Progress*
and *Robinson Crusoe*.

One of the first recognitions of Goldsmith's genius

was the nomination of him in 1769 by the Royal
Academy to the position of honorary professor of history. It must not be supposed, however, that Dr. Goldsmith, for all his recognition, ceased that picturesque
existence which colored so quaintly his youthful career.
He still kept up a speaking acquaintance with his old
friend, poverty. He was still fond of gay garments, and
he might often be seen, caparisoned in his bloom-
colored coat, bag-wig, and sword, strutting about the
Temple Gardens. He still, too, blundered as if by instinct into odd experiences, and was as always the butt
of his friends. There was sometimes a touch of malice
in the sallies of Garrick, who had some cause, perhaps,
and of Boswell, who was after all Boswell, but the rest
were always in good fun. One joke played on him by
Burke illustrates especially his naïve simplicity. Burke,
having passed him staring at some ladies in the square,
accused him, when they met at Sir Joshua's, of exclaiming that the crowd must be "stupid beasts" to stare
so at those "painted Jezebels," while a man of his parts
went unnoticed. Goldsmith denied having said it, but
upon Burke's replying, "If you had not said so, how
should I have known it?" he answered feebly: "I am
very sorry — it was very foolish; I do recollect that
something of the kind passed through my mind, but I
did not think I had uttered it." "Sir, he was a fool,"
said one who had known him, to the poet Rogers. "If
you gave him back a bad shilling, he'd say, Why, it's as
good a shilling as ever was *born*. You know he ought to
have said *coined*. *Coined*, sir, never entered his head.
He was a fool, sir." But he held his own with his pen
and in the *Retaliation*, called forth by one of Garrick's
thrusts, he met his playful friends on their own ground.

It is perhaps of a piece with Goldsmith's character in general, yet rather remarkable for one of his tenderness, that he never became seriously attached to any lady. Miss Reynolds, it is true, ceased to consider him ugly when she had heard the *Traveller* read aloud. There were, moreover, two sisters, Catharine and Mary Horneck, nicknamed "Little Comedy" and the "Jessamy Bride," of whom Goldsmith was very fond. "Little Comedy" was soon married to a Mr. Bunbury, so it was on the "Jessamy Bride" that Goldsmith showered most of his awkward attention. This affection may have inspired, Irving thinks, the vast addition of gay silken things at this time to the poet's wardrobe. His friends rallied him much about the "Jessamy Bride," and she on her part treasured a lock of hair that was taken after his death — a touching tribute to the gentle, loving man whose blunders and ugly features helped him into the affections of men and shut him out almost wholly from the love of women.

While yet in middle life, however, Goldsmith came to an untimely death. His health failed rapidly, extravagances had renewed his debts, and an attempt at prescribing for himself only precipitated the fever from which he never recovered. On April 4, 1774, he died rather suddenly, in his forty-seventh year. "Sir Joshua is of opinion," wrote Johnson to Boswell, "that he [Goldsmith] owed not less than two thousand pounds. Was ever poet so trusted before?" "Poor Goldy" was greatly mourned. Sir Joshua, who was much affected, "did not touch the pencil for that day, a circumstance most extraordinary for him who passed *no day without a line*." A large body of men distinguished in letters and politics followed him to his grave, which stands alone in the Court of the Middle Temple. It is significant of his lifelong inability to attain and maintain a position in the innermost circles of respect that he thus lies alone with no comment but his name in Temple Court, while Johnson and Garrick, who achieved such overwhelming honor in their lifetime, lie side by side in Westminster Abbey. There is a touch of pathos in the man even after his death.

" Goldsmith," says Coleridge, " did everything happily," and in so saying really explains the charm of the man. When we know the simplicity and generosity of his life, his gentleness and his awkwardness — in short, the pathos and the humor of him, then we shall not only grow to love the village preacher in the *Deserted Village* and Dr. Primrose, unsophisticated, foolish, and loving, in the *Vicar of Wakefield*, and the incomparably amusing scenes of *She Stoops to Conquer*, but, far more than this, we shall be privileged to join that great host of his readers who have unaffectedly laughed and wept with him. No person, once he is understood, has so contagious a spirit as Goldsmith. He is probably the most picturesque and certainly the most lovable figure among English writers.

EDMUND BURKE

No great English writer has been more closely connected with politics than Burke. He was much less an adroit politician than an able writer, yet now, when the smaller men who passed him in pursuit of office are forgotten, he is remembered not only for his impressive style, but also for his broad political wisdom. "There was a catholicity about his gaze," says Mr. Augustine Birrell. "He knew how the whole world lived."

Next to Burke's great store of knowledge, his most striking characteristic is his fervor. In Parliament he was called "the Irish Adventurer;" once, in his indignation at a navy scandal, he threw "the fine gilt book of estimates" at the Treasurer of the Navy; another time Fox and Sheridan had to hold him by the coat-tails; when he was aroused, he burst into a torrent of invective. "He was so violent, so overbearing, so arrogant, so intractable," said Lord Lansdowne, "that to have got on with him in a cabinet would have been utterly and absolutely impossible." It is easy to see why such a man, an Irishman untamed to the last, consistently a supporter of the minority, should have been kept out of high office. The remarkable thing is that, almost single-handed, he could hold the field so long.

Edmund Burke was born in Dublin on January 12, 1729 (N. S.). His father, Richard Burke, a solicitor in good standing, was a Protestant; his mother, of the family of Nagle, was a Roman Catholic. Young Burke's early education was chiefly at the school of a Quaker,

Abraham Shackleton, at Ballitore. From here in 1743
Burke went up to Trinity College, Dublin, where he
took his degree of B. A. in 1748. He was not conspicuous as a good student, but he knew his Latin well,
showed plenty of ability, and spent much time in reading. In 1750 he decided to study law and was entered
at the Middle Temple, London. He never took seriously
to the work, however, and when he gave it up soon
after, his angry father withdrew the allowance of £100.
Yet during these years of desultory study Burke acquired that wide and exhaustive knowledge which
was his best equipment. He " understands everything,"
W. G. Hamilton said later, " but gaming and music."
Mr. Birrell draws a good picture of this time of preparation. Burke, he says, " was fond of roaming about the
country, during, it is to be hoped, vacation-time only,
and is to be found writing the most cheerful letters to
his friends in Ireland (all of whom are persuaded that
he is going some day to be somebody, though sorely
puzzled to surmise what thing or when, so pleasantly
does he take life), from all sorts of out-of-the-way
country places, where he lodges with quaint old land-
ladies who wonder maternally why he never gets drunk,
and generally mistake him for an author until he pays
his bill."

Help from home failing, Burke took to his pen. In
1756 he published his *Philosophical Inquiry into the
Origin of our Ideas on the Sublime and the Beautiful*, a heavy treatise begun when he was nineteen ; and
his *Vindication of Natural Society*, a satirical imitation of Bolingbroke, which called much attention to the
young author. As a result his father was pleased to
send him £100. Three years later (1759) Burke un-

dertook to write Dodsley's *Annual Register*, for which
he received £100 a year and which he continued till
1788.

Before he began to work for Dodsley Burke was a
married man. Some years back he had given up, on account of weak health, his noisy lodgings near Temple
Bar and had gone to live with his physician, Dr. Nugent.
There he fell in love with the doctor's daughter, Jane, to
whom he was married in the winter of 1756. Among
his friends he was well known for his "orderly and amiable domestic habits."

It is unfortunate that so little is known of the third
decade of Burke's life, for by the end of it he was already
a man of respected opinion. It is very significant that
in 1758 he was able unchallenged to dispute the great
Dr. Johnson at Garrick's Christmas dinner. The following year he accepted the position of private secretary to
William G. ("Single Speech") Hamilton, and in 1761
went with Hamilton to Ireland. But Burke was not
the mere servant his employer would have had him, and
when Hamilton sought to bind him by favors, Burke
indignantly gave up his pension of £300 and left Hamilton for good. This was in 1764. In the same year he
joined the famous Literary Club.

In the Club he was a greatly respected member. Men
loved him easily — especially Johnson, who admired his
mental powers, Garrick, who helped him through many
financial troubles, and Reynolds, who made him one of
his executors and left him, in 1792, £2000. Of course
the Tory Johnson abominated Burke's politics. "Sir,"
he said in 1774, "he is a cursed Whig, a *bottomless*
Whig, as they all are now." But politics aside, the doctor had much admiration for the man. Burke, he said,

" does not talk from a desire of distinction, but because
his mind is full."

The following year, 1765, Burke became private secretary to Rockingham, First Lord of the Treasury. In
December he was sent up to the House of Commons for
Wendover. " Now we who know Mr. Burke," said Dr.
Johnson, " know that he will be one of the first men in
the country." Unfortunately for Burke, Rockingham
was removed in 1766 to make way for Grafton, of Chatham's ministry.

The eclipse of Rockingham in 1766 gives a chance
for another look at Burke's private life. In 1768 he
purchased a large estate near Beaconsfield, in Buckinghamshire. Where Burke got the money has never
been satisfactorily explained. A large part of the
£20,600 was covered by mortgage, and most of the
rest was borrowed, but it is supposed that Burke made
something by his interest in the speculations of his
brother Richard and his cousin William. It is certain
that after their collapse in 1769 Burke was constantly
in financial trouble. Still, he continued to live at Beaconsfield, keeping four black horses, and at an annual
expense of £2500. It is known that he received much
help from his friends. Besides that from Garrick and
Reynolds, the Marquis of Rockingham gave him great
assistance when in his will he directed that all Burke's
bonds held by him, bonds amounting to £30,000, should
be canceled. Whatever is thought of Burke's free
acceptance of help, it must not be forgotten that he
himself was very generous and that the charge of dis-
honesty in business, made by his detractors, is quite
unfounded. Very fond of planting and farming, he was
eager to have a " retreat " from London ; indeed, Bea-

consfield seemed to him as necessary a luxury as Abbotsford did to Walter Scott. One of Burke's best sides, too, that of the scholar, the philanthropist, and the quiet rural philosopher, is seen at Beaconsfield.

It is necessary, before following Burke farther in his career, to remember clearly the changes of administration during the next twenty years and the position which he took in 1770 : the first to avoid confusion, the second to judge fairly of his so-called apostasy in 1791. The Chatham ministry, then, which in 1766 put Rockingham out of office, was so liberal in its Whiggism that it brought about in 1770 the Lord North ministry, equally illiberal in its Toryism and directly provocative of the American war. After twelve years of misrule, " the King's friends," with Lord North at the helm, gave way to Rockingham. But he died only three months after return to power; Shelburne was unable long to hold the Whigs together; and in the spring of 1783 grew up the strange Coalition Ministry, nominally under the Duke of Portland, but really under the Whig Fox and the Tory North. In December of the same year the ministry of the younger Pitt came into power.

During all these changes between riotous Whiggism and tyrant Toryism Burke held on the same course : he was a conservative Whig. To be sure, he befriended Irish Catholics, though he himself was a Protestant, and he took up the cause of America. This position, however, was taken because he believed firmly in the constitutional liberties of the people and in religious toleration; he had from the outset that quality which came out so strongly in the French crisis, — a veneration for tradition and established order; he hated license and anarchy. That he later modified his opinions is true,

but that he turned coat is false. He was never, indeed,
a very free-thinking Whig, in the days when Whiggism
ran riot, and he was never, in his bitterest denunciation
of the French Revolution, a Tory at heart.

Burke's parliamentary position, from the first against
the King, was clearly registered by his protests against
excluding Wilkes, no doubt notorious, but nevertheless
elected, from his seat in the House. Soon after followed
Burke's *Thoughts on the Present Discontents* (1770),
an attempt to recall the policies of 1688. Lord Chatham wrote in complaint to Rockingham, who showed
the letter to Burke. Burke never got over his wrath at
Chatham's disapproval, though he admitted " the great
splendid side " of his adversary's character.

In general, three great questions occupied Burke :
America, India, and France. In his attack on England's treatment of America he was at his best. Disappointments had not yet made him bitter, nor repetitions
shrill; he brought to the subject more information and
more sane judgment than any other man in Parliament; and he expressed his views with an eloquence
and dignity that set him far above all others in the
dispute. In 1774, elected member for Bristol, then the
second city in England, he made his *Speech on Taxation*, a protest against the tea tax. The following year
(March 22, 1775) he spoke for three hours on *Con-
ciliation with the American Colonies*. Holding to the
belief that taxation without representation is unjust,
seeing that representation in the case of the distant
American Colonies was impossible, and foreseeing the
disaster of coercion, he suggested that the colonies be
permitted to make voluntary grants, that they be given
the power of refusal, " the first of all revenues." Burke's

speech contained maxims for all time; to us to-day it seems to have found a reasonable remedy for the American complaint; but his far-reaching wisdom was ill-adapted to the understanding of the scheming politicians about him. He might tell them that "An Englishman is the unfittest person on earth to argue another Englishman into slavery," that "The ocean remains. You cannot pump this dry;" — his oracular sentences were in vain. The "King's friends" were hopelessly in the majority, and Burke's proposition was defeated — 78 yeas, 270 noes. Two years later came his famous *Letter to the Sheriffs of Bristol on the Affairs of America.* Closely associated with him in this fight against Lord North's ministry was the young and brilliant statesman, Charles James Fox, from 1774 to 1782 Burke's firm friend and ally.

In 1782, on the return of Rockingham to power, Burke fully expected high office, and felt keenly the appointment to so subordinate a position as Paymaster of Forces. He put into practice, however, his theory of economical reform, brought forward two years before, by regulating his salary at £4000 instead of pocketing the large "balance," as his predecessors had done. Under the Coalition Ministry (1783) he was again paymaster, but on Pitt's accession to power in December of the same year he lost his position and never again held office. His popularity in Parliament, too, was waning; in 1780 he had been defeated for Bristol and thereafter sat for Malton. Soon after Pitt's coming in, in fact, Burke was in great disfavor. Once when he rose to speak, so many noisily left the room that he sat down. "I could teach a pack of hounds," he cried out in the House one day, "to yelp with greater melody and more comprehension." Much of his time was now spent in retirement at Beaconsfield.

But Burke, as every one realized, was an authority on India. He had already been attacking the corruption in the government there; so when, in 1786, he worked up his charge against Warren Hastings, he found both Fox and Sheridan ready to support him. On May 10, 1787, he appeared at the bar of the House of Peers and solemnly impeached Hastings of "high crimes and misdemeanors." The trial began on February 13, 1788, in Westminster Hall. Burke spoke during four sittings. Investigations followed and the trial dragged through several years. In 1794 Burke made his famous nine days' speech in reply to the defense of Hastings and thus finished his work for the impeachment. Hastings was finally acquitted, but Burke's investigations were really what first prompted reform in the administration of India.

While the trial of Hastings was going on, Burke found time for his third great interest, France. He first touched the subject in a letter, October, 1789, to a Frenchman, M. Dupont. Not long afterwards, the open sympathy of many English for the uprising in France caused him to write his *Reflections on the Revolution*, published in November, 1790. In these reflections he was no longer the self-contained upholder of constitutional liberty; disgusted by the bloody spectacle of a king dragged through the streets, horrified by the irreverent subversion of ancient, respectable institutions, he came forth the defender of established order. He saw only chaos and crime in the Revolution; he missed its main significance. Sheridan and Fox, who saw great promise in the capture of the Bastile, opposed Burke, who they thought was growing positively monarchical. But it must not be supposed that Burke took suddenly to shouting for George III. He had always resisted the tyranny of kings and would still have done so, no doubt, if he had not given his whole animosity to what he thought a much worse tyranny, — that of mobs and atheists. Thus he became, by force of his own reasoning, over-conservative; he even went so far as to oppose Fox's bill (1790) for the repeal of the Test and Corporation Acts. The King was naturally delighted with the *Reflections*, said it was "a good book, a very good book; every gentleman ought to read it." Its author had certainly lost his old cool judgment, but he was still eloquent and noble. As a result there was a strong reaction against the Revolution, and the Whig Party was almost demolished.

The most serious result for Burke himself was the final alienation from his old friend, Fox. The Whigs were indignant, and Burke, far from a Tory, was thus practically cut off from all party. Yet he was still an important figure : he was in correspondence with French royalists, and the Catholics of Ireland still looked to him for help. In 1792 he published his *Appeal from the New to the Old Whigs*, and in the fall of the same year took his stand on the ministerial side. Such a position made it necessary for him to resign (in 1793) from the Whig Club.

In 1794 Burke's days of active service came to an end. The death of his son, who had just taken his seat for Malton, was a heavy blow; and the last three years of his life he passed in retirement at Beaconsfield. There his chief interests were managing his farm, looking after poor neighbors, caring for the education of the children

of French refugees, and writing indignant pamphlets.
One of these, the *Letter to a Noble Lord* (1795),
was a reply, in which he justified himself, to an attack
on his acceptance of pensions. He had been offered a
peerage, but since he had no son to inherit it, he preferred pensions amounting to £3700. Other important
pamphlets during these last days were *Letters on a
Regicide Peace* (1796), marked by his failing judgment and rising indignation. By this time he had begun
to suffer from internal abscesses; he declined rapidly
and died on July 9, 1797. He was buried, according to
his wish, at Beaconsfield, in spite of Fox's generous
suggestion of Westminster Abbey. " There is but one
event," wrote Canning shortly after, " but that is an
event for the world — Burke is dead."

It can hardly escape notice that the chief schemes
Burke advocated failed of adoption, or that he himself
was never a cabinet minister. He was practically always
in the minority. But the real cause of his failure, as
well as of his greatness, lay in the fact that his nature
was essentially poetic and philosophical. He scorned
preferment at the compromise of his views or his ideals,
and of course he failed, in the reign of George III, as
a politician. The great strength of his political wisdom,
feared but only half appreciated by most of his contemporaries, was that it was not " partial," " pinched,"
" occasional," like Lord North's, but that it was fundamental, for all time. " A great empire and little minds
go ill together; " " whenever a separation is made between liberty and justice, neither is in my opinion safe; "
— such sentences abound in Burke. " I have learnt
more," said Fox, " from my right honorable friend than
from all the men with whom I ever conversed."

THE AGE OF ROMANTICISM

THE period which extends roughly from 1780 to 1830 is usually called the Age of Romanticism. It was distinctly a time of reaction, a reassertion of the poetic nature always strong in the English people. Towards the end of the eighteenth century there came a general protest against the cold conformity to rule that had been the aim of writers under Anne and the early Georges. The result was that imagination got the upper hand and that the age became one of enthusiasm and poetry instead of one of sophistication and prose. Yet men had been taught a lesson by the school of Pope. The Elizabethans, as the Rev. Stopford Brooke points out, had followed chiefly the instincts of nature; the Augustans, on the other hand, had lost themselves in artificial devices. It remained for the Romanticists to combine the two — art and nature. This period, therefore, produced many great poets; it stands, in fact, next to the great age of Elizabeth in literary significance.

The beginnings of the Romantic reaction can be traced underground into the very strongholds of the Augustans. Faint signs of it begin in the hey-day of Pope's despotism; and though Dr. Johnson, still true to the Augustan traditions, made fun of the ballads which his friend Percy collected in 1765, and scourged Macpherson for forging in *Ossian* what Johnson held to be contemptible stuff, yet ballad and epic were alike trumpet-calls in the Romantic movement.

The most general characteristics of this period are freedom from restraint and a love for the strange and the picturesque, what Walter Pater has called " strangeness added to beauty." For purposes of study, however, it will be found convenient to subdivide into five heads, though it must be remembered that no writers so defy glib classification as the Romantic writers and that the ticketing of poets with this or that characteristic is a fatal practice. (1) Men, wearying of the artificial fripperies of the Queen Anne age, began to seek natural beauty. At first they had resort only to quiet, rural, noon-day nature; but soon the interest deepened into a fondness for wild and awe-inspiring scenery, for the mountains and the storm-swept sea. (2) Another feature was the revival of the Middle Ages, a keen interest in ancient tales of mystery and romantic deeds, a love of the picturesqueness and pageantry of olden times. This is the widest characteristic of the time; it has, in fact, given the name *Romantic* to the period. (3) A phase in common with the French Revolution was a growing sympathy with the life of the poor, a sympathy felt more keenly by individual poets, such as Burns and Wordsworth, than by the people as a whole. (4) A very natural development, too, which resulted from greater freedom of thought and a more inquiring spirit, was a more genuine, fundamental philosophy. In many cases of morbid or highly emotional men this brought about over-wrought self-analysis, with the double result of great advance in thought and of frequent melancholia. Such Hamlet-moods may be found in nearly all the poets. (5) Finally, the verse-form kept pace with the freedom of thought. Poets, emancipated from the tyranny of the heroic couplet, interested in the literatures of all ages, tried many different metres. At first they followed chiefly Spenser and Milton, but soon they revived ballad stanza, the Italian "ottava rima," the sonnet, and a variety of lyrical measures.

In such an age of emotion and spontaneity most of the greater writers were of course poets. There were, to be sure, many able prose writers, such as Scott, Lamb, De Quincey; but it is a significant fact that nearly all the prose-writers tried their hand at poetry: the age was decidedly a *poetic* age.

ROBERT BURNS

It is significant that in speaking of the greatest
Scotch poet we nine times in ten call him *Bobbie
Burns* — a pleasant familiarity inspired only by a few
great writers, such as Kit Marlowe and Dick Steele.
To the readers of Burns's songs, he will ever be the
blithesome Ayrshire farmer-boy who whistled and sang
at the plow-tail. Indeed, as Carlyle points out, in one
aspect he never wholly grew to full manhood; he died
a youth in his thirty-seventh year, full of the exuberant
emotions and delusions of youth, still unsettled in moral
conviction. Yet in another sense he grew up all too
soon; blossomed and flourished in a day, exhausted his
strength like an unpruned plant. These two sides of
Burns's nature remain distinct to the end. The one
showed him at his best, truly a great genius, sincerely
affectionate, of a fine independent spirit, bursting with
fullness of song. The other manifested itself, by strange
contrast, in his inconstancy, in his moral irresolution,
in a deal of false pride. At first glance it is difficult
to believe that *Bobbie* Burns, who wrote *The Cotter's
Saturday Night* and *Bonnie Doon*, was the same person
as *Rab the Ranter*, who drank away a good portion
of his life, made irreverent songs about the clergy, and
was the lover of a dozen women. As we come to a
knowledge of the man's life, however, and of the circumstances in which he was placed, we perceive that he was
precisely the person in whom these two characters could
find expression — with a splendid and tragic result.

Robert Burns, the son of William Burness [or Burnes] and Agnes Brown, was born on the 25th of January, 1759, in an " auld clay bigging " at Alloway, about two miles from the town of Ayr, Scotland. His father, a poor farmer, did his best for the education of his sons. He instructed them in arithmetic, borrowed books for them on history and theology, and loved to turn aside from his labors or to give up his evenings for " solid conversation " with them. Robert in after life spoke often of the sound training he had received from his father — a man with a good understanding, he wrote to Dr. Moore, of " men, their manners, and ways," and of a " stubborn ungainly integrity." This education at Ayr made up all of Burns's regular training, except for an early period at the village school and instructions from the excellent Murdoch, a needy teacher engaged by Mr. Burness and some neighbors while the family lived at Mt. Oliphant. But the boy read so eagerly that by manhood he had acquired a respectable stock of book-learning, to say nothing of an education which his natural keenness and sympathy assimilated from everything he touched. At this early date the story of Sir William Wallace, he afterwards wrote, " poured a Scottish prejudice into my veins, which will boil along there, till the flood gates of life shut in eternal rest."

When Robert was seven his father moved to a farm at Mt. Oliphant, about two miles away. Here for eleven years the father and growing sons toiled to squeeze out of barren soil a wretched existence — the life which Burns afterwards referred to as "the unceasing moil of a galley-slave." In 1777 the family took another farm, at Lochlea, in the parish of Tarbolton. Robert now began to show great tenderness for the Tarbolton lassies, in consequence of which he is found attending a dancing-school in the village. The Tarbolton Club, of which he was the leading spirit, was a curious gathering of country youths, who debated such questions as love and social duties. When Burns and his brother Gilbert moved in 1783 to a farm at Mossgiel, the club broke up; it had taken its character and its life from its chief member, the genial, witty plowboy.

In appearance Burns was tall and sinewy, with swarthy features, a slight stoop at the shoulders, from handling the plow, and large strong hands. His big dark eyes glowed like coals of fire when he spoke. " I never saw," said Scott, " such another eye in a human head, though I have seen the most distinguished men of my time." In conversation he excelled : the sharpness of his retorts, the pathos of his appeals, the modulation of his voice to the subject, the rapidity yet clearness of his articulation struck every one ; the Duchess of Gordon said he " carried her off her feet." " When animated in company," comments Allan Cunningham, " he was a man of a million ; his swarthy features glowed ; his eyes kindled up till they all but lightened ; his plowman stoop vanished ; and his voice — deep, manly, and musical — added its sorcery of pathos or of wit, till the dullest owned the enchantments of his genius."

After the death of his father, in 1784, a growing restlessness beset Burns. The farm at Mossgiel, on " high land with a wet bottom," yielded no better than Mt. Oliphant and Lochlea. Yet he stuck — a little irresolutely, perhaps — to the plow. A few years before, he had gone to Irvine to learn the trade of a flax-dresser, but nothing except bad companions had come of it. He was not indeed so much an incompetent farmer as a poverty-stricken farmer, tilling barren soil and distracted by interests which had nothing to do with his work. As far as drawing the straightest furrow or sowing the most seed-corn in a day went, he had few superiors. He loved contests of rural activity. Once when he was equaled by a fellow worker in the harvest field, " Robert," said his rival, " I 'm no sae far behind this time, I 'm thinking." " John," answered the poet, " you 're behind in something yet — I made a sang while I was stooking."

For all his geniality and gift of song, however, Burns was increasingly unhappy. In his very " sangs " made while he was " stooking " lay a seed of the growing discontent : he was already conscious of his genius and he longed for leisure and wealth, that he might versify. If at this time he had decided fairly for the one or the other — farming or poetry — he might have been a happier, more successful man ; and, incidentally, the world might have been poorer of some of its best songs. One cannot regret the poetry that Burns did allow himself, but rather the vacillation which consumed the good years of his life. Added to this fretting uncertainty, numerous and distracting love affairs conspired with the beginnings of too convivial habits, contracted at Irvine, to throw him into unrest. He was looked on, moreover, with suspicion by his religious superiors. A controversy between the ministers of the Old Light and the New Light in the Western Kirk had called forth from the poet *Holy Willie's Prayer*, a poem full of the jovial, irreverent wit which his promiscuous comradeship and his keen insight were sure to breed when he contemplated the austere elders of the kirk. The whole matter — his flippancy and rare humor — is comprehended in one stanza of the poem; the keen ridicule must have been a veritable thorn in the side of the grave Calvinistic divines. "Holy Willie" prays:

> " O Thou, wha in the heavens dost dwell,
>   Wha, as it pleases best thysel',
> Sends ane to heaven, and ten to hell,
>   A' for thy glory,
> And no for ony gude or ill
>   They 've done afore thee ! "

Of Burns's early love affairs the most serious were those with Mary Campbell and Jean Armour. For his "Highland Mary" he felt a truer passion than for any. In their affectionate farewell when he was leaving for Edinburgh they met by a brookside, wet their fingers in the brook, exchanged Bibles, and swore eternal troth. But "fell death's untimely frost" snatched away his love; his only consolation was that her name inspired two of his tenderest melodies, *Highland Mary* and *Mary in Heaven*.

The affair with Jean Armour is not so pleasing to remember. Soon after moving to Mossgiel Burns had met this girl, the amiable daughter of a master-mason. All through 1785 his courtship continued with varying passion until finally by a forbidden marriage she bore him children. It is unpleasant to reflect that it was almost immediately after his separation from Jean — the indignant mason having refused to countenance the marriage — that Burns plighted his troth with Mary Campbell by the brookside. It was not till he moved to Ellisland in 1788 that he finally took Jean as his lawful wife; and for all his verses to "bonnie Jean" and his occasional praise of her figure or "wood-note wild," there was less of the fire of his better affection shown the poor girl than was granted to many other women. Indeed, his letters to his friends Smith and Richmond, to whom he confided his heart's secrets without reticence or delicacy, show often a most ungenerous attitude towards the woman he owed protection. " I have waited on Armour since her return home," he writes Richmond; "not from any the least view of reconciliation, but merely to ask for her health and — to you I will confess it — from a foolish hankering fondness — very ill placed indeed." And again, to Smith, when one might have expected his sin to be heavy upon him, he writes of another attachment — of a young lady who "flew off in a tangent of female dignity and reserve, like a mounting lark in an April morning. . . . But I am an old hawk at the sport, and wrote her such a cool, deliberate, prudent reply, as brought my bird from her aerial towerings, pop, down at my foot, like Corporal Trim's hat." He says himself that he had a way when he met a lovely lass of " battering himself into a warm affection ; " and he stands, Stevenson comments, " positively without a competitor " in that " debilitating and futile exercise." All through his life he was susceptible to feminine charm. Women inspired his best song; they were, in many instances, his truest friends and advisers ; and they were the chief cause of his inconstancy and waywardness. To Robert Riddell he wrote: " I have been all along a miserable dupe to love."

In judging Burns, however, we must take into account, as Carlyle has so emphatically pointed out, not the amount of deflection alone, but the proportion of the deflection to the size of the orbit. Burns was doubtless given to joviality succeeded by remorse; he did fling his "honest poverty" into rich men's faces; he did treat with disrespect the grave elders of the kirk; he did approximate what Stevenson calls the professional Don Juan. But these failings must be weighed against his virtues: his spontaneous affection and generosity; his intense patriotism; and, chiefly, his great gift of song. To ask restraint from Burns in his love affairs would be to ask that many of his best songs had not been written. It should be clear, moreover, that his vices as his virtues were a result of the man and his environment; bursting with passion, endowed with an insight which pierced unerringly through the religious and social mockeries of his day, dogged his life long by those two arch-foes, poverty and pride, he fell on unsympathetic times.

Burns's poetry, on his own authority, was in him the result of love. "I never had the least thought or inclination of turning poet," he says, "till I once got heartily in love, and then rhyme and song were, in a manner, the spontaneous language of my heart." Many of the verses addressed to the fair were not, it must be understood, the result of serious attachment; mere woman-kind acted on his fancy "like inspiration." "I can no more desist rhyming on the impulse," he writes to Miss Davies, "than an Eolian harp can refuse its tones to the streaming air." In the years at Lochlea and Mossgiel nearly all of his best longer poems were written; in fact, only *Tam o' Shanter* and some of the songs belong to a later period. His first publication (1786) in the Kilmarnock Edition, included such poems as *The Cotter's Saturday Night, The Jolly Beggars, A Winter Night, Address to the Deil, To*

J. Lapraik, the *Epistles to Davie, To a Mouse, To a Mountain Daisy,* and *The Twa Dogs.*

> " Give me ae spark o' nature's fire ! "

he says, —

> " That 's a' the learning I desire;
> Then though I drudge thro' dub an' mire
>   At pleugh or cart,
> My muse, though hamely in attire,
>   May touch the heart."

With the £20 made from the sale of his first volume Burns renewed his intention to embark for Jamaica, a scheme he had long considered as an escape from the difficulties at home. But the acclamation with which his poems were received and the enthusiastic invitations of friends induced him to visit Edinburgh. He had sprung into national fame. On his way he found the milkmaid and plowman singing his songs; at inns the guests and servants got out of bed to hear him talk; and the *literati* of Edinburgh opened their arms to him.

Nothing could have been more characteristic of Burns than his life in Edinburgh. He was fêted by the great and honored by the acquaintance of rich and learned alike, yet in no single instance did he display servility or embarrassment. With " manners direct from God," he was at ease in the innermost circles of aristocracy and by his ready, unaffected wit and brilliant conversation charmed whole assemblies. Among his more intimate friends were : Professor Dugald Stewart ; Professor Walker ; Dr. Blair, the aged divine ; Mackenzie, author of the *Man of Feeling ;* Robertson, the famous historian; Mrs. Dunlop, direct descendant of William Wallace ; Lord Monboddo, the whimsical judge; the Duchess of Gordon; James, Earl of

Glencairn; and the accomplished John Francis Erskine, Earl of Mar. Among all these notables he moved with the confidence of a peer.

For a moment Burns's fortunes took a brighter turn. The Edinburgh edition of his poems (1787) yielded him above £500, though the payment was in part delayed. After making a tour of the Scotch border, with which he was not greatly impressed, he returned to Mossgiel. Here, however, discontent soon developed. The difficulties of farming the barren soil and the constant reminders of his affair with Jean Armour led him to return to Edinburgh. The second trip to the capital, however, was not so happy as the first. His circle of stanch friends was diminishing; society was tired of its plaything; Burns was established as a famous poet, but he was no longer the literary lion of the hour. Much more immediately significant to the poet, he was poor and without a fixed occupation. By his brilliant conversation he could still, to be sure, force momentary entrances where he would, but dining occasionally at the tables of aristocracy only brought home the scantiness of his usual "hamely fare." A trip to the Highlands with a friend, John Nicol, did little to dispel the dark clouds he saw ahead. With the Mossgiel failure behind him and with a dangerous tendency to conviviality, he became increasingly unsettled in his ways and bitter in his attitude towards the rich. He began to talk much, often violently, about his "Rock of Independence." He had never bowed down to the "pride o' rank," and now, when he saw that servility was necessary to material success, he burst out in disgust and anger; in every fibre of him there vibrated his father's "stubborn ungainly integrity;" he could not contain himself before the presumptuous insolence of

"yon birkie ca'd a lord." Sometimes his outbursts, especially in his letters, are personal and ill-tempered, but
for the most part he inspires sympathy and indignation.

> "For a' that, and a' that,
>   Our toils obscure, and a' that;
> The rank is but the guinea's stamp,
> The man's the gowd for a' that."

In the spring of 1788, then, Burns, disgusted, indignant, and remorseful by turns, left Edinburgh and, taking Jean Armour as his lawful wife, moved to a farm
at Ellisland, on the River Nith, about six miles north
of Dumfries. Ellisland, like Mossgiel, yielded little success. "Mr. Burns," said Allan Cunningham's father,
"you have made a poet's not a farmer's choice;" and
Burns himself, though he admired the scenery, spoke
later of the land as the "riddlings of creation." To
eke out his small income he accepted a position in the
excise, and finally, the farm going from bad to worse,
he made the fatal step of moving in 1791 to Dumfries,
with his government office, £50 a year, as his only
regular means of support.

As an excise officer Burns worked diligently enough,
but he had a contempt for his superiors which cost him
advancement, and a kindness of heart which led him
to wink at the little smugglings of the poor. One night,
when the clatter of horses at the gallop took him from
his bed to the window, he turned to his wife and whispered, "It's smugglers, Jean." "Then I fear ye'll be
to follow them?" she answered. "And so I would," said
he, "were it Will Gunnion or Edgar Wright; but it's
poor Brandyburn, who has a wife and three weans, and
is no doing owre weel in his farm. What can I do?"
Another time he led a force through the water and with

drawn sword carried a well-armed brig, but received a reprimand afterwards for buying four of the cannon and sending them to the Directory in France. It was on this occasion, while waiting for a fellow-officer who had gone for arms and men, that he composed the rollicking song, *The Deil's awa' wi' the Exciseman*, the very burden of which embodies the reckless humor with which he regarded his government position. He had not been gauger long, in fact, before he was charged with revolutionary principles. Besides the affair of the cannon, he had sat covered at the theatre while *God save the King* was being sung, and he had done a deal of talking, for the times, about despots and liberty. The reproof from his superiors rather provoked than silenced more talk, about which there is just a suggestion of bravado. He took up the cause of France in verse, and once at a dinner, when Pitt's health was proposed, he cried, "Let us drink to the health of a greater and better man — George Washington." He was instructed that it was his "business to act, not to think." To which he might well have replied with his own lines: —

"Here's freedom to him that wad read,
 Here's freedom to him that wad write;
 There's nane ever feared that the truth should be heard
 But them wham the truth wad indite."

The end was now very near. In 1795 the poet's health failed rapidly, and the following winter a dangerous condition was brought on by sleeping in the street one snowy night, after late convivality. Sea-bathing afforded less relief than the doctor had hoped, and at the same time Burns was depressed by a melancholy sense of his failings, of his inability to revive his weakening powers. On meeting a friend in the streets of Dumfries, he said,

"I am going to ruin as fast as I can ; the best I can do is to go consistently." Once, when his friend Mrs. Riddell entered the room, his first words were : "Well, madam, have you any commands for the other world ?" As he lay on his death-bed in the summer of 1796, he remarked to the doctor, with a flash of his old humor: "I am but a poor crow, and not worth picking ; " and to Gibson, a fellow volunteer, — for Burns had enlisted for a short time in the volunteer service of Dumfries, — he said, smiling, "John, don't let the awkward squad fire over me." He died on the 21st of July, 1796. His fellow townsmen were sufficiently aware of his genius, and, above all, fond of his kindly personality, to give him public funeral. His body was borne to the old kirk-yard by the volunteers, who, despite his request, fired three ragged volleys.

About Burns there has gathered a great fund of anecdotes, naturally bred of his brilliant conversation and his quick humor. There is a story told by one James Thomson, the son of a neighbor at Ellisland : "I remember Burns weel," said he ; "I have some cause to mind him. . . . Once I shot at a hare that was busy on our braird ; she ran bleeding past Burns : he cursed me and ordered me out of his sight, else he would throw me into the water. I'm told he has written a poem about it." "But do you think he could have thrown you in ? " was asked. "Thrown ! Aye, I'll warrant could he, though I was baith young and strong." Another time, at a wedding feast, Burns told some young fellows to stop quarreling or "he'd hing them up in verse on the morrow." A clergyman once attempted to censure Burns's *Holy Fair*, but he made a poor-fist of his criticism ; Burns's eye began to twinkle, and all present

looked for a sharp reply. " No," he said ; " by heaven,
I 'll not touch him —

" ' Dulness is sacred in a sound divine.' "

Of the Edinburgh *literati* he made the famous remark
at Dr. Blair's table, that they were " like the wife's
daughter in the west, — they spin the thread of their
criticism so fine, that it is fit for neither warp nor waft."
His Edinburgh wit often had a bitter turn to it, as he
suppressed his rising indignation. To a lady who re-
monstrated with him about his drinking he answered :
" Madam, they would not thank me for my company if
I did not drink with them. I *must* give them a slice
of my constitution."

During the years at Ellisland and Dumfries Burns's
principal poetical work consisted of songs, chiefly for
Thomson, an Edinburgh collector, or for Johnson's
Musical Museum. Some of the pieces were old songs
rearranged for music ; most were original compositions.
Burns seems to have been incapable now of sustained
effort, but many of his best songs date from these later
days — such songs as : *Highland Mary, Bonnie Doon,
Auld Lang Syne, Coming thro' the Rye, O my Luve 's
like a Red, Red Rose,* and that stirring battle-slogan,
Scots wha hae wi' Wallace bled, composed while galloping across the wild Galloway moors in a tempest.

In his songs rests Burns's chief fame. The world,
now that a century has passed, is quite willing that he
should " bear the gree ; " in his kind he stands supreme.
And these songs, singing themselves in the man's heart,
since they were scattered all through his life, give us
the truest account of his nature. " He put more of himself into all he wrote," says Allan Cunningham, " than

any other poet, ancient or modern; to which may be
added the important corollary, amply proved in the
songs, that he was a man of noble character — a loving,
a humorous, a patriotic, a kindly man. The very fact
that nearly all his biographers have zealously taken sides
— for or against him — testifies to the infectious fire of
his personality, even after his death. The world has
much forgiveness ready for the man who can write with
the mingled humor and pathos of Burns's *Address to
the Deil* : —

> " ' An' now, auld Cloots, I ken ye 're thinkin',
>   A certain Bardie's rantin', drinkin',
>   Some luckless hour will send him linkin'
>   To your black pit ;
>   But, faith ! he 'll turn a corner jinkin',
>   An cheat you yet.' "

Turbulent, chaotic, driven by his genius and reined
in by his poverty, his life never wholly worked itself
out — " a life of fragments," Carlyle has called it. Step
aside he often did, to pluck the bright flowers by the
way ; but if he seems to have lacked a central guiding
principle in life, let it be remembered that it was no
easy thing for a man with his nature and in his circumstances to be sure of a fixed principle, that his very
genius gave him no precedent on which to act. If he
reached no clear moral manhood, let it be remembered
that he started bravely on a new journey, while his
countrymen remained at home. Decades ahead of his
time, he must needs march alone, not attended, as was
Tennyson, by the trumpets of his generation; yet he
reached a summit and looked into the nineteenth century, the promised land which he might not enter. His
own words are his fairest epitaph : —

" The poor inhabitant below
　Was quick to learn, and wise to know,
　And keenly felt the friendly glow,
　　And softer flame,
　But thoughtless follies laid him low,
　　And stain'd his name !"

WALTER SCOTT

"THE great magician," "the wizard of the North" — the two names so frequently given to Scott — call to mind immediately his power of conjuring with the song and story of the past. No picture of him is complete, however, until he is shown as the great-hearted laird of Abbotsford. Among his contemporaries he was frequently surpassed in poetry; he clearly excelled only in his novels. But as a man of a big, warm heart he had no rival, scarcely a second. He always contrived to find the best side of friend or enemy; he knew how to forget injuries; his heart and his purse went together to the poor; his dependents, his family, his friends, even strangers — who always found the hospitable doors of Abbotsford open to them — returned him affection as if it were his unquestionable right. Even many creditors, in the hour of his trial, joined the ranks of his loving admirers. So great, indeed, was the power of love in the man that generations of Scotchmen have looked to him with undoubting, filial affection; and to that great family have long since been added thousands and tens of thousands wherever English is spoken or read.

No man fills up quite so completely as Scott the whole period of Romanticism. Besides his work as a lawyer, he attained excellence and renown as an antiquarian, a poet, an essayist, a historian, and a novelist. In studying his life it will be found convenient, though his humor may often demand digressive anecdote, to divide it into three periods; that of his youth, education,

Walter Scott

In 1820. After the painting by Sir Thomas Lawrence, P.R.A., in the Royal Gallery, Windsor Castle

and poetry (1771–1814) ; that of his novels (1814–1826) ; and that of his noble struggle to pay off an enormous debt (1826–1832).

Walter Scott, the son of Walter Scott, a writer to the signet (or attorney at law), and Anne Rutherford, daughter of a professor in the University of Edinburgh, was born in the Scotch capital, in a house at the head of the College Wynd, on August 15, 1771. He was one of twelve children ; but there was always a high mortality among the Scotts, and only five of the children lived to maturity. " My birth," Scott says, " was neither distinguished nor sordid ; " but "it was esteemed *gentle.*" One of the ancestors of whom he was proudest was Walter Scott of Harden, commonly called *Auld Wat,* "whose name I have made to ring in many a ditty." Descent from him and " his fair dame, the Flower of Yarrow," Scott adds, was " no bad genealogy for a Border Minstrel."

Scott says he was " an uncommonly healthy child " at first, but when he was eighteen months old a severe fever so affected his right leg that he was lame for life. For remedy he was sent to his grandfather's place at Sandy-Knowe — Smailholme Grange, near " Tweed's fair flood." There he improved so rapidly that he was soon able to ride a Shetland pony over the moors. His lameness, indeed, did not long prevent his walking or his developing into a very robust, active man. The greatest gain from Sandy-Knowe, however, was the boy's early interest in Border story and song. His memory for some things was not remarkable, but in the matter of ballads to hear was to remember. He tells how his vigorous recitation of " Hardicanute " quite silenced a visiting clergyman, who asserted that one "might as well speak in a cannon's mouth as where that child was."

In his fourth year Scott was taken to Bath to try the waters, but without material advantage. The trip to London, however, and the return via Prestonpans fed his already growing interest in history. In 1777 he was considered well enough to visit his parents in Edinburgh. It was at this time that Mrs. Cockburn found the boy reading his mother the description of a shipwreck. " His passion rose with the storm," she wrote. " He lifted his eyes and hands. ' There 's the mast gone,' says he; 'crash it goes ! — they will all perish !' After his agitation he turns to me. ' That is too melancholy,' says he; ' I had better read you something more amusing.' " On going to bed he told his aunt that he liked Mrs. Cockburn; "' for I think she is a virtuoso like myself.' And on his aunt's asking, ' Dear Walter, what is a virtuoso ? ' he answered, ' Don't ye know? Why, it 's one who wishes and will know everything.' "

In 1778 Scott was sent to the grammar school division of Edinburgh High School. At first he was under Mr. Luke Fraser, and afterwards under the Rector, Dr. Adam. He was a great reader, but not a very good scholar, though he was brilliant at times. He "glanced," he says, " like a meteor from one end of the class to the other." Lockhart gives a good illustration of the kind of learning which the boy possessed to a startling degree. On some dolt's calling *cum* a substantive, the master asked, " Is *with* ever a substantive ? " Scott, when the others had gone down before this question, promptly replied : " And Samson said unto Delilah, If they bind me with seven green *withs* that were never dried, then shall I be weak, and as another man." In

the Bible, ballads, and folk-lore he could already compete with all boys and many men. But he had no Greek
and only a handy knowledge of Latin. His good humor among his companions, his "inexhaustible" tales,
and his generous spirit made him, he says, "a brighter
figure in the *yards* than in the *class*." "I was never a
dunce, nor thought to be so," he adds in a footnote,
"but an incorrigibly idle imp, who was always longing
to do something else than what was enjoined him." As
a narrator, a *maker*, he was, as Mr. Andrew Lang puts
it, already "made." "He was a bold rider, a lover of
nature and of the past, he was a Jacobite, and the friend
of epic and ballad."

In 1785 Scott entered Edinburgh University and at
the same time began reading law in his father's office.
It was at this period that he became the familiar friend
of William Clerk, the Darsie Latimer of *Redgauntlet*, with whom he for a while studied daily and with
whom he became an authorized advocate in July, 1792.
Scott, who had taken rather unwillingly to the law,
always considered it a "dry and barren wilderness of
forms and conveyances." He worked, however, with a
perseverance which either belies his assertion of natural
indolence or bears witness to heroic effort. "When actually at the oar," he says, "no man could pull it harder
than I, and I remember writing upwards of 120 folio
pages with no interval either for food or rest." This
effort is equaled only by his writing in one day, after
his health had broken down in old age, the copy for sixty
pages of print. During all his law studies, however, and
his somewhat intermittent attendance at the University,
he found time for wide and curious reading, occasional
versification, and good fellowship. He tried his hand at

drawing, painting, and singing, but was a rather conspicuous failure.

In appearance Scott was large and strong—"all rough and alive with power," says Dr. John Brown, who continues: "Had you met him anywhere else [than in Edinburgh], you would say he was a Liddesdale store-farmer, come of gentle blood; 'a stout, blunt carle,' as he says of himself, with the swing and stride and the eye of a man of the hills — a large, sunny, out-of-door air all about him." His high head, rising almost literally to a peak on top, later earned him the nickname of "Peveril of the Peak" among his fellow lawyers.

How much Scott had to struggle with at this period is not commonly emphasized. About the second year of his legal apprenticeship, he says, he suffered from bursting a blood-vessel, and recovery was slow. In his nineteenth year, moreover, he fell in love with a Miss Margaret Stewart Belches. For five years he worshiped at her shrine, and was certainly very much broken by her marriage, in 1796, to William Forbes. Scott managed, however, to keep manfully quiet. He was no doubt less sensitive than Byron and Keats, but he was also, it must be remembered, made of sterner stuff. One is apt to be misled by his outward cheerfulness, to forget that his optimism was won with a struggle. "He did not 'make copy,'" comments Mr. Andrew Lang, "of his deepest thoughts or of his deepest affections."

By 1797, however, when his heart was "handsomely pieced," as he expressed it, he fell in love with Miss Charlotte Margaret Carpenter (or Charpentier), a lady of French parentage. On Christmas Eve they were married. The record of their long happiness and of the home which they made for their children and friends is a very pleasant chapter. Mrs. Scott was a ministering angel among the neighboring poor, the children were everywhere beloved, and the father's congeniality and hospitality would almost be famous if he had never written a line. No family bears scrutiny better.

Soon after his marriage Scott moved to Lasswade, just outside of Edinburgh. In 1799 he was made sheriff depute of Selkirkshire, and five years later took up his abode at Ashestiel, on the Tweed, the river of his boyhood and his heart. In 1806 he undertook the duties of a clerk of session, though he did not begin to receive the salary, £1300, until May, 1812.

To cover Scott's literary work a step backwards is necessary. His first serious performance, remarkable in its choice of a romantic subject, was a translation of Bürger's ballad, *Lenore*, in 1796. In 1799 he brought out a free translation of Goethe's *Goetz von Berlichingen*, and in 1800 he wrote the *Eve of St. John*. His first great work, however, was his *Border Minstrelsy*, a collection of old songs and ballads, which few were better qualified than he to assort and put together. Many of them, indeed, he wrote out from memory, for their only life had been in the mouths of the peasantry, from whom he had picked them up as he rode about the country. These ballads, with notes and introductions by Scott, were printed by his old schoolfellow, James Ballantyne, in 1802. Of the Ballantynes much serious later. In connection with the search for ballads appears another of Scott's friends, John Leyden, the eccentric and ingenuous scholar who in six weeks prepared for his medical examination for an Indian appointment — an effort which usually took several years. Lockhart tells how Leyden once went in search of a ballad, how, two days later, a party at dinner was astonished by " a sound like that of the whistling of a tempest through the torn rigging of the vessel which scuds before it," and how a few minutes later Leyden "burst into the room chanting the desiderated ballad with the most enthusiastic gestures, and all the energy of what he used to call the *saw-tones* of his voice." The same zeal carried the poor fellow into a shut-up house in India, in search of rare books, with the result that he caught a fatal fever.

Scott's first popular success in literature did not come, however, till the publication of the *Lay of the Last Minstrel* in 1805. In spite of the faults which the *Edinburgh Review* of course discovered, the *Lay* had an unprecedented success. In 1808 came *Marmion* and secure fame. The stirring, martial swing of the poem, unlike anything yet written, appealed to nearly every one. Jeffrey, in the *Edinburgh Review*, still found fault, but his voice sounds small. Scott himself, in the bewildering applause of two nations, managed to keep his head, though he admitted that *Marmion* had given him " such a *heeze* " (hoist), he had " for a moment almost lost his footing." When he visited London the following year (1809), he found his fame before him. Mr. Morritt of Rokeby, a friend of Scott's, well expresses in his journal the attitude of the author of *Marmion:* " 'All this is very flattering,' he would say, ' and very civil; and, if people are amused with hearing me tell a parcel of old stories, or recite a pack of ballads to lovely young girls and gaping matrons, they are easily pleased; and a man would be very ill-natured who would not give pleasure so cheaply conferred.'" Scott's good wife seems to have been much more agitated over his fame than Scott himself. The *Lady of the Lake* in 1810 surpassed its predecessor in sale, though perhaps not in popularity. It is said, indeed, that so great was the interest aroused in the scenes of Scott's poems that the increased travel noticeably affected the revenue from the post-horse duty. To-day, when everybody travels, Stratford-on-Avon is about the only " literary shrine " which draws more visitors than the Trossachs and Loch Katrine.

Yet poetry was only one side of "the great magician's " literary activity. In 1808 he finished a long life of Dryden and in 1814 a similar work on Swift, both of which have outlived by their own merit most of the biographies written at that time. Besides them, moreover, Scott found time to write many sketches and short criticisms for magazine publication. A great man for exercise, he was able, nevertheless, to do without it; a new kind of work, prose after poetry, he said, was sufficient " refreshment to the machine." In 1808 he gave willing support to the Tory *Quarterly*, in opposition to the Whig *Edinburgh Review*. From boyhood Scott had been a king's man; he had then sided with the Cavaliers of the seventeenth century, he said, as King Charles II had chosen his religion, "because it was the more gentlemanlike " of the two. Gifford, however, proved an injudicious editor, and the *Quarterly* went the acrimonious way of the *Edinburgh*.

It was in 1806 that Scott, long interested in the brothers Ballantyne, first put £6000 into their printing establishment, and a few years later aided in the junction of it with Constable's publishing house. Scott became a silent partner and was frequently called on to

sustain the irregular, ingenuous business ways of the
Ballantynes. As yet all went fairly well.

Legal and social duties in these days often took
Scott up to Edinburgh, where he lived at 39 Castle
Street and, incidentally, did some of his writing. The
story of Marjorie Fleming, by Dr. John Brown, is a
delightful picture of Scott's familiar ways with children; when he was tired of work, the story runs, he
would fetch little Marjorie, aged eight, in his arms,
Maida the dog gamboling in the snow beside him,
carry the " wee wifee " to Castle Street, and there
recite his lesson to that remarkable child, or listen to
her comments on Shakespeare. The incidents of Dr.
Brown's book may not be taken from actual fact, but
he has ably caught the spirit of Scott.

On the flood of his literary success the poet, who had
always been eager for a large estate, bought, in 1811,
the farm of Abbotsford, on the Tweed. There he lived
chiefly the rest of his life. He built a large house,
planted trees, and laid out his grounds with keen interest. In May, 1812, the family migrated from Ashestiel,
five miles up the river. Scott wrote of the " procession
of my furniture, in which old swords, bows, targets,
and lances made a very conspicuous show. A family of
turkeys was accommodated within the helmet of some
preux chevalier of ancient border fame; and the very
cows, for aught I know, were bearing banners and
muskets. . . . This caravan, attended by a dozen of
ragged, rosy peasant children, carrying fishing-rods and
spears, and leading ponies, greyhounds, and spaniels,
would, as it crossed the Tweed, have furnished no bad
subject for the pencil, and really reminded me of one
of the gipsy groups of Callot upon their march." At

Abbotsford Scott opened his hospitable doors to friends and visitors. Washington Irving tells how his host sent his son Walter to show him the neighboring Dryburgh Abbey, and then how the good-hearted "laird," insisting that what was intended for a call should be prolonged to a visit, entertained him with many a merry tale. On the poet's wife's exclaiming, during some narration, "Why, Mr. Scott, Macnab's not dead, is he?" Scott replied, "Faith, my dear, if he's not dead they've done him great injustice — for they've buried him!"

There has been considerable adverse criticism of Scott's manner of life at Abbotsford — as if he had coined his literary ideals and in turn converted the coin into a vast accumulation of earthly things. The halls at Abbotsford, hung with armor and trophies of the chase, were, it is often said, the sign of a petty worldliness — a child's passion for baubles — unbecoming in a man who should be rearing intellectual castles. It is true that Scott did go in more deeply than he knew — through the mismanagement of the Ballantynes and through his own two-handed generosity; Abbotsford was, as Mr. Lang says, his "private Moscow expedition." Yet even if his defense were not found in his last, noble struggle, there would still be ample justification of his actions. Scott lived in the spirit of the Middle Ages. To reproduce faithfully in word and deed the chivalry and pageantry of the past was his life. What more fitting expression of such a man could there have been than his *Marmion*, his *Ivanhoe*, his Abbotsford? The large-hearted gentleman took his chivalrous ideals from his ancestors; and in beautifying Abbotsford, as in his works and in his honor to women and courtesy to guests, he played his part sincerely. He had, moreover,

a not unworthy Scottish ambition to provide his posterity with a fitting ancestral estate ; he would fain have
his descendants known as "the Scotts of Abbotsford."

The poet's residence at Abbotsford, when he was not
on legal duty, was, then, a full working out of his best
self. He usually wrote for two or three hours before
breakfast, and by noon was his "own man," as he said.
When he did not spend the rest of the day in writing
or entertaining guests, he went riding or shooting with
his son or visited the Border peasantry. Among these
simple folk the "Shirra" or the "laird," as they called
him, was a deservedly great man. At Abbotsford, moreover, he was able to gratify to the full his affection for
dogs and horses. Among the latter, Captain, Lieutenant,
Brown Adam, and Daisy reigned up to Waterloo, as
Mr. Hutton quaintly puts it ; while Sybil Grey and the
Covenanter or Douce Davie filled the later period. Camp,
Maida, and Nimrod were his favorite dogs. When Camp
died Scott gave up a dinner party, and to Maida he
erected a marble monument.

Of Scott's children — Walter, Charles, Anne, and
Sophia — none long outlived him. Sophia, however,
from whom the line is continued to the present day,
through adding the name of Scott to Hope, and in the
third generation to Maxwell, married John Gibson Lockhart, for twenty-seven years editor of the *Quarterly*
and author of the best life of his father-in-law — indeed,
of one of the few great biographies.

In later years, when the press of visitors became
thick, Scott used sometimes to escape to Lockhart's
near-by cottage of Chiefswood. "The clatter of Sybil
Grey's hoofs, the yelping of Mustard and Spice, and his
own joyous shout of reveillé under our windows, were

the signal that he had burst his toils and meant for that day to take his 'ease in his inn.' On descending he was to be found seated, with all his dogs and ours about him, under a spreading ash that overshadowed half the bank behind the cottage and the park, pointing the edge of his woodman's axe for himself, and listening to Tom Purdie's lecture touching the plantation that most needed thinning."

During all this pleasant life Scott wrote prodigiously. While still at Ashestiel he had published *The Vision of Don Roderick* (1811), *Rokeby* (1812), and *The Bridal of Triermain* (1812). Then the greater success of Lord Byron's *Childe Harold* induced him to give up poetry. Though he 'continued for some years to write verse, he did so with less zeal and less power than in the hey-day of *Marmion*. *The Lord of the Isles* (1815), *Waterloo* (1815), — for which he made a short visit to Belgium, — and *Harold the Dauntless* (1817) were his last long poems. In 1813 he was offered the laureate-ship, but he modestly declined it, in favor of Southey.

The eclipse of Scott by Byron in 1812 really lasted only two years; for in 1814 Scott's first novel, *Waverley*, appeared. One third of it had been written nine years before, but the fragment had been put aside as not worth finishing. It was taken up for a brief moment in 1810, but again laid aside. One day, in 1814, while hunting for some fishing-tackle, Scott came across the old manu-script, finished it in three weeks, and, to satisfy a whim, published it without his name. But it did not need his name; its success surpassed that of his poems. He forth-with followed up the popular favor with a great number of novels, most of which are now known to every school-boy. For years he persisted in concealing his connection with them, and the public spoke of their author as " the great unknown." *Guy Mannering* came out in 1815, and was quickly followed by a succession of Scotch stories, — *The Antiquary* (1816); *The Black Dwarf* and *Old Mortality*, in the *First Series of Tales of My Landlord* (1816); *Rob Roy* (1818); *The Heart of Midlothian*, in the *Second Series of Tales of My Landlord* (1818); and *The Bride of Lammermoor* and *The Legend of Montrose*, in the *Third Series* (1819). During the year 1819 Scott suffered much from intense pain in the stomach, so much so that when he had finished dictating *The Bride of Lammermoor* he could not remember a single incident of the story. " But," he later wrote, " I have no idea of these things preventing a man from doing what he has a mind."

The year 1820 was a proud one for the novelist. On the accession of George IV he was made a baronet — henceforth Sir Walter. The same year, too, saw some of his best literary work : *Ivanhoe, The Monastery*, and *The Abbot*. By this time he was making, from his writings alone, upwards of £10,000 a year. More significant still, the sale of his novels not only put poetry out of countenance, but so affected the mind of the reading public that poetry has never since been able to compete with prose in popularity. Lord Byron's works were still widely read, of course, but the rising poets, Shelley and Keats, were scarcely known. It is no small thing to have influenced the post-horse revenue by one's poetry and then, when no less a person than Byron has stolen one's fire, to write poetry out of fashion by the success of one's novels.

For five years more Scott continued in his prosperous career. In 1821 came *Kenilworth* and *The Pirate;* in

1822 *The Fortunes of Nigel* and *Halidon Hill;* in 1823
Peveril of the Peak, Quentin Durward, and *St.
Ronan's Well;* in 1824 *Redgauntlet;* and in 1825 *The
Bethrothed* and *The Talisman.* The public of course
preferred certain novels to others, but in the glamour of
Scott's greatness all sold well, whether he kept to his
favorite Scottish subjects, as in the earlier *Waverley* tales,
or tried his hand at other themes, such as those of the
English *Ivanhoe* or of the French *Quentin Durward.*

In 1826, while he was working on *Woodstock,* the
crash came. Sufficiently afflicted by the death of Lady
Scott in May, he was in the same year brought low by
the complete failure of both firms with which he was
connected — Constable, the publisher, and the Ballantynes, printers. The collapse was due to general mismanagement, chiefly on the part of the Ballantyne
brothers. Scott, a silent partner, found himself responsible for the large debt of £117,000. With cheerful
face he reconciled himself to giving up Abbotsford and
set himself to the task of writing off the debt. "Nobody
in the end can lose a penny by me," was one of the first
things he said. "Give me my popularity," he cried,
"and all my present difficulties shall be a joke in four
years." He soon finished *Woodstock* and followed it
in the next year (1827) with his long *Life of Napoleon,* to study for which he made a trip to Paris. The
novel brought him £8000 and the *Life* £18,000. Popularity was still his. A little reckless of his art, perhaps,
conscious only of the duty he had set himself, he turned
out novels with feverish haste. In 1827 appeared the
First Series of Chronicles of the Canongate, including *The Two Drovers, The Highland Widow,* and *The
Surgeon's Daughter;* in 1827-30 *The Tales of a*

Grandfather; in 1828 *The Fair Maid of Perth (Second Series of Chronicles of the Canongate)*; and in 1829 *Anne of Geierstein.* In 1830 came the *Letters on Demonology and Witchcraft.* Then the strain began to tell; his "magic wand," as he put it, was broken. His last two novels (1831) — *Count Robert of Paris* and *Castle Dangerous (Fourth Series of Tales of My Landlord)* — were the weak results of his failing powers. "The gentleman," says Lockhart, "survived the genius."

Without his last effort Scott's life would have been merely interesting ; with it, it was sublime, one of the most heroic. "There was nothing in Scott," says Mr. Hutton, "while he remained prosperous, to relieve adequately the glare of triumphant prosperity." When, however, he was ready to renounce the dearest idols of that prosperity and to strive in his old age with the single idea of clearing his name from debt and of leaving his family unembarrassed, he showed a fullness of stature hitherto unknown. Many young men have achieved through renunciation a noble old age, but few old men have been able to rise, as Scott did, superior to the thousand things which have become daily habit. Material prosperity never softened Scott. Indeed, there is something fine in the valuation he set on this world's goods — things to be dearly prized and accumulated while all went well, but to be unhesitatingly renounced when honor was at stake ; for to pay off the debt Scott took to be his only honorable course. He loved mightily his possessions, yet he made no show of giving them up : hence the greater credit. He had already revealed chivalry, courtesy, affection, and great literary skill — but always against no odds. In his adversity he revealed fortitude and endurance — characteristics which make his gentleness and tenderness all the more striking; for it is only in a strong man that tenderness is admirable.

One of the finest things in connection with the struggle was the unwillingness of friends and dependents to desert him. Even some of the poor offered what they had. But Scott declined all help; he had resolved to get himself the victory with his "own right hand." His creditors, however, not only positively refused to accept Abbotsford, but they insured its being left to his descendants. "The butler," says Lockhart, "was now doing half the work of the house at probably half his former wages. Old Peter, who had been for five and twenty years a dignified coachman, was now plowman in ordinary. . . . And all, to my view, seemed happier than they had even done before." "If things get round with me," cried Sir Walter one day, "easy shall be Pete's cushion!"

The struggle, however, was too vast and the man too old. In February, 1831, he had a slight stroke of paralysis. Soon a growing weakness of both mind and body forbade further work. Altogether, Sir Walter had written off £40,000 of the debt, but at the end he was led by kind friends to believe that he had accomplished his whole task. As a matter of fact, the sale of his works alone did clear the whole debt, though not till fifteen years after his death. In vain hope of recovery he visited Italy in the winter of 1831–32. But the news of Goethe's death, March 22, 1832, made him eager to get back to his beloved Tweed. He had said to Irving, years before, "If I should not see the heather at least once a year, I think I should die." Returned to Abbotsford, he at first rallied, even thought of renewed labors; but when the pen dropped from his paralyzed fingers, he sank back among his pillows and wept. " Friends," he said, " don't let me expose myself; get me to bed — that's the only place." After lingering for a few months, he died on the 21st of September, 1832, and was buried in Dryburgh Abbey, the resting-place of his ancestors. A few days before his death he called Lockhart to his bedside. " My dear," he said, " be a good man, — be virtuous, — be religious, — be a good man. Nothing else will give you any comfort when you come to lie here."

Whether Scott's genius falls short of that of his great contemporaries, such as Coleridge, Byron, Shelley, is a matter for literary discussion; but the regularity of his life, instead of being certain disproof, as some ingeniously argue, is possibly the best evidence of great genius. For the perfect man might conceivably be not only the greatest genius, but also the person most in sympathy with his human surroundings; it is often the incompleteness rather than the greatness of genius which makes it inapt to social routine. Certainly it must be pleasant to all (except perhaps to those who are determined a genius must be eccentric) that Scott was a man without spot or blemish in the eyes of the unromantic world. His life is, indeed, reassuring, a veritable justification of genius, and no doubt a comfort, to boot, to those who would not object to a little genius along with their respectability. The normality of Scott's character, moreover, is doubly significant when it is remembered that he lived in the most wildly romantic period of English literature and that he himself was " the great Romancer." His heart was in an idealized past; his interest was always, as Mr. Chesterton has pointed out, not in the intricacies of impossible things, but in actual living — when all is said and done, the most romantic thing in the world. It was, indeed, this genuineness, this total absence of all make-believe in Scott, this real romantic spirit, in his life as well as in his work, which found him the first place in the hearts of his friends and readers. It is usually with a glow of generous exaggeration that one applies to a man the fine tribute of Antony to the dead Brutus; but in the case of Scott one is decently within bounds, one feels that even aged moderation would admit " the elements so mixt " in Scott, —

> " That Nature might stand up
> And say to all the world, This was a Man."

Mr. Andrew Lang, one of his best biographers, speaks, at the close, of " three generations who have warmed their hands at the hearth of his genius, who have drunk of his enchanted cup, and eaten of his fairy bread, and been happy through his gift."

WILLIAM WORDSWORTH

IT is hard for people of to-day, who are used to living with nature and studying it, to understand fully what a completely new message Wordsworth brought to the English-speaking peoples. Until the middle of the eighteenth century there was almost no serious interest in nature, and even then, in such poets as Gray, the new interest was comparatively on the surface — a comfortable, midsummer pleasure in gently rural things. Burns, in a certain sense as close to nature as any one, nevertheless treated it for the most part as a background. Cowper made indeed a great advance, and to him and Burns Wordsworth owed much. In all the Lake poet's predecessors, however, there was lacking his complete intimacy with nature, his loving interest in it, and especially his religious inspiration from it. Before his day nature had been only a companion, if not quite an impersonal thing; with him it became a prophet. Burns might love the " banks and braes of bonnie Doon," but he could not finish the poem without recalling a love for which " bonnie Doon " was merely a setting. Cowper might love the fair broad valley of the Ouse and the trees about Weston Underwood, but he loved his seclusion more. Wordsworth, in distinction, loved earnestly and simply the mere earth about him for its own sake; for the English Lakes he had the affection of a mediæval mystic for the Church. And to him is chiefly due the interest of the nineteenth century in the deeper meaning of nature, an interest which we to-day take for granted.

An understanding of this communion of Wordsworth's with nature is, in fact, essential in the briefest account of his life. For the mere facts of his existence — except for one dramatic moment in France — are uninteresting and meaningless without such an introduction. Born in the mountains of Cumberland, he returned thither when he was less than thirty and there lived, in almost uneventful simplicity, the remainder of his life. The reader who thirsts for the exploits of a Ralegh or the elopements of a Shelley finds little enough in Wordsworth. Yet this extremely simple life, when his communion with nature is understood, becomes one of the most interesting; those who really care for Wordsworth love him.

Few men, indeed, demand of the reader more initiation than Wordsworth does. No better method can be found than acquiring an intimacy with that part of England which meant so much to him; a fact especially borne out by those who have visited the Lakes — not via motorbus vociferous, but on foot into the inmost recesses that he loved — down the valley of the Duddon, along the banks of Esthwaite Water, or up the Langdale Valley to Blea Tarn. Among the mountains and lakes of this region, one catches at last glimpses of the man's true personality. But always it is necessary to

> " Bring with you a heart
> That watches and receives."

There is at first sight nothing very grand about the scenery of the Lake District, the whole of which covers an area of scarcely thirty miles square. The mountains are in fact very small. But so close together do they

stand, so profuse is the abundance of crag and waterfall
and lake, and so perfect are the proportions, that even
little peaks are remarkably impressive. At every hill-
top one is surprised by the view: a deep blue lake, a
" beck" chattering down a gorge, ribbons of silver water-
falls never dry on the green slopes, sheep grazing among
the gray, mist-covered crags of Helvellyn, a "tarn"
glistening high up in a mountain hollow. In spring the
dales are bright with flowers, and in late summer whole
hillsides are yellow with gorse and purple with heather.
But it is not the impressiveness so much as the almost
human personality of the region that " takes " one most,
a personality which grows and develops and, like a true
friend, is inexhaustible and inspiring. Little by little
one finds what Wordsworth found. To the visitor who
fails to do this Wordsworth is a shut book, an inpene-
trable mystery, not infrequently an object of derision.

Another thing that puts the wayfarer in the Lake
District into a Wordsworthian frame of mind is the
human life actually there. On all sides there is an atmosphere of industry and integrity, a communal spirit,
that the merest traveler cannot fail to remark. And as
one gradually becomes conscious of these things, gets to
know the simplicity and honesty of the people, one finds,
too, that one is getting to understand Wordsworth.

The traveler discovers, moreover, as if a happy addition to the original stock, a pleasant atmosphere of literary people. The road from Coniston all the way to
Keswick is a succession of shrines for the literary pilgrim. At Brantwood, on Coniston Water, Ruskin spent
his last years; Hawkshead, where Wordsworth went to
school, lies quaintly at the head of Esthwaite Water;
Dr. Thomas Arnold built at Fox How, between Amble-

side and Grasmere; near-by stand the houses once
occupied by Harriet Martineau and Felicia Hemans;
Hartley Coleridge lived at Nab Cottage, just below
Rydal Mount; and at Grasmere and Rydal are Wordsworth's homes. Farther on, at Keswick, stands Greta
Hall, the dwelling of Southey and Coleridge. All these
knew and revered the poet of the Lakes.

Cockermouth lies in the extreme northwest corner of
the Lake District, and there, on April 7, 1770, William
Wordsworth was born. His father was John Wordsworth, attorney at law, and his mother, Anne Cookson.
Of his sister Dorothy we shall see more later. Of his
three brothers, Richard, John, and Christopher, John
died when a young man, and Christopher lived to be
Master of Trinity College, Cambridge, and father of two
illustrious prelates, — Charles, Bishop of St. Andrew's,
and Christopher, Head Master of Harrow, Canon of
Westminster, and Bishop of Lincoln.

In his boyhood Wordsworth became an orphan, his
mother dying in 1778 and his father in 1784. He was
left, too, in considerable poverty, but intelligent and
generous uncles saw him through a good education. He
was sent, in 1779, to the grammar school at Hawkshead,
from which in October, 1787, he went up to St. John's
College, Cambridge.

The chief feature of Wordsworth's character is apparent from the first. While at Hawkshead, although
he showed a serious interest in studies, he displayed
much more a fondness for nature. Every spot about
Esthwaite Water and Windermere was explored. He
walked early with the rising sun, he spent hours alone
among the hills, he led his companions in quest of the
raven's nest. The experiences of this early period —

what he calls the "fair seed-time of my soul"—have been recorded by him in the *Prelude*.

>"Ere I had told ten birthdays,"

he says,

>>"'t was my joy
>>With store of springes o'er my shoulder hung
>>To range the open heights where woodcocks run
>>Along the smooth green turf."

He saw in nature

>"Gleams, like the flashings of a shield,"

and

>>"the earth
>>And common face of nature spake to him
>>Rememberable things."

He tells, too, how he would sometimes turn aside from his fellow-skaters

>"To cut across the reflex of a star
>That fled, and, flying still before me, gleamed
>Upon the glassy plain."

Of all these boyhood experiences perhaps the most significant was the vision of the "huge peak, black and huge,"—the top of Wetherlam,—that seemed to stride after him as he rowed across Esthwaite Water.

>"Huge and mighty forms, that do not live
>Like living men, moved slowly through the mind
>By day, and were a trouble to my dreams."

From then on he was a consecrated priest of nature. And as such he considered himself; "not in vain," he says to the Spirit of the Universe,—

>"By day or star light thus from my first dawn
>Of childhood didst thou intertwine for me
>The passions that build up the human soul;
>Not with the mean and vulgar works of man,
>But with high objects, with enduring things,—
>With life and nature—purifying thus

The elements of feeling and of thought,
And sanctifying, by such discipline,
Both pain and fear, until we recognize
A grandeur in the beatings of the heart."

" I made no vows, but vows
Were then made for me; bond unknown to me
Was given, that I should be, else sinning greatly,
A dedicated Spirit."

Wordsworth as a boy was perhaps too kindly dis-
posed to be called austere ; he had, however, a Miltonic
seriousness from the first. There was plenty of joyous-
ness in him, but little mirth, just as in the man there
was positively no humor. Yet it is a great error to
infer, as many have done from the calmness of his
writings, that he was a youth of little passion. His
nature was particularly sensitive and excitable, and the
calmness of later years was, as Mr. Myers has pointed
out, rather the result of a deliberate philosophy than of
coldness of temperament.

Cambridge did not have the transforming power
over Wordsworth that one might have expected. Just
at the close of the eighteenth century the old university
was peacefully asleep, and the poet drifted quietly
through its meditative atmosphere without any striking
experiences. The hold of his earlier life was strong
enough still to possess him, and he went forth, something more of a scholar, but still the Hawkshead boy,
unsophisticated in the ways of men and ignorant of
the great revolution that was transforming Europe. He
did not understand the language of these new things
— that was all. His noble and sensitive nature must
otherwise have responded instantly — as it later did —
to the message of France ; the Revolution as yet spoke
no prophecy to him.

He took the degree of B. A. in January, 1791, and with no settled occupation went to London. But for him London, too, had at first no message. Before he could grow up, before he could humanize his interest in nature, he must undergo an experience. The intricate, passionate life of a great city which meant so much to a man like Browning made only an external impression on Wordsworth. In November of the same year he went to France. There the Revolution was raging, but he passed through Paris almost unmoved. As Dr. Hancock has put it, he was like one coming late to a theatre; he failed to get the trend of the plot.

Finally at Orleans a transformation took place. There Wordsworth met the nobly-born republican general, Beaupuis. At first the ardor of Beaupuis did not appeal to him. One day, however, when they were walking together, the general pointed out a little girl leading a heifer, a type of the half-starved humanity ground down by the heel of the aristocracy. " It is for that," said Beaupuis, " that we are fighting." Immediately Wordsworth saw. From that moment his sympathy for the republican cause became a passion.

> " Bliss was it in that dawn to be alive,
> But to be young was very heaven ! "

he cried. He was eager even to throw in his lot with that of the republicans and to take up arms. Fortunately for him, however, friends called him back to England just as war between the two countries was imminent. But he had had *his* experience. He was a changed man.

Such a soul-searching ordeal was nevertheless not to be lightly passed through. When the young Republic and England came to war, when Wordsworth found all his fair hopes trailed in the mud by the new power without even the dignity of antiquity, he was thrown almost into despair. His eyes had been opened and he had beheld a nightmare. Nor did London, big, brutal, throbbing with intensest life, make the problem less complex; to take his puzzle there was like taking nitro-glycerine into a powder-magazine. It was impossible to return now to the childish faith; it was equally impossible to live with the nightmare.

After nearly two years of this confusion and despair Wordsworth found a twofold cure. The first was in intelligent thought; he turned instinctively to the philosophy of the movement. For a while the only logical plan seemed to be to follow William Godwin's theories, which asserted that reason was the sole guide. But cold reason in the light of facts had been as disastrous a leader as the undisciplined enthusiasm of Rousseau, who said that man should follow his simple, primitive instincts, that is, "return to nature;" the scheme in France had simply not worked. To a man of Wordsworth's sensitive, idealistic temperament, moreover, the harsh materialism which Godwin's doctrines implied was particularly distasteful. There were "strange misgivings" of the soul which it could in no way answer; there were higher instincts, elemental forebodings of a God and of a truth which veritably "passeth human understanding." Godwinism, pushed to its logical extreme by a man for whom the sky and the stars and the morning sun had any message, was absurd; and Wordsworth naturally fell back on nature, the firm, tried friend of his youth. In no merely figurative sense did he lift up his eyes unto the hills from whence came his help.

The other and far greater cure was found in the companionship of his sister Dorothy. In 1795 she came to live with him, and together they took a little house at Racedown, in Dorset. A fortunate bequest of £900 from a friend, Raisley Calvert, who died in 1795, and £1000 from his father's estate made it possible for Wordsworth to give himself up wholly to poetry. Here, under the influence of simple nature and his sister's loving sympathy, he again saw clearly. Those who think, however, that he regained his old *boyhood* faith miss the whole development of the *man ;* he rather acquired a new faith — the stronger, surer faith of a grown man, founded indeed on the imperishable revelations of his youth, but strengthened by a new interest in mankind. The conflict, to use an excellent, well-worn expression, had *humanized* him. Nature now carried a new, a fuller, a deeper meaning. "For I have learned," he says,

> "To look on nature, not as in the hour
> Of thoughtless youth ; but hearing oftentimes
> The still sad music of humanity,
> Nor harsh nor grating, though of ample power
> To chasten and subdue. And I have felt
> A presence that disturbs me with the joy
> Of elevated thoughts : a sense sublime
> Of something far more deeply interfused,
> And the round ocean and the living air,
> And the blue sky, and in the mind of man :
> A motion and a spirit, that impels
> All thinking things, all objects of all thoughts,
> And rolls through all things."

These lines, written on July 13, 1798, a few miles above Tintern Abbey, amount to a confession of faith.

During the next fifteen years, in fact, Wordsworth's best poetry was written. He had published as early as

1792 two poems, *The Evening Walk* and *Descriptive Sketches*, which attracted the attention of young Coleridge. At Racedown he finished *Guilt and Sorrow* and wrote a tragedy, *The Borderers*, and a poem called *The Ruined Cottage*, which he later inserted in *The Excursion*. In 1797 he and his sister moved to Alfoxden, not far from Nether-Stowey, in order to be near Coleridge, with whom he had developed a warm friendship. The next year appeared *The Lyrical Ballads*, started conjointly by the two poets to defray the expenses of a walking tour, but finally expanded into a volume. This book, which included *The Ancient Mariner*, almost wholly by Coleridge, and Wordsworth's *Lines Written above Tintern Abbey*, brought both writers into considerable notice, not only because of the admitted excellence of some of the poems, but because of such trivial pieces as *The Idiot Boy* and because of the preface's expounding a new theory of poetry, — that any topic, however homely, if taken from " real life," might be a poetic topic.

Wordsworth and his sister spent the following winter at Goslar, in Germany. *Ruth, Nutting, A Poet's Epitaph*, and *Lucy Gray* were written there, and The *Prelude*, an introduction to the long projected poem of *The Recluse*, was planned. The *Prelude*, dedicated to Coleridge, was not finished till 1805, and not published till after Wordsworth's death. The *Lucy Gray* poems, about which Wordsworth was singularly reticent, suggest by their earnest emotion some very real attachment. It has been remarked that it is ungenerous to inquire further ; it may be added that it is now also futile. *Lucy Gray* may after all have been only a type of various youthful idealizations of women rather

than a single person; still, there are some who, convinced of her individuality, will search for her as men
still seek the " dark lady " of Shakespeare's sonnets.

In December, 1799, when Wordsworth was just
under thirty years old, he returned to the Lakes, never
again to leave them for any great length of time. For
the first thirteen years of the century, except for a tour
in Scotland and a visit to Coleorton Hall, in Leicestershire, he lived in or near Grasmere. His first residence
there, with his sister, at Dove Cottage, has become one
of the most interesting of all literary shrines. It is a
pity, however, that the memorials are so exclusively to
the Wordsworths, for their successor, De Quincey, is
just as closely associated with the house. It is a little
white cottage, perched against a hillside, with the back
garden right under the second-floor windows, and with
diminutive, irregular, low-ceiled rooms.

It must have been a memorable experience to have
visited Wordsworth there. His closest friends and most
frequent visitors were Coleridge and Southey, who lived
at Keswick. On a rock at the end of Thirlmere, just
half way between Grasmere and Keswick, are cut significant initials — W. W., S. T. C., D. W., and M.
H. This rock, fragments of which are now pathetically
preserved in a cairn piled just beyond the straining-
well of its destroyer, the Manchester Water Company,
was their favorite meeting-place.

The initials M. H. stood for Mary Hutchinson, of
Penrith, to whom Wordsworth became engaged in 1800.
Two years later the marriage took place. It came just
at the flood-tide of his spiritual prosperity, when in his
greatest vigor and clearness of mind he was writing
down those records of his new and larger faith, when he

had just returned with a whole heart to the hills. Mary Wordsworth has, to be sure, been eclipsed in the mind of posterity by the more sensitive, more expressive Dorothy; but she was no less than Dorothy his constant companion and inspiration; — and something of a poet, too: it was she, in fact, who suggested the two most famous lines of that famous poem, *The Daffodils*, —

> " They flash upon that inward eye
> Which is the bliss of solitude."

In 1808 the growing family moved to Allan Bank, at the other end of the town. Three years were spent there, two more in the parsonage at Grasmere, and then, in 1813, the poet took up his last residence, at Rydal Mount, overlooking Rydal Water and commanding a fine view of distant Windermere. Here for thirty-seven years he lived his simple life, writing considerably, caring for his sister Dorothy, now become an invalid, laying out his garden and planting his trees, and walking with his friends and children among his well-loved hills.

In his later years Wordsworth was much visited by men of letters and admirers, to whom he had an ingenuous way of quoting only his own poetry. " Gradually it became apparent to me," says Carlyle, " that of transcendent unlimited there was, to this critic, probably but one specimen known, Wordsworth himself! " Sometimes the old poet went up to London, but except for his fascinating eye and an occasional flow of language he was not attractive to even literary London. Few men have been so wholly without humor. Dickens is reported to have said of him, " Dreadful old bore! " — a remark, it may be added, that reveals the limitations of Dickens as well as of Wordsworth. Carlyle was

almost as impatient of him, his monotonous remarks, his
feeble handshake, and called him a " small " though
" genuine " man, but did, in one or two phrases, strike
off a memorable picture of the old bard. " A man
recognizably of strong intellectual powers, strong character," the Scotchman says; " given to meditation, and
much contemptuous of the unmeditative world and its
noisy nothingnesses; had a fine limpid style of writing
and delineating, in his small way; a fine limpid vein of
melody too in him (as of an honest rustic fiddle, good,
and well-handled, but wanting two or more of the strings,
and not capable of much !)." Once Carlyle, in a discussion with Sterling, made some remarks, which he
thought would " perhaps please Wordsworth too," who
sat "almost next to me," but who " gave not the least sign
of that or any other feeling." Carlyle thus describes
him : "The eyes were not very brilliant, but they had
a quiet clearness; there was enough of brow and well-
shaped; rather too much of cheek ('horse face' I have
heard satirists say) ; face of squarish shape and decidedly longish, as I think the head itself was (its
'length' going horizontal); he was large-boned, lean,
but still firm-knit, tall and strong-looking when he stood,
a right good old steel-gray figure, with rustic simplicity and dignity about him." To do Wordsworth justice, allowance must be made for his great age (about
seventy) when Carlyle saw him, and for the grotesque
humor and occasional spleen of the limner. One more
glimpse, from Carlyle, cannot well be omitted, for its
own sake as well as for the picture of the poet: " I
look upwards, leftwards " (during dessert at a large
dinner-party), "the coast being luckily for a moment
clear; then, far off, beautifully screened in the shadow

of his vertical green shade, which was on the farther side of him, sat Wordsworth, silent, slowly but steadily gnawing some portion of what I judged to be raisins, with his eye and attention placidly fixed on these and these alone. The sight of whom, and of his rock-like indifference to the babble, quasi-scientific and other, with attention turned on the small practical alone, was comfortable and amusing to me, who felt like him but could not eat raisins."

The dining and the visitors, however, made up in reality a very minor feature of Wordsworth's life. At Rydal he lived in great simplicity. He was indeed never well off, for his poetry brought no addition to his slender income. In 1802 he received £1800 as his share of an old family debt then paid; and ten years later he was appointed distributor of stamps for Westmoreland, with £400 a year. On his resigning this position in 1842, Sir Robert Peel managed to get him a pension of £300 from the civil list. In 1827, moreover, Sir George Beaumont had begun his annual gift of £100 for a trip to Scotland.

Of the poems written between the *Lyrical Ballads* (1798) and Wordsworth's death (1850), a division, as has been suggested, can be conveniently made. For ten or fifteen years he was filled with the full inspiration of his message. After *Tintern Abbey* came many of his best lyrics — such as *To the Cuckoo, My Heart leaps up, To the Daisy, She was a Phantom of Delight, I Wandered Lonely as a Cloud,* — the song which a heart, so full as the lines written above Tintern prove his to have been, spontaneously gave forth. Many of his sonnets, too, — especially the patriotic ones in 1802 and 1803, — were composed in this his best period. Of his shorter narrative poems written at this time *Michael, Resolution and Independence, The Brothers*, and *Margaret* are the best known. In 1805 the *Ode to Duty* was written and in 1806 the *Ode on Intimations of Immortality* was finished. *The White Doe of Rylstone* belongs to the year 1808; *Laodamia* and *Dion* were both done in 1814, the year which may best be taken as the beginning of the second division. In this year was finished the *Excursion*, his longest poem, the second part of the projected *Recluse*, of which the *Prelude* had been made an introduction. The *Excursion*, like the *Prelude*, is a naïve statement in blank verse of his experiences and his philosophy, and to it we are indebted for much autobiography.

Even more important than the *Excursion*, in studying Wordsworth's life, is the great *Ode on Intimations of Immortality*. At first he states the theory that the boy, coming " from God, who is our home," is more wholly spiritual than the man ; then that the man, under the influence of material surroundings, daily must travel farther from the east, gradually grows away from spiritual things, loses the divine presence which in the boy " is not to be put by," comes at last to

> " Forget the glories he hath known,
> And that imperial palace whence he came."

If Wordsworth had stopped here, the philosophy of the poem would be dreary enough and incompatible with his other work ; it would have to be regarded as a freak, the offspring of a despondent mood. But he saves himself by contradicting himself, by saying that in us is " something that doth live," a " shadowy recollection " of the childhood glory.

> "Hence, in a season of calm weather,
> Though inland far we be,
> Our souls have sight of that immortal sea
> Which brought us hither."

There still exists that

> "primal sympathy
> Which having been must ever be."
>
> .   .   .   .
>
> "The innocent brightness of a new-born day
> Is lovely yet ;
> The clouds that gather round the setting sun
> Do take a sober coloring from an eye
> That hath kept watch o'er man's mortality."

Is not here a complete record of his childish idealism,
of his period of conflict and despair, and of his maturity that brought back the idealism tempered and tried
and infused with a love for man ? He could finally say,
at the end of the poem, —

> "To me the meanest flower that blows can give
> Thoughts that do often lie too deep for tears."

On account of this soberer faith that came with
" years that bring the philosophic mind," because of his
recanting from the wilder principles of the French
Revolution, Wordsworth was accused by some of desert-
ing the cause. Browning's *Lost Leader*, which the author himself would not admit to be the " very effigies " of
Wordsworth, has been no doubt responsible for an ac-
cusation so false. Wordsworth's change was the natural
result of maturity. Coleridge, too, recanted. All his
great contemporaries did so, in fact, except Byron and
Shelley, who were both constitutionally unable to put
up with social laws. It is ridiculous to think that Wordsworth ever deserted for " a handful of silver " or for

" a riband to stick in his coat ; " and of course Browning never meant that directly of *him*.

Until his death Wordsworth continued to write much. Among the great mass of indifferent poems in this second period (1814–50) there shine out *The Duddon Sonnets* (1820) ; one or two odes, such as that *To a Skylark*, beginning " Ethereal minstrel" (1825) ; and *Yarrow Revisited* (1831). During the years 1821–22 he wrote a great quantity of sonnets collected under the title *Ecclesiastical Sonnets*, and during a trip to Italy in 1837 he composed several poems included under the title *Memorials of a Tour in Italy*. In 1829–30 he spent much time over a translation of part of the *Æneid*. At this time, too, he wrote considerable prose, the most interesting of which is his description of the *Scenery of the Lakes* (1822). His magnum opus, *The Recluse*, was never finished. Of the three books planned, the first, called *Home at Grasmere*, — to go between *The Prelude* and *The Excursion*, — was published in 1888. A large part of what was intended for the third book is scattered among other poems. A fitting recognition finally accorded him came in the appointment to the post of poet-laureate, left vacant by the death of Southey in 1843.

Wordsworth's last days were very tranquil. At the age of eighty, after taking a cold which developed pleurisy, he died quietly at noon, on April 23, 1850. His grave was put between those of his sister Dorothy and his daughter Dora in Grasmere Churchyard, and to these was added, nine years later, that of his wife.

In spite of the laureateship and of his great age, the poet did not win very wide recognition till years after his death. There was not enough of the spectacular in

him to storm popular citadels, when Scott, Coleridge,
and Byron were claiming attention. And immediately
after his death Tennyson, with a more universal voice,
held the ear of England. It was necessary, moreover,
for the world, under the guidance of such excellent
interpreters as Matthew Arnold, to grow to a comprehension of his meaning. There is in him a splendid
spiritual power, an imperishable word to those who will
truly listen.

> " He is retired as noontide dew,
>   Or fountain in a noonday grove :
>   And you must love him, ere to you
>   He will seem worthy of your love.
>
> " The outward shows of sky and earth,
>   Of hill and valley, he has viewed;
>   And impulses of deeper birth
>   Have come to him in solitude.
>
> " In common things that round us lie
>   Some random truths he can impart; —
>   The harvest of a quiet eye
>   That broods and sleeps on his own heart."

SAMUEL TAYLOR COLERIDGE

" As to my shape," Coleridge said in a letter describing himself, " 't is a good shape enough, if measured — but my gait is awkward, and the walk of the whole man indicates *indolence capable of energies*." Here are expressed the two most striking things about Coleridge : he was a very capable man, and he somehow usually failed to achieve the results he promised. He was one of the keenest critics of his time, he was a widely versed scholar, and he had a poetic skill rarely surpassed. Nor did he fail for want of divine fire ; back of his scholarship and skill lay an especially bright genius. But physical irresolution possessed him from the first ; he fell into indolence and then into opium-eating ; and from a condition where he saw the bright visions of youth pass unrecorded, he sank rapidly to a condition where the visions grew feebler and more indistinct. As if to make his life more tragic, his reason remained good to the end ; he saw clearly the awful penalty he was paying. There is something very sad in the humor of Lamb, in writing of Coleridge in 1810 : " Coleridge has powdered his hair, and looks like Bacchus, Bacchus ever sleek and young. He is going to turn sober, but his clock has not struck yet." As early as 1794, when he was only twenty-two, Coleridge saw and expressed the tragedy of his life : —

> " Sloth-jaundiced all ! and from my graspless hand
> Drop Friendship's precious pearls, like hour-glass sand."

Yet in spite of this curse of irresolution, Coleridge

did manage, because of a very great genius within him, to write a little great prose and poetry. Most of his work, however, is unfinished — as his whole life was. On this account people to-day are prone to underestimate his genius. It must have been necessary to know the man, to hear him talk, to see his eye, if one would comprehend his real magnitude. For in discourse, which does not require the resolute girding up of loins that writing does, he was at his best. Among his contemporaries he would have been the undisputed successor of Dr. Johnson — if such a dictator had been possible after the French Revolution.

Samuel Taylor Coleridge, the youngest of thirteen children, was born October 21, 1772, at Ottery-St. Mary's in Devonshire. His father, the Rev. John Coleridge, was vicar of the village and a schoolmaster. His mother, John Coleridge's second wife, was Anne Bowdon. So many poets are spoken of as precocious in boyhood that a superlative is necessary in Coleridge's case. No great writer of the nineteenth century, except the marvelous Macaulay, was so precocious a child. He mixed little, he says, with other boys, but spent most of his time reading " incessantly " or acting out what he had read. "And I used to lie by the wall and mope ; and my spirits used to come upon me sudden, in a flood ; and then I was accustomed to run up and down the churchyard and act over again all I had been reading, to the docks and the nettles and the rank grass." The Rev. John, fearing the effect of fairy tales on the imaginative infant, burned the child's books. " So," he goes on, " I became a dreamer, and acquired an indisposition to all bodily activity. I was fretful and inordinately passionate ; . . . despised and hated by the boys . . .

and flattered and wondered at by all the old women. And before I was eight years old I was a *character*." These are important words; they show in the child the man almost completely foreshadowed : the flashing, imaginative mind, the great learning, the irresolution, the disaster, and Coleridge the *character*. For of all his great contemporaries only Shelley can compete with him in strangeness of ways.

Such a boy, as may be imagined, was an odd figure at school. He was at a dame school from three to six, and at his father's grammar school from six to nine. Then his father died, and with him even a meagre financial support. Through Mr. Francis Buller, however, an appointment to Christ Hospital School in London was obtained, and on July 18, 1782, Coleridge became a blue-coat boy. The first six weeks were spent in the Junior School at Hertford, but in September he was removed to the Under Grammar-School in London and initiated into the mysteries of " milk porritch, blue and tasteless," and " pease soup, coarse and choking." "Come back into my memory," writes his schoolfellow Charles Lamb in *Christ's Hospital Five and Thirty Years Ago*, "like as thou wert in the dayspring of thy fancies, with hope like a fiery column before thee — the dark pillar not yet turned — Samuel Taylor Coleridge — Logician, Metaphysician, Bard! — How have I seen the casual passer through the cloisters stand still, entranced with admiration (while he weighed the disproportion between the *speech* and the *garb* of the young Mirandula), to hear thee unfold, in thy deep and sweet intonations, the mysteries of Jamblichus or Plotinus (for even in those years thou waxedst not pale at such philosophic draughts), or reciting Homer in his

Greek, or Pindar — while the walls of the old Grey
Friars reëchoed to the accents of the *inspired charity
boy !* " Lamb tells, too, of the hot summer nights when
Coleridge gazed from the roof at the stars, and of the
whole holidays when they roamed the fields about London or went to see the grim sights of the Tower; and
he recounts, with incomparable drollery, the doings of
the Head Master, the Rev. James Boyer, with his "Ods
my life, sirrah! I have a great mind to whip you!"
When, years afterwards, Coleridge heard that this rig-
orous teacher was on his death-bed, he remarked: "Poor
J. B.! May all his faults be forgiven, and may he be
wafted to bliss by little cherub boys, all heads and
wings, with no *bottoms* to reproach his sublunary infirmities."

Coleridge was a brilliant if wayward scholar, and he
won easily a Christ Hospital "Exhibition" Scholarship
at Jesus College, Cambridge, which he entered in the
fall of 1791. He passed most of his time there till 1794,
but his attendance was irregular and he never took a
degree. He was of course in the forefront of those interested in the Revolution, and his rooms soon became
a centre for youthful philosophers, poets, and champions
of liberal views. A minute of a Literary Society is
doubly significant: "Time before supper was spent in
hearing Coleridge repeat some original poetry (he having neglected to write his essay, which is therefore to
be produced next week)." First, it is evident that his
verse was already a matter for admiration among his
friends; indeed, he had already written (1793), besides
many imitations and pieces of little merit, his *Lines
on an Autumnal Evening*, and his poem *To Fortune*
had just appeared in the *Morning Chronicle*. Second,

it is plain that he had already begun to neglect things; and there is no record that " next week " ever came for that essay.

Coleridge's longest absence from Cambridge was during the winter of 1793–94, when he enlisted as Silas Tomkyn Comberbach in the 15th Regiment of Light Dragoons. This sudden departure was brought on by debts and despondency. He made a very sorry horseman, but he managed by writing love-letters for his comrades to get his horse and accoutrements cleaned for him. In two months, however, he had had enough; by April, 1794, his discharge was procured; and after being admonished, he was reinstated by the Master of Jesus College.

The following summer and fall brought two important events into Coleridge's life — Pantisocracy and his love affair with Mary Evans. The first was a scheme concocted by Southey, Coleridge, Burnett, and Lovell — a plan born of the socialistic dreams that the French Revolution inspired in youthful minds. Briefly stated, " Twelve gentlemen of good education and liberal principles are to embark with twelve ladies in April next" for some " delightful part of the new back settlements " of America. The banks of the Susquehanna were the chosen spot. Here all were to enjoy the fruits of the soil and freedom of thought and action, out of which, they somehow imagined, was to arise a sort of Utopian blessedness. But the expedition never started, because at first funds were lacking, to supply which Coleridge and Southey took ardently to writing and to lecturing at Bristol, and because later there were disagreements, and ardor cooled.

Coleridge's love for Mary Evans seems to have been

long-standing and sincere — deeper in fact than any affection he later felt. In the summer of 1794, with his
head full of Pantisocracy, he had, to be sure, paid court
to Sarah Fricker, sister of Southey's betrothed. But the
following winter his love for Mary Evans returned and
he rallied a forlorn hope in a letter of direct proposal.
She refused him, however; yet his quiet manner of accepting the conditions, so far as his letter of reply is
any indication, was very creditable.

Cambridge was become, as might be expected, a place
of slight charm for him, and about the middle of December, 1794, he left it for good. The winter was
spent in unsettled life in London, where his work was
chiefly writing sonnets for the *Morning Chronicle*. It
was at this time that he passed those rare evenings with
Charles Lamb at "The Salutation." "*Those were* days
(or nights)," said Lamb, "but they were marked with
a white stone. Such were his extraordinary powers,
that when it was time for him to go and be married,
the landlord entreated him to stay, and offered him
free quarters if he would only talk."

Coleridge evidently did feel it was time to go and be
married. And so — Mary Evans failing — he renewed
suit with unbecoming haste to Sarah Fricker. He was
at Bristol with Southey early in 1795, and more lectures and Pantisocracy followed. On the 4th of October of the same year he was married to Miss Fricker
and moved into a cottage at Clevedon near the Somer-
set coast.

Among the literary results of the life in the West
were the publication of *Robespierre* in 1794, a play
written conjointly by Coleridge and Southey, and the
acquaintance with Amos Cottle, a bookseller who in-

spired Byron's " Phœbus! What a name!" In March,
1796, Cottle brought out Coleridge's *Poems on Various Subjects*, which included most of his earlier verse
and *Religious Musings*.

At the suggestion of friends enthusiastic over Coleridge's liberal views, the poet made a tour of the North
to secure subscriptions for his proposed periodical,
The Watchman. He preached by the way, he says,
" as a hireless volunteer, in a blue coat and white waistcoat, that not a rag of the woman of Babylon might
be seen on me. For I was at that time and long after
. . . a zealous Unitarian in religion." He returned
with nearly a thousand names, and *The Watchman*
appeared on March 1, 1796. But it came to a speedy
death with the tenth issue on May 13. " The reason
is short and satisfactory," says the " Address to the
Reader:" " the work does not pay its expenses."

During the following autumn Coleridge first touched
opium. He had been suffering from depression and
neuralgia, and on the 3d of November he took " between 60 and 70 drops of laudanum," he wrote to his
friend Poole, " and sopped the Cerberus just as his
mouth began to open." True, it was some years before
taking opium became a habit, but he had now learned
the terrible cure, to which he so helplessly turned when
other ills combined with bodily to tempt him.

There followed on this period of depression, nevertheless, the brightest and most productive days of Coleridge's life. The best part of his friendship with
Wordsworth, his greatest poetic work, and his most
conspicuous growth all belong to the next five years.
After 1802 domestic difficulties, estrangement from
friends, shiftless and injurious habits, and the loss of

his poetic gift crowded ruin upon him; he was never again quite his own man. But in 1797, when he and Mrs. Coleridge moved with their infant Hartley to a house at Stowey, he was still rising to greatness.

Coleridge first met Wordsworth in June, 1797, when the latter was living with his sister Dorothy at Racedown, in Dorset. A close friendship at once possessed all three. Wordsworth was in Coleridge's eyes the noblest man alive — the only man to whom he always granted superiority. There was, on the other hand, a fire and a fascination about the young preacher and poet of Stowey which took the Wordsworths completely, which brought them indeed to Alfoxden, near Stowey, to live. Dorothy Wordsworth thus describes Coleridge: "He is a wonderful man. His conversation teems with soul, mind, and spirit. . . . At first I thought him very plain, that is for about three minutes: he is pale, thin, has a wide mouth, thick lips, and not very good teeth, longish, loose-growing, half-curling rough black hair. But if you hear him speak for five minutes, you think no more of them. His eye is large and full, and not very dark, but gray — such an eye as would receive from a heavy soul the dullest expression; but it speaks every emotion of his animated mind; it has more of 'the poet's eye in fine frenzy rolling' than I ever witnessed." And Coleridge, in describing himself to Thelwall, says: "As to me, my face, unless animated by immediate eloquence, expresses great sloth, and great, indeed almost idiotic, good nature. 'T is a mere carcase of a face: fat, flabby, and expressive chiefly of inexpression. . . . I cannot breathe through my nose, so my mouth with sensual thick lips is almost always open."

But before the great production which resulted from the friendship with Wordsworth, the second edition of Coleridge's poems was published in the summer of 1797. In the same volume were verses by Charles Lamb, his friend of school-days, and by Charles Lloyd, a sensitive, melancholy youth who had been living as a kind of disciple with Coleridge. Soon after this Coleridge quarreled with Lloyd, and as a result was estranged for a time from Lamb. During the same summer Sheridan asked Coleridge to write a play for Drury Lane, and by October *Osorio* was finished. It was then rejected, but came up successfully sixteen years later in the rewritten *Remorse*.

Coleridge's greatest achievement, *The Ancient Mariner*, which alone would insure his position as a very great poet, was the first fruit of the friendship with Wordsworth. In November, 1797, the three friends went on a walking tour through North Devon, and to defray expenses hit on writing a joint poem. Coleridge rapidly sketched a plan and soon took to himself the greater part of the work. The poem, still unfinished, was not sent to the *Monthly Magazine* as proposed, but "grew and grew," says Wordsworth. Finally, on the 23d of the following March, Coleridge went to dine at Alfoxden and took with him the finished ballad — "inimitable," as he himself called it. The poem, for some time very unpopular, but now among the best known in the language, was published as part of Coleridge's small contribution to the *Lyrical Ballads*, brought out by the two poets in September, 1798.

The spirit of poetry was indeed on Coleridge as never before or since. In 1797 he began *Christabel*, like most of his work never finished, and the following year

he contributed to the *Morning Post* some of his
best work, — the *Ode to France*, *Frost at Midnight*,
and *Fears in Solitude*. Coleridge, who had been, as
Wordsworth, an enthusiastic champion of the French
Revolution, had now recanted, as had his friend, when
he saw France —

> " Mix with kings in the low lust of sway,
> Yell in the hunt, and share the murderous prey."

In April of the same year the quarrel with Lloyd had
driven the dejected Coleridge to " a lonely farmhouse
between Porlock and Linton." There he had recourse
to an " anodyne." One of the results was another link
in the chain of the habit about to possess him inex-
orably ; the other result was *Kubla Khan*. For Coleridge dreamed a whole poem and proceeded, on awaking
from the opium dream, to write it down. When, however, he had written fifty-four lines he was called out
on business, and later the marvelous vision had fled.
Yet there remains the perfect fragment.

Professor Brandl has pointed out how common
melancholia, depression, and overwrought imagination
were among writers at the close of the eighteenth century; how common indeed was the opium cure. The
lives of Dr. Johnson, Collins, Fergusson, Burns, Cowper, Blake, Coleridge, Lamb, Lloyd, De Quincey, Byron, Shelley, Leigh Hunt, and Keats (not to mention
minor authors) — all were touched by a haunting sadness. Of these De Quincey and Coleridge were conspicuous as opium-eaters ; but one feels that almost any
of these men, by the slightest twisting of the threads
of life, might have shared a similar fate. To-day such
a list would read like a catalogue of degenerates ; but
one must not judge too harshly of men whom imagina-

tion possessed at times as a nightmare. It is indeed
to the great credit of many that they waved back so
bravely the insidious comfort.

To return to Coleridge in 1798. He had now become
a considerable figure. Nearly every Sunday he preached
in Unitarian chapels, drawing by his ardor and eloquence many young men. How marvelously he talked
may be guessed from the admiration of young William
Hazlitt, who heard him preach in Shrewsbury: " The
preacher then launched into his subject like an eagle
dallying with the wind."

In the fall of this year, just as the *Lyrical Ballads*
were coming out, he joined the Wordsworths in a trip
to Germany, with the purpose of getting the language
and the philosophy of that country. On reaching the
continent, the Wordsworths went to Goslar for a dismal
winter; Coleridge to Ratzeburg to learn the language.
Early in 1799 he moved to Göttingen, and there, at
the university, worked "harder than, I trust in God
Almighty, I shall ever have occasion to work again."
He became a great student of German metaphysics —
in fact, was largely responsible for introducing them to
the English. He always, however, spoke German with
an "abominable accent," and referred constantly, it
is said, to a pocket-dictionary. After a walking tour
through the Harz Mountains he returned to Stowey in
July, 1799.

But Coleridge did not stay long at home. From the
English Lakes, where he had been visiting Wordsworth,
he went to London to write political articles for *The
Morning Post* and *The Courier*. He did work consistently hard for a time, and so well that Stuart offered
him half shares in the two papers; "but I told him

I would not give up the country and the lazy reading of old folios for two thousand times two thousand pounds." He was working, too, on a translation of Schiller's trilogy, *Wallenstein*, a work which, as time went on, filled him with "unutterable disgust," but which he managed to finish by the following April.

In July, 1800, he moved with his family to Greta Hall, Keswick, where Southey was already living. The two families shared the house with tolerable amicability, a fact which does great credit to the methodical Southey. There is a story that Southey went every now and then to his friend's study to retrieve chairs which Coleridge had in all friendliness appropriated.

At first Coleridge was in high spirits. The scenery about Keswick pleased him much, and the Wordsworths, now living near-by at Grasmere, were still his best friends. One gets little glimpses of the life in Dorothy Wordsworth's journal: "At eleven o'clock Coleridge came when I was walking in the still, clear moonshine in the garden. He came over Helvellyn. . . . We sat and chatted till half-past three." Another time: "We were very merry. . . . William read *Ruth*." It was under this inspiration that Coleridge wrote the second part of *Christabel*.

The following winter, however, brought sickness, bodily and mental. He suffered greatly from rheumatic pains and swollen knee-joints. The unhappiness in his home, too, began seriously about this time. Mrs. Coleridge's only fault, it was said, was fretfulness — not without cause, for she had much to bear in the irresolution of her husband, especially when her sister, Edith Southey, offered such a contrast in fortune. Yet, as Mr. Dykes Campbell points out, "fretting is one of the habits which bring about consequences that seem disproportionate." Coleridge was no doubt chiefly to blame, but his wife brought to him, besides fretfulness, no sympathy and no comprehension; and it is not in the least remarkable that what had at first been merely feeble love had not only cooled into indifference, but had hardened into dislike. Coleridge perhaps owed her consideration, but that was not to be expected from a sick man. A thinly-lined purse, moreover, in spite of the yearly pension of £150 which the Wedgewoods had given him in order that he might write poetry, added to his cares. He sought in opium relief at first from bodily pain, then from mental and spiritual. Sometimes there were bright moments of regained health, of hope and renewed purpose, but they were usually forerunners of further sickness and dejection. It was in the latter spirit that he wrote, in the fall of 1801, his *Ode to Dejection*, one of the saddest poems in the English language, a poem which marks the end of his strongest poetic impulse; it records

> " A grief without a pang, void, dark, and drear,
> A stifled, drowsy, unimpassioned grief,
> Which finds no natural outlet, no relief,
> In word, or sigh, or tear."

Greta Hall had now become almost intolerable, and much of Coleridge's time was spent at Dove Cottage with the Wordsworths. Once he walked vigorously through Scotland, doing " 263 miles in eight days, in the hope of forcing the disease into the extremities. . . . While I am in possession of my will and my reason, I can keep the fiend at arm's length; but with the night my horrors commence. During the whole of my journey, three nights out of four, I have fallen asleep struggling and resolving to lie awake, and awaking have blest the scream which delivered me from the reluctant sleep."

The story of Coleridge's life has here reached its climax; in the *Ode to Dejection* the catastrophe is already shadowed forth. The "dark pillar" Lamb writes of has now been turned. The rest of his existence — dragged through thirty years — is the story of projects deferred and promises broken, of family discord and of moral weakness. Yet one is too apt to make much of the contrasts, to catch at the sensational and in this case condemning incidents. There were many bright years scattered through — notably 1809, 1817, and the last years. Out of the wreck of his earlier genius there arises finally the sage of Highgate, the wonderful talker who drew all wise men to hear him — a little infirm and broken perhaps, "an archangel slightly damaged," as Lamb quaintly puts it — but still an archangel, still the most marvelous, the most dominating figure of his day.

During the years 1802–04, to return to the order of events, Coleridge was more than ever ill and dejected. He planned a trip to the Azores, he purposed to write for periodicals, to finish *Christabel*, he talked of a great work, *Organum verè Organum* — but nothing came of the projects. He did finally get off for Malta in the spring of 1804. The climate, however, did not agree with him as he had hoped, and after a year and a half there — during part of which one is surprised to find him serving as acting secretary to the Tory governor, Sir Alexander Ball — he returned via Italy to England.

But he did not go directly home; "he recoils so much," said Wordsworth, "from the thought of domesticating with Mrs. Coleridge." That winter he and his

wife agreed to a kind of separation. Coleridge saw her
frequently again, not without friendliness, but the
breach was never really mended. Indeed, he had become
unfit to look after a home. " He ought not to have a
wife or children," Charles Lamb wrote to Crabb Robinson ; " he should have a sort of diocesan care of the
world — no parish duty."

Towards the end of 1808, during a suspension of
opium-taking while he was living with the Wordsworths,
Coleridge rallied himself to the project of bringing
out a weekly periodical. In June, 1809, although six
months behind the promise in the prospectus, *The
Friend* began to appear. But No. III came out seven
weeks late, and the scheme fell through altogether with
No. XXVII (March 15, 1810). The mere fact of composition at Grasmere and publication at the distant village of Penrith, connected by no direct post, was sufficient to forecast the failure which Coleridge's delays
made certain.

In October, 1810, he joined Basil Montagu, who was
returning to London, and thus, except for a short visit
in 1812, left Greta Hall for good. He lived almost
wholly until 1816 at the house of John Morgan, a sympathetic friend who dwelt at No. 7, Portland Place,
Hammersmith. At this time he took up journalism
again, writing rather intermittently for the *Courier*.

But the greatest events of these years were the production of *Remorse* and the *Lectures*. Lord Byron got
the Drury Lane Committee to accept *Remorse*, the rewritten *Osorio*, and it was put on the stage January
23, 1813. It ran for twenty nights and Coleridge made
by it £400. The *Lectures* on Shakespeare, unwritten
and for the most part unprepared, but among the most

brilliant achievements of his life, were given in the fall
and winter of 1812. During the following two years
similar lectures — conversational, brilliant — were given
in Bristol. Frequently Coleridge came late — at Bristol
two or three days late. There is an amusing story,
illustrative of his powers, telling how, some years later,
he received one morning a letter asking him to deliver
a lecture that very evening — on what subject was not
indicated. He got there on time for once, and was much
astonished when the president of the London Philosophical Society announced to a crowded hall: "Mr.
Coleridge will deliver a lecture on 'The Growth of the
Individual Mind.'" "A pretty stiff subject," Coleridge
whispered to Gillman, who had accompanied him; but,
says Gillman, "he plunged at once into his lecture —
and most brilliant, eloquent, and logically consecutive
it was." Coleridge's monopoly of conversation for thirty
years had not been in vain. These apparently careless
talks have established his fame as a critic.

In 1814 miseries beset him again. He had shaken
the affection of most of his friends and had brought on
himself censure from Southey. He often neglected to
answer letters, lacked sometimes even the courage to
read them. The education of his sons was left largely
to kind friends. He talks again of a great work, this
time on "Christianity, the one true philosophy," pro-
poses to write for the *Courier*, and does nothing. In
the fall the Morgans accompanied him to Calne, Wiltshire, and there, thanks to Mrs. Morgan, who did much
towards breaking him of the opium-habit, he regained
sufficient vigor to get ready his *Biographia Literaria*
— a history of his thought rather than of his life — and
the *Sibylline Leaves*, published finally in 1817.

There is but one more chapter to Coleridge's life. In April, 1816, he moved to the house of Dr. Gillman in Highgate, near Hampstead, the haunt of Keats and Leigh Hunt, where he "played," wrote Lamb to Wordsworth, " at leaving off laud-m." Here, except for a few brief visits and a trip up the Rhine with the Wordsworths in 1828, he lived the rest of his life. He was too far shattered to leave off laudanum altogether, but Dr. Gillman superintended and restricted the doses ; so that Coleridge passed his last years in comparatively even health.

It must not be imagined, however, that he spent this time in comfortable opulence. He was never well off. The Wedgewood pension had been withdrawn in 1812, and Coleridge had been living on the charity of the Morgans and what little, his lectures and writings brought him. " Woe is me ! " he wrote in 1818, " that at 46 I am under the necessity of appearing as a lecturer." Poverty, too, spurred him to write. In 1817 was published the drama *Zapolya*, though it was never acted. To the years 1816 and 1817 belong the two *Lay Sermons*, indicating Coleridge's complete change from his early radical views to faith in the institution of the English Church. At Highgate he resorted to a kind of philosophic teaching, the few members of his class paying what they liked. This class later developed into the following of enthusiastic young men who hung on every precept. His *Aids to Reflection*, published in the spring of 1825, was hailed by them with delight. About the same time he was appointed to an associateship in the Royal Society of Literature, a nomination which brought him a hundred guineas a year, and when this **was** lost on the death of George IV, John Hookham

Frere made it up to him annually. In consequence Coleridge wrote less and talked more. There was still much said of the *Magnum Opus*, to fill several volumes, but nothing came of it. The only important publication, in fact, between 1825 and his death was his collected *Poetical and Dramatic Works* in 1828. The year after his death, his nephew, Henry Nelson Coleridge, brought out *Table Talk*, an interesting record of Coleridge's *obiter dicta* during the last twelve years (1822–34). The *Confessions of an Inquiring Spirit*, written by Coleridge about 1824, was first published in 1840.

During the days at Gillman's the philosopher became a picturesque and well-known figure. Some of his old friends now began to see more of him — especially Charles Lamb, mellowed into a kindly age. His wife and daughter came to the " Grove," as Gillman's house was called, to visit him ; his nephew was often there ; a remarkable young man, Joseph Henry Green, became his ardent disciple, and sought, after the master's death, to express the inexpressible Coleridgean system of philosophy ; and many other young men, such as John Sterling, were under the spell of his talk and thought. Others who sought out the Sage of Highgate were Landor, whose *Imaginary Conversations* were now appearing ; Edward Irving, a brilliant young preacher; Harriet Martineau, from the Lakes ; Emerson, whose youthful Unitarianism found no favor with the recanter ; Crabb Robinson, a kind of Boswell to Wordsworth and Coleridge, and Carlyle, just rising to prominence. After 1824, " Thursday " became a regular evening for such visitors.

Carlyle has left the world a famous picture of the

aged Coleridge. Carlyle, it must be remembered, was
gloomy and vigorous, had plenty of philosophy of his
own, and was intolerant of senility; yet his picture, if
only for the outward aspect, is worth quoting in part,
and in places does, after all, much justice to Coleridge.
" Coleridge," he says, " sat on the brow of Highgate
Hill in those years looking down on London and its
smoke tumult like a sage escaped from the inanity of
life's battle, attracting towards him the thoughts of
innumerable brave souls still engaged there. . . . He
was thought to hold — he alone in England — the key
of German and other Transcendentalisms; knew the
sublime secret of believing by the ' reason ' what the
' understanding ' had been obliged to fling out as in-
credible; and could still, after Hume and Voltaire had
done their best and worst with him, profess himself an
orthodox Christian, and say and point to the Church
of England, with its singular old rubrics and surplices,
at Allhallowtide, *Esto perpetua.* A sublime man, who
alone in those dark days had saved his crown of spiritual manhood, escaping from the black materialisms
and revolutionary deluges with ' God, Freedom, Immortality,' still his; a king of men. The practical intellects of the world did not much heed him, or carelessly
reckoned him a metaphysical dreamer; but to the rising
spirits of the young generation he had this dusky sublime character, and sat there as a kind of Magus, girt
in mystery and enigma." " Brow and head," Carlyle
goes on, " were round and of massive weight, but the
face was flabby and irresolute. The deep eyes, of a
light hazel, were as full of sorrow as of inspiration;
confused pain looked mildly from them, as in a kind
of mild astonishment. The whole figure and air, good

and amiable otherwise, might be called flabby and
irresolute; expressive of weakness under possibility of
strength. He hung loosely on his limbs, with knees
bent, and stooping attitude; in walking he rather shuf-
fled than decisively stept; and a lady once remarked
he never could fix which side of the garden-walk would
suit him best, but continually shifted, corkscrew fashion, and kept trying both; a heavy-laden, high-aspiring,
and surely much-suffering man. . . . I still recollect
his ' object ' and ' subject ' . . . and how he sang and
snuffled them into ' om-m-ject,' and ' sum-m-ject ' with
a kind of solemn shake or quaver as he rolled along."
And once more: " He began anywhere; you put some
question to him, made some suggestive observation; instead of answering this, or decidedly setting out towards
an answer of it, he would accumulate formidable ap-
paratus, logical swim-bladders, transcendental life-pre-
servers, and other precautionary and vehiculatory gear
for setting out; perhaps did at last get under way —
but was swiftly solicited, turned aside by the flame of
some radiant new game on this hand or on that into
new courses, and ever into new."

There is a story, very likely untrue, but very amusing
and exaggeratedly characteristic of Coleridge's length
of discourse. Lamb, the story runs, once met him in a
crowded street, was caught by the button, and drawn
into a doorway. Thereupon the Sage of Highgate, still
holding to the button, began a dissertation, and, after
his manner, closed his eyes " as he rolled along." Lamb
was interested enough, but his business was pressing,
so he cut off the button and escaped. Hours later, it
is said, he returned to find Coleridge still holding the
button, still in impassioned utterance.

Not long before his death, Coleridge was blessed by
a hitherto unknown serenity. But it was not for a great
while. On July 20, 1834, he fell ill, and for a few days
suffered much. At the last, however, he was quiet and
happy. He died on July 25, and was buried in Highgate. "His great spirit haunts me," wrote Wordsworth
years later. "Never saw I his likeness, nor probably the
world can see again;" and under the stress of more
immediate grief he paid this tribute to his friends Coleridge and Lamb: —

> "Nor has the rolling year twice measured,
> From sign to sign, its steadfast course,
> Since every mortal power of Coleridge
> Was frozen at its marvellous source;

> "The rapt One, of the godlike forehead,
> The heaven-eyed creature sleeps in earth:
> And Lamb, the frolic and the gentle,
> Has vanished from his lonely hearth.

> "Like clouds that rake the mountain-summits,
> Or waves that own no curbing hand,
> How fast has brother followed brother
> From sunshine to the sunless land."

CHARLES LAMB

"I was born," says Lamb, "and passed the first seven years of my life, in the Temple." These words tell a great part of Lamb's story. No other man except Dr. Johnson gives one such intimate, easy acquaintance with the innermost places of the "city," from Fenchurch Street to Temple Bar. And from no other life do we get so delightful and familiar a glimpse of the literary people of his day — the day of Wordsworth, Coleridge, Southey, De Quincey, and Keats. But the quality which Lamb possesses above all others is the power to give, in his letters, real life and substance to the lesser writers of his day; with him we meet that whole society of strange and fascinating men and see them again moving about the streets of London — such men as Hazlitt, Landor, and Leigh Hunt; Lloyd, the misanthropic poet; H. C. Robinson, the indefatigable diarist; Godwin, the bankrupt philosopher; Tom Hood, "that half Hogarth," as Lamb called him; Haydon, the florid artist; Taylor and Hessey, proprietors of the *London Magazine* and friends of genius; Moxon, the publisher; the Cowden Clarkes, of Enfield, friends of Keats; Fanny Kelly and Charles Kemble, from the stage; and Talfourd, lawyer, dramatist, and first biographer of Lamb. And how many others, forgotten but for Charles Lamb, come to life at his name! — Barton, the Quaker poet; Thomas Manning, the first Englishman to enter Llassa, Thibet; Valentine Le Grice, friend of boyhood days and brilliant punster; James Kenney, the dramatist; George Burnett, Pantisocrat, who died in a work-house; Thomas Barnes, editor of *The Times;* the Burneys, incomparable at whist; and poor George Dyer, kindly, half-mad poet, hugging "his intolerable flannel vestment closer about his poetic loins" — a fellow infinitely picturesque. Of most of these and of many more Lamb was the intimate friend; by every one he was beloved.

It is this lovable quality in Lamb, in fact, which is his most striking characteristic. "Val" Le Grice noticed — and every one repeats it because it is so true — that men rarely spoke of Lamb except as "Charles Lamb," and Le Grice found therein a subtle touch of affection. To no other writer can "gentle" be more aptly applied.

The quaint humor of Lamb, best seen in his *Elia* essays, has become proverbial. But many, remembering only jests, think of him far too often as a mere wag, a professional wit. Such persons of course miss the real cause of his fame; they fail to grasp the far deeper humor which plays along the borderland of pathos, the humor which really distinguishes a man in a century. Few men have made more puns, few men have had a more instinctive relish for "excellent fooling;" but Lamb's most genuine humor has a touch of sadness in it; *Elia* is "full," as Barry Cornwall put it, "of a witty melancholy;" and those who knew Lamb said he was at his best when serious. "No one," says Hazlitt, "ever stammered out such fine, piquant, deep, eloquent things, in half a dozen sentences." A volume of anecdotes, however amusing, cannot hide the pathos of his life.

Charles Lamb was born in Crown Office Row in the Temple, London, on February 10, 1775. His father,

John Lamb, was in the service of one Samuel Salt, a
"bencher" of the Inner Temple. Of this parent (under
the name of Lovel) Charles Lamb gives an account in
one of his *Elia* essays: "He was a man of an incor-
rigible and losing honesty. A good fellow withal, and
'would strike.' . . . L. was the liveliest little fellow
breathing, had a face as gay as Garrick's, whom he was
said greatly to resemble . . . , possessed a fine turn for
humorous poetry — next to Swift and Prior, — moulded
heads in clay or plaster of Paris to admiration, by
the dint of natural genius merely; turned cribbage
boards, and such small cabinet toys, to perfection;
took a hand at quadrille or bowls with equal facility;
made punch better than any man of his degree in England; had .the merriest quips and conceits, and was
altogether as brimful of rogueries and inventions as
you could desire." Charles Lamb's mother was an Elizabeth Field, of Blakesware, in Hertfordshire; and it
is from this connection that Lamb's interest in that
county arose, whence his essays on "Blakesmoor in
Hertfordshire," "Mackery End," and all the delightful reminiscence of "Grandmother Field." Of the six
children only two besides Charles survived infancy:
John and Mary, twelve and ten years his seniors. John
went early into the South Sea House and practically
separated from his family. Of Mary more presently.

Charles was a nervous, imaginative boy. "The night-
time solitude," he says, "and the dark, were my hell.
The sufferings I endured in this nature would justify
the expression. I never laid my head on my pillow, I
suppose, from the fourth to the seventh or eighth year
of my life — so far as memory serves in things so long
ago — without an assurance, which realized its own

prophecy, of seeing some frightful spectre." About his education little is known till he was sent, when still a small boy, to the day-school of a Mr. Bird, off Fetter Lane. When he was only seven a place was procured, probably through the efforts of Mr. Samuel Salt, in Christ Hospital School.

The famous "blue-coat" school, attended by Coleridge and Leigh Hunt, has been well described by the latter. "We rose to the call of a bell, at six in summer, and seven in winter. . . . From breakfast we proceeded to school, where we remained till eleven, winter and summer, and then had an hour's play. Dinner took place at twelve. Afterward was a little play till one, when we again went to school, and remained till five in summer and four in winter. At six was the supper. We used to play after it in summer till eight. In winter we proceeded from supper to bed." The meals Hunt describes as follows: " Our breakfast was bread (half of a three-halfpenny loaf) and water, for the beer was too bad to drink. . . . For dinner, we had the same quantity of bread, with meat only every other day. . . . On the other days, we had a milk-porridge, ludicrously thin; or rice-milk, which was better. . . . For supper, we had a like piece of bread, with butter or cheese." Lamb, it seems, was somewhat envied for the hot rolls which were sent in to him and for frequent visits to his home. Otherwise he was subjected to the heroic regimen set forth by Hunt. But there were numerous holidays when the penniless boys, always in their blue coats and yellow stockings, roamed the streets or near-by country in quest of adventure. How they lived and grew, and how the master, James Boyer, ruled with a rough hand, and what friends Charles Lamb made there, — more especially Coleridge, the Le Grice boys, and " Jem " White, immortalized in the Chimney-sweep essay, — are not all these things recorded in Lamb's " Recollections of Christ's Hospital " and " Christ's Hospital Five-and-Thirty Years Ago " ? Of his learning it is sufficient to say that he was a good Latin scholar, knew little Greek, and did not become a " Grecian " (or boy of highest rank), but was made a " Deputy Grecian." His greatest education was in the reading of old and curious literature, for which all through life he had a quaint fondness.

In November, 1789, when he was only fourteen, Charles left school and soon after "went to work." For a short time he was in a Mr. Paice's office ; next he was a very humble clerk in the South Sea House, where his brother John worked; finally, in April, 1792, he obtained a position of clerk in the accountant's office of the East India House, and there he stayed for thirty-three years of uncongenial, daily labor.

Soon after Lamb entered the East India House his family moved to Little Queen Street. Those were the times of the rare evenings in the company of Coleridge at the " Salutation." Lamb himself had begun to write poetry. His earliest effort was made in 1789, and by 1794 he had taken to it seriously. The immediate cause seems to have been " Alice W——," of whom nothing is known except that she has been identified by Canon Ainger with an Ann Simmons who lived near Blakesware, that some of Lamb's earlier sonnets were addressed to her, and that she was probably the dream-wife in his tenderest essay, " Dream-Children," written twenty-five years later.

For six weeks in the winter of 1795–96 Lamb was

in a madhouse, some believe as a result of his disappointment in love. There was of course a strong tendency to madness in his family, but it is important to note, in correction of various reports, that this was Lamb's first and last attack. Soon after coming out of the confinement, he wrote to Coleridge: " I look back upon it at times with a gloomy kind of envy: for, while it lasted, I had many, many hours of pure happiness. Dream not, Coleridge, of having tasted all the grandeur and wildness of Fancy till you have gone mad."

Poor Mary Lamb, his sister, had a worse attack, and in September, 1796, in a fit of insanity killed her mother. " I was at hand," wrote Lamb to Coleridge, "only time enough to snatch the knife out of her grasp. She is at present in a madhouse, from whence I fear she must be moved to an hospital. God has preserved me to my senses: I eat, and drink, and sleep, and have my judgment, I believe, very sound." " I look upon you," wrote Coleridge in reply, "as a man called by sorrow and anguish and a strange desolation of hopes into quietness, and a soul set apart and made peculiar to God."

Then followed, indeed, some hard years for Charles Lamb. With his old aunt Hetty and his now half-imbecile father he moved to 45, Chapel Street, Pentonville. His evenings were spent playing cribbage with his father, "who," he wrote, " will not let me enjoy a meal in peace — but I must conform to my situation, and I hope I am, for the most part, not unthankful."

It was under these depressing cares that Lamb wrote his best and saddest poem, *The Old Familiar Faces*, full of a sorrow inexpressible, one would have said, if he had not expressed it. He had already been in print.

Four of his sonnets had been attached to Coleridge's
Poems of 1796, and to the title of Coleridge's second
edition (1797) were added the words *Poems by Charles
Lamb and Charles Lloyd.* *The Old Familiar Faces*
was published in 1798, in a small volume of verse by
Lamb and Lloyd. " I have had playmates," says Lamb,

> " I have had companions,
> In my days of childhood, in my joyful school-days —
> All, all are gone, the old familiar faces."

The lament was particularly for Coleridge, now living
far away at Stowey, and for Lloyd, under an alien roof.
And, as if to make the sorrow still more real, Lamb
was soon after the writing of this poem alienated from
Coleridge, on account of his friend's difference with the
melancholy Lloyd. By 1800 the friendship was renewed
and happily never broken again.

In 1799, when his father died, — his aunt had died
two years before, — Lamb took his sister, who was again
well, to live with him ; and thenceforward, as her guardian, he cared for her tenderly the rest of his life. All
who knew her testify that, except in moments when the
insanity returned, she was a person hardly less delightful than her brother. " I will, some day," Lamb wrote
to Coleridge a month after the tragedy, "as I promised,
enlarge to you upon my sister's excellences : 't will seem
like exaggeration ; but I will do it." Certainly she was
a great help to him ; and together they bore bravely a
burden either alone would have endured with difficulty.
Unfortunately, the malady did at times recur. She could
tell, however, when these times were coming, and then
the brother and sister might be seen, it is said, walking
hand in hand, with tears in their eyes, to the asylum at
Hoxton.

It was difficult of course for two such persons to keep one place of lodging. For some time they moved about frequently, though always in London, till in 1801 they settled in the Mitre Court Buildings, in the Temple. In 1809 they changed to 4, Inner Temple Lane; from 1817 to 1823 they were in Russell Street, Covent Garden, except for a short trip to France in 1822; and after 1823 lived in Islington, Enfield Chace, and Edmonton. They were never well-to-do, but Mr. Lucas has called attention to the fact that their poverty has been exaggerated. Lamb worked hard for an increasing salary; and by middle life he was able to add to his savings considerable money earned by his pen.

Soon after the beginning of the century Lamb found his way into a small literary recognition. In 1798 he had published *A Tale of Rosamund Gray* and *Old Blind Margaret*. In 1802 came a play, *John Woodvil;* and in 1803 he sent Manning his well-known lines to Hester Savory, "a young Quaker," he says, "you may have heard me speak of as being in love with for some years while I lived at Pentonville, though I had never spoken to her in my life. She died about a month since." In 1805 Godwin, who had become a publisher of children's books, asked Lamb and his sister to do the *Tales from Shakespeare*. Charles did the tragedies, Mary the comedies, and the now well-known little book was published in 1807. Meanwhile, in 1806, Lamb and his sister had brought out *Mrs. Leicester's School;* and in the same year *Mr. H.*, a farce by Lamb, had been put on the stage. *Mr. H.* failed signally, and the author himself joined in the derision. In 1808 appeared the *Adventures of Ulysses*, now one of his most familiar books among children; and in the same year came out a more substantial work, his *Specimens of English Dramatic Poets Contemporary with Shakespeare*. *Elia* and renown were yet to come, but henceforward Lamb was a recognized writer.

One of the most memorable qualities of Lamb was his indescribably delightful flavor of old English writers — the Jacobean dramatists, Sir Thomas Browne, Izaak Walton, and "hearty, cheerful Mr. Cotton." " Hang the age ! " he once cried; " I will write for antiquity." In one of his later essays, that on " Old China," Bridget Elia (Mary Lamb) asks him if he remembers the old days when they saved every penny to buy " that folio Beaumont and Fletcher, which you dragged home late at night from Barker's in Covent Garden ? " No one brings back so pleasantly as Lamb the spirit of old authors ; there is a relish in his mere mention of them. In another essay, on " Books and Reading," he runs on: "The sweetest names, and which carry a perfume in the mention, are Kit Marlowe, Drayton, Drummond of Hawthornden, and Cowley. . . . Milton almost requires a solemn service of music to be played before you enter upon him. But he brings his music, to which, who listens, had need bring docile thoughts and purged ears. . . . Winter evenings — the world shut out — with less of ceremony the gentle Shakespeare enters."

This little man, with his quaint flavor of the past, became, by 1810, a familiar figure among London literary men. So striking was his appearance that many have left some description of it. He had a large, long head, an aquiline nose, a high forehead, black stiff hair, a small spare body, and smaller legs. " He had a horror," he says of Elia (that is, himself), " which he carried to a foible, of looking like anything important

and parochial. He thought that he approached nearer
to that stamp daily." Indeed, he did dress more and
more, despite his aversion, like a Methodist preacher.
When long trousers came in he continued, like Coleridge, to wear knee-breeches; and his dress, says Barry
Cornwall, "indicated much wear." In a letter to Manning, Lamb called himself "a compound of the Jew, the
gentleman, and the angel." "His features," says Leigh
Hunt, "were strongly yet delicately cut: he had a fine
eye as well as forehead; and no face carried in it
greater marks of thought and feeling." Elia thus goes
on to describe his habits: "He herded always, while it
was possible, with people younger than himself. He
did not conform to the march of time, but was dragged
along in the procession. . . . The impressions of infancy had burnt into him, and he resented the impertinence of manhood." Lamb's manner of moving was
rather tentative, though he was a great walker; he
stuttered considerably, too; and his whole appearance
to such resolute young men as Carlyle, who visited
Lamb at Enfield in 1831, and called him "pitiful, rick-
ety, gasping, staggering," was that of a querulous, little old man. But Lamb, who detested arrogance and
self-assurance, could hit back if necessary. He formed
a much better estimate of Carlyle and his race than
the great prophet formed of him.[1] Once, Leigh Hunt
says, "when somebody was speaking of a person who
valued himself on being a matter-of-fact man," Lamb
replied, "'Now, I value myself on being a matter-of-lie
man.'"

Charles Lamb's quaint humor was of course irresist-
ible, — except to a few Scotchmen, — and by it and good

[1] See the essay "Imperfect Sympathies."

literary taste he drew many to his simple lodgings to talk, to dine, to play cards. Most of all, men were drawn by his indefinable gentleness. For a while, "Thursday evenings" (really late Wednesday) became regular times for visitors; and while the ardent youth gathered at Highgate to admire Coleridge, talking transcendentalism, men of all sorts found their way to Inner Temple Lane, Russell Street, and Islington to enjoy Charles Lamb.

Lamb, it must be admitted, was given to conviviality, sometimes to too much. It is not fair, however, to judge the amount by his frequent efforts to renounce the bottle and the pipe or by his essay "Confessions of a Drunkard," which some pious souls have been pleased to take as strictly autobiographical and to treat as a religious tract. "The truth is," says Barry Cornwall, "that a small quantity of any strong liquid disturbed his speech, which at best was but an eloquent stammer." It would be perilous to attempt to condone Lamb's intemperance, but it would be as presumptuous to assert that, in his case, drinking did him more than mere physical harm. Above all, it must be remembered that one hundred years ago drunkenness was not such an offense as it is to-day.

Lamb's stutter is responsible for many of the most amusing anecdotes about him. Once, at the seaside, when he was to be "dipped" for his health, he said to the men who were to do the "dipping," as he shivered on the steps of his bath-house, "I am to be di-di-dipped" — so the men had understood, and on hearing the word "dipped" they promptly submerged him. He came up gasping. "I tell you," he said, "I am to be di-di-dipped" — under he went again. After

the third performance he got it out: "I am to be—
I *was* to be di-di-dipped only *once !* "

One of Lamb's best friends, and one of the best
actresses during the second decade of the century, was
Fanny Kelly. On July 4, 1819, he wrote an article on
Miss Kelly as " Rachel," for the *Examiner*, in which
he makes " a stranger who sat beside us " say of her,
" ' What a lass that were to go a-gypsying through
the world with.' " Mr. Lucas adds to the quotation: " Knowing what we do of Charles Lamb's little
ways, we can be in no doubt as to the identity of the
stranger who was fabled to have sat beside him." It
is not so surprising, after this, to find him in love
with her. In fact, only two weeks later he proposed
by letter. She replied kindly, but refused him ; and
he, treating the matter with admirable good humor,
answered on the same day as the proposal, July 20,
" Dear Miss Kelly: Your injunctions shall be obeyed
to a tittle. I feel myself in a lackadaisical, no-how-ish
kind of a humor. I believe it is the rain, or something,"
— and so on, with the result that they remained good
friends. This action is of course no indication that
Lamb's affections were not deep, but rather a sign
that he, now in middle age, had learned the rare grace
of saving a situation by humor. This, the kindliness
growing upon him, and his wide and sympathetic
observation of men and their foibles, made *Elia* possible.

Those famous essays, the name for which Lamb took
from a clerk in the South Sea House of his early days,
began in August of the following year (1820) in the
London Magazine. He had been writing occasionally
for periodicals, notably " Recollections of Christ's Hos-

pital " (1813) in the *Gentleman's Magazine*, and various papers for the *Reflector* and the *Examiner*. The
first number of *Elia* was " Recollections of the South
Sea House." Then followed those beloved by all readers of Lamb : " Christ's Hospital Five-and-Thirty Years
Ago," " New Year's Eve," " Mrs. Battle's Opinions on
Whist," " A Chapter on Ears," " Mackery End," " The
Old Benchers," " Grace before Meat," " Dream-Children," " The Praise of Chimney-Sweepers," " A Dissertation upon Roast Pig," and others not so familiar
but quite worthy parts of the collected *Essays of Elia*
in 1823. *The Last Essays of Elia*, finally published
in book form in 1833, include some not printed in
the first volume or those written after its publication.
They number, too, many of the best : " Poor Relations," " Detached Thoughts on Books and Reading,"
" The Superannuated Man," " The Child Angel," and
" Old China."

It is chiefly for *Elia*, of course, that Lamb is remembered. No one has approached him in this kind
of familiar essay, either in the delicacy of his playful
humor or in the tenderness of his sympathy. They are,
in fact, most important in his biography ; for Lamb is
Elia. They must not, to be sure, be too strictly interpreted as literal records of his life, but he is never
quite absent ; most of them give charming, half-con-
cealed glimpses of their gentle author.

From Lamb's *Letters*, too, one may get a pleasant
and fairly complete picture of the man ; they contain
his unfailing wit, the sadness of his early days of
manhood, and the tenderness of his genial maturity.
" Who, I wonder," says Mr. Birrell, " ever managed
to squeeze into a correspondence of forty years truer

humor, madder nonsense, or more tender sympathy! "
In fact, these excellent *Letters* and *Elia* give almost
the whole man — too changeful, too *uncapturable*, to
be put in a phrase, and on that account always freshly
interesting. Scarcely any figure in the whole range of
literature can be known so intimately as a human
being, aside from his literary fame. He clung tenaciously to life and living men and women. "I am in
love with this green earth," he says in "New Year's
Eve." " . . . I would set up my tabernacle here. . . .
A new state of being staggers me." And in 1827 he
wrote to Robinson, after the death of an old friend,
Randal Norris, " I have none to call me Charley now."

In March, 1822, Lamb wrote to Wordsworth, in
referring to the East India House, " Thirty years have
I served the Philistines, and my neck is not subdued
to the yoke." Three years later, he was retired on a
pension of £441 a year. " I walk about, not to and
from," he says quaintly in " The Superannuated Man,"
an essay published in May, 1725 ; " . . . I grow into
gentility perceptibly. . . . I have worked task-work,
and have the rest of the day to myself." But he had
been too long in the service ever to get used to so
much leisure. He called Enfield " this vale of deliberate senectitude," and half wished for the old bondage. The household was brightened, however, by the
adoption, in 1823, of a little girl named Emma Isola.
Ten years later she married Moxon, the publisher.
Lamb continued to write occasionally through these
last years : some of his last *Elia* essays, *Album Verses*
(1830), and *Satan in Search of a Wife* (1831). On
December 22, 1834, he stumbled and fell, was not
strong enough to recover from the blow, and " sank

into death," says Talfourd, " as placidly as into sleep,"
on December 27, 1834, in his sixtieth year.

Those who would enjoy to the full Lamb's numerous
clever sayings and the best anecdotes about him should
follow him through the excellent *Life* by Mr. E. V.
Lucas. Here there is space for only a few. At Haydon's
"immortal dinner," in 1816, when Keats, Wordsworth,
and Lamb talked so rarely, there was also present a
pompous comptroller of stamps, who insisted on an intimacy with Wordsworth, and who asked, among other
strange questions, " Don't you think Newton a great
genius?" "I could not stand it any longer," says
Haydon. "Keats put his head into my books. . . .
Wordsworth seemed asking himself, 'Who is this?'
Lamb got up, and taking a candle, said, 'Sir, will you
allow me to look at your phrenological development?'
He then turned his back on the poor man and at every
question of the comptroller he chanted —

> 'Diddle diddle dumpling, my son John
> Went to bed with his breeches on.'

. . . Keats and I hurried Lamb into the painting-
room, shut the door and gave way to inextinguishable
laughter. . . . All the while we could hear Lamb struggling in the painting-room and calling at intervals,
'Who is that fellow? Allow me to see his organs once
more.'"

There is a story that one evening Lamb, who had
urged Wordsworth to expunge the lines in *Peter Bell* —

> "Is it a party in a parlor
> All silent and all damned?"—

as he passed a window through which were visible a
company sitting in silent plush solemnity, shook the

railings and called out : " A party in a parlor, all silent
and all damned ! "

Another time Coleridge said, " Charles, I think you
have heard me preach ? " " I n-n-never heard you do
anything else," replied Lamb.

But Lamb's jokes, however excellent, are not, it
must be remembered, the greater part of him. In his
" uncomplaining endurance," says Barry Cornwall, "and
in his steady adherence to a great principle of conduct,
his life was heroic." " There was no fuss or cant about
him," is one of Hazlitt's many tributes ; " nor were
his sweets or sours ever diluted with one particle of
affectation." The world is coming to see that in doing
no more than enjoy Lamb's puns and happy phrases it
has done him scant justice ; that his life was made sad
by a tragic duty and sublime by his quiet, manly bearing of his burden.

THOMAS DE QUINCEY

AFTER Coleridge and Lamb one may well be prepared for extremes of genius ; but one finds, in following Thomas De Quincey, that one has not half guessed the vagaries which human nature can take. De Quincey, in fact, is the most various, the most elusive in character of all the great Romanticists ; and it is only by coming to him with no preconceptions that one can possibly reconcile his intellectual power with his tendency to dreams, his strong will with his enslavement to an injurious habit, his shyness and solitude with his love of human society, and his minutely logical mind with his disorderly methods of life. As he himself said, " not to sympathize is not to understand."

On account of the sensational title of one of his books De Quincey has been too exclusively associated with opium-eating. With his use of the drug this narrative must deal later ; here, however, it is important to notice that he was not a dreamer because he took opium, but, as Mr. Page, his chief biographer, has pointed out, he rather took opium the more readily because he was a dreamer, because he had what he himself called a " constitutional determination to reverie." Yet to call him merely an inspired dreamer is superficial and inadequate. He was, Coleridge not excepted, the most magnificent dreamer of a body of men given to great visions ; but he was much more. He called himself " an intellectual creature," in both pursuits and pleasures, from his school-days ; and this characteristic, intellectual force,

can never rightly be dissociated from any glimpse of
him, whether in his dreams, in his humor, in his philosophy, or in the mere events of his life. Such an intellect, moreover, which could be the informing power of
such emotional dreams, must have been intensely sympathetic; and one is not surprised, therefore, to learn
of his hatred of pedantry, his love of human beings,
and, when his physical frailty is recognized, the almost
immeasurable pain which he suffered.

In spite of De Quincey's remark concerning biography, that "one is so certain of the man's being born,
and also of his having died, that it is dismal to be under
the necessity of reading it," the dates of his own birth
and death are especially full of meaning; for he was
born early enough to be a contemporary and friend of
the great Romanticists, and yet lived, not in aged repose,
but in active literary work, to be the contemporary and
friend of Victorian writers; he was born before the
French Revolution and he outlived the Crimean War;
Carlyle, Ruskin, Macaulay, Dickens, Thackeray, and
Tennyson were all famous years before his death. The
exact date of his birth, which took place in Manchester,
was August 15, 1785. He was the fifth child of Thomas
Quincey, a merchant, and a Miss Penson. The family
name had been English since the Conquest and was
entitled to the prefix *De*, which the son adopted, writing
it, however, with a small *d*.

Soon after the boy's birth the family lived at "The
Farm," near Manchester, and in 1791 moved to Green-
hay. Thus a great part of his childhood was spent in the
country, his fondness for which was almost instinctive
and lasted throughout his life. The earliest things he
remembered were: " first, a remarkable dream of terrific

grandeur about a favorite nurse, which is interesting to myself for this reason — that it demonstrates my dreaming tendencies to have been constitutional and not dependent upon laudanum; and secondly, the fact of having connected a profound sense of pathos with the reappearance, very early in the spring, of some crocuses." Before he was two he felt " the passion of grief," and soon afterwards " awe the most enduring, and a dawning sense of the infinite." Still more was he affected by the death of his sister Jane, though not so remarkably as by that of his sister Elizabeth when he was only five. He crept into the room where Elizabeth lay. " From the gorgeous sunlight," he says, " I turned round to the corpse. . . . I stood checked for a moment; awe, not fear, fell upon me; and whilst I stood, a solemn wind began to blow — the saddest that ever ear heard. It was a wind that might have swept the field of mortality for a thousand centuries." Not long afterwards the little fellow's father, dying of consumption, was brought home. How graphically he describes the first sight, indelible after years! — " the sudden emerging of horses' heads from the deep gloom of the shady lane; the next was the mass of white pillows against which the dying patient was reclining." In no other writer is the record of childhood impressions more important; like Coleridge, he foreshadowed his manhood from his birth.

When he was eight De Quincey was sent to a day-school at Salford, near by. He now came under the terrorizing dominion of an older brother. Fear and docility were uppermost. " What I was told to do I did, never presuming to murmur or to argue, or so much as to think about the nature of my orders. Doubtless, and willingly I allow it, if those orders were to run away, I obeyed them more cheerfully." In his classes the boy made remarkable progress and soon showed himself an excellent scholar. For better opportunities he was sent in his eleventh year to Bath Grammar School. There he developed his great interest in Greek. " At thirteen," he says, " I wrote Greek with ease, and at fifteen my command of that language was so great, that I not only composed Greek verses in lyric metres, but would converse in Greek fluently, and without embarrassment. . . . 'That boy,' said one of my masters, . . . 'could harangue an Athenian mob better than you or I could address an English one.' "

From Bath De Quincey went for a short time to Winkfield School in Wiltshire, which he left to make a trip to Ireland in 1800, with his friend Lord Westport. Of the various influences on his life at this time, that of a Miss Blake, for whom he felt a bashful admiration, was the strongest. " Ever after," he says, " throughout the period of youth, I was jealous of my own demeanor, reserved and awestruck in the presence of women ; reverencing often, not so much *them*, as my own ideal of woman latent in them." The intellectual inspiration from Lady Carberry and the Rev. John Clowes, a clergyman in Manchester, were also of no small account in his early influences.

In 1801 De Quincey was sent, against his will, to Manchester Grammar School. He was already prepared for Oxford. A small, delicate boy, he positively shrank from the pugilistic pastimes of his fellows ; and he felt no respect for his pedantic teacher. When July of the next year came round, therefore, he took the matter into his own hands and ran away. After his father's death he was heir to £150 a year, but could not get it until he came of age. By the influence of his uncle, Colonel Penson, however, who saw the boy was not to be brought back to Manchester bondage, he was allowed a guinea a week. Through the summer he roamed about the mountains of North Wales and slept in the open air.; but when winter came on he resolved, in spite of thereby forfeiting his allowance, to wander up to London and collect sufficient funds for Oxford.

Now followed those days so vividly described in the *Confessions:* how he wandered penniless and faint about the streets, slept in an empty house in Greek Street with a little waif, made innocent and affectionate acquaintance with the homeless creatures of the sidewalk (his references to Ann of Oxford Street contain some of his most touching pathos), and dreamed indelible, immortal dreams. This period in London was his "experience," his initiation into "human sorrow and strife too profound to pass away for years," and must be taken, along with his early childhood, as the most determining influence of his first twenty years.

By 1803 De Quincey came to an arrangement with his relatives and was entered at Worcester College, Oxford. There he again shone as a brilliant scholar, but failed of a degree because, after passing a remarkably good written examination, he left suddenly, unable to face the *viva voce* test, in which he was expected to do equally well. Just why he went so abruptly has never been quite explained. He was in good repute at Oxford; "generally known," says Dr. Cotton, then Provost of Worcester, "as a quiet and studious man." After all, he was De Quincey.

While an undergraduate, in 1804, De Quincey first

took opium to relieve severe neuralgia. So much has been said in connection with his use of the drug that it is important to understand clearly his beginning of the habit. Dr. Eatwell, who has carefully reviewed the whole case, testifies that De Quincey's condition, hereditarily and as a result of his starvation in London, brought on a malady of the stomach similar to what the East Indians call "Peetsool," a malady for which opium is considered the only relief. This and his constant neuralgia, not "sensuous gratification," as Dr. Eatwéll points out, were the real and pardonable cause of De Quincey's resort to opium. It is hard for an ordinary man to conceive what anguish so frail and sensitive a person must have suffered. The serious slip, of course, was to take the fatal cure without medical advice and restriction and, once taken, to continue to such an extent that the horrors of opium were tenfold worse than the pains of disease. Though he showed at times great strength of will in his battle with the poison, yet moments came when all the benefits of good resolutions were swept away by sudden over-indulgence ; he himself admits that he " could not face misery with sufficient firmness." While he was at Oxford, however, opium was only an occasional cure, and his dreams there, in which Levana, afterwards the mysterious goddess of the *Suspiria*, often appeared to him, were chiefly the result of his " constitutional determination to reverie."

De Quincey had for some time been an admirer, almost a worshiper, of Wordsworth and Coleridge ; in his frequent trips to London he had become familiar with Lamb and the Coleridgean circle ; and therefore, on leaving Oxford in 1808, he gladly turned his steps to the Lake District, to visit the Wordsworths at Allan

Bank, Grasmere. In February, 1809, he moved into Dove Cottage, where he lived for many years, until his own family and many books forced him to find more room. In spirit he was really far more a member of the " Lake School " than any except Wordsworth.

To give a list of De Quincey's friends through these and later years would include most of the great literary names of the day, those mentioned above and Hazlitt, Hood, and Talfourd being among the closest. Chief among his Lake friendships, and always enduring, was that with John Wilson of Elleray, commonly known as " Christopher North," the sturdy author of *Noctes Ambrosianæ*. In later years the affection for Wordsworth cooled, and gave rise to some of De Quincey's " faint praise " in his *Reminiscences;* friendship was no longer possible, but to say that they quarreled or that they lost all admiration for one another is a great overstatement.

De Quincey's marriage, in 1816, to Margaret Simpson, daughter of a Westmoreland " statesman," or farmer, brought much happiness into his life. To her, watching patiently through years of her husband's suffering, too high praise cannot be given ; and he himself tenderly said as much after her death. Three years after his marriage he suddenly found himself face to face with poverty, for his open-handed generosity had exhausted much of his £150 a year. What he had so far written was inconsiderable, but he had always led a scholarly, literary life ; and now, though thirty-five years old, he turned immediately to his pen as a source of income. As a result he poured forth for over thirty years the most brilliant and various literature that magazines have ever known from one pen. His first regular work was as editor of the Tory *Westmoreland Gazette* in 1819. In 1821 he went up to London, joined the staff of the *London Magazine*, and in October and November published in that periodical his best-known work, *The Confessions of an English Opium-Eater*. The first part of it tells of his early life and his predisposition to dreaming; and the whole book is, in fact, not so much a discussion of opium as of dreaming, and, incidentally, of the influence which opium has on dreams. Later it was considerably added to and published in his *Collected Works* (1853–60).

What this influence of opium was no one knew better than he, for by 1821 he had passed through his worst experiences with the enemy. It was in 1812 that he first sank into over-indulgence and in 1813 that he reached the high mark of 8000 drops of laudanum per day. The effect was worse than the gnawing pains in his stomach which he strove to relieve; he was cast into profound melancholy. By an effort of the will (and in this he was far stronger than poor Coleridge) he threw off the yoke for some years, regained his health, and, as has been seen, married in 1816. The following year, however, he fell again into " the gloom and cloudy melancholy of opium." There is not space here to transcribe more than a sentence or two from the *Confessions:* " In the early stages of my malady the splendors of my dreams were indeed chiefly architectural; and I beheld such pomps of cities and palaces as were never yet beheld by the waking eye, unless in clouds. . . . But now, that which I have called the tyranny of the human face began to unfold itself. Perhaps some part of my London life might be answer-

able for this. Be that as it may, now it was that upon
the rocking waters of the ocean the human face began
to appear : the sea appeared to be paved with innumerable faces, upturned to the heavens ; faces, imploring,
wrathful, despairing, surged up by thousands, by
myriads, by generations, by centuries: my agitation
was infinite, my mind tossed and surged with the
ocean."

Twice again, after freeing himself by a great effort
of the will, De Quincey fell to excess. The last time,
in 1844, he fought it off by regular exercise : " Within
a measured space of forty-four yards in circuit," he
says, . . . " I had within ninety days walked a thousand miles. And so far I triumphed. But because still
I was irregular as to laudanum, this also I reformed."
If there is something a trifle abject about the struggles
and failures of the sick little man, there is something
truly great about his final victory, with the remark
" this also I reformed," when he was past middle age.
For after 1844 he was able to control the dose as he
felt necessary, and he never again went to excess.

Only for brief periods, it must be realized, was De
Quincey incapacitated for work. He wrote with great
fluency and vigor, though with little regularity. His
intellect held strong to the end. In 1826 he became a
contributor to *Blackwood's Magazine*, and in 1830
moved to Edinburgh to be near his work. Until his
Collected Works he published only two volumes besides the *Confessions*, of which numerous editions were
in demand: *Klosterheim* (1832), a novel ; and *The
Logic of Political Economy* (1844). For *Blackwood's* he wrote *Murder Considered as One of the Fine
Arts*, biographies of *Kant* and *Dr. Parr*, *The Cæsars*,

The Revolt of the Tartars, the essays on *Style* and *Rhetoric*, *The Philosophy of Herodotus*, *Suspiria de Profundis*, and *The English Mail-Coach*. To *Tait's Magazine* he contributed *Joan of Arc*, *The Spanish Military Nun*, and his *Literary Reminiscences*. The *Encyclopædia Britannica* included his articles on *Goethe*, *Pope*, *Schiller*, and *Shakespeare*.

All of these works, in one way or another, show his many-sided power; none so much as the *Suspiria*, unless perhaps his famous *Confessions*, so deeply or so eloquently expresses his insight into dreams and his ability to make real and magnificent the characters of dreams. In it there is lacking much of the familiar De Quincey, the quaint, scholarly humorist; but in it is especially revealed the most important De Quincey, the inspired interpreter of dreams. "I know them thoroughly," he says, "and have walked in all their kingdoms. Three sisters they are, of one mysterious household; and their paths are wide apart; but of their dominion there is no end. Them I saw often conversing with Levana, and sometimes about myself. . . . Madonna moves with uncertain steps, fast or slow, but still with tragic grace. Our Lady of Sighs creeps timidly and stealthily. But this youngest sister moves with incalculable motions, bounding, and with a tiger's leaps. She carries no key; for, though coming rarely amongst men, she storms all doors at which she is permitted to enter at all. And *her* name is *Mater Tenebrarum*, — Our Lady of Darkness."

In his last years De Quincey became a familiar figure. He was shy, deliberately sought solitude, and was hence not widely known in Edinburgh society; but he was intimate with many literary men. Professor Masson tells amusingly how it was really easy to get De Quincey to dine with you " if you knew the way." " He would promise — promise most punctually, and, if he saw you doubted, reassure you with a dissertation on the beauty of punctuality ; but when the time came, and you were all met, a hundred to one you were without your De Quincey. But send a cab for him, and some one in it to fetch him, and he came meekly, unresistingly, as if it were his doom, and he conceived it appointed that, in case of resistance, he should be carried out by the nape of the neck. . . . And was it not a treat? Hour after hour there was the stream, the sweet and subtle eddying-on of the silver talk."

Of De Quincey's personal appearance there are many descriptions. Mr. J. R. Findlay says : " He was a very little man (about 5 feet 3 or 4 inches) ; his countenance the most remarkable for its intellectual attractiveness that I have ever seen. His features, though not regular, were aristocratically fine, and an air of delicate breeding pervaded the face. His forehead was unusually high, square, and compact." And Carlyle, with an eye for a memorable phrase, writes: " You would have taken him, by candlelight, for the beautifullest little child ; blue-eyed, blonde-haired, sparkling face — had there not been something too which said, ' Eccovi, this Child has been in Hell.' "

There is abundant record of De Quincey's odd ways. Sometimes on an inspiration for work he would stop dressing, continue forgetful of the cooling coffee by him, and, if a visitor called, hurry into incongruous clothes and put on his shoes without noticing that he wore only one sock. Almost daily he set something about the house on fire, " the commonest incident being," says his daughter, Mrs. Baird Smith, "for some one to look up from work or book to say casually, ' Papa, your hair is on fire,' of which a calm 'Is it, my love?' and a hand rubbing out the blaze was all the notice taken." He had a way of polishing all shillings that came into his hands. But his strangest habit was that of filling room after room with chaotic manuscript. When he was thus "snowed up," he moved to another place. In this way he had at his death half a dozen rooms, at expense wholly beyond him, rented in various parts of Edinburgh. Once, it is said, he filled a bath-tub with his turbulent papers. " When it was my frequent and agreeable duty to call on Mr. De Quincey," says Hood, " and I have found him at home, quite at home, in the midst of a German Ocean of literature in a storm, flooding all the floor, the tables; billows of books tossing, tumbling, surging open — on such occasions I have willingly listened by the hour, whilst the philosopher, standing with his eyes fixed on one side of the room, seemed to be less speaking than reading from 'a handwriting on the wall.' "

In conversation De Quincey had at least one advantage over Coleridge: he was a good listener as well as talker. " When fully kindled up and warmed by his subject," says one writer, " his whole talk is poetry ; and his slight, attenuated frame, pale countenance, and massive forehead, with the singular sweetness and melody of his voice and language, impress one as if a voice from the dead — from some ' old man eloquent ' — had risen to tell us of the hidden world of thought and imagination and knowledge." " ' Oh, for one hour of Dundee ! ' — one hour of De Quincey ! " cries Charles Knight. " Better three hours, from nine till midnight, for a rapt

listener to be 'under the wand of the magician,' spell-
bound by his wonderful affluence of talk, such as that
of the fairy whose lips dropped rubies and diamonds."

De Quincey's abundant humor must not be passed
by. " Both Lamb and myself," he says, " had a furious
love for nonsense — headlong nonsense." This is readily
granted by all who know his letters and that excellent
piece of extravagance, *Murder Considered as One of the
Fine Arts*. But he was capable, too, of the subtle turn
worthy of Lamb himself. In describing the advantages
of Grasmere he writes to Knight: " New potatoes of
celestial earthiness and raciness, which with us last to
October; and finally milk, milk, milk — cream, cream,
cream (hear it, thou benighted Londoner!), in which
you must and shall bathe; " — a letter doubly humorous
when one remembers how rarely De Quincey himself
could eat anything even approximating a meal. In writing to an old schoolfellow in 1847, he said that he had
had no dinner since parting from him in the eighteenth
century.

The pathos in De Quincey's life, however, even more
than in Lamb's, outweighs the humor. His affection
for children is very touching. " Mr. Kinsey " was always
welcome to the Wordsworth children, and long after
Kate Wordsworth's death he saw her, he says, walking
among the hills. It was particularly hard on such an
affectionate nature to lose one son in 1833, another in
1835, and his wife in 1837. Still more, he was by no
means well off; friends, chief among them Coleridge,
had long ago used up most of his patrimony, and he
continued to give away the chief part of what he earned.
" His presence at home," says his daughter, " was the
signal for a crowd of beggars, among whom borrowed

babies and drunken old women were sure of the largest share of his sympathies." His poverty, in fact, is the one thing in De Quincey's life easy to explain.

In 1840 he took a cottage, Mavis Bush, near Lasswade, with his daughters. He was a great walker, and, even when seventy, frequently trudged to Edinburgh and back even after dark, a distance of fourteen miles. Sometimes he disappeared for weeks at a time. His daughters knew his habits, how when a change of scene was necessary there was no holding him, knew also that he was with kind friends in Edinburgh, and that he would some day turn up at home. Towards the end of his life he spent most of his time in lodgings in Lothian Street, Edinburgh. Late in 1859 he was very low, rather from old age than from sickness, and on December 8 he died. He was buried in the West Churchyard of Edinburgh. In his last hours there was some delirium, during which he was heard to cry, "Sister! Sister! Sister!" — calling thus in his last words on his little sister Elizabeth, of whom he had written: "Pillar of fire, that didst go before me to guide and to quicken — pillar of darkness, when thy countenance was turned away to God, that didst too truly reveal to my dawning fears the secret shadow of death, — by what mysterious gravitation was it that my heart was drawn to thine?"

GEORGE GORDON NOEL BYRON

SCHERER says Byron "posed all his life long," and
Matthew Arnold, catching Swinburne's phrase, speaks
of Byron's "splendid and imperishable excellence of
sincerity and strength." There is plenty of evidence
to support both judgments. Byron himself, on looking
in a mirror just after he had been sick, remarked to a
friend, "How pale I look! I should like, I think, to
die of a consumption; because then the women would
all say, 'See that poor Byron, — how interesting he
looks in dying!'" Almost whenever he got a chance he
exposed his suffering heart to a compassionate humanity
and talked of himself without modesty or reticence;
hence what the Hon. Roden Noel has called his "gaudy
charlatanry, blare of brass, and big bow-wowishness;"
— hence, too, when the suffering was real, what the
Germans have aptly called *Weltschmerz*. There was,
on the other hand, a dauntless Viking spirit in Byron's
breast, a sincere opposition to tyranny and bigotry.
This very characteristic, which was his deepest and
most abiding, which made him hate the sham and falseness of himself as well as of others, is in both his life
and his work the predominant note. It is on this, in
fact, that his fame depends; and, by strange irony, it
was by this vigorous, defiant spirit, which scorned and
resented correction, that he wrought his own downfall.

No man in the whole history of English literature
has become so suddenly famous as Byron did on the
publication of *Childe Harold*, and no poet has had

heaped upon him such wrathful denunciation by the virtuous and the zealous misinformed. As a result, he has figured in exaggerated, superlative terms. Because he was a peer, because he wrote excellent verses, because he was beautiful, he has received absurd adulation. Because he made certain very serious moral and social slips, because he had the grim humor to pretend he was much worse than he really was, because scandal-mongers spread almost unimaginable lies about him, he was practically driven from England and has been, since his death, the victim of unjustified calumny.

A further consequence of the exaggerated attitude towards Byron has been the falsification of the mere facts of his life, as well as of the inferences in regard to his character. He has been pictured, for instance, as a beautiful, black-haired Adonis, albeit with a club-foot, reclining, as he wrote verses, on a tombstone at Harrow, while his fellow scholars formed an admiring circle about him. As a matter of fact, however, when Byron was at Harrow, as Mr. Jeaffreson has pointed out, he was fat and shy, his hair was auburn, and he did not have, literally, a club-foot. Further, biographers have spoken of his vigorous, manly appearance when they could have found all sorts of proof that he was robust only in his arms and shoulders, that his legs were weak, and that his face, far from having the rugged vigor they imagine, was beautiful rather than handsome, femininely delicate in outline and expressive of feminine sensibilities. In later life he was accused of the blackest crimes in the calendar. Unfortunately he could not have cleared himself wholly if he had tried, but it must be kept in mind that he did not do half the things, good or bad, attributed to him.

Byron

After the engraving by Finden from the painting by G. Sanders in 1807

To call Byron a *bad* man is, after all, beside the point. He was a *weak* man. Intensely passionate, badly brought up, spoiled by the adulations of society, constitutionally reckless of authority, he literally followed his impulses. This and the fact that he could be wholly possessed by rapidly succeeding and widely differing moods account in a large measure for his abrupt, seemingly inconsistent changes: his "silent rages," his affection and hatred almost at the same moment, his recklessness and remorse, his sentimental melancholy, and his fundamental sincerity. It is futile, of course, to gloss over Byron's faults, but it must be remembered that his discreditable quarrel with his wife and his dissolute life in Venice, as well as the facts that he was a "noble lord" and had an adorable face, are no longer the only important features of his life or the cause of his great fame — however they may have brought about a newspaper notoriety in his day. What is far more significant now, when all the little creatures who shared his scandals have disappeared, is the evidence of genius, the Titanic soul in him. It throws light on the story of his life to know that Lady Caroline Lamb lost her head over him, but it is much more illuminating to know that Scott and Goethe, two of his greatest contemporaries, considered him a very great genius.

George Gordon Byron, born January 22, 1788, in Holles Street, London, was the only son of Captain Jack Byron and Catharine Gordon of Aberdeen. His descent can be traced from the Norman Buruns, recorded in the Domesday Book. Sir John Byron — "Sir John the little with the great beard" — was the first of the family to come by Newstead Abbey, near Nottingham, granted him by Henry VIII, and the poet was the last owner.

Both of Byron's paternal grandparents, Admiral John
Byron — known as " foul-weather Jack " — and Sophia
Trevanion, were the grandchildren of the fourth Baron
Berkeley, and may reasonably have inherited the vehement Berkeley temperament. His father — known as
" mad Jack " in the Horse Guards — first ran off with
the Marchioness of Carmarthen, and soon after her death
in 1784 hastened to repair his fortunes by suit to
Catharine Gordon. She did not prove so rich as he had
anticipated ; he soon exhausted what little she had, and,
after five years, separated from her. The following year
(1791) he died in France.

Mrs. Byron was thus left with £150 a year and a
three-year-old boy. Shortly after the poet's birth the
parents had moved to Aberdeen, and there, among her
friends, Mrs. Byron might have managed fairly well.
But she was irritable, quick-tempered, and very unrea-
sonable in the education of her child. He, on his part,
though he had fits of affection for her, felt little filial
respect. She spent half her time in caressing him and
half in abusing him. In her more violent tempers she
pursued him with poker and tongs and called him a
" lame brat." In answer he developed his "silent rages,"
which kept the awestruck mother at a distance. Once
he seized a knife and threatened to commit suicide.
Another time the domestic feud was so great that Mrs.
Byron hastened to the apothecary and told him not to
sell her son any poison — only to find that the son had
given like instructions in regard to her.

At school Byron was too shy and rebellious to do
very well. He was easier to lead, one of his teachers
said, by a silken thread than by a cable. He first went
to Mr. Bowers's school in Aberdeen from 1792–93, then

was under tutors, and in 1794 entered the Aberdeen Grammar School. There was about the boy a girlish sensitiveness which continued all through his life and often, when people imagined him a hardened sinner, brought tears to his eyes. In 1798 by the death of his great-uncle — the " wicked old lord " — he inherited the Newstead estate and the family title; and he was henceforth " Dominus " in the roll-call. So sensitive was he, however, that when " Dominus " was first read out he burst into tears.

It is remarkable enough for any boy in his ninth year to fall in love. Even Dante was in his tenth. Byron, however, seems to have fallen in love in his ninth year more genuinely than many people manage in their twenty-fifth. Mary Duff was the young lady, and years later, when Mrs. Byron told him of Mary's marriage, Byron, after his manner, burst into tears. Besides this affair, moreover, he had two very serious passions before he went to college. Perhaps the tenderest affection of his whole life was for Margaret Parker in 1800. Whenever he spoke of her in later times he was lifted to his best self. It was due to her, he says, that he made his " first dash into poetry." Some believe that the tender lines to " Thyrza " are in memory of her. For she died when still a girl, and Byron thus lost his " good angel " when he was a mere boy. His next love was Mary Anne Chaworth, who lived at Annesley, near Newstead. In the summer of 1803, Byron, fat, with auburn locks combed straight over his forehead, paid awkward court to her. But he was a hopeless suitor. Miss Chaworth was older than he, and evidently felt no affection for her fat, lame, sentimental lover.

Those who think Byron's whole life was a pose assert

that he was from the first a professional lover and that
his boyhood affairs were the preliminary steps of a
despicable career. They assume that fickleness neces-
sarily implies affectation. But Byron was too much a
creature of impulses to pose in any but trivial matters.
He pretended, to be sure, in the bitter humor of his
later years, that he was a professional lover; but he
was really wholly possessed, even in his later passions,
by strong affection. Therein lies the tragedy of his
life, for when the passion, true and vehement while it
lasted, gave way to the swiftly succeeding impulse,
he presented one of the best examples of sincere fickleness in history. If he had been merely "putting on,"
he would have mixed a little more comedy with the
tragedy.

In 1799 Byron's mother thought that the owner of
Newstead should have a more fashionable education
than either Aberdeen or Nottingham could offer. She
therefore took him up to London and sent him to Dul-
wich Academy. The head master, Dr. Glennie, seems to
have had a sympathetic understanding of the boy, but all
his efforts were frustrated by the descents of the hysterical mother, who frequently took the child away for
a couple of days and undid discipline with parties and
caresses.

In 1801 Byron was sent to Harrow. His lameness,
the result of a contracted Achilles tendon, and much
augmented in childhood by the brutal treatment of
ignorant physicians, really prevented him from taking
part in most sports, except riding and swimming. It
has been pointed out that he played cricket, but Mr.
Jeaffreson has pointed out that he played poorly. His
sensitiveness in regard to this lameness lasted all through

his life. In childhood he had retorted to his mother's
reproaches, "I was born so, mother;" and he remembered the incident well enough to put it in his last
work, *The Deformed Transformed.* On his death-bed
he even asked to be blistered in such a way that his
feet should not be exposed. Leigh Hunt says that in
walking Byron hopped like a bird. Thus handicapped
in athletics, fat and shy, impulsive and sullen by turns,
Byron found Harrow at first an uncongenial home.
"I was a most unpopular boy," he says, "but *led* latterly." His friendships, as always, were marked by a
girlish sentiment; he invariably referred to them as
"passions." In his studies he made no mark. Indeed,
he was considered poor in Latin, worse in Greek, and
very poor in mathematics. In declamation he excelled.
Most of his education, on the whole, seems to have
come from his wide reading.

In 1805 Byron went up to Trinity College, Cambridge. There he was never a congenial member. In
the first place, his defiant spirit revolted against what he
considered the bigotry and smug respectability of his
superiors. His zeal for scholarship, moreover, did not increase in the presence of what he felt was pedantry. On
the whole he found Cambridge a fitter place for revelry
than study. He discovered that he could easily shock
the worthies there, and this pleased him so much that
he straightway acted as if shocking people was his cue.
He kept a coach, valet, and dogs, — Boatswain, the great
Newfoundland, and Nelson, the savage bulldog, — and
finally he brought a bear to Cambridge, to "sit for a
fellowship," he said. The worst side of Byron's early
life is seen at Cambridge — his pride, conceit, and vulgar
ostentation. It must be said in his favor, however,

that he was frolicsome rather than vicious. Underneath, moreover, there are plenty of evidences of sincerity — in his opposition to bigotry and cant and in his choice of friends. His best friend at college, as indeed his stanchest defender after his death, was John Cam Hobhouse (Lord Broughton).

Most of the violent excesses attributed to Byron during his years at Cambridge are not only unfounded, but against all fact. For while there he commenced the strict regimen which had so much effect on his life. He was short, five feet eight inches, and when he was nineteen weighed over two hundred pounds. He then began — chiefly to relieve the physical discomfort, for he was almost too fat to walk on his feeble legs — a process which amounted nearly to starving. He gave up drink, and subsisted for weeks on biscuits and soda-water. To aid in reducing his flesh he took up various exercises, chiefly boxing, in which he excelled by impetuous onset rather than by skill or endurance. It was not until after a period of this discipline that there emerged the delicately beautiful Lord Byron who was the talk of London society. Such diet, naturally, soon played great havoc with his digestion. Occasionally, in a fit of hunger, he would gorge a mess of fish, rice, and potatoes drenched with vinegar. He found, however, that his intellectual powers were so much improved with the reduction of flesh that he continued the severe diet through most of his life. In 1811, to relieve his suffering, he began to take opium, and, though he never went to the excesses of De Quincey, he was never again wholly free from the habit.

While at Cambridge Byron stepped into literary notice. He had collected and privately printed his

juvenile verses in November, 1806, but on the suggestion of a friend that certain lines were too broad, he
unhesitatingly (and rather unnaturally for him) burned
the edition. The revised copy was printed in January,
1807. His first public edition of verse, however, did
not appear till March, 1807, when he brought out
Hours of Idleness. These the *Edinburgh Review*
attacked after its vituperative manner. Byron of course
suffered by his studied conspicuousness at Cambridge.
He therefore avoided the university and spent most of
his time at Newstead or London till he had ready his
famous reply, *English Bards and Scotch Reviewers*.
The clumsy reviewer had reckoned without his host.
For Byron, who had already written 380 lines of the
satire, got it ready, by some alterations and additions,
for publication by the spring of 1809. The attacks he
makes are unjustified, and he later so regretted their
extravagance that he suppressed the fifth edition ; but
he had shown the reviewers that he too could " hunt a
poetaster down," and, vastly more, he had taken a conspicuous place in the literary world.

Byron now found little to interest him at Cambridge,
and left in the fall of 1808 without a degree. On
March 13, 1809, he took his seat in the House of Lords,
but was disappointed at the cold reception accorded him,
and soon resolved to go abroad. It was this spring that
he was joined by several cronies who entered Newstead
between a bear and a wolf, spent the days in boxing,
fencing, riding, and pistol-shooting, and the nights in
gaming, feasting, and ribald song. The young gentlemen dressed up as monks, and out of a skull found in
the garden drank perdition to reviewers. But the stories
of Byron's excesses at this time are exaggerated ; for

while his friends were carousing he himself persisted in his severe diet, read a great deal, and sat up at night writing. Just before leaving for the Continent, he heard that the reviewers were preparing a second attack, so he wrote, in a humor prophetic of *Don Juan*, " I yet hope to light my pipe with it in Persia."

On July 2 he sailed with his friend Hobhouse from Falmouth for Lisbon. Byron was abroad about two years, after which time he found himself in considerable debt and was forced to return. Most of his travels were in Spain and Greece, where he had numerous exciting and romantic adventures, though by no means all of those recorded in *Childe Harold*. The greatest feature of the trip, however, was the composition of the first two cantos of *Childe Harold*. He had also written some shorter poems — such as *Maid of Athens* — and a satire called *Hints from Horace*. This last he thought worth publication, but Murray, the publisher, preferred *Childe Harold* to the satire, and published it on February 29, 1812. Byron, who as yet considered taking pay for his pen below him, gave the £600 to his friend Dallas.

Byron literally " awoke and found himself famous." All London went mad over the young poet. When it was discovered that he was beautiful, with an expression of " dainty melancholy," when, as the Countess Guiccioli hath it, " fame lit up his noble brow," he was courted and petted without end. Byron, who had once thought of calling the poem *Childe Burun*, was of course, in spirit at least, the unhappy, sentimental pilgrim of the poem, as he was in spirit the chief figure of all his works. And the possibility, the delightful danger that he might himself have had all the romantic experiences of the *Childe* fascinated not only young ladies.

On the flood-tide of this unprecedented success Byron wrote in the next two years several of his narrative poems — the *Giaour* (1813), the *Bride of Abydos* (1813), the *Corsair* (1814), and *Lara* (1814). Their vogue was phenomenal; 14,000 copies of the *Corsair* sold in a single day; Scott was completely eclipsed. *Parasina* and the *Siege of Corinth* (published in 1816) were also written in this period of popularity.

Lady Caroline Lamb — "beautiful silliness," as Miss Milbanke called her — met the poet and wrote in her diary, " Mad, bad, and dangerous to know." Whatever was the truth about poor Byron, whose head might very well be turned by this time, Lady Caroline, who herself deserved the judgment she made of him, determined to know him. For a few months she drew the young poet in her train. Then he managed to see what a scandal was brewing and turned her away with one of the most tactful letters he ever wrote. Her mother-in-law, Lady Melbourne, also feared a scandal and hoped, by introducing her niece, Miss Anne Isabella Milbanke, as a possible match for Byron, to keep talk in the family.

Miss Milbanke, however, was not thrust upon Byron. He fell deeply in love with her, and even after a refusal persisted for two years till he was accepted. It is convenient to prove certain arguments by saying that Byron married her for money or, as he himself often asserted to her and others, out of spite ; but there is good evidence that such was not the case. Her fortune of £10,000 and prospects of more when Lord Wentworth died were scarcely inducements to the owner of Newstead, who at the time of his proposal had arranged to sell his estate for £140,000. Whatever he said in obvious jest, good or ill natured, or whatever she in indignant and self-righteous old age reported to Mrs. Stowe is not much to the point. It is to the point, however, that in later years he often spoke of her, when he had good cause to speak otherwise, with great respect and even with affection. In fact, he never in his best moments got over his love for her, and several times he hoped for a reconciliation.

The marriage took place on January 2, 1815, and the young couple soon settled at 13, Piccadilly Terrace, London. They did not live in great splendor, to be sure, for Byron was not yet clear of his debts. But they did live very happily — at least for eight months. Byron thus wrote to Moore in February : " My spouse and I agree to admiration. Swift says, ' No *wise* man ever married,' but, for a fool, I think it the most ambrosial of all possible future states."

It is almost idle now, and certainly impossible in so short an account, to discuss all the details of the miserable quarrel which gave birth to so much gossip and slander. It is chiefly important to keep the characters of the two clearly in mind. Lady Byron was accomplished, attractive, and conspicuous for her high ideals and purity of thought. Unfortunately she was hopelessly dignified, coldly austere. She lacked, in fact, the two things most needed for companionship with Byron : a sense of humor and a sympathetic comprehension of his genius. She had very strict notions of piety, was easily shocked, and came to look on herself as an emissary direct from God for the regeneration of her wicked husband. Byron's sensitiveness and impulsiveness, which he had learned to mask under cynicism and bitter jesting, have already been noted. By August, 1815, when his diet of biscuits and soda-water and his doses of

laudanum had attacked his digestion, he was unwontedly
irritable. Above all must be remembered his great
selfishness — even Hobhouse admits that; an unconscious, insatiable selfishness. He could bid those

> " Whose agonies are evils of a day "
> " Control
> In their shut breasts their petty misery; "

he could give generously to the poor and his friends;
he could give himself gladly to the cause of freedom:
but always there stepped in the spirit of the melancholy
Childe Harold, to exact the uttermost farthing of consolation; and when this was denied him by the unfeel-
ing world, as it must always be, the spirit of Don Juan
followed, jesting bitterly.

It is not necessary, then, as some have thought, to
invent a great crime which should suddenly come between Byron and his wife. The ill-feeling developed
slowly after August. In the first place, Byron talked
of a trip abroad, and said brutally, to a wife with no
sense of humor, that if she could not accompany him
he should go without her. He began, moreover, to tell
various tales of his wickedness. When he saw this
shocked her serious righteousness, he was immensely
amused. Another grievance was his absence from meals.
He could not bear to sit through a long repast while
his fare consisted of the aforesaid biscuits and soda-
water; but this action she very reasonably construed
as the expression of a dislike for her. Still another
trouble was religious dissension. " He broke me," she
said afterward with a tragic seriousness almost amusing
to-day, " on the rock of predestination." Then, too, those
" silent rages " of his boyhood continued, and no doubt
a look could do as much injury as anything he said.

Such silence, moreover, was often followed by violent outbursts of temper, as when he dashed a watch to pieces on the hearth and then attacked the broken, unresisting timepiece with a poker. But one cannot help being amused, even if one must condemn Byron's conduct, when there enters to his lordship his dignified lady with the question, "Byron, am I in the way?" and he replies, "Damnably!" As a writer in the *Quarterly Review* for October, 1869, says, "His monomania lay in being an impossible sinner, and hers in being an impossible saint." But Byron was no doubt chiefly at fault. His daughter Ada was born on the 10th of December, 1815, and just at a time when Lady Byron deserved every consideration he was brutally inconsiderate. She generously thought him mad.

It is worth noting, however, that there was no talk of a separation when, on January 15, 1816, Lady Byron went north to Kirkby Mallory to visit her parents. The letters were still affectionate. A few days later, when she heard from a physician that Byron was not mad, she first resolved on a separation; for she asserted that what he had said and done, if he was in his right senses, was unpardonable. At first her relatives on both sides urged reconciliation, and lawyers said there were not sufficient grounds for divorce. A few weeks afterwards, however, was discovered or invented the additional evidence which convinced even lawyers that a separation was necessary. The matter did not come to public trial; Byron acquiesced, though he never knew, he asserted, what the mysterious additional evidence was. His silence, however, convicted him in the eyes of society, which jumped to all sorts of conclusions and showed an unsurpassed fertility of invention. The proposal of separation was made by Lady Byron's father on February 2, 1816, and the deed signed on April 22.

Byron's actions during the spring throw much light on his character. On the 8th of March he wrote to Moore: " I do not believe — and I must say it, in the very dregs of all this bitter business — that there was ever a better, or even a brighter, a kinder, or a more amiable and agreeable being than Lady Byron. I never had, nor can have, any reproach to make of her while with me. Where there is blame, it belongs to myself; and, if I cannot redeem, I must bear it." Yet almost at the same time he wrote the verses beginning " Fare thee well." He was no doubt strangely sincere when he wrote them; but he misrepresented the whole case when he allowed them to be published, for in them he poses before the world as a " sad true lover " deserted by his wife. His truer and more frequent mood was that of the letter to Moore. Similarly, in later times he usually spoke of her with respect and affection, but when he relapsed into sentimentality or vulgarity he attacked her in verse — notably in the *Dream* and in *Don Juan*, where he called her his "moral Clytemnestra" and " Miss Millpond." Certainly the worst thing he did was to contract a connection in the very spring of 1816 with Jane Clermont, the stepsister of Shelley's wife, Mary Godwin. A year later she bore him a daughter, Allegra, who died, at the age of five, in an Italian convent.

The storm of popular imprecation which followed Byron's separation from Lady Byron was as great as the popular enthusiasm for him four years before, though not quite so cyclonic. Certain people had found dangerous theology, they thought, in *Childe Harold*, and many who believed Byron actually did what the hero of the poem was made to do, if not quite indignant, were nevertheless shocked. Moreover, he had been applauding Napoleon while nine-tenths of England were in ecstasy over Wellington. He was, furthermore, unpopular with men, who disliked, on the one hand, his conspicuous favor among their women, and, on the other, his ostentatious disapproval of their pheasant-shooting and of their Anglo-Saxon tastes for food and drink. In 1816, then, when what they considered his unspeakable villanies were on every tongue, nearly all England turned against him. " Far worse men than he," says the Hon. Roden Noel, . . . " made a queer sort of vicarious atonement for their own vices by an immoderate and unjust condemnation of his. He became their whipping-boy." Those who found Nero too mild a comparison frankly likened him to Satan.

On the 25th of April, 1816, Byron left England with a mutual hatred. " I felt," he said, " that if what was whispered and muttered and murmured was true, I was unfit for England ; if false, England was unfit for me." He went via the Rhine to Geneva, where he was joined by the Shelleys.

The influence of Shelley on Byron was good. Byron was inspired by Shelley's ardor to a studious, intellectual life, and while at Geneva did much of his best work. He wrote the third canto of *Childe Harold*, *Prometheus*, the *Prisoner of Chillon* (in two days, while on a tour of the lake with Shelley), part of *Manfred*, and the stanzas to his stepsister, Augusta. This sister's unwavering faith in him and her frank rebuke of his errors, as well as his affection for her, present one of the pleasantest pictures in his life.

In October Byron crossed the Alps with Hobhouse and proceeded via Milan and Verona to Venice. Now comes the most miserable chapter of his life. At Venice he plunged into the worst sort of dissipation, to a degree that shocked even the Venetians. He gave up, moreover, his habit of starving himself. At first he became coarse and fat; then his overstrained constitution gave way.

When he had lived thus for about a year, enfeebled health, disgust, and affection for the young Countess Guiccioli, who lived at Ravenna, brought him back to his better self. His connection with Theresa Guiccioli, who ran off with him to Venice, was culpable enough, to be sure, but it kept him clear of further vice. It is great credit to the Countess that she discovered his better qualities, loved him for them, and by her love kept them uppermost in him for the remainder of his life. The best evidence of his good impulses at this time is, besides his return to sobriety, his generosity to the poor, his many individual acts of kindness, and his interest in the cause of Italian freedom. The *Carbonari* made him the chief of the *Mericani*, or fighting troops.

For the rest of his stay in Italy Byron was at Venice, Ravenna, Pisa, whither Shelley attracted him, and Genoa. His literary output during these six years in Italy was enormous. Even at Venice he wrote a great deal. In 1817, besides finishing *Manfred*, he composed the *Lament of Tasso;* in 1818, *Beppo;* and in 1819, *Mazeppa* and the first two cantos of his greatest work, *Don Juan*. In it the character of the mature Byron is excellently revealed: the vigorous Viking spirit; the flashing satirist; the bitter jester; the occasionally vulgar intriguer; and the romantic soul, with its love of freedom and nature. In 1821, his biggest year, he pro-

duced cantos iii–v of *Don Juan, Marino Faliero,
Sardanapalus, The Two Foscari,* and *Cain.*

Byron had long since got over his scruples about
taking money for his publications. In all he received
from Murray £12,580 for his writings between 1816
and 1821. By the latter date, moreover, he was very
comfortably off. Newstead had at last been sold, in
1818; and in 1822, on the death of Lady Noel, Byron
came in for a half share of the Wentworth property,
on his taking the name of Noel. For the last two years
of his life, therefore, he signed " George Gordon Noel
Byron."

Byron's Pisan days, when he lived at the Palazzo
Lanfranchi, present the pleasantest picture of his Italian
life. There he lived quietly in the excellent company of
Shelley and his friends, chief among whom were Trelawny, who accompanied Byron to Greece, Williams, who
was drowned with Shelley, Tom Medwin, a schoolfellow
of Shelley's, and Mrs. Shelley. At the palazzo the
Counts Gamba, father and son, and the daughter, the
Countess Guiccioli, lived with Byron till their sympathy with the *Carbonari* brought the authorities down
on them. Byron, who had been chief of the *Mericani*
at Ravenna, was still an agitator of the liberal cause.
He had written : " The king-times are fast finishing!
there will be blood shed like water, and tears like mist,
but the peoples will conquer in the end. I shall not live
to see it, but I foresee it." Such declarations and the
enthusiasm he stirred up among the common people soon
set the police of Pisa as well as of Ravenna against him.

There is an amusing story of a row which grew out
of this animosity. While Byron and his friends were
returning to Pisa on horseback from a park where they

went to practice pistol-shooting, a trooper rode rather roughly through them and nearly unhorsed an Irishman, one Taafe, who indignantly called Byron's attention to the insult. Byron put spurs to his horse and chased the offender through the gates of Pisa. As the trooper clattered past the Palazzo Lanfranchi one of the servants rushed out and wounded him with a stable fork. The poet, on returning to the gates, found that the guard had mustered before the rest of his party could get through, and that in, the ensuing scuffle Shelley had received a sabre-cut on the head, and Taafe, well in the rear, the reproaches of the Countess and Mrs. Shelley.

In 1822 began Byron's connection with Leigh Hunt's *Liberal*. Byron had long felt a desire for a periodical at his command. It was to start this venture that he invited Hunt to Italy. Byron was to own the paper ; Hunt, well known for his daring liberalism, was to edit it. Hunt arrived at Leghorn in the summer of 1821, just before Shelley's death by drowning, and, together with Mrs. Hunt and many little Hunts, took up his dwelling on the ground floor of the Palazzo Lanfranchi. From the first, however, the two writers did not get along well. Hunt was by this time a querulous, mercenary champion of liberty, and the cockney of him exasperated Byron. The *Liberal* proved to be unsuccessful and short-lived. Its best contributions were from Byron : *The Vision of Judgment* (1822), *Heaven and Earth* (1822), and *Morgante Maggiore* (1823).

In the Villa Saluzzo, at Albaro, about a mile outside of Genoa, Byron wrote a great deal. Cantos iv–xvi of *Don Juan* were published in 1823 and 1824. To the former year also belong : *Werner, The Age of Bronze,* and *The Island ;* to the latter, *The Deformed Trans-*

formed and his *Parliamentary Speeches* made in 1809.

Byron was, however, distinctly a spirit of action. He often spoke of his writing as mere play, to be given up when serious work began. " Do people think," he said to Trelawny in Greece, " that . . . I came to Greece to scribble more nonsense? I will show them I can do something better. I wish I had never written a line, to have it cast in my teeth at every turn. Let's have a swim." In 1823 the struggle of the Greeks against the Turks attracted him. They needed money, which he went about raising, giving unsparingly of his own, and they needed brave, intelligent leaders. He dreamed perhaps of great glory in this last enterprise of his; he could rarely forget himself and the spectacular. Still, when his whole life is taken into account, this effort to redeem his shattered character is greatly to his credit. He had little to sacrifice, to be sure, and much to gain, — but it is perhaps fairer to say that he felt, in the bottom of his vigorous heart, that he had still a high ideal to serve. How near he came to great gain may be guessed from Trelawny's remark that " had Byron lived to reach Salona as commissioner of the [English] loan, the dispenser of a million crowns would have been offered a golden one."

Setting out with Trelawny and the younger Gamba in July, 1823, Byron went first to Cephalonia, where he spent six months, to make sure how and where he should lend his services. It was during this time that, on a visit to Ithaca, he was taken with such violent indigestion, while he was being done especial honor as chief guest at a monastery, that he seized a torch, cursed the Abbot in virulent Italian, and rushed from the hall.

Later, in his fury, he threw furniture at his friends who sought to pacify him.

On arriving at Missolonghi on January 4, 1824, he was received with honor by Mavrocordatos, the Greek chieftain, and was made *Archistrategos* (commander-in-chief) of Marco Bozzaris's Suliotes. He did not see actual fighting in Greece, but the record of his services there does him great credit. He kept in good control a very rebellious band, the Suliotes, and did, besides, many little acts of kindness to prisoners and friends. There must have been something both magnificent and lovable about his appearance and manner. The same man who had captivated London society and played havoc with a dozen hearts inspired soldiers with zeal and affection and filled all who came in touch with him latterly, from the poet Shelley to the fighter Trelawny, with unbounded admiration. Hardened warriors wept by his death-bed, and all Greece went into mourning.

The story of Byron's last days can be briefly told. On February 15 began a series of epileptic fits; on April 11 he was taken with fever; on the 18th he spoke his last words, " Now I shall go to sleep; " and on the 19th he died, in his thirty-seventh year. His remains were taken to England; but, since the Dean of Westminster refused them burial in the Abbey, they were placed in the family vault of Hucknall - Torkard Church, near Newstead. The small gentry of Nottingham drew their prudish skirts about them, but Byron's friends, the poor, flocked in crowds to his grave.

In looking back over the life of Byron one feels that he was just beginning to find himself — to live down the sentimental *poseur* in him and to reveal the strong, sincere spirit underneath — when he was cut short.

In the shipwreck of his life there rises, as in *Don Juan*,

" the bubbling cry
Of some strong swimmer in his agony."

It must be admitted that Byron was always an image-breaker ; he was strong only in destruction ; he had no hopeful theory. " When he thinks," said Goethe, " he is a child." Byron himself wrote in 1813 : " I have simplified my politics into an utter detestation of all existing governments." But his defiance, it must be remembered, was at its best splendidly sincere, full of " imperishable strength," and the images he shattered were often idols of Baal. " To tell him not to fight," says Professor Nichol, " was like telling Wordsworth not to reflect, or Shelley not to sing." In his nobler moments and at what he finally achieved, Byron was the better self of his heroes : Harold, Don Juan, Cain, Manfred, Bonnivard — the

" Eternal spirit of the chainless mind."

His friend Shelley, who understood what was best in him, called him " the Pilgrim of Eternity."

PERCY BYSSHE SHELLEY

"MAD SHELLEY," "the immortal child," "a creature of impetuous breath," "a beautiful and ineffectual
angel," — these are some of the epithets that have been
applied to Shelley. And in them lies what is most striking in his personality: his visionary idealism, his ingenuous earnestness, his passionate love of beauty and
truth, his high ethereal spirit, unconscious of bodily
existence. He described himself as "A pardlike spirit
beautiful and swift." His poetry is similarly individual;
it has been called a "lyrical cry." He himself is his
"Cloud," who sings, —

> "I bind the sun's throne with a burning zone,
>   And the moon's with a girdle of pearl ;
>   The volcanoes are dim and the stars reel and swim,
>   When the whirlwinds my banner unfurl."

He himself is the leaf borne along the "Wild West
Wind;" he is his "Skylark" — an "unbodied joy" —

> "In the golden lightning
>   Of the sunken sun."

It is the coursers of his own Promethean mind who
are "wont to respire"

> "On the brink of the night and the morning,"

and to drink of "the whirlwind's stream."

On August 4, 1792, Percy Bysshe Shelley, the son
of Sir Timothy Shelley and Elizabeth Pilfold, was born
at Field Place, near Horsham, in Sussex. His father,
a stanch Whig in the House of Commons, was fairly

obsessed by conventional respectability and a commonplace belief in tradition — qualities which must have
early provoked the opposition of his meteor-spirited son.
Shelley's mother left the boy an inheritance of her great
beauty ; the immediate attention of all was attracted by
his slender frame, deep blue eyes, ruddy complexion,
and curling golden brown hair. This boyish appearance he retained all through life, even though his hair
turned prematurely gray. Trelawny describes him at
their first meeting, only two years before Shelley's
death, as "blushing like a girl."

Shy, impulsive, and enthusiastic for studies not in
the curriculum, Shelley did not get along well at school.
After two years at Sion House Academy, Isleworth, he
was sent, when twelve years old, to Eton. Among his
fellows he was conspicuously abnormal. He delighted
not in their sports, his shyness precluded companionship
except with one or two, and his independent nature
rebelled openly against the system of fagging. "Mad
Shelley," the boys dubbed him ; he was "surrounded,"
says one of his schoolfellows, "hooted, baited like a
maddened bull." Yet he was preparing himself in his
own way — by private reading and experiments in science, forbidden as a dangerous study for the young.
One of his experiments was to set fire with a burning-
glass to a valued old oak. There are some lines in the
Revolt of Islam descriptive of these Eton days — lines
ringing with Miltonic prophecy of his high calling : —

> " And from that hour did I with earnest thought
> Heap knowledge from forbidden mines of lore,
> Yet nothing that my tyrants knew or taught
> I cared to learn, but from that secret store
> Wrought linkèd armor for my soul, before
> It might walk forth to war among mankind."

Shelley's literary efforts· began early. In childhood he scribbled verses with fluency, and he delighted in amusing his sisters with strange tales or in leading them through imaginary romantic escapades. His first published book was the novel *Zastrozzi*, an extravagant reflection of the wild romances he had been reading, especially those of Mrs. Radcliffe and Godwin. *Zastrozzi* came out just before he left Eton and was followed in the fall of the same year (1810) by a similar romance, *St. Irvyne or the Rosicrucian*. The *Original Poetry by Victor and Cazire* was another work of that year.

From Eton Shelley went to University College, Oxford, in 1810. Of his short life there a most interesting account is given by his constant companion, Thomas Jefferson Hogg. The two were thrown together the first night at supper, continued their discourses in Hogg's room, and became forthwith inseparable. In Shelley's rooms, where they usually took supper, everything was in confusion : retorts supported by costly books, beakers used alternately for tea and *aqua regia*, stains on furniture and carpet — and in the midst of it Percy Bysshe Shelley, radiant, transfigured with enthusiasm, discussing vehemently in his shrill voice the wonders of science or the perfectibility of man. Hogg's account is full of Shelley's peculiarities — eccentricities which have become familiar to all : how he stepped on his hands when going upstairs ; how he read as he walked, whether in the country or the crowded streets of London ; how he slept after supper on the hearth-rug, with his little round head exposed to the heat of a blazing fire; how, in spite of his occasional awkwardness, " he would often glide without collision through a crowded assembly." Byron

compared him to a snake — an animal which always had
a strange fascination for Shelley. But Hogg saw beyond
the eccentricities : he has dwelt lovingly on Shelley's
generosity and quick sympathy, on his nobility of character and veneration for true greatness.

Hogg's testimony, moreover, is of the greater value
because it throws light on Shelley's atheism. The dread
word atheist is so apt to inspire, even to-day, the horror
which bristled in the hearts of the Oxford powers that
it is necessary to see just what kind of atheist Shelley
was. " I never could discern in him any more than two
fixed principles," says Hogg. " The first was a strong
irrepressible love of liberty ; of liberty in the abstract.
. . . The second was an equally ardent love of toleration
of all opinions, but more especially of religious opinions.
. . . He felt an intense abhorrence of persecution of
every kind, public or private." Add to this the further
testimony : " Shelley was actually offended at a coarse
or awkward jest, especially if it were immodest or un-
cleanly." And as a third consideration : " In no individual, perhaps, was the moral sense ever more completely developed than in Shelley." His atheism, then, was
not a blind revolt of immorality against traditions and
customs, as some have thought ; it was the philosophy
of a man who, inspired by the French Revolution, set
up Reason as his guide. He had indeed a profound
reverence for the divine spirit of " nature," or of " necessity," the very devotion to which, he would have put it,
forbade his using for it the name of God, a word associated through many centuries with the tyranny and
bigotry and sordid selfishness of the church. For the
personality of Christ he had a deep veneration ; for the
authority of dogmatic Christianity, for institutionalism,

he had complete contempt. As a result, because his premises were more defective than his noble aspirations, and because he was possessed by a militant ardor, he went in his youth to an extreme — to atheism. Yet not altogether unreasonably : to Trelawny, who in the last year of Shelley's life asked him why he called himself an atheist, he replied : " It is a good word of abuse to stop discussion, a painted devil to frighten the foolish, a threat to intimidate the wise and good. I used it to express my *abhorrence of superstition.* I took up the word as a knight takes up a gauntlet in defiance of injustice."

When these revolutionary views of Shelley's finally appeared in printed form, February, 1811, in a pamphlet called *The Necessity of Atheism,* he was peremptorily asked by the authorities whether he had written the booklet. His whole spirit, however, rebelled against what seemed to him rude inquisitorial arrogance ; he refused to answer, and together with his friend Hogg, who too would not commit himself, he was expelled March 25, 1811. Hogg tells how Shelley sat with his head in his hands, crying " Expelled! expelled! " Yet it was not so much his own misfortune that depressed him as the thought that there could exist in England an institution where a man should be punished for daring to think. With Hogg he took lodgings in London, his father having denied him Field Place unless he would separate from his free-thinking friend.

Shelley's resistance to tyranny and his support of the downtrodden soon led him into difficulties more serious than expulsion from college. When he was living with Hogg in London his sisters were in a school at Clapham, and while visiting them he became acquainted with Harriet Westbrook, the sixteen-year-old daughter of a wealthy, retired innkeeper. The acquaintance developed a correspondence; that in turn a close friendship. Harriet fell hopelessly in love with Shelley, and he, a very emotional youth of nineteen, half returned the affection. Soon her letters spoke of persecution at home, and the effect on Shelley was immediate; his spark of passion was fanned by his sympathy for the wronged into a considerable flame, and he offered, half chivalrously, to marry her — she need only to call him if the domestic conditions could not be endured. Soon she did call him; without a moment's hesitation he joined her, took her to Edinburgh, and there married her, August 28, 1811, under the Scotch law. On March 24, 1814, they were again married in London.

There is no doubt that Shelley failed to find in Harriet the finely tempered spirit that his poetic nature craved. Yet his precipitate action was quite consistent with his impetuous, generous character. He had been for the most part nurtured on idealistic dreams, and for a while all went well enough. Accompanied by a ubiquitous sister-in-law, Eliza Westbrook, he and his wife visited Hogg, who was now studying law in York. York Minster incidentally called from the young iconoclast the comment, — a " gigantic pile of superstition." From York they traveled to Keswick, where Shelley called on Southey, whose poetry had fascinated him in boyhood. Thence the young couple went to Ireland, where Shelley threw himself with characteristic ardor into the cause of Catholic emancipation. He wrote a pamphlet, which he distributed broadcast: sometimes he threw it from the balcony of his dwelling and sometimes, much to Harriet's amusement, stuck it in the hoods of women's capes on the street. Conscious of failure, however, he left for Wales; was soon at Lynmouth, Devon, where he amused himself by setting adrift on Bristol Channel bottled copies of his pamphlet; and finally returned, after a little more than a year's absence, to London.

Shelley's father was irate. His son and heir had attained, to his way of thinking, an average of zero. To be expelled from Oxford for atheism was bad enough; to elope with an innkeeper's daughter was an intolerable offense. Shelley's allowance of £200 a year, which he had been receiving for some time, was now cut off, and only the benevolence of his maternal uncle, Captain Pilfold, rescued him from abject poverty. Yet the lack of funds was small deprivation to Shelley. Whenever he had money he gave much to the poor and his friends. For himself he knew few bodily needs: already he had begun his abstemious vegetarian habits. To Hogg's entreaties to join him in a pudding, he replied that "a pudding was a prejudice." If hunger assailed him in the public street, he would dive into a bake-shop, purchase a roll, and proceed down the street, book in hand, munching as he went.

In February, 1813, *Queen Mab*, chiefly written when he was eighteen, was finished and printed for private distribution. Shelley later spoke of it as "villanous trash," and never intended to include it among his published works. In any account of his life, however, it has a twofold importance: as his first considerable work of any excellence, and as an exposition of his atheism. The idealistic, visionary philosophy, regardless of human limitations, ignorant that most

men were incapable of his Ariel-flight, could be well
expressed only in poetry ; it was in fact a poetic philosophy, and as such most characteristic of Shelley.

An important figure, in the person of William Godwin, whose anarchistic principles, expounded in his
Political Justice, had largely influenced the philosophy
of *Queen Mab,* now appears in Shelley's life. Shelley
wrote to Godwin from Keswick, a correspondence grew
up, and later, in London, a close intimacy. Yet more
significant in the young poet's life was Mary Woll-
stonecraft Godwin, the pale daughter with the "piercing
look." For some time she and Shelley never actually
met, though they were well known to each other by hear-
say ; but one eventful afternoon, when Shelley called
at Godwin's house, it is said, the door was opened by
her, a feminine voice cried, "Shelley!" and on the
instant came reply, "Mary!"

Meanwhile domestic peace had departed from the
Shelley household. Sister-in-law Eliza had excited
Percy's "unbounded abhorrence;" Harriet and Shelley
had a petty quarrel, Harriet left her home, and the
youthful husband and father was plunged again into
dejection. His fair dreams — Oxford and Harriet —
had alike lost lustre. In Mary Godwin only did he find
a kindred spirit — the upshot of all which was that
Shelley, defying sacred as well as social laws, or, as he
would have put it, unshackled by such traditional su-
perstitions as marriage rites, eloped with her on July
28, 1814.

The fugitive couple crossed to France and Switzerland, but after six weeks returned to London. Here
poverty and the inconsistent indignation of the anar-
chist Godwin for a while beset them. The following

January (1815), however, Shelley's grandfather died, leaving considerable property. Shelley, who went immediately to Field Place to claim his share of the inheritance, was refused admittance by the still wrathful parent; but he treated the repulse with admirable composure, sat on the steps, and read *Comus*. Finally he was allowed £1000 annually, and affairs for a while took a brighter turn. It was during the following summer, while living at Bishopsgate, on the borders of Windsor Park, that he composed *Alastor*.

Godwin, however, although he willingly enough accepted financial aid, would not yet tolerate Shelley as his son-in-law. A despicable figure he made, as Matthew Arnold puts it, " preaching and holding the hat." Shelley, indignant, once more left England, in May, 1816, and spent the summer at Geneva, chiefly in the company of Lord Byron. He was back again in October, however, only to meet the severest catastrophe of his life. In December the body of Harriet was found in the Serpentine. Further, as if to fill full the cup of his dejection, suit for the guardianship of Harriet's children was brought against him; a suit in which the avowed atheist stood no chance against indignant orthodoxy. Indeed, about the only comfort derived from the whole winter was a reconciliation with Godwin, Mary and Shelley having been formally married on December 30, 1816.

It would be pleasant to pass quickly over Shelley's relations to Harriet, the least attractive side of his life. Such offenses as his are in themselves of course to be wholly condemned; but at the same time, without condoning the act, it is important to remember the kind of man he was. When he was in Switzerland with

Mary he urged Harriet to join them — a remarkable
invitation, to be sure, but by its ridiculous impossibility
the best proof of his utter failure to comprehend what
was due his wife. So sensitive a man as Shelley could
never have written such a letter in jest or brutality; he
simply did not understand why things should not be so.
In forming an opinion of him, moreover, one must take
into account his scrupulous personal purity. Leigh
Hunt attacks with vehemence Shelley's severest de-
nouncers, "the collegiate refusers of argument and the
conventional sowers of wild oats." For from these two
things — conventional moral cant and youthful dissipation followed by so-called respectability — Shelley revolted completely.

No one, of course, can pardon Shelley just because
he held strange theories and lived up to them. Yet his
breaking of the most sacred conventions, it must be emphasized, was not the result of a libertine passion. He
believed sincerely in what he did. For this consistent
madness he had to pay by a twofold suffering: in remorse over the wretched suicide with which he was inextricably tangled, and in the loss of his two children,
whom he passionately loved. "The conventions which
he despised and treated like the dust beneath his feet,"
comments J. A. Symonds, "were found in this most
cruel crisis to be a rock on which his very heart was
broken."

During the chancery suit for his children Shelley
lived with Mary at Great Marlow, on the Thames.
All through these sad days he was a ministering angel
among the poor of the neighborhood. He kept a list of
the needy, whom he relieved out of his own pocket; he
visited the sick in their beds; and once, Leigh Hunt

tells us, he carried a sick woman whom he found on
Hampstead Heath from door to door seeking to find
shelter until he brought her to Hunt's house, where
she was cared for: Nor was his generosity only to the
poor. His friend Peacock, the novelist, received annually £100; once he gave Leigh Hunt £1400; and he
continued to pay Godwin's debts, in all about £6000.

In spite of dejection, however, Shelley's life at Great
Marlow was not without its compensations. It was at
this time that he became intimate with Hunt and
Lamb. The former gives an amusing account of Shelley's games with the Hunt children, how he would sail
paper boats with them, or play at " frightful creatures,"
from which pastime they snatched a " fearful joy."
Through Hunt he met Hazlitt and Keats, but neither
of them took to him so kindly as he to them; Keats
especially stood off from the aristocracy that went with
Shelley's name.

The year at Great Marlow, too, brought added literary store from the poet. He finished his long poem of
Laon and Cythna (revised and published January,
1818, as the *Revolt of Islam*) while floating in his boat
under the beech groves by the Thames. Besides this,
the poem *Mont Blanc* and the *Hymn to Intellectual
Beauty*, conceived during his second visit to Switzerland, were written; and he began *Prince Athanase* (unfinished) and *Rosalind and Helen* (finished in Italy).

Early in the spring of 1818 Shelley left England
behind him forever. His broken health — he had been
threatened with consumption — and the unfortunate
events of the past year, together with urgent invitations
from Lord Byron, who was in Venice, were the chief
causes of his going.

The remaining four years of Shelley's life may be conveniently divided into two periods: the first year and a half, during which his places of residence were numerous and unsettled; and the two years and a half at Pisa and Lerici. He and his party arrived at Milan early in April, and, after a few weeks at Como and a month's visit to the Gisbornes at Leghorn, took up summer residence at the Bagni di Lucca. During the fall they occupied, at Byron's invitation, his vacant villa at Este in the Euganean Hills, overlooking Padua, Venice, and "the waveless plain of Lombardy." Since the severity of a winter in North Italy was feared, on account of Shelley's poor health, he and his wife journeyed via Rome to Naples. Though he shunned crowds or strangers, Shelley depended for cheerfulness on two or three companions; and the lack thereof at Naples, together with continued illness, threw him into low spirits. Only occasional moments — such as visits to Pæstum or Pompeii, where he heard

> "The mountain's slumberous voice at intervals
> Thrill through those roofless halls" —

relieved the monotony of his loneliness. "I could," he says in the *Stanzas written in Dejection*,

> "lie down like a tired child,
> And weep away the life of care
> Which I have borne and yet must bear."

Spring in Rome was a much happier time. Antiquity spoke eloquently to Shelley's heart; sitting among the ruined baths of Caracalla, wandering about the Colosseum, or treading the spring flowers of the Campagna, he fashioned some of his greatest verse, — *Prometheus* and *The Cenci*. The following summer was spent at

Leghorn, and the fall at Florence, where the son who
inherited the family estates, Sir Percy Florence Shelley,
was born. Finally he took up residence early in 1820
at Pisa.

Under the sunny Italian sky Shelley soon grew
stronger, and with his strength came his best literary
work. First, at Lucca he finished *Rosalind and Helen*,
at his wife's request, and translated Plato's *Banquet*. A
visit to Venice in August, 1818, inspired *Julian and
Madallo*, in which are given portraits of the author and
Byron. At Este he wrote those melodious octosyllabics,
Among the Euganean Hills, and began *Prometheus
Unbound;* and Naples at least inspired the immortal
Stanzas. But the year 1819 was his banner-year. In
it at Rome, Leghorn, and Florence he finished *The
Cenci*, nearly completed *Prometheus*, wrote the *Mask
of Anarchy*, translated Euripides's *The Cyclops*, and
sang many of his incomparable lyrics, chief of which
are the *Indian Serenade* and the *Ode to the West
Wind*. His manner of composition, usually in the open
air, was truly poetical. We remember *Alastor*, written
under the great trees of Windsor Park, and the *Revolt
of Islam*, in a boat on the Thames ; we have seen him
among the ruins of Rome and on the Bay of Naples ;
at Pisa he did most of his work on the roof, with only
a glass covering between him and the scorching Italian
sun. The *Ode to the West Wind* was " conceived and
chiefly written," he says in the introductory note, " in
a wood that skirts the Arno," in communion with the
whirling leaves and tempestuous gusts from the " wind-
grieved Apennine." In it is expressed especially the
poet's vague, insubstantial being, like a cloud or a leaf
at play with the wind — the intangible, Ariel-like Shel-

ley, unknown to the other self throbbing with sympathy
for mankind. If there is something inspiring about the
warm affection and high ideals of the human Shelley
of Hampstead Heath, there is at the same time something perhaps greater, certainly rarer, about the fancy-
flights of the child of nature — a purer, freer spiritu-
ality than can be met in any other poet. To the West
Wind he says : —

> " Make me thy lyre, even as the forest is :
> What if my leaves are falling like its own !
> The tumult of thy mighty harmonies
> Will take from both a deep, autumnal tone,
> Sweet though in sadness. Be thou, Spirit fierce,
> My spirit ! Be thou me, impetuous one ! "

At Pisa Shelley was happy among friends. His
schoolfellow and cousin, Thomas Medwin, joined him ;
and Captain and Mrs. Edward Williams, — Mrs. Williams was the " Jane " of some of his later poems, —
charmed by Medwin's tales of Shelley, came from Switzerland and soon took up their abode in the same house
with him and Mary. Captain Edward Trelawny, the
friend of the Williamses and faithful to the poet unto
death, followed not long after. Of greater significance,
Lord Byron quitted his Ravenna home for a palace
in Pisa. Shelley, who was always a little silenced by
Byron's fame and a wistful boyish admiration for his
genius, saw clearly enough, however, to write to Hunt :
" He has many generous and exalted qualities, but the
canker of aristocracy wants to be cut out." The two
great poets were nevertheless very close companions ;
Shelley gradually overcame his shyness, and Byron said
that his friend was the most truly noble spirit he had
known. Shelley always charmed his listeners with his

manner and his abundant conversation. His voice, very shrill, was eager and piercing rather than discordant.

During Pisan days Shelley's genius continued to thrive. In the first year, 1820, he wrote the charming *Letter to Maria Gisborne*, the *Witch of Atlas*, *The Sensitive Plant*, and his fanciful version of *Œdipus*. The following year produced some of his best work: *Epipsychidion*, inspired by Emilia Viviani, a beautiful Italian girl cloistered against her will, a girl into whose clear spirit he read his intellectual, unattainable ideal of woman; *Adonais*, the surpassing elegy on John Keats, by far the most completely finished of Shelley's poems; *Hellas*, an imaginative "improvise," he calls it, in celebration of Liberty; and an essay, the *Defence of Poetry*, in which he showed his power of writing noble prose. During the first six months of 1822, the last of his life, he wrote three fragments: *An Unfinished Drama; Charles the First*, a drama; and *The Triumph of Life*, in *terza rima*, a poem which gives presage of a clearer, more tranquil maturity. Sprinkled through the three years are many fragmentary translations from Greek, Latin, Italian, Spanish, and German, and a host of shorter pieces such as *The Cloud, The Skylark, Arethusa, Ode to Liberty, Hymn to Pan*, and *Ode to Naples*, — poems full of his "lyrical cry."

The last days were now at hand. In the summer of 1822 the Shelleys and the Williamses took a small house, the Casa Magni, near Lerici, on the Gulf of Spezia. They procured a sailing skiff, which they dubbed *Don Juan*, and Shelley, ignorant of seamanship but enthusiastic over sailing, spent most of his time on the water with Williams, who knew something of navigation. One day, early in July, they put forth, Williams at the helm and Shelley with his book, for Leghorn, where Leigh Hunt had just arrived. On the 8th, after happy days with Hunt, the two set sail again for Lerici — into the teeth of a storm. Through days of misery Mary and Jane watched and waited. Finally, on July 19, the ill news was brought them by Trelawny; the bodies had been washed ashore — Shelley with a manuscript of the *Indian Serenade* and two volumes in his pocket, Sophocles and Keats, the latter turned back as in the act of reading. The bodies were burned, Hunt, Byron, and Trelawny attending. Shelley's heart, however, withstood the flames, and the intrepid Trelawny snatched it unconsumed from the pyre. The poet's ashes were then collected and buried at Rome, near the grave of Keats. The epitaph, composed by Leigh Hunt, had at first the two simple words, *Cor Cordium*, but Trelawny added those lines so indelibly characteristic of Shelley and his watery grave : —

> "Nothing of him that doth fade,
> But doth suffer a sea-change
> Into something rich and strange."

JOHN KEATS

KEATS, whose name will ever be associated with beauty in English poetry, whose devotion to an ideal and remarkable realization thereof in a mere handful of years are unsurpassed in the history of English literature, is especially inspiring as a *man*. Indeed, one of his friends, Archdeacon Bailey, writes of him as one " whose genius I did not, and do not, more fully admire than I entirely loved the man." And his friend Reynolds says, " He was the sincerest friend, the most lovable associate . . . ' that ever lived in this tide of times.' " Of extreme sensitiveness, endowed with a vivid imagination, confronted by poverty, consumption, and a passionate love which could never come to its fulfillment, Keats the man wins followers as readily as Keats the poet.

The son of Thomas Keats and Frances Jennings, and the first of five children, he was born in London on the 29th of October, 1795. His father, first an ostler in the livery stable of Mr. John Jennings of Moorfields, had married his employer's daughter and risen to a position of respectability in his trade, if not, as Lord Houghton would have it, to " the upper ranks of the middle class." It is sufficient, as Lowell points out, that Keats's " poetical pedigree is of the best, tracing through Spenser to Chaucer, and that Pegasus does not stand at livery in the largest establishments in Moorfields."

In his earliest youth Keats showed signs of a quick and fiery spirit, and, if the enthusiastic but often erroneous Haydon is to be believed, of a tendency to make verses. The boy had a trick, it was said, of answering questions by making a rhyme to the last word spoken. As a young child, when his mother was very ill, he stood guard at her door with an old sword, and allowed no one to disturb her. At her death, report says, he was so overcome that he hid for days under the master's desk at school.

John, with his younger brothers George and Tom, was sent to the school kept by the Rev. John Clarke at Enfield. Perhaps the most remarkable features of his school-days were his pugnacity and his enduring friendships. He was a little boy and his brother George, of larger limb, often had to take his part; but he possessed, says one of his schoolfellows, " a terrier-like resoluteness." Again, " he would fight any one — morning, noon, and night, his brother among the rest. . . . No one was more popular." Indeed, a schoolmate thought afterwards that Keats as a boy had promised greatness, though rather a military than a poetic. Yet " he was not merely the favorite of all, like a pet prize-fighter, for his terrier courage," writes Charles Cowden Clarke, the son of the head master and one of Keats's warmest friends ; " but his high-mindedness, his utter unconsciousness of a mean motive, his placability, his generosity, wrought so general a feeling in his behalf that I never heard a word of disapproval from any one, superior or equal, who had known him."

At school Keats had the reputation of being a "regular " student, but he received no great education — small Latin and no Greek. Yet so keen was his perception and so great his power of making what he saw and heard his own that he came forth, as did the grammar-schooled boy of Stratford, with a far vaster equipment than many a university man. Soon, under the influence of the somewhat older Clarke, he acquired a love of the English poets — especially of Spenser, whose romance, says Clarke, "he *ramped* through like a young horse turned into a spring meadow."

It is a little surprising, perhaps, to find this young enthusiastic lover of Chaucer and Spenser leaving Mr. Clarke's in 1810 and apprenticing himself to Mr. Hammond, a surgeon of Edmonton. But the orphaned son of a liveryman must be about learning a trade. He seems later to have quarreled with Mr. Hammond, who allowed the indentures to be canceled; and Keats, at about nineteen, went up to London to study at St. Thomas's and Guy's hospitals. He passed with credit, July, 1815, his examination at Apothecaries' Hall. But his imagination was too keen for the work. "The other day, during the lecture," he once said to Cowden Clarke, "there came a sunbeam into the room, and with it a whole troop of creatures floating in the ray; and I was off with them to Oberon and fairy-land." At the same time the purpose of consecrating his life to poetry was growing upon him. His verses had been praised in a circle of friends; above all, Leigh Hunt, .editor, poet, enthusiastic supporter of Liberty and friend of literary aspirants, and Clarke, whose reading of Chapman's Homer with Keats one night in 1816 had called forth the famous sonnet—

"Much have I travelled in the realms of gold " —

urged him to the new profession. In 1817 he published his first volume of verse, with a dedication to Leigh Hunt in an effusive sonnet.

For the few remaining years of Keats's life London and Hampstead were his chief places of residence. In fact, though he changed his home several times, his environment, except for short trips to Stratford, Oxford, Scotland, Winchester, and the Isle of Wight, and the fatal journey to Rome, was substantially that of London and its neighborhood.

Keats had many friends during these last years, and all of them held him in high esteem. Leigh Hunt had for a year or two the greatest share of his affection; together they wrote verses and discussed poetry, art, religion — all things — with great fervor. It is to Keats's credit that he was later less dazzled by Hunt's superficial splendor. Through Hunt, Keats met Shelley, already famous for his poetry and Godwinism; Haydon, the vigorous, whole-souled, egotistical painter; John Hamilton Reynolds, a writer of little note, but one of the finest natures that ever lived; and James Rice, "of infinite jest" and lovable personality. Others whom he met intimately in various ways were an artist, Joseph Severn, later his constant companion in Rome; Charles Wentworth Dilke, for many years editor of the *Athenæum;* Charles Armitage Brown, one of Keats's closest friends, with whom he lived for some time at Hampstead; and a young clergyman named Benjamin Bailey, later Archdeacon of Colombo. Three greater men, with whom Keats was not so intimate as with those already named, must nevertheless be added to the list of his friends: Wordsworth, Lamb, and Hazlitt. The meeting with Coleridge in Caen Wood is remarkable for Coleridge's prediction after Keats had passed on; to a friend he said, "There is death in that hand." The common testimony of Keats's friends to his good

temper, graceful wit, rare humor, and generosity is
worth remembering. Especially famous was Haydon's
"immortal dinner" on the 28th of December, 1817,
where Keats first met Wordsworth. "Wordsworth's
fine intonation as he quoted Milton and Virgil, Keats's
eager inspired look, Lamb's quaint sparkle of lambent
humor, so speeded the stream of conversation," says
Haydon, "that I never passed a more delightful time."

Keats now gave himself up entirely to poetry. So
vivid were his sensations that he threw himself into his
work as he had thrown himself into his schoolboy pugnacity. Poetry became an absorbing passion with him;
the slightest emotion he felt to the finger-tips. In
writing to Reynolds from the Isle of Wight, whither
he had gone to work on *Endymion*, he says: "I find I
cannot exist without Poetry — without eternal Poetry
— half the day will not do — the whole of it — I began
with a little, but habit has made me a Leviathan. I had
become all in a Tremble from not having written anything of late — the Sonnet [1] over-leaf did me good. I
slept the better last night for it — this Morning, however, I am nearly as bad again." As Lowell puts it
excellently, "Every one of Keats's poems was a sacrifice of vitality; a virtue went away from him into every
one of them." The exquisite sensitiveness of Keats, living thus intensely on his art, came to be almost a disease; he was worn out by his constant nervous energy.
"O for a life of sensations rather than of thoughts!"
he once cried. The minutest sensations excited such
bewildering intellectual activity that the overloaded
imagination longed for rest. Along with his extreme

---

[1] Refers to the sea sonnet beginning "It keeps eternal whisperings
around." The sonnet was inclosed in the letter to Reynolds.

sensitiveness, there developed in Keats a tendency to melancholia; "a horrid morbidity of Temperament," he calls it. "It is," he continues, "the greatest Enemy and stumbling-block I have to fear."

In 1818 Keats's first considerable production, *Endymion*, came out. In the preface the author apologizes for his "inexperience, immaturity, and every error denoting a feverish attempt, rather than a deed accomplished." Again, with remarkably clear insight, "The imagination of a boy is healthy, and the mature imagination of a man is healthy ; but there is a space of life between, in which the soul is in a ferment, the character undecided, the way of life uncertain, the ambition thick-sighted : thence proceeds mawkishness." Clearly Keats was in this "space of life between" when he wrote *Endymion*, but just as clearly he quite perceived and understood his "mawkishness," of which the comprehension is half the cure. The poem received overwhelming censure from the reviews, especially from the *Quarterly*. Keats became, in their hands, a cockney poet, "the puling satellite of the arch-offender and King of Cockaigne, Hunt ; " he was advised to return to his "plasters, pills, and ointment boxes."

Yet the idea that Keats suffered intensely from these attacks, that he was a weakling "snuffed out" by the reviewers, — an idea born chiefly of Shelley's *Adonais* and Byron's doggerel, "Who killed John Keats ? I, said the Quarterly," — is largely false. We have already seen his calm, clear self-analysis in the Preface. "I hate a mawkish popularity," he wrote to a friend ; and after the reception of *Endymion*, instead of retorting, as did Hunt, or bringing suit, as did Hazlitt, he quietly set about perfecting himself. "This is a mere matter of the

moment," he says; " I think I shall be among the English poets after my death." A man so nervously sensitive
must have winced, to be sure, under the bludgeon blows
of his adversaries. " He suffered," as Lowell points out,
" in proportion as his ideal was high and he was conscious of falling below it." Yet it was his own unerring
self-censure that cut far deeper than outside comment.
It is essential, if Keats's character is to be interpreted
aright, to understand that the effect of the attack was
only temporary. Sensibility, it must be remembered, is
very different from sentimentality. Keats was, his
brother George tells us, " as much like the Holy Ghost
as Johnny Keats," and Matthew Arnold, taking up the
phrase, says: " The thing to be seized is, that Keats
had flint and iron in him, that he had character."
Indeed, it is the man's robustness, more especially in
spite of his high nervous tension, which should excite
remark.

With so active a spirit, with a brain already " troubled
with thick-coming fancies," — an intellectual sickness
which friendships and an abundant fund of humor could
not overcome, — Keats fell the prey to two things which
far more than the reviewers drove him to an untimely
death: a love affair, which took complete control of
him, spiritually and physically; and a hereditary disease,
consumption, which mocked his passionate love and his
efforts to write. At the same time poverty, due to a
Mr. Abbey's mismanagement of his mother's not uncomfortable legacy, became a very real issue.

Fanny Brawne, who lived near Brown's house in
Hampstead, where Keats was living in the winter of
1818–19, was the object of Keats's affection. What
was at first only " a chat and a tiff" passed rapidly

into violent passion and " a restless physical jealousy,"
as Mr. Colvin calls it. By April, 1819, he was probably
engaged to her, yet Keats's poor health and poverty
made immediate marriage inadvisable ; and as it was
put off and he saw disease slowly tightening its grip
upon him, the passionate lover was almost consumed
with despair.

It is from now on that his love letters to Fanny
Brawne date, and the overstrained passion that breaks
out in them, what Matthew Arnold calls "the abandon-
ment of all reticence and all dignity, of the merely sensuous man," has been caught at by many as a measure
of his real character. But this view, naturally supported
by the *Adonais* idea, is almost wholly unfair. In the
first place, his letters to his friends show to the last his
good humor, courage, and nobleness. In the second
place, only parts of his letters to Fanny Brawne, which,
by the way, were written to her, not to the public,
exhibit " the merely sensuous man."

Let us look at one of the most " abandoned " letters.
" You have absorb'd me. . . . I could die for you. My
Creed is Love and you are its only tenet. You have
ravished me by a Power I cannot resist; and yet I
could resist till I saw you ; and even since I have seen
you I have endeavoured often ' to reason against the
reasons of my Love.' I can do that no more — the
pain would be too great. My love is selfish. I cannot
breathe without you " (October 13, 1819). This letter,
to be sure, was written nearly four months before his
first violent attack of consumption. But he had been
ill long before this. He had suffered from sore throat
during the whole preceding winter and spring ; yet it
was not a physical sickness which racked him most.

Consider the situation: A man sensitive to the utmost degree, confronted by a poetic ideal the very service of which took a " virtue " out of him; a man whose brother had just died of consumption; a man himself already in weak health — nothing, in short, but nerves and imagination left. The complete and overwhelming irony of his fate, and, as if by an impossibly deeper irony, the nervous temperament with which he must wage his battle against such odds, wholly explain, if not excuse, his occasional loss of self-control. His energy has already been consumed by his passion for poetry. And now he falls in love with a woman, not playfully, nor just " deeply," but with all his nervous imagination. Is it not natural enough that he should write " I cannot breathe without you " ? Then the foreseen tuberculosis and poverty and the utter loss of all cherished hopes — except poetic immortality — take hold of him : the wreck is complete. Yet — and this is the point for remark — he writes in March, 1820 (*after* the first serious illness) with a delightful touch of humor : " There is a great difference between going off in warm blood like Romeo and making one's exit like a frog in a frost." On the whole, he bore up with admirable courage.

To return to the course of events which introduce the last chapter of his life. In the summer of 1818, Keats, after seeing his brother George, with a newly married wife, off for America, made a walking tour, with his friend Brown, through the English Lake District and Scotland. A letter to Reynolds gives an amusing account of his visit to the cottage of Burns. Here he met " a mahogany-faced old Jackass who knew Burns. . . . His gab hindered my sublimity : the flat dog made me write a flat sonnet." During his tour Keats underwent

great physical strain. In the Isle of Mull he caught
a violent cold, from the effects of which he never quite
recovered. It was the following winter, when he was
making the acquaintance of Fanny Brawne, that he
suffered continually from sore throat. In December,
when consumption had carried off his brother Tom,
he was induced to move to Brown's home, Wentworth
Place, Hampstead. After a year of recurring colds he
met his fatal illness on February 3, 1820. On seeing
a drop of blood from his mouth, he said quietly to
Brown: "It is arterial blood — I cannot be deceived
in that color. . . . I must die."

It is interesting to note that Keats's best poems were
written in the year preceding his serious illness. He had
served his apprenticeship in *Endymion ;* the volume of
1820, containing *Lamia*, *Isabella*, the famous Odes,
the *Eve of St. Agnes*, and *Hyperion* are of his maturity. In two years, with the coming sickness imminent upon him, he completely answered and silenced
the reviewers, not by vituperation or satire, but by genuine work which bore its own fruit. No comments of
contemporaries offer such abundant testimony as does
this 1820 edition of poems to the real vigor of his character and the nobleness of his ideals. He served poetry
truly — not for a "mawkish popularity." What he
might have done had he lived to even greater maturity
must ever be sad conjecture.

Much of the best work on the poems was done at
Winchester, where Keats, having willfully absented himself from Hampstead and Fanny Brawne, spent the fall
of 1819. After his return to London he did little work
except for an attempt at recasting the fragment *Hyperion*. Soon the disease was upon him. During the spring

and summer it grew intermittently worse; he was told another winter in England would kill him; and he finally consented to go to Italy — though he said it was " like marching up to a battery." A brave and generous companion was found in Joseph Severn, his artist friend, who sailed with him on September 18, 1820. On the boat was written his last poem, the famous sonnet beginning, " Bright star, would I were steadfast as thou art."

The two travelers arrived at Naples late in October and journeyed thence to Rome, where Keats soon grew too weak even to write letters. A note of November 1, written to Brown, is full of his torture. At home he had kept to himself the consuming fire of his passion; now he breaks out in despair: " I can bear to die — I cannot bear to leave her. O God! God! God! Everything I have in my trunks that reminds me of her goes through me like a spear. The silk lining she put in my traveling cap scalds my head. . . . Despair is forced upon me as a habit. . . . Oh, Brown, I have coals of fire in my breast." In his last letter (November 30) he speaks, with a flash of the old humor, of " leading a posthumous existence." Towards the end he would not hear of recovery, but longed for the ease of death — in a manner reminiscent of his line, —

"I have been half in love with easeful Death."

Once he said, " I feel the flowers growing over me," and another time gave for his epitaph, —

" Here lies one whose name was writ in water."

On the 23d of February, 1821, he died. He was buried in the Protestant Cemetery, near the pyramid of Gaius Sestius.

The sensitiveness of Keats should be especially remembered, for it was not only stronger than that of any other great English poet, but it underlay all his actions; it was responsible for his weakness and his strength. It gave rise to his youthful mawkishness and to his " horrid morbidity of temperament;" but it gave rise, too, to many noble qualities which easily outweigh these defects, — to his eager affection, to his generosity, and chiefly to an ambition which soon sought a far higher service than popular applause. It is indeed worth noting that Keats overcame his youthful mawkishness more surely than men who had less cause for melancholy. This sensitiveness, it must not be forgotten, was responsible for his genuine devotion to an ideal—a devotion that produced the little but great poetry which has put him, as he humbly hoped, among the English poets after his death. "He is," says Matthew Arnold, — "he is with Shakespeare." Many who have pitied the poor, inspired weakling of their imaginations, the Keats killed by the reviews, give up reluctantly the tragic story they have believed. Fortunately for English poetry, John Keats was not so mawkish as some of his admirers; he had " flint and iron " in him. There is, even then, surely enough tragedy to his life; and rather than a pathetic weakness to mourn, there is something infinitely greater, — an enduring strength and nobleness to admire.

THE VICTORIAN AGE

THE chief characteristic of the Victorian Age, which, roughly speaking, may be placed between 1830 and 1900, was *variety of interest*. No other time except the Elizabethan has been so full of enterprise. But the England of Victoria, though it possessed the vigor and resourcefulness, lacked the freshness and imagination of the England of Elizabeth; hence, instead of being an age of discovery and poetry, it was rather one of invention and prose. If " More beyond " was the motto of the aspiring Elizabethans, " More within " may be said to have been the motto of the inquiring Victorians.

The original impulse to this age of great development came, of course, from the French Revolution, which broke down the barriers of superstition and absolute monarchy, and demanded new political, religious, and social organization. At first, however, the influence in England was seen only in the visionary poetry of the Romanticists. The first practical expression of the new spirit was the Reform Bill in 1832, which secured for England representative government. From then on interest in political advancement was widespread, the more so since England, in her colonies, became a world-empire. A little after the first political ferment came the religious conflict, brought on largely by the scientific study of evolution. Science destroyed the old systems, threw many people into confusion and agnostic despair, and finally forced on the world a new and larger, less dogmatic faith. The third most striking change, the social, appeared in a great improvement in the material comfort of the people. More and better schools grew up; cities became cleaner, better lighted; steam and electricity promoted intercourse of men and nations. This development, like the religious, may be almost wholly attributed to science. Urged on by its inquiring spirit, culture spread amazingly; four of the six English universities were established in the nineteenth century; study was for the first time put on an accurate, "historical" basis; the cheapness of paper now put books, magazines, and newspapers within the reach of all; and the "general reader" sprang into being. Yet, at the same time, the commercialism which the new mechanical interests inspired grew out of all proportion. The prosperity of the people was also its curse, for it brought about a narrow eagerness for mere luxury and a consequent lowness of artistic and moral ideals; it came perilously near making man into a machine. Of this the best evidence is the atrocious architecture of the years from 1850 to 1875 and the absorption of the majority of men in mere money-making business. If Macaulay reflects the progress and success of his times, Carlyle and Ruskin, it must not be forgotten, are strong in disgust at the way such success was attained; their cry is for spiritual as well as material progress.

This age of diversity and scientific inquiry had two chief literary expressions — both in prose: (1) The *novel*, which reached its maturity in Victorian days, analyzed and expressed far more than any other kind of writing the complexity of a very various life. Equally significant has been the perfecting of the short story, a form of fiction peculiarly adapted to the hurried, complicated life of the nineteenth century. (2) The *essay*, which through magazines reached a wide reading public, gave a medium to most of the great writers on scientific, religious, moral, social, and historical subjects.

The poetry of the Victorian Age was generally surpassed, especially in bulk, by the prose. In two instances, however, those of Tennyson and Browning, it clearly held its own. This period, though not so essentially a poetic age as the preceding one of Romanticism, offered much, especially in the realm of spiritual conflict, for poetic expression. There was, too, a vastness of enterprise, a universality of interest which called for great poetry. Yet, with the exception of a few master-hands, most of the work was self-conscious, imitative, or unimaginative.

THOMAS BABINGTON MACAULAY

EVERY one has heard of Macaulay's wonderful memory and clear style in writing; but after these have
been noticed, the man is too often dismissed as commonplace. It is asserted by some that Macaulay, the
prejudiced Whig and complacent materialist, lived in
unaspiring prosperity; that, except in a few freaks of
memory and a mastery of a second-rate kind of writing,
he presents a very dull figure when compared to other
great literary men — to Coleridge, for instance, with his
fascinating dreams and brilliant philosophy, even to
Goldsmith, with his picturesque squalor. Coleridge's
life, to be sure, is startling, one of the most interesting
in history, and Goldsmith's is incomparable in its kind.
If not to live sensationally, moreover, is to be uninteresting, Macaulay is for the most part uninteresting; he
does not compete with Shelley and Byron. Yet lack of
interest in general is an absurd charge to bring against
Macaulay, however he may suffer by comparison with
Coleridge, Goldsmith, Shelley, and Byron; those who
have accepted this error on faith should hasten to read
Trevelyan's Life of his uncle.

It must nevertheless be admitted, when the best has
been said for Macaulay, that he is without spiritual interest — a conspicuous lack in a great man. "He appears
to have been almost wholly wanting," says Mr. Morrison, "in intellectual curiosity of any kind. . . . It would
not be easy to quote a sentence from either his published
works or his private letters which shows insight or medi-

tation on love, or marriage, or friendship, or the education of children, or religious faith or doubt." He had, that is, no dreams of "that untraveled world;" he never guessed nor cared to guess what lay "beyond the sunset." He was wholly a man of this world, of the average man's kind, albeit of great magnitude; and one feels that, although he is so far unparalleled, such another might conceivably appear. Hence the world does not treat his death as the irreparable loss that it sees in the death of a great genius. Wordsworth wrote of Coleridge: "Never saw I his likeness, nor probably the world can see again;" for Coleridge was truly unique, an *inimitable* man. One may be indeed interested in Macaulay, even impressed by his greatness, but one is never awestruck.

For all this, almost any one who starts to glance through Macaulay's letters finishes by reading them carefully and comes to feel that he has been in touch with a very interesting and great personality. And those who in reading have discovered the man's calm courage against financial and political odds, his labors for reform, and the stainlessness of his character, find his life not only interesting, but in a manner inspiring. Nor was it altogether without sensation. The sudden and wide popularity of his writings; his brilliant eloquence when as a young man he held the House of Commons under his spell so that old men remembered nothing like it since Fox and Canning; his whole part in the great revolutionary movement of 1832, when the system of "Rotten Boroughs" was done away with, — all give evidence of something akin to sensation. In his own day, moreover, though his literary fame was great, he was especially notable as a talker, as the elegant orator in the House of Commons and as the man who charmed the gatherings at Holland House.

Thomas Babington Macaulay was the son of Zachary Macaulay, of Scotch Presbyterian descent, and Selina Mills, the daughter of a Bristol Quaker. The father, who was for a time the governor of Sierra Leone, and who became in 1800 secretary to the company which had founded that colony, gave his whole life to the abolition of slavery. He was a stern man, with little understanding of the brilliancy and humor of his son, a man with more interest in a good tract than in a witty gathering at dinner, with most interest, however, in untiring good works. Macaulay's mother, more brilliant and sensitive than her quiet, religious husband, understood her son much better. On October 25, 1800, while she was on a visit at Rothley Temple, in Leicestershire, the home of her sister-in-law, who had married a Mr. Thomas Babington, the boy who took his uncle's name was born. He was the first of a family of nine children.

For nearly his whole life Macaulay's home was London; indeed, he never took any great interest in the country or even in any other city. London he knew by heart. While he was still very young his parents took a house in Birchin Lane. Soon after, they moved to the High Street, Clapham, on the south side of the Thames.

Macaulay's boyhood sayings and doings are as well known as anything about him; and they deserve, in fact, considerable mention, for in them appear without the complications of maturity his animation, his precosity, and his faithful work. Trevelyan tells how the boy lay by the hour in front of the fire, with a book before him and a piece of bread-and-butter in his hand. He did not care for toys, and talked, the maid said, "quite printed words." Another time, after a servant at Strawberry Hill had spilled some hot coffee on the boy's legs, when Lady Waldegrave later asked him how he was feeling, he replied solemnly, "Thank you, madam, the agony is abated." Once, when a servant at home had thrown away some oyster-shells which marked a spot sacred to him, Tom went to the drawing-room and, heedless of visitors there, pronounced seriously, "Cursed be Sally; for it is written, Cursed is he that removeth his neighbor's landmark."

Macaulay early began to write. Before he was eight he compiled a *Compendium of Universal History*, showing in it a startling amount of information, — even though Oliver Cromwell figures as "an unjust and wicked man," — and three cantos of a romance in verse, the *Battle of Cheviot*, in the manner of Scott. Soon after, the remarkable child composed a long blank verse poem called *Fingal, a Poem in XII Books*. But his greatest boy-work was the heroic poem, *Olaus Magnus, King of Norway*, from whom he sought to trace his own descent.

But Macaulay was not a spoiled child. His mother always concealed her wonder before him. When very young he was sent to the private school of a Mr. Greaves in Clapham, and whenever he begged to stay at home after dinner, he always met the same well-known reply, "No, Tom, if it rains cats and dogs, you shall go." Yet his interest in reading did not prevent his being a lad of good spirits and fun; and when he returned from school he filled the household of children with mirth. Mrs. Hannah More, next to his mother, had the greatest

influence over his boyhood; he often visited her at
Barley Wood, and through her suggestion and aid commenced his library.

In 1812 the boy was sent, much against his will, to
Mr. Preston's school at Little Shelford, near Cambridge. Two years later Mr. Preston moved to Aspen-
den Hall, Hertfordshire, and there Macaulay prepared
for college. He was wholly without skill in sports, but
on account of his frank manner and brilliant conversation he was not unpopular. In his studies, especially the
classics, he excelled, though he stole what time he could
for his incessant reading. How superior he was to the
average boy of thirteen, both in thought and expression,
most of all in the maturity of his sense of humor, is
evident from such a letter as the following : —

                              SHELFORD, April 11, 1814.

MY DEAR MAMA, — The news is glorious indeed.
Peace! peace with a Bourbon, with a descendant of
Henri Quatre, with a prince who is bound to us by all
the ties of gratitude! . . .

I am sorry to hear that some nameless friend of papa's
denounced my voice as remarkably loud. I have accordingly resolved to speak in a moderate key except on the
undermentioned special occasions. *Imprimis*, when I
am speaking at the same time with three others.
Secondly, when I am praising the *Christian Observer*.[1]
Thirdly, when I am praising Mr. Preston or his sisters,
I may be allowed to speak in my loudest voice, that
they may hear me.

I saw to-day that greatest of churchmen, that pillar
of Orthodoxy, that true friend to the Liturgy, that

------

[1] Edited by Macaulay's father.

mortal enemy to the Bible Society, Herbert Marsh,
D. D., Professor of Divinity on Lady Margaret's foundation. I stood looking at him for about ten minutes,
and shall always continue to maintain that he is a very
ill-favored gentleman as far as outward appearance is
concerned. I am going this week to spend a day or two
at Dean Milner's, where I hope, nothing unforeseen
preventing, to see you in about two months' time.

Ever your affectionate son,

T. B. MACAULAY.

At Trinity College, Cambridge, which Macaulay entered in October, 1818, he made a record in some ways
more brilliant than that at school, though he failed of
highest honors because of inability at mathematics. He
won, however, a Trinity fellowship, which gave him
£300 a year till 1831. During his college days, too, his
powers of conversation brought him more fame than
they ever could to a boy at school. His special strength
was argument and epigrammatic reply, and his rooms
soon became a centre of brilliant discussions, which he
was ready to carry to any hour of the night. Among
his friends at college were Derwent Coleridge and
Henry Nelson Coleridge, respectively son and nephew
of the great poet. His closest friend was the remarkable Charles Austin of Jesus College. Of these two
young men and their conversation Trevelyan tells that
they happened, while on a visit to Lord Lansdowne at
Bowood, to get talking one morning at breakfast.
" When the meal was finished they drew their chairs to
either end of the chimmey-piece, and talked at each
other across the hearth-rug as if they were in a first-
floor room in the Old Court of Trinity. The whole com-

pany, ladies, artists, politicians, and diners-out, formed
a silent circle round the two Cantabs, and, with a short
break for lunch, never stirred till the bell warned them
that it was time to dress for dinner."

After his college days Macaulay studied law and was
called to the bar in 1826. He always took more interest
in government than in law, however, and, latterly, more
in the study of government than in politics. At first,
when he was not traveling on the Northern Circuit, he
lived with his parents in Great Ormond Street. In 1829
he took chambers near by at 8, South Square, Gray's
Inn.

But Macaulay the essayist soon overshadowed Macaulay the lawyer. He began to write publicly in 1823
with contributions to *Knight's Magazine*. In 1825 his
Essay on Milton was published in the famous *Edinburgh Review*, and with it came widespread fame.
Murray, Byron's publisher, said it would be worth the
copyright of *Childe Harold* to have Macaulay on the
staff of the *Quarterly*, the Tory rival of the *Edinburgh
Review*. The essays, which have done so much to fix
Macaulay's fame, continued to appear from time to time,
usually in the *Edinburgh Review*. Some of them were
written during his busiest days, when the only moments
he could find for such work were between five in the
morning and breakfast. Yet he managed, in spite of
necessary haste, to maintain a remarkably consistent
excellence; once he gained the popular ear, he never
lost it. To-day his best essays are known as well as
novels. No man has done so much to introduce the general reader to unknown fields of history, biography, and
literature and to inspire an unexpected and fruitful interest. Among the essays contributed to the *Edinburgh*

Review, the best known are: Milton (1825), Hallam's Constitutional History, Frederick the Great, Horace Walpole, William Pitt, Sir William Temple, Lord Clive, Von Ranke's History of the Popes, Leigh Hunt, Lord Holland, Warren Hastings, Addison (1843). For the *Encyclopædia Britannica*, 8th edition (1853-1859), he wrote: Atterbury, Bunyan, Goldsmith, Johnson, and Pitt. It has been said that nearly all that many well-informed people know of history and literature has been picked up from Macaulay's essays.

The successful writer, however, was by 1830 gaining greater prominence with his tongue than with his pen. Breakfasting together had become very popular among the great men of London, and in the days when conversation was an art Macaulay easily won his way to a conspicuous position. If wits and great ladies were interested to meet the author of the brilliant articles in the *Review*, they were still more eager to know the remarkable talker. At Holland House, where he was a frequent guest, he became familiar with Rogers, Campbell, Tom Moore, and Sydney Smith. He was a friend of Sir James Mackintosh, and he knew the great French diplomatist, Talleyrand. Such notes as the following are common in the diaries of great men who knew him: " Breakfasted with Hallam, John Russell, Macaulay, Everett, Van de Weyer, Hamilton, Mahon. Never were such torrents of good talk as burst and sputtered over from Macaulay and Hallam " (Lord Carlisle's Journal, June 27, 1843).

Yet Macaulay was far from attractive in appearance. He was described by the poet Praed as " a short, manly figure, marvelously upright, with a bad neckcloth, and one hand in his waistcoat pocket. Of regular beauty he had little to boast; but in faces where there is an expression of great power, or of great good humor, or both, you do not regret its absence." " While conversing at table," says Trevelyan, "no one thought him otherwise than good-looking; but when he rose, he was seen to be short and stout in figure." When Lady Lyndhurst met him in 1831, she said : " I thought you were dark and thin, but you are fair, and, really, Mr. Macaulay, you are fat."

The only test of Macaulay's endurance through adversity came soon after he began to practice law. Political defeat in later life merely meant more time for his cherished studies ; his fame was secure. But in 1826, when he was not rich, when his literary fame was small, and when he had not yet entered politics, the recent failure of the firm of Babington and Macaulay, which threw the family expenses largely on him, put him to a genuine test. So strait were his circumstances that he was forced to sell even his Cambridge gold medal. Through the whole matter, however, he bore up with admirable good humor, and with his cheery ways kept up the spirits of the company in Great Ormond Street. It is his best praise that he treated his position not as a matter of grim, noble duty, but as a matter of course.

Lady Trevelyan, Macaulay's sister, in a few words addressed to her children gives a large glimpse of the family life at this time, a life a little limited in means, perhaps, but certainly not lugubrious. " In the morning there was some pretense of work and study. In the afternoon your uncle always took my sister Margaret and myself a long walk. We traversed every part of the city, Islington, Clerkenwell, and the parks, returning just in time for six o'clock dinner. What anecdotes he used to pour out about every street, and square, and court, and alley! There are many places I never pass without the tender grace of a day that is dead coming back to me. Then, after dinner, he always walked up and down the drawing-room between us chatting till tea-time. Our noisy mirth, his wretched puns, so many a minute, so many an hour! Then we sung, none of us having any voices, and he, if possible, least of all; but still the old nursery songs were set to music and chanted. My father, sitting at his own table, used to look up occasionally, and push back his spectacles, and, I dare say, wonder, in his heart, how we could so waste our time. After tea the book then in reading was produced. Your uncle very seldom read aloud himself of an evening, but walked about listening, and commenting, and drinking water."

Macaulay's first political position was a seat in the House of Commons for Calne. He entered in February, 1830, and made his first speech on the 5th of April of the same year, in favor of removing the Jewish disabilities. From the beginning he took a foremost position through his oratory. He wrote strongly in argument, but men who heard him speak said his written arguments were nothing to his eloquence in debate. "Whenever he rose to speak," says Gladstone, "it was a summons like a trumpet-call to fill the benches." In the spring of 1831 he was found, of course, on the Whig side ardently supporting the Reform Bill. When the bill became an act on June 7, 1832, he was appointed one of the commissioners of the Board of Control. In January, 1833, under the new system of election, he was sent up as member for Leeds. The following year he accepted a seat in the Supreme Council of India,

and in February sailed with his sister Hannah for Calcutta. Out of his salary during the four years of Indian
service he saved about £20,000 ; and from then on his
family was comfortably off. Besides his regular work
as legal adviser to the Council, he undertook the chair-
manship of the Committee of Instruction, as well as the
presidency of a commission appointed to draw up the
Penal Code and the Code of Criminal Procedure.

Very few men have read so constantly or so much as
Macaulay. Even in India, when his work was very exacting, he found time to read an almost fabulous
amount. In 1835 he writes, of classics alone, " During
the last thirteen months I have read Æschylus twice,
Sophocles twice, Euripides once, Pindar twice, Cal-
limachus, Apollonius Rhodius, Quintus Calaber, Theocritus twice, Herodotus, Thucydides, almost all of
Xenophon's works, almost all Plato, Aristotle's *Politics*, and a good deal of his *Organon*, besides dipping
elsewhere in him ; the whole of Plutarch's *Lives*, about
half of Lucian, two or three books of Athenæus, Plau-
tus twice, Terence twice, Lucretius twice, Catullus,
Tibullus, Propertius, Lucan, Statius, Silius Italicus,
Livy, Velleius Paterculus, Sallust, Cæsar, and lastly
Cicero." But his reading was not always of this nature.
" There was a certain prolific author," says Lady Trevelyan, " named Mrs. Meeke, whose romances he all
but knew by heart." Indeed, Macaulay seems to have
devoured without great discrimination whatever literature he could lay his hands on. He never spent much
time in reflection or revery — a possible indication of
shallowness. Once, for instance, he was crossing the
Irish Channel in order to verify certain points for his
History, at a time when one would suppose he might

have had much matter for reflection, yet his acquisitive intellect did not pause an instant; the light being too poor to read, he amused his mind by reciting to himself half of *Paradise Lost*. The quantity and rapidity of his reading, moreover, and the memory which retained half of *Paradise Lost* and most of *Pilgrim's Progress*, when his lack of meditation and of selection are considered, are not, as Mr. Morrison well points out, so much a title to honor as a sign of unprecedented consumption, as even a defect. Macaulay's Ben Jonson would have said doubtless: " Would he had meditated a thousand times! "

Macaulay on his return to England in 1838 spent some time in Italy, and there made observations for his *Lays of Ancient Rome*. About the only poetry he had written since Trinity days was the poem called *The Armada*, published in 1833 in *Friendship's Offering*, a collection of indifferent verse by various hands. The *Lays* were finally published in 1842. They were very popular; eighteen thousand copies sold in the first ten years, forty thousand in twenty years; and to-day every one knows "Horatius at the Bridge."

Soon after reaching England in 1839 Macaulay became member for Edinburgh. In the same year Lord Melbourne made him Secretary of War, an office which he held for two years. By this time, however, his interest in active political life was fast giving way to his eagerness to finish his great life-work, *The History of England*, which he first seriously thought of in 1838. He did hold office again, as Paymaster-General under Lord John Russell in 1846, and in 1852 he was reelected for Edinburgh. Failing health, however, and the absorbing work on the *History* kept him almost wholly from Parliament. In 1857, two years before his death, he was made Baron Macaulay of Rothley, and thus went down to history as *Lord* Macaulay. Though he took his seat in the House of Lords, he never spoke there. He accepted, however, the Lord High Steward-ship of the Borough of Cambridge.

The *History of England* in its original conception was intended to cover the period from the accession of James II to the death of George IV. Five volumes of this enormous work were written, but the author got no further than William III. In July, 1852, he suf-fered an attack of heart disease, followed by asthma. With death thus apparently near he worked single-mindedly at the great undertaking. Frequently his journal in later years records, instead of dinners at Holland House with Talleyrand or breakfasts with Hallam and Lord John Russell, the simple statement: " My task," or " My task and a little more." The first two volumes of the work were published by Longmans in 1848, and two more in 1855 ; the fifth volume, after his death, in 1861. None of Macaulay's other works, though popular, compared in phenomenal sale to the *History*. In 1856, 26,500 copies sold in ten weeks, and in a generation upwards of 140,000 copies sold in the United Kingdom alone.

After the attack in 1852, Macaulay's health failed rapidly. He lived from 1841 to 1856 at the Albany, just off Piccadilly, but for his last years he sought a quieter home, Holly Lodge, in Kensington. There, on the 28th of December, 1859, he died. He was buried with great ceremony in the Poets' Corner, Westminster, at the foot of Addison's monument.

In remembering Macaulay it is necessary to discount

a good many glib, superficial estimates that have become current. Lord Melbourne is said to have remarked: "I wish I were as cocksure of any one thing as Macaulay is of everything." There was, it is true, painfully little hesitation about Macaulay, but he was distinctly not a conceited man; he had, moreover, a better right to be "cocksure" about most things than the average man; his mere knowledge was not only extraordinarily great, but accurate; he knew that his memory was well-nigh infallible. His lack of spiritual depth has already been noticed; but it is a very hasty and false conclusion to infer that he was without great intellectual depth, or without a very striking genius. He is furthermore charged with deficiency of real humor. He was not, certainly, a great humorist, he was in no sense a Lamb or a Thackeray; but one suspects that those who prefer the charge have not read his correspondence. The fairest view, after all, considers the almost unanimous opinion of his contemporaries; such an estimate does not forget his spotless integrity, his capacity for painstaking work, his brilliant conversation, his controlling eloquence in the House of Commons, and, above all, his authorship of the *Essays* and *The History of England*. Greater even than his vogue as essayist and historian is his influence on the writing of English prose, especially in journalism. In spite of many literary reactions, nearly every journalist who wishes to impress the larger public takes refuge in the force and the clearness, the antithesis and the brevity invariably associated with the name of Macaulay.

THOMAS CARLYLE

"MAN, son of Earth and of Heaven," says Carlyle, "lies there not in the innermost heart of thee, a Spirit of active Method, a Force for work!" "All true Work is Religion: and whatsoever Religion is not Work may go and dwell among the Brahmins, Antinomians, Spinning Dervishes, or where it will; with me it shall have no harbor." Here is the great message of Carlyle, by far the most outstanding feature of his life — *genuine, earnest work.* This gospel he preached in words of fire. Many no doubt have held such a philosophy, but no man in the nineteenth century has brought to this philosophy the genius of Carlyle; hence of no modern man can it so justly be said that he spoke "with tongues." It has become a commonplace to call him the *prophet* of the century.

Yet this is by no means the whole or commonly accepted view of Carlyle. It is still customary to hear him spoken of as a dyspeptic cynic, a hard-hearted misanthrope, and, worse yet, a hypocrite who, preaching fine practices, was in his private life a bully and a tyrant. This view is the result of Froude's treatment of his master. In the nine volumes, including Personal Reminiscences, Biography, and Letters of Carlyle, written or edited by Froude shortly after Carlyle's death, an unfair impression was given; for Froude, feebly asserting that his master was white, painted him black. So great, moreover, was the volume of Froude's work, and so overwhelming the authority with which he spoke,

THOMAS CARLYLE

From the portrait by J. A. McNeill Whistler

that, in spite of careful and adequate corrections by such scholars as Professor Masson and Professor Norton, the popular prejudice has largely lived on ; and now, inveterate after twenty years, it is in some minds almost an incurable disease. The only fair estimate, after all, is based on a consideration of the *whole* correspondence, in the authentic editions, of Carlyle, his wife, and his friends.

Carlyle's cruelty and insincerity, after such a consideration, cannot stand. Even his cynicism, often bitter and towards the end violent, is not the most fundamental thing about him. " I have called my task," he wrote to Miss Welsh in June, 1826, " an Egyptian bondage, but that was a splenetic word, and came not from the heart, but from the sore throat." Almost all through his life Carlyle suffered also from sleeplessness and dyspepsia, a " rat gnawing at his stomach." " Some days," he wrote in 1823, " I suffer as much pain as would drive about three Lake poets down to Tartarus." But there was more than this. " His misery," says Professor Masson aptly, " was the fretting of such a sword in such a scabbard, or in any scabbard." Carlyle and his wife used often to joke about " the raal mental awgony in my ain inside." By disposition, too, he was moody and melancholy ; and in moments of despair he was cynical enough. But the Yahoo-raillery of Swift was never his. " The former," says Mr. Augustine Birrell, " pelts you with mud, as did in old days gentlemen electors their parliamentary candidates ; the latter only occasionally splashes you, as does a public vehicle pursuing on a wet day its uproarious course." The doubt, moreover, which was at the bottom of the cynicism was emphatically not his chief quality. He

was certainly most unlike the cocksure Macaulay; he
did doubt all through his life — doubted Christianity,
things of this world and the world to come, doubted
himself. But though he speaks of himself as "solitary,"
" eating my own heart," " bearing the fire of hell in an
unguilty bosom," there were also, as Professor Masson
points out, " moments of inexpressible beauty, like
auroral gleams on a sky all dark." And Dr. Gordon,
who knew him well, said that he was " the pleasantest
and heartiest fellow in the world, and most excellent
company." Nor must Carlyle's humor and his great,
boisterous laugh at his own ferocity be forgotten;
" those who have not heard that laugh," says Mr. Al-
lingham, " will never know what Carlyle's talk really
was." Whenever he was thrown back on ultimate
things, moreover, "cornered," as it were, or whenever
others looked to him for faith, he came out strongly.
" Courage " was always his watchword to his suffering,
doubting wife; self-confidence after a soul-searching
struggle is the main point of *Sartor Resartus.* " Thou,
too, shalt return *home* in honor," he says in *Past and
Present,* " to thy far-distant Home, in honor; doubt it
not — if in the battle thou keep thy shield ! " — this is
the gospel he strove to preach.

Thomas Carlyle, born at Ecclefechan, Dumfriesshire,
December 4, 1795, came of Annandale peasant stock.
His father, James Carlyle, was a rugged stone-mason,
" wholly a man of action," says his son, " with speech
subservient thereto ; " . . . with language "full of metaphor, though he knew not what metaphor was." The
mother, Margaret Aitken, was a trusting, sympathetic
soul, who learned to write in later years that she might
correspond with her son. Not much is known of the

boy's early years. He says that he cried a great deal.
In *Sartor Resartus*, his most autobiographic work, is
pictured a man much influenced in childhood by nature,
especially by rugged mountain scenery. Carlyle learned
reading and arithmetic at home, at five went to a very
elementary village school, and at nine entered the Annan Grammar School. There he was shy and put upon
by the other boys, till finally he broke his promise to
his parents not to hit back. In 1809 he walked to Edinburgh, eighty miles, and entered the university, with the
purpose, at his father's wish, of preparing for the Scottish Kirk. At Edinburgh he did well in Latin and
mathematics, but despised philosophy as then taught,
and never mastered Greek.

Carlyle did not, however, enter the ministry. He
went, instead, through an uncertain, unhappy period of
teaching, studying, and hack-writing before he finally
experienced, in 1821, what he called his " fire-baptism."
First, in the summer of 1814 he taught mathematics in
the Annan Academy, "a situation flatly contradictory
to all ideals or wishes of mine." Two years later he received a position as master in a school at Kirkaldy, Fife.
Here the master of a rival school, Edward Irving, " Tris-
megistus Irving," received him warmly and first taught
him, he says, " what the communion of man with man
means." The two became firm friends, and Carlyle years
afterwards wrote a striking record of Irving's brilliant,
brief career. Through Irving he was weaned of his
mathematical bent, and he transferred his interest to
history, devouring Gibbon in leisure moments. Through
Irving, too, he was persuaded to give up Kirkaldy soon
after the marvelous friend had himself abandoned it for
Edinburgh and the ministry. Carlyle went up to the

capital, started to study mineralogy, which introduced him to German, if nothing else, translated French scientific papers, and so struggled along, an aimless, befogged student, but with some sort of light flickering dimly ahead in the fog. At last Brewster gave him some work for his *Edinburgh Encyclopædia*, to which he contributed sixteen articles. Thus he dragged on, " living in a continual indefinite pining fear."

In 1821 the remarkable crisis came. It is recorded in·*Sartor Resartus*, — Teufelsdröckh's years of doubt and groveling fear and unhappiness, and finally his encounter with the " Everlasting No." The story is written hot out of Carlyle's own experience; one has only to substitute him for Teufelsdröckh and Leith Walk for the Rue St. Thomas de l'Enfer. Bunyan, praying by the roadside or fighting the fiend in the night-watches, had staked all on the success of his struggle; not less did the issue matter to Carlyle, who, if not religious, yet was full of what he called " religiosity." " All at once," says Teufelsdröckh, " there rose a Thought in me, and I asked myself : 'What *art* thou afraid of? Wherefore, like a coward, dost thou forever pip and whimper, and go cowering and trembling? Despicable biped! what is the sum-total of the worst that lies before thee? Death? Well, Death ; and say the pangs of Tophet too, and all that the Devil and Man may, will, or can do against thee! Hast thou not a heart ; canst thou not suffer whatsoever it be ; and, as a Child of Freedom, though outcast, trample Tophet itself under thy feet, while it consumes thee? Let it come, then ; I will meet it and defy it!' And as I so thought, there rushed like a stream of fire over my whole soul ; and I shook base Fear away from me forever." " The Everlasting No had said : ' Behold,

thou art fatherless, outcast, and the Universe is mine
(the Devil's) ; ' to which my whole Me now made answer : '*I* am not thine, but Free, and forever hate
thee ! ' " " It is from this hour that I incline to date my
Spiritual New-birth, or Baphometic Fire-baptism ; perhaps I directly thereupon began to be a Man." So Carlyle did not take orders for the Kirk, but from this time
on he strove diligently to prepare himself to preach his
gospel of genuine work and hatred of iniquity and baseness. Heretofore he had been rudderless ; now he had
a helm and a port. True, it was fifteen years before he
found his audience, but after 1821 he was possessed of
a purpose, " directly thereupon began to be a Man."

Next to this encounter with Apollyon in Leith Walk,
the thing which most influenced Carlyle was the love of
Jane Baillie Welsh, the bright, accomplished daughter
of a Haddington surgeon. Here again Edward Irving,
who had led him up to Edinburgh and the momentous
spiritual conflict, took him down to Haddington and
introduced him to Miss Welsh. She had once been a
pupil of Irving's and was six years younger than Carlyle, who was now twenty-six. Many stories are told of
her clever, capricious youth — how she crawled along
outside the rail of the bridge over the Nith, a feat
among boys ; how, when she had been forbidden the
masculine pursuit of Latin, she learned to decline *penna*,
hid herself under the library table, and at the appropriate moment emerged, reciting her *penna, pennœ*, and
begging that she might be a boy. As she grew older
she became very beautiful, with black hair and slender,
graceful figure. She was a brilliant, intellectual woman, and soon saw that Carlyle was head and shoulders
above her other suitors, that he was, indeed, a genius ;

and she never lost faith in him. After five years during which he worked on at Edinburgh, reading and translating German, or (1822–24) acted as private tutor in the Buller family, he struggled into sufficient means to keep a very frugal household. So October 17, 1826, he married and settled at Comley Bank, Edinburgh.

The contest over Froude's perversions has waged hottest in connection with Carlyle's treatment of his wife. Of specific charges more in appropriate places. It is sufficient here to say that, from the letters now accessible, the Carlyles seem to have been very much in love, before and after their marriage. It is true, no doubt, that they often quarreled over little things, but it is equally true that behind his rugged exterior and her sharp tongue there was an infinity of tenderness and affection. It would be ʿutile to quote one or two passages to prove this; opponents could easily find detached sayings in contradiction, such as Mrs. Carlyle's to a friend: " My dear, whatever you do, never marry a man of genius." Those who are infected with the heresy or interested in the whole story should read the whole correspondence. The authentic letters of Carlyle and his wife are the most convincing proof of a very genuine and enduring love.

More than half of the sharp sayings, moreover, have been misinterpreted. If the irrepressible humor and the delight of both in grim jests are taken quite seriously, the Carlyles were, it must be admitted, in perpetual quarrel. The weak health of both, the childless household, the depressing melancholy, and the loneliness that always hedges genius — for both were of startling, sensitive genius — must, of course, have provoked many tiffs between two natures intolerant of obstacles and naturally impetuous. "Woe to the house where there is no chiding," wrote Mrs. Carlyle in her note-book ; and certainly she would have been the first to find things dull if she had been forbidden to " chide." Carlyle himself held that it was "not good to be 'at ease in Zion.'" Chiefly, both overflowed with humor, even about their poor " ain insides ; " they were, along with their complainings and melancholy, persons " of infinite jest." Indeed, when one finds nothing, except the genius, which might not occur in any remotely similar family, and then contemplates the vast volume of discussion thereabout, one is tempted to think that there has been " much speaking."

To return to the course of events — Carlyle struggled slowly into literary recognition. His methods were just the opposite of the fluent Byron's, with his "fatal facility," and success was won only after arduous toil. His first considerable effort was a translation of Goethe's *Wilhelm Meister* in 1824. He became now intensely interested in German thought, wrote the *Life of Schiller* (1825), translated specimens of *German Romance* (1827), and started a correspondence with the patriarchal Goethe. Until the great German's death in 1832 the two exchanged letters and gifts. Goethe, indeed, was one of the first to recognize the Scotchman's worth. " Carlyle," he said to Eckermann in 1827, " is a *moral* force of great importance ; there is in him much for the future, and we cannot foresee what he will produce and effect." Jeffrey, the " wonderful little man," who had outgrown the prejudices of youth which made him so hostile to rising genius, was another who saw Carlyle's possibilities. Several essays by Carlyle for the *Edinburgh Review* and the *Foreign Review* were the result. Much the most famous of these was that on *Burns*.

But the young prophet, uncomfortable in Edinburgh, in the spring of 1828 moved his household gods to Craigenputtock, an old farm of the Welshes in a barren country, sixteen miles from Dumfries and civilization. There, except for the winter of 1831–32, spent at 4, Ampton Street, London, he lived for the next six years, studying hard and writing some of his best work.

The shade of Froude again rises, for the life at Craigenputtock he pictures as a life to which no considerate husband would subject such a tender wife as Mrs. Carlyle. But she, it seems, was content. True, she dated her letters from " The Desert " and often reviled the place ; but, humor not extracted, there remains on the whole less sincere complaint at Craigenputtock than in London. It must be remembered that at this time the Carlyles were very poor, that the husband's voice was as yet not greatly heard in the land, and that the upward pull seemed, to two dyspeptic, melancholy persons, a long and dreary one. London would doubtless have offered more diversion, but probably not the solitude necessary for the writing of *Sartor Resartus*. At all events, there was not the drudgery Froude imagines. Mrs. Carlyle did not *have* to milk the cows or bake bread, nor is there evidence that she did so except as an occasional amusement ; she took, it seems, great delight in her domestic ministrations ; and they had one servant instead of two at her particular wish. Again, read the correspondence : it takes an ingenious or a hasty man to discover that life went strikingly ill at Craigenputtock.

Much the most important thing Carlyle did there was

the writing of *Sartor Resartus*, the record of his experience ten years before. But it did not wholly free him, as *Werther* had freed Goethe, from inward conflicts; for the obvious reason that *Werther* deals with an interest of sentimental youth, easily outgrown, while *Sartor* deals with an interest of spiritual manhood, in such men as Carlyle never outgrown. His self-questioning and melancholy, more or less commensurate with his state of health, continued all through his life. There were "auroral gleams," as Masson said; but they were on a "sky all dark" — often dark as thunder-clouds. "When I look at the wonderful Chaos within me," Carlyle wrote to Goethe in 1830, "full of natural Supernaturalism, and all manner of Antediluvian fragments; and how the Universe is daily growing more mysterious as well as more august, and the influences from without more heterogeneous and perplexing; I see not well what is to come of it all, and only conjecture from the violence of the fermentation that something strange may come."

With *Sartor Resartus*, hailed by Mrs. Carlyle as a work of great genius, the author, in the fall of 1831, journeyed to London. But publishers feared its rough, grotesque style, and for two years none would take the book. At length Fraser, for whose magazine Carlyle had begun to write, notably his essay on *Johnson*, consented to bring out *Sartor* in his periodical. It began in December, 1833, and ran through several numbers. The work brought Carlyle some prominence, but chiefly as a literary curiosity; few as yet recognized his greatness.

Carlyle soon realized, however, that life in London, be it never so noisy and expensive, was a necessity for a writer for periodicals; so in June, 1834, he moved to 5, Cheyne Row, Chelsea. Here, to keep out the noises of the street, he had a double wall built to his study on the top-floor; and his wife finally managed to buy off the neighbors' cocks, whose crowing banished all slumber. For a time the small family lived very frugally indeed — two candles being the allowance of light for the drawing-room. Carlyle's routine of the day was to work during a long morning (dinner at three o'clock), to answer letters and ride in the afternoon, and to read, usually with his wife, in the evening. As yet the stream of curious visitors was small.

With the publication in 1837 of *The French Revolution*, when Carlyle was forty-two, came his first real fame. He had been known before as the champion of German literature; now he was recognized as a great writer, and as a vivid and discerning, if not unprejudiced, historian. One of the most striking stories about him is in connection with the burning of the first volume of the manuscript of *The French Revolution*. He might complain enough over little matters, be "a roaring Thor when himself pricked by a pin," as Mrs. Carlyle puts it; but when the distracted Mill rushed in to tell of the fire, Carlyle, to whom writing meant exhausting labor, talked calmly for two hours and then, when Mill had gone, turned to his wife with: "Well, Mill, poor fellow, is terribly cut up; we must endeavor to hide from him how very serious the business is to us."

At the suggestion of Miss Martineau, Carlyle now began (1837) to give a series of lectures on German literature. These were so successful, in spite of his apprehension, that they were soon followed by others, the most famous of which were those on *Heroes and Hero-*

Worship (1840). But he did not like to speak in public. "O Heaven!" he wrote to Emerson in 1839, "I
cannot 'speak'; I can only gasp and writhe and stutter,
a spectacle to gods and fashionables — being forced to
it by want of money."

Heroes and Hero-Worship, published as a book in
1841, is here particularly important because it reveals
his character and principles. "The history of what man
has accomplished in this world," he says, "is at bottom
the History of the Great Men who have worked here."
To illustrate this point, he treats of the hero as *divinity*
(Odin), as *prophet* (Mahomet), as *poet* (Dante and
Shakespeare), as *priest* (Luther and Knox), as *man of
letters* (Johnson, Burns, and Rousseau), and as *king*
(Cromwell and Napoleon). The point is that the great
man, the shaper of world-destinies, is the genuine, original man, "not a second-hand, borrowing or begging
man," — standing if need be, like Johnson, on his own
feet "on frost and mud, if you will, but honestly on
that." Such a man is the true "king" of men, a leader,
in whatever form — divinity, prophet, poet, priest, man
of letters, actual king — the age may demand; and the
reverence for such leadership is essential to all people.
Democracy, as Carlyle saw it about him, was to him an
abomination, the first-cousin of anarchy.

Carlyle's gospel, then, was against the tendency of
the times. Such movements as the great reform of 1832
were not progress, he thought — unless into darkness
and "the mask of Gehenna forevermore." Like Ruskin,
he fought the mechanical spirit of his age. "I do not
want cheaper cotton, swifter railways," he cried; "I
want what Novalis calls 'God, Freedom, Immortality.'"
"Will the whole upholsterers and confectioners of mod-

ern Europe undertake to make one single shoeblack
happy!" As Mr. Nichol puts it, interpreting Carlyle,
"The electric light can do nothing to dispel the darkness of the mind." This philosophy was all very well
at first: there was Hebraic simplicity and strength in
the voice crying at Craigenputtock; there was a merited
rebuke in Carlyle's rugged sincerity, in his inexorable
demand for genuineness. In *Chartism* (1839) and *Past
and Present* (1843) his preaching was still reasonable.
As time went on and he repeated himself, however
(especially in *Latter-Day Pamphlets*, *Frederick the
Great*, and *Shooting Niagara*), his voice became shrill
and his curses violent. In condemning the age of steam
as a bar to spiritual progress he was led into absurd,
ruthless condemnation of most present things; he even
included such men as Darwin in his anathema. Then
it was, in the sixties, that men got their idea of the
gloomy, savage satirist. But even *then* there still endured
a tenderness and trustfulness wholly lacking in the last
days of Dean Swift.

In the forties, however, when Carlyle was at his best,
he was by no means the emaciated, gloomy figure of
later years. Emerson, who visited him at Craigenputtock, describes him as a man then "tall and gaunt,
with a cliff-like brow, self-possessed and holding his extraordinary powers of conversation in easy command;
clinging to his northern accent with evident relish; full
of lively anecdote, and with streaming humor which
floated everything he looked upon." He had a great
shock of dark hair, no beard until middle life, and a
"bilious-ruddy or ruddy-bilious" complexion, says Dr.
Garnett, "according as Devil or Baker might be prevailing with him." In private he was a great talker,

explosive, humorous, animated; he even surpassed his clever wife.

Among great men Carlyle had many friends and acquaintances. Emerson began a correspondence with him in 1834 and continued it till 1872, during which long period hardly a year passed without several letters. Of the great men of London Coleridge was gone, but Carlyle when he first came to London had known the old sage of Highgate, "a kind of *Magus*, girt in mystery and enigma." Irving, his old friend and Coleridge's disciple, was dead too. John Sterling, another disciple, who lived till 1844, said dying to Carlyle: "Towards England no man has been and done like you." Wordsworth he knew, but did not admire; in Southey he found greater sympathy. Others whom he knew were Leigh Hunt, still lingering; Walter Savage Landor, the shaggy old lion; Dickens, a young man, but advanced in fame; and Tennyson, rising to success. There is a story that he and Tennyson sat speechless, smoking for a whole evening by the fireside at Cheyne Row, and that when Tennyson got up to go Carlyle broke silence with, "We've had a grand evening, Ælfred; coom again." Later he became familiar with Kingsley, Browning, and Ruskin.

In Carlyle's fame *Sartor Resartus* and *Heroes and Hero-Worship* have taken perhaps the most prominent place, but the great bulk of his work was in history. The next long labor after *The French Revolution* was his edition of *Cromwell's Letters and Speeches* (1845). His third and greatest effort was the *History of Frederick II* (1858–65). Between these two came *Latter-Day Pamphlets* (1850), the *Life of John Sterling* (1851), and *The Nigger Question* (1853).

The labor on *Frederick* was tremendous and taxing.
" My days were black and spiritually muddy," he says ;
" hers, too, very weak and dreamy, though *un*complain-
ing ; never did complain once of *her un*chosen sufferings and miserable eclipse under the writing of that sad
book." When it was finished he was past sixty and
subsequently wrote very little, only *Shooting Niagara :
and After ?* (1867), an attack on Socialism ; *The
Early Kings of Norway : also an Essay on the Portraits of John Knox* (1875) ; and parts of the *Reminiscences*, published in 1881 after his death.

It was during the writing of *Frederick* that there
occurred the difference, if it can be called such, between
Carlyle and his wife. Froude, who gives the exaggerated
impression, bases his views chiefly on the inaccurate
evidence and unclean imaginations of one person, an
intimate but not greatly respected friend of Mrs. Carlyle's ; " a flimsy tatter of a creature," as Carlyle puts it.
The only offense of Carlyle's which is worth discussing is
his affection for Lady Ashburton, the brilliant mistress
of Bath House. This affection, in the light of facts,
turns out to be nothing more than the warm admiration
which Carlyle had for a very clever woman and which
Lord Ashburton was sensible enough to countenance.
But the neglect of Mrs. Carlyle and her jealousy are
Froude's points. For some neglect Carlyle must stand
guilty, but it was unconscious and far less than that
caused by *Frederick*. For the jealousy Mrs. Carlyle,
who particularly loved to excel in wit, and who saw herself surpassed only in this one instance, is alone responsible. Even then, both the neglect and the jealousy
have been exaggerated. Mrs. Carlyle went frequently
to Bath House when her health allowed and did not

seriously complain until she was attacked in 1856 by a
nervous disorder which was quite naturally accompanied, doctors have testified, by a morbid jealousy. In
1857, when Lady Ashburton had died and Mrs. Carlyle had recovered from her strange sickness, the latter
accepted gifts of Lady Ashburton's things — certain
evidence that in normal health she did not take the
matter seriously. The morbid complaints, moreover,
which she wrote in her Journal during her sickness,
were not known by Carlyle till he read them after her
death, and then not all of them; so that his misunderstanding of her unhappiness, attributing it, as he did,
to her ill health, was quite reasonable; and his subsequent grief over the pain he had caused her was to be
expected. It is hard to believe, with Froude, that Carlyle felt the necessity of expiating by confession to the
world some horrible and so far undiscoverable wrong
he had done.

The saddest chapter of his life, indeed, is that which
deals with his wife's death in 1866 and the writing of
the *Reminiscences.* He had been elected Lord Rector
of Edinburgh University in 1865; the health of both
husband and wife, though hopelessly shattered, was
better than for some years; the increased sale of his
books had set him in easy circumstances; he was surrounded by friends who flocked to Cheyne Row to do
him honor. Then the blow fell. While he was off at
Edinburgh making a successful inaugural address, on
the 21st of April, 1866, his wife, driving in Hyde Park,
died suddenly of heart failure. For the rest of the
year he could do little but read her letters mournfully
and write of her — his " bright fellow-pilgrim," as he
called her. "I say deliberately," he wrote in " Jane

Welsh Carlyle," included in the *Reminiscences* by Froude, who tore off Carlyle's solemn injunction that the chapter should never be published, " her part in the stern battle — and, except myself, none knows how stern — was brighter and braver than my own. Thanks, darling, for your shining words and acts, which were continual in my eyes, and in no other mortal's. Worthless I was your divinity, wrapt in your perpetual love of me and pride in me, in defiance of all men and things."

Carlyle survived his wife fifteen years, most of which were spent in thinking of her. He shrank from public honors. He did accept, in 1874, the Prussian Order, " Pour le Mérite," but he declined, in an admirable letter, Disraeli's offer of the " Grand Cross of the Bath." It is this Carlyle — old, bent, with gray beard and hair, wearing a slouch hat, and riding towards dusk in Hyde Park — that is so vividly remembered by many still alive. His fierce, impatient spirit was much softened; those who saw him near the end found him gentle, with only occasional flashes of indignation. Yet he was still very sad, waiting earnestly for death. In the next to last letter he wrote, February 8, 1879, he says to Dr. John Carlyle, his much-loved brother: " Alas! Alas! The final mercy of God, it in late years always appears to me, is that He delivers us from a life which has become a task too hard for us." On February 5, 1881, he died. He was buried, according to his wish, among his people at Ecclefechan.

Many, with Lowell, admitting the sincerity and usefulness of Carlyle's early prophecy, and the excellence of his vivid style, think that he came, by violent repetition of the same theories, to be unconsciously one of the shams he himself had abominated. That Carlyle was, after all, in his less heaven-sent moments one of those poor human pedestrians he " splashed with mud in his uproarious course," that he was splendidly sincere and inspiriting and yet cynical, is the human tragedy of his life. Without this confusion of elements he would have been indeed either a bully or a saint — and incidentally *Sartor Resartus* would not have been written. " What can you say of Carlyle," said Ruskin, " but that he was born in the clouds and struck by lightning ? "

A more favorable estimate is Mr. Augustine Birrell's : he calls Carlyle " one who, though a man of genius and of letters, neither outraged society nor stooped to it ; was neither a rebel nor a slave ; who in poverty scorned wealth ; who never mistook popularity for fame ; but from the first assumed, and throughout maintained, the proud attitude of one whose duty it was to teach and not to tickle mankind."

The central principle of that teaching was war on sham and cant and idleness — a gospel well suited to cure the great sin of the Victorian Age, complacent, opulent materialism. Carlyle discovered, along with Goethe and Schiller, what, indeed, most of the noble souls of the nineteenth century did at last fall back on as the one important philosophy.

> " Industry that never wearies,"

says Schiller in *Die Ideale*,

> " That slowly works, but ne'er destroys,
> That to the eternal structure layeth
> But grain of sand for grain of sand,
> Yet of time's debt as surely payeth
> Days, minutes, years, with cane'lling hand."

And near the close of Goethe's *Faust* the angels sing :

"Who always striving labors on,
    Him can we grant salvation."

"Cry 'Speed, — fight on ; fare ever there as here !'"

is Browning's last word. "Look up," says Carlyle, "my wearied brother : see thy fellow-workmen there, in God's Eternity ; surviving there, they alone surviving : sacred Band of the Immortals, celestial Bodyguard of the Empire of Mankind." Carlyle may have doubted in many little things and in some great things ; may, as far as a smiling face and a good digestion go, have been a pessimist; was certainly a lonely and an unhappy man : but in the one great thing he was an earnest, an exuberant optimist.

JOHN RUSKIN

THE most obvious thing about Ruskin is his sensibility. Other characteristics — his integrity, his simplicity, his attitude towards art, his fatherly affection for the English poor, his querulous indignation — are the most striking at certain times ; but underlying all these and animating his whole life is an extreme emotional sensitiveness. Of this there is abundant evidence. In early youth he was uncommonly affected by nature and art. Though discipline made him sober and serene, he always gave important things an emotional interpretation. Whenever he came in contact with women, moreover, he was ruled by the same sensibility, whether it was to revere them as a class, as in *Queen's Gardens*, or to fall in love with them individually, as he did many times. In old age one of the things he most liked was to be surrounded by innumerable, beautiful, ecstatic maidens, to whom he could teach, in half-fatherly way, his *Ethics of the Dust*. Still another evidence is his positive distress for the poor. " I simply cannot paint," he says in *Fors Clavigera*, " nor read, nor look at minerals, nor do anything else that I like, and the very light of the morning sky . . . has become hateful to me, because of the misery that I know of, and see signs of where I know it not, which no imagination can interpret too bitterly."

This sensibility, as in the case of two very different men, Burns and Keats, was Ruskin's weakness and strength. It caused him many a futile effort and

many an hour of misery. Yet few natures have been
better endowed for inspiring people through beautiful language to an appreciation of the beautiful and
the noble in life. For it must not be imagined that
such sensibility precludes careful thought. Ruskin
called himself " analytic " and " reasonable," even as a
child ; in fact, his power of mere intellect was very
great. His reasoning, however, was in spiritual things ;
his intellect was governed by ideals rather than by
material facts ; and he never was so blind as to depend
on mere intellect in matters where only spiritual insight
could perceive. " You cannot judge with judgment,"
he says, " if you have not the sun in your spirit and
passion in your heart." He had the intellectual virility
of a man, but he had the quick sensibility of a woman.

As a consequence Ruskin stands, with Carlyle, as one
of the great prophets of the Victorian Age. It is of
small matter whether his views on art were sound or his
social reforms practicable ; it is of great matter that he
pointed the way, that he made unflinching war on the
ugly, the mean, and the sordid.

John Ruskin was born at 54, Hunter Street, Bruns-
wick Square, London, on February 8, 1819. Of his
plebeian ancestry he was very proud. He tells in *Fors*
that his mother was a sailor's daughter, one of his
aunts a baker's wife, the other a tanner's, and adds
that he does n't know much more about his family,
except that there used to be a green-grocer of the name
in a small shop near the Crystal Palace. His father,
John James Ruskin, of Scotch descent, was a wine
merchant, upon whose grave the son wrote, " He was
an entirely honest merchant." Ruskin's mother, Margaret Cox, was also of Scotch descent. Her well-trained

mind, strict discipline, and constant interest in the boy's welfare had much to do with shaping his habits and thoughts. It must not be imagined, however, that she was stern. She was in a sense very indulgent. So great was her care for her only son that she coddled him by her caution. Things which other boys did he was not allowed to do; not even allowed to put up the step of the carriage — " lest I should pinch my fingers; " nor permitted " to go to the edge of a pond, or be in the same field with a pony."

At first Ruskin's schooling was chiefly in the Bible. " My mother forced me," he says in *Præterita*, his autobiography, " to learn long chapters of the Bible by heart; as well as to read it every syllable through, aloud, hard names and all, from Genesis to the Apocalypse, about once a year; and to that discipline — patient, accurate, and resolute — I owe, not only a knowledge of the book, which I find occasionally serviceable, but much of my general power of taking pains, and the best part of my taste in literature." As time went on, other studies were added, and the whole morning was consumed in work. In the afternoon the boy was allowed to walk with his nurse or to play in the garden at Herne Hill, whither the Ruskins had moved in 1823. But the Scotch parent, with her evangelical strictness, did not allow him a confusion of toys. " I had a bunch of keys to play with," he says, " as long as I was capable only of pleasure in what glittered and jingled; as I grew older, I had a cart and a ball; and when I was five or six years old, two boxes of well-cut wooden bricks. With these modest, but, I still think, entirely sufficient possessions, and being always summarily whipped if I cried, did not do as I was bid, or tumbled on the stairs, I

soon attained serene and secure methods of life and
motion ; and could pass my days contentedly in tracing
the squares and comparing the colors of my carpet."

Nearly all of Ruskin's education was at home. He
early read Scott, and Pope's Homer, from whom, he
says, he learned his Toryism. He always had an artist's
love for kings and castles — but only as decoration for
the land ; for himself he desired a humble cottage. On
Sundays his literary diet, besides the Bible, was *Pilgrim's Progress* and *Robinson Crusoe*. As he grew
older, he was allowed to sit quietly in his corner and
listen to Mr. Ruskin read aloud. Thus he became
familiar with Shakespeare, Christopher North's *Noctes
Ambrosianæ*, and, oddly enough in such a family, with
Byron and Smollett. By himself he early developed an
interest in geology, which he kept up throughout his life.
When he was fifteen he was sent to the private school
of the Rev. Thomas Dale, and a Mr. Rowbotham came
in to teach him mathematics. Much the most educative
influence, however, his mother with her Bible always excepted, was exerted by his frequent travels. The sherry
business took Mr. Ruskin all over England, and it
was the custom for his wife and child to accompany
him in a stately chaise. More important still was the
influence of the Continent.

In 1832 Mr. Telford, a partner of Mr. Ruskin's,
gave the boy a copy of Rogers's *Italy*, illustrated by
Turner, and thus " determined," says Ruskin, " the main
tenor of my life." The following year the little family
visited Germany, Switzerland, and Northern Italy.
From now on, indeed, sometimes for pleasure, sometimes
for the boy's health, which was never strong, the visits
to Switzerland were frequent. Ruskin, writing in later

life, counted the first sight of the Col de la Faucille, a
pass in the Alps, as one of the chief determining influences of his artist's life ; it " opened to me in distinct vision the Holy Land of my future work and true
home in this world." Of the influence of foreign cities,
he says : " There have been, in sum, three centres of
my life's thought : Rouen, Geneva, and Pisa."

Long before he saw the Alps, however, Ruskin began to write and to draw, at first in a very imitative
way. " The earliest dated efforts I can find," he says,
. . . " are six ' poems ' . . . ' finished about January,
1827.' The whole of it, therefore, was written and
printed in imitation of book-print, in my seventh year."
His interest in drawing began a little later, but by 1831
he showed sufficient promise to have a Mr. Runciman
come in to give him lessons.

Among his few playfellows Ruskin was shy and unsophisticated. He seems to have preferred the companionship of girls. When he was only eight he became
very fond of his little Scotch cousin, Jessie Richardson,
and agreed with her that " we should be married when
we were a little older." About four years later, he says,
a Miss Andrews, " an extremely beautiful girl of seventeen," sang " Tambourgi, Tambourgi," and " made me
feel generally that there was something in girls that I
did not understand and that was curiously agreeable."
But these were only the beginnings of more serious
sensibilities.

When Ruskin entered Christ Church College, Oxford, in 1836, then, he was an extremely delicate, sensitive youth, well disciplined in self-control, already
ardently attached to art and nature, shy, and hopelessly
ignorant of men and their ways. His mother came up to

Oxford to live near him, his father visited him on Sunday, and his fellow collegians at first looked on him as a kind of joke. Soon, however, he showed himself, in spite of his girlish ways, to be a man of such parts that he was sought out by the best intellects at Oxford. He ranked very well, studied hard, and won the Newdigate Prize for poetry. He was intended by his fond parents for the Church, but he early revolted from any such idea. His father's ideal, he says, was " that I should enter at college into the best society, take all the prizes every year, and a double first to finish with; marry Lady Clara Vere de Vere; write poetry as good as Byron's, only pious; preach sermons as good as Bossuet's, only Protestant; be made, at forty, Bishop of Winchester, and at fifty, Primate of England."

At Oxford Ruskin came into some literary prominence. His first printed piece had been an Essay in 1834 on the geological strata of Mont Blanc, in Loudon's *Magazine of Natural History*. In 1835 *Friendship's Offering*, an annual, contained three of his poems. While he was at college he wrote, under the assumed name of " Kata Phusin " (i. e. According to Nature), several papers for Loudon's *Architectural Magazine*. Readers thought they were written by an Oxford don.

In 1840, however, just before taking his degree, Ruskin was forced, by an attack of consumption, to leave for Italy. How much his ill health was the result of the news of the marriage of Clotilde Domecq is of course conjecture, but the relapse came directly after he heard it. At all events, the affair was very serious. M. Domecq, the French partner of Mr. Ruskin, came with his four daughters to visit at Herne Hill when John was seventeen. John was forthwith " reduced to a heap

of white ashes." "In company I sat jealously miserable
like a stock-fish. . . . I endeavored to entertain my
Spanish-born, Paris-bred, and Catholic-hearted mistress
with my own views upon the subjects of the Spanish
Armada, the Battle of Waterloo, and the Doctrine of
Transubstantiation." By way of variety, the sentimental youth wrote her verses and letters in bad French.
But Clotilde, or Adèle as he called her, to rhyme with
"shell, spell, and knell," laughed over them in " rip-
pling ecstasies of derision." In short, she four years
later married Baron Duquesne, and almost immediately
Ruskin's health gave way. For two years he was an
aimless invalid in Italy.

The Italian life, however, bore its fruit; for it led
to the production of Ruskin's first great work, *Modern
Painters*. The first volume (1843), which was chiefly
in praise of Turner, brought down the hostility of
orthodox critics, especially of *Blackwood's*. But many,
poets in particular, welcomed the young champion of
new theories. His proud father gave out the identity
of the " Graduate of Oxford " who had written the
book, and urged his son to continue the work. The
result was frequent trips to the Continent, and by degrees the rest of *Modern Painters*, vol. ii in 1846,
vols. iii and iv in 1856, and vol. v in 1860. The
Turner heresy, however, was somewhat amended, for
in 1844 the wonders of the Venetian school, more especially of Veronese and Tintoretto, for the first time
dawned on Ruskin.

With the publication of the first volume of *Modern Painters* Ruskin, only twenty-four, took a leading position among writers on art; and some of the
more discerning judges saw what now counts for much

more than his critical opinions, — his mastery of descriptive English. *Seven Lamps of Architecture* was published in 1849, *Pre-Raphaelitism* in 1850, and *Stones of Venice* in 1851–53. Ruskin, indeed, became one of the apostles of the Pre-Raphaelites, who included such men as D. G. Rosetti, Burne-Jones, Millais, Holman Hunt, and William Morris.

During all this art interest Ruskin's sensitiveness to feminine charm did not cease. In 1847 "a Scottish fairy, White Lady, and witch of the fatallest sort," — Charlotte Lockhart, granddaughter of Sir Walter Scott, — crossed his path and again reduced him to "a heap of ashes." But Charlotte Lockhart married Hope Scott, and Ruskin spent the summer of 1847 in despondency and religious depression.

The next year, moreover, took place the most unfortunate event in his life, — an event which he skips wholly in *Præterita*. His parents, determined that he should marry, finally persuaded him to offer himself to Euphemia Chalmers Gray, the daughter of old Perthshire friends and a great beauty. As ill luck would have it, she accepted him. They were married April 10, 1848, but never got along together. She adored London and society; he abominated them. Some years later she brought suit for nullity of marriage, he quietly acquiesced, and she soon married the famous painter, John Everett Millais. Nor was this Ruskin's last unfortunate affair; indeed, but for the few last years of peace before the grave, the story of his life grows increasingly sad.

The year 1860 is generally taken to mark the beginning of Ruskin's interest in social reform. Yet he had always, ever since he saw clearly outside the Cal-

vinistic blinders put upon him in youth, been more or
less zealous to uplift the poor and to denounce the vulgar. In all his writings on art he had considered the
usefulness of beauty, art in its moral aspects. Beauty,
simplicity, sincerity, and their usefulness, — this was
the basis of Ruskin's teaching. In early life the artistic side predominated; in later life the ethical.

In the thick of his crusade against the "philosophy
of steam," however, he continued his work on art. In
1869 he was elected Slade Professor of Art at Oxford,
a position which he held for ten years and again for a
year in 1883–84. His lectures were finally published
in book form as: *Lectures on Art* (1870), *Aratra Pen-
telici* (1870), *Michael Angelo and Tintoret* (1870),
Eagle's Nest (1872), *Ariadne Florentina* (1872),
Love's Meinie (1873), *Val d'Arno* (1873), *Art of
England* (1873), and *Pleasures of England* (1884).
He also wrote a sort of model guide-books: *Mornings
in Florence* (1875–77), *Academy of Fine Arts in
Venice* (1877), and *St. Mark's Rest* (1884).

The books in which Ruskin figures as a teacher are
among his best known. *Unto This Last* was published
in 1862, *Munera Pulveris* in 1863, *Ethics of the Dust*
in 1865, *Sesame and Lilies* in 1865, *Crown of Wild
Olive* in 1866, and *Fors Clavigera* in 1871-78. Even
in such works as *Mornings in Florence* he is chiefly
intent on showing the usefulness of art, the simple sincerity and hence excellence of such men as Giotto,
and the comparative worthlessness of such mere "goldsmith's work" as Ghirlandajo's.

The material philosophy of "Gradgrind," the apo-
theosis of machinery and mammon, — this was what
Ruskin attacked. Dickens had made fun of the same

thing; Carlyle had cursed it. In *Unto This Last*, published first in Thackeray's *Cornhill Magazine*, Ruskin says: " There is no wealth but Life — Life, including all its powers of love, of joy, and of admiration. That country is the richest which nourishes the greatest number of noble and happy human beings ; " and again, in *The Mystery of Life and its Arts*, the third lecture of *Sesame and Lilies*, he speaks of " the reckless luxury, the deforming mechanism, and the squalid misery of modern cities." " I should like," he says in *Fors*, " to destroy most of the railroads in England, and all the railroads in Wales. I should like to destroy and rebuild the Houses of Parliament, the National Gallery, and the East End of London ; and to destroy, without rebuilding, the new town of Edinburgh, the north suburb of Geneva, and the city of New York." Many thought the man was mad ; some were enthusiastic over his attack on " commercialism." " No other man in England," wrote Carlyle to Emerson, " that I meet has in him the divine rage against iniquity, falsity, and baseness that Ruskin has, and that every man ought to have." In this attack on the " Iron Age " Ruskin was untiring, even when he wrote in *Præterita* of his childhood. " I do not venture to affirm," he says playfully, " that the snow of those Christmas holidays was whiter than it is now, *though I might give some reasons for supposing that it remained longer white.*"

But Ruskin did much more than write books. He worked with his own hands among the poor. He had always held a theory that one should know at first-hand what one taught ; so, as he had at one time climbed on scaffolds to examine frescoes, he now broke stones on the road and swept London crossings. Further than this, he started a model tea-shop; he founded collections of art at Oxford and Cambridge; he insisted that his books should be beautifully printed, and for that purpose established the printing house at Orpington; and he gave Miss Octavia Hill the money necessary to support her scheme of poor-relief. He soon gave away, in fact, all of the £157,000 left him by the rich wine-merchant. All over England the traveler runs across little institutions of orderly, honest labor, founded by Ruskin. Far up Tilberthwaite Ghyll, among the mountains of the Lake District, one may buy linen at a cottage industry which received its first impulse from him.

Much the greatest of his projects, however, was the Company of St. George, set forth in *Fors Clavigera*, a series of letters to workingmen. The idea of this company, which was scarcely more than a project, was based on three Material things — Pure Air, Water, and Earth; and on three Immaterial things — Admiration, Hope, and Love. " The task of St. George," says Mr. Frederic Harrison, " was to slay the dragon of Industrialism; to deliver the people from all the moral and physical abominations of city life, and plant them again on the soil of an England purified from steam, from filth, and from destitution. In this regenerated country there were to be no competition, no engines, no huckstering, no fraud, no luxury, no idleness, no pernicious journalism, no vain erudition or mechanical book-learning." In course of time " Bishops " and " Centurions," to satisfy Ruskin's Tory taste, were to be introduced; and wine was allowed, if it was more than ten years old! The effort failed indeed, after seven years of thought and work; but it was the vanguard of the better class of socialistic movements

which have followed, the first futile effort of an earnest
lover of mankind to do the work of the twentieth
century.

Unfortunately, in his attitude toward steam and cities
Ruskin soon grew bitter; his voice was often shrill and
querulous. The truth is that it was the natural cry of
the forlorn hope, and a very sad cry. Consider the odds
against him. In the first place his health, always weak,
had suffered grievously from several severe lung afflic-
tions. Next, his projects were chiefly failures; his single
efforts against the " dragon of Industrialism " seemed
unavailing; and it cost him dear to care so much and
yet to fail. Further, he was again disappointed in love.
Far back, in 1858, he had given drawing lessons to one
Rosie La Touche, aged ten, and as years went on he
fell in love with her, after his wont. She, however, was
a Roman Catholic, and could not think, says Mr. Collingwood, of being " yoked with an unbeliever." So in
1872 she refused him. Three years later she died, and
he, by way of consolation, fell into a half-delirious love
of a vision of St. Ursula. The disappointment in 1840
was serious enough; but the suffering of the old man
in 1872 is pathetic beyond words. But this is not all.
The death of his father in 1864 and his mother in 1871
did not leave so sensitive a nature unscarred. Still more,
he suffered in 1878 from a mental malady, during the
attacks of which he may hardly be held responsible for
his utterances. Lastly, repelled by the Calvinism of his
youth, bewildered by the turmoil of religious opinion
caused by the war between dogma and science, he had
fallen, along with Carlyle and other free-thinkers, into
fits of pessimism when it seemed as if nothing could save
the world. Is it to be wondered at that he grew queru-

lous? His life at this time has been compared to Swift's, without the savage cynicism, but with all the tragic, forlorn despair. Indeed, he saw the sad likeness himself. "The peace in which I am at present," he wrote to Professor Charles E. Norton, "is only as if I had buried myself in a tuft of grass on a battlefield wet with blood."

Towards the end, happily, there came over him a serener mood. His health improved slightly, and he amused himself with writing *Prœterita* (1885–89), suggested by Professor Norton. When his mother died he gave up the house at Denmark Hill, London, where the family had lived since 1843, and bought Brantwood, on Lake Coniston. Here, under the kind care of his cousin, Mrs. Arthur Severn, he spent his last days peacefully, reading, entertaining visitors, and filling the simple mountain folk with his kindliness. He passed many hours, it is said, gazing wistfully across the lake toward the mountain, Coniston Old Man. He was now out of the maelstrom and on the quiet stream, "too full for sound or foam." He died quietly, January 20, 1900, and was buried, without pomp or black pall, both of which he detested, in Coniston churchyard.

Yet those who know only the last years of Ruskin too often think of him as a gentle, venerable man. Through the greater part of his life his spirit was tossed within him. In his turbulence and his unattained ideals, when one remembers the frail, suffering body and mind, lies the tragic touch that gives his prophecy sublimity. For he was a prophet — alone with Carlyle the greatest of the century. However critics may disagree as to the rightness of his views on art and sociology, all are unanimous that his spirit was right, that his influence was beneficent. The twentieth century will probably not establish a St. George's Company, but it must look for inspiration to the man who could dream of such a company. "I grew," he says in *Præterita*, "also daily more and more sure that the peace of God rested on all the dutiful and kindly hearts of the laborious poor; and that the only constant form of pure religion was in useful work, faithful love, and stintless charity."

MATTHEW ARNOLD

IF one were asked to select a typical Englishman of the nineteenth century, several reasons could be urged for the choice of Matthew Arnold. He had the physical characteristics; he was a large, handsome man, intensely fond of the outdoor life, and a real lover of nature. He belonged to that upper middle class which has produced England's finest men and women. He loved the beaten cause, and was profoundly attached to Oxford as "the home of beaten causes," as the citadel of conservatism. He loved the English Church. No one has paid a higher tribute to the English nobility in its best estate than Arnold paid in his illustration of a passage in Homer by the anecdote of Lord Granville. He was more than conservative in his admiration of the classics and in his insistence upon their value for education and culture. Yet throughout his life Matthew Arnold was the most persistent and effective critic of English life and English temperament. He named the upper classes "barbarians," and railed at the great middle class as "Philistines." He did more to undermine the dogmas of his own church than those scientific opponents of religion whose attitude he so deplored. He lauded the very qualities, say of the French or of the German mind, at which Englishmen were wont to scoff, and poured remorseless satire on that inaccessibility to ideas which marked his countrymen. Breaking away from the practice of English poets, he maintained that the beauty of the whole poem should be achieved

even at the cost of beauty in the parts; and in his own
poetry, as in his admirable critical essays, he held to
this theory of art. His criticism was avowedly based on
the principles of his master, the foreign Sainte-Beuve.
By his vocation an inspector of schools, he condemmed
the national system; and while he was proud enough
in his heart of Rugby and Winchester, proud of his
father's great record, he was unwearied in an affectionate contempt of English public schools — "those absurd cock-pits," he calls them — and their lamentably
inadequate instruction. So, too, with university education. Nobody ever dealt out keener satire upon its
defects; nobody ever really loved and appreciated Oxford more than Matthew Arnold. The truth is that,
like the England of his day, he was made up of two
elements. One held fast to the traditions of his race
and his creed; the other welcomed whatever seemed
good in the world of new and of foreign ideas.

Matthew Arnold was born at Laleham, in the Thames
valley, December 24, 1822. His father, the greatest
of English head-masters, Dr. Thomas Arnold, transmitted to this eldest son more of the qualities which
made Arnold of Rugby so influential and so famous
than the son's contemporaries would have allowed. Dr.
Arnold was a fearless liberal; so was the son. But a
liberal in 1832 could still be a pillar of the English
Church and an ardent supporter of the party which
passed the reform bill; the liberalism of the second half
of the century, that of the enlightened men like Arnold
himself, not that of what he calls " the vulgar liberals,"
was forced into quite different channels. In personal
characteristics father and son were not unlike. Both
were uncompromising in their ideals of conduct, of per-

sonal purity, and in their love of truth, their hatred of
a lie. The vehement altruism of the elder man, his insistence on active and vital religion, what was called
"muscular Christianity," was equally prominent in the
son, though he had another conception of Christianity
itself, and allowed his vein of playfulness and satire to
take the place of the earnestness and directness which
so well became Dr. Arnold as a preacher and a teacher
in direct contact with youth. How keenly the son appreciated his father's noble nature can be read in the
beautiful lines of *Rugby Chapel*. His mother was
Mary Penrose, daughter of a clergyman; and while the
letters which Arnold wrote her with unfailing regularity
until her death in 1873 show no great store of epigram
and phrase, they are not only the outcome of a deep
affection, but clear evidence that she appreciated her
son's work and sympathized with his ideas. She must
have transmitted to him something of the charm and
delicate flavor which he displayed in his best efforts, as
well as that accessibility to ideas which he always professed. Dean Stanley wrote Arnold upon her death:
"She retained the lifelong reverence for your father's
greatness, without a blind attempt to rest in the form
and letter of his words;" and Arnold comments: "This
is exactly true."

In 1828 Thomas Arnold was elected head-master
of Rugby, and moved thither with his family; but two
years later Matthew was sent back to Laleham as a
pupil of the Rev. Mr. Buckland, an uncle, and remained
there until 1836, when he went to Winchester. His
biographer notes the cleverness which enabled the boy
to take a high place in the school and so to escape much
of the "austerity" of the Winchester system. After a

year, he entered Rugby, living with his father in the school-house. Readers of *Tom Brown's School-Days* will recall the scene where Tom is sent to the doctor's rooms and finds that awful person in familiar play with the children, a picture drawn from life. We hear of a poem, *Alaric at Rome*, winning a school prize for the boy of seventeen; and the next year, 1841, after obtaining a classical scholarship at Balliol College, Oxford, and then a " school-exhibition," he goes into residence in the university which he loved so tenderly and scolded with such amiable persistence.

Matthew Arnold is the poet of Oxford. His two poems, *Thyrsis*, a monody on the death of his friend Arthur Hugh Clough, and *The Scholar-Gypsy*, abound in allusions to " that sweet city with her dreaming spires " and to the beautiful country about it. They are not only a kind of poetical guide-book to the place, but they have in more subtle ways the Oxford note, a note which Arnold himself sounds in nearly all his written work. Like Oxford, he was apparently supercilious, apart, exactly the opposite of the popular or " genial " man. Like Oxford, too, he was not really supercilious, not at all the " superior person," but simply one who was not to be taken in by the shows of things or by popular clamor,—one who knew his own position and the value of his own opinion and was frank enough to state his exact estimate of himself. " I have just seen an American," he writes his mother from Paris, in 1865, " a great admirer of mine, who says that the three people he wanted to see in Europe were James Martineau, Herbert Spencer, and myself. His talk was not as our talk, but he was a good man." It would be easy to comment on this as insufferable conceit; but it is nothing of the kind. He writes just what he thinks; and what one would most like to investigate is the sincerity of the American. The attitude of Arnold is, of course, his own; but it is impossible not to recognize in it the influence of his Oxford training. Of his university experience the facts are easily told. A charming, witty, keen, and robust companion, noted among a group of notable young men, he won a fair share of the honors and absorbed all the delights of Oxford life. In 1842 he gained the Hertford scholarship, and in 1843 the Newdigate prize for a poem on Cromwell. For this poem he received ten pounds from the publishers, and saw the sale of some seven hundred copies. He took only a second class in the final classical schools, but his ability was conceded, and in March, 1845, he was elected Fellow of Oriel College. That is the record of events; for the inner work, the making of his character, his own words will suffice, not only in the various special tributes which he pays to Oxford, such as the famous passage in the introduction to his *Essays in Criticism*, but in the summary, so to speak, which opens his address on Emerson: " Forty years ago, when I was an undergraduate at Oxford, voices were in the air there which haunt my memory still. . . . No such voices . . . are sounding there now." He goes on to tell of Newman and the sermons at St. Mary's " in the most entrancing of voices; " and he speaks once more of those " last enchantments of the Middle Age which Oxford sheds around us." It is the spirit of the passage, not its letter, which reveals Arnold's indebtedness to his university; without understanding how great this indebtedness was, one cannot comprehend him as a man.

A brief experience in teaching classics to the fifth

form at Rugby was followed, in 1847, by Arnold's permanent engagement as private secretary to Lord Lansdowne, a member of the English government. He came into this indirect public activity at a time when affairs were of the most exciting kind. The revolutions of 1848 were breaking out on the Continent, and England had its own alarms. "It will be *rioting* here, only," wrote Arnold to his mother after witnessing the doings of a great mob in Trafalgar Square; and he was a true prophet. But he saw clearly the abuses of the political and social system in England, and had already turned to those ideas which he afterwards preached so strenuously as the only hope for true reform. Meanwhile he continued his poetical efforts, but in a very unobtrusive way. *The Strayed Reveller and Other Poems* appeared in 1849 in an edition of five hundred copies, of which few were sold. The rest were withdrawn, and the book is now very rare; "A" was the only clue to authorship afforded by the title-page. In 1852 he published *Empedocles on Etna, and Other Poems;* but again few copies were sold, and the edition was withdrawn. The year before, he had been appointed inspector of schools under government, and was thus enabled to set up a household. June 10, 1851, he married Frances Lucy, daughter of Sir William Wightman, a judge of the Court of Queen's Bench. The letters which he wrote to his wife, the "Flu" of his other correspondence, now from a school in Ipswich which he is examining, now from the other side of England, now from Paris, show not only the tremendous amount of work which Arnold had to do away from home, but also the full happiness and helpfulness of his married life. Writing in October, 1851, he refers cheerfully to the "moving about," and says they "can always look forward to retiring to Italy on £200 a year;" in such a case he will do what he can "in the literary way" to increase the income. His harmless and playful irony, turned as readily on himself as on others, gives one a wrong impression of the amount of hard work which he did and of the responsibility which he felt. "I write this very late at night," runs a passage in his letter to a friend, "with S——, a young Derby banker, *très sport*, completing an orgy in the next room. When that good young man is calm, these lodgings are pleasant enough." Nothing could be more typical of Arnold than this bright bit of information; the reader smiles at the irony, envies the easy mood, admires the phrase, and passes lightly over a following sentence about the "battle of life as an inspector of schools." Indeed, most of the work by which we know Matthew Arnold was written, like the letter, "very late at night," while the work by which he lived and supported his family was full day's labor punctually and conscientiously done. Moreover, while he was well aware of the quality of his verse, and knew that it could never take the public by storm as Tennyson's poetry did, and while he was bound to satisfy his artistic conscience first and let the popular approval come as it might, he was nevertheless fairly hopeful that he might win his way as a poet. Of his three main activities, poetry occupied his younger manhood, social and religious reform his later days, and literary criticism his entire maturity. In 1853 appeared *Poems, by Matthew Arnold;* it contained the new *Sohrab and Rustum* and many pieces from the other two anonymous volumes, but perhaps more important than anything else in the book was his critical preface. It is not too much if one calls this preface the begin-

ning of a new epoch in English criticism. In 1855
came out a second series of poems, of which the most
notable was *Balder Dead*. He writes to his sister that
he thinks *Balder* will " consolidate the peculiar sort of
reputation " which he got by *Sohrab and Rustum*.
As a matter of fact, he never earned much money from
his poems, though one is not to take too seriously his
remark to the tax commission that they saw before
them " an unpopular author." He could be complacent
on occasion, and never underrated his poetical powers
in earnest; thus he records the remark of Lord John
Russell that Matthew Arnold was the only young poet
of really great promise. He likes to note that a review
in the *Times* "has brought *Empedocles* to the rail-
way bookstall at Derby." In 1857 he was elected Professor of Poetry at Oxford; and the next year he
published his *Merope* as a kind of manifesto of his
poetical creed. In 1867 appeared his *New Poems*, and
if he had printed nothing but *Thyrsis*, the monody on
the death of his friend, the poet Clough, this would
have been a notable volume.

But it was criticism in which Arnold was to make his
main appeal to the public. His Oxford lectures *On
Translating Homer* were published in 1861, and led
to considerable controversy both of the pleasant and
of the unpleasant kind. In 1865 came out the *Essays
in Criticism*, a most important book. If not a popular
author, he was now one of the best known men of letters in England; for already, amid the judgments on
books and writers, had begun to peep out those stric-
tures on the social, political, and religious shortcomings
of his countrymen by which he made his widest appeal.
He was now, since 1858, living in London ; and the old

monotony of provincial visits was further broken by a long tour on the Continent as a commissioner to investigate foreign methods of education. This was in 1859; again in 1865 he spent eight months abroad on the same errand. Articles in magazines, a collection of lectures such as the *Study of Celtic Literature*, an occasional pamphlet like his *England and the Italian Question*, revision of his poems, and the hard round of his professional duties, fill up these years. In 1868 he lost his youngest child. The entry in his commonplace book is pathetically brief; and Mr. Russell found him on the day after the child's death " consoling himself with Marcus Aurelius." The family had moved to Harrow, so as to be near the school; and here they lived until 1873, when they moved to Cobham, which was Arnold's home for the next fifteen years, until his death.

Probably as a result of increasing interest in the whole human question, Arnold's work now dealt somewhat less with books and somewhat more with life. His *Friendship's Garland*, 1871, is one of the most successful of his works, and satirizes that object of Arnold's keenest criticism, the great middle class of England, the Philistines, with an almost exuberant humor. A more serious attack on the social ideas of Englishmen is his *Culture and Anarchy*. Taking a phrase from Swift in praise of " sweetness and light," Matthew Arnold now threw in the teeth of his countrymen the reproach of their almost total lack of these supreme qualities. It was an easy step, too, from manners and politics to religion. In 1870 he began his plea for a more rational view of the religious question with a book — its contents had appeared in the *Cornhill Magazine* — on *St. Paul and Protestantism;* it was followed in 1873

by *Literature and Dogma*, where certain bishops of the
English Church were not too respectfully treated, and
in 1875 by *God and the Bible*.

He was now regarded as the first literary critic of
his age and country, although the public was not inclined to rate his religious contributions as important.
Many of his friends, even, thought this work a waste
of time, and mourned for the poetry that he might have
produced. Opposition of course was active; and he declined a second election as Oxford professor of poetry,
for fear of the " religious row " which would ensue. A
leading article in the *Athenæum* seriously considered
his claims to the title of best English poet, placing him
in some respects ahead of Tennyson and Browning. But
he wrote little poetry in these years; two poems, however, the beautiful *Ode* on the death of his friend Dean
Stanley and the pathetic *Geist's Grave*, will always
be regarded as supporting the regrets of his friends
that he produced so little verse. Meanwhile he did excellent service to the cause of poetry in general by writing the introduction to Ward's collection of English
Poets, and by publishing selections from Wordsworth
and from Byron.

In 1883 Gladstone assigned him a pension of £250
from the literary fund, and the same winter he visited
America to give a course of lectures. These *Discourses
in America* — one on " Numbers," attacking the problem of good government and social organization, one on
" Literature and Science," and one on " Emerson " —
showed him in undiminished vigor of thought and phrase.
The newspapers made gentle fun of his manner, and
there was nothing popular in the course; but it won
him many new friends and earned him a fair amount

of money. His daughter married an American, and Arnold made another visit in the States in 1886. This time his enjoyment of the journey was marred by ill health. He had inherited from his father a tendency to heart disease, and was now aware of its actual presence ; but in his letters, he speaks calmly of the prospect of sudden death. In 1885 and 1886 he was still busy investigating foreign schools, though he complains of the cold, and, at times, of his own suffering. In November, 1886, he retired from his active duties as inspector of schools. In April, 1888, he went to Liverpool to meet his daughter, who had sailed thither from New York. On. Tuesday, the 15th, while hastening towards the docks, he fell, and died without regaining consciousness.

CHARLES DICKENS

WHATEVER the minor merits or defects in the character of Dickens, two great features stand out clearly — his kindliness and his courage. To the whole human race he reached a hand of cheer and comfort. Children loved him. It was this great heart of his that caused Thackeray's children to ask their father why he did not write books like Mr. Dickens's, and grown persons to cry, at mention of his name, "God bless him!" His unfailing good spirits through the last years of illness close fittingly a story of sweetness and courage. Once in a speech, in which he spoke of the actor's having "sometimes to come from scenes of sickness, of suffering, ay, even of death itself, to play his part," he added that "all of us, in our spheres, have as often to do violence to our feelings, and to hide our hearts in fighting this great battle of life, and in discharging our duties and responsibilities." Frequently in ill-health, married to an uncongenial wife, during his boyhood subjected to ignominious labor, Dickens had as much cause as the average man to be sad; yet, outwardly, and generally in his family, he was cheerful. Perhaps the very struggle which he had to make saved him, taught him the larger optimism. Certainly a great deal was due to his natural mirthfulness, his inexhaustible humor. Still, as has often been observed, mirth is by no means cheerfulness, and humor is played about by pathos. Dickens's cheerfulness was won hardly and could never have been won but for his courage.

These chief characteristics of Dickens are, as every one knows, shadowed forth in his books with ever-changing, never-ending pathos and humor. Whatever purpose they had, — to reform this prison or that charity school, or to give thousands wholesome amusement, or to ridicule the "Circumlocution Office,"—they have accomplished the greater purpose of preaching the chief trait of their author. In nearly all his books, behind the gloomy pictures of oppression and poverty, behind the loud humor and buffoonery, is his gentleness, his genial mirth, his simple faith in mankind. Every one has laughed and wept over his books; no writer of the nineteenth century, perhaps of any century, has so given his heart to English-reading people.

There are of course certain other traits very obvious in Dickens. He was feverishly ambitious, often for mere worldly fame. He had a pride that sometimes was almost akin to vanity. In little things he was unreasonably irritable. Further, still, though he had a fine sense of honor and courtesy, he had, it must be granted, a certain bluntness of artistic sensibility — a cheap love of melodramatic effect; in the man, as in his books, there is too frequently a suggestion of overdone pathos, of humor that borders on caricature, of theatrical show. Personally, he was always overdressed. Many have sought to account for this lack of taste by Dickens's lack of fine breeding, by his extremely humble origin. It would be indeed remarkable if the son of a Mr. Micawber — for such a man was Dickens's father — developed the austere taste of an Arnold or a Newman; Dickens was nurtured literally in the streets of London, not in an academic grove. Yet in his actions and his manners he was in no sense vulgar. The humble-origin argument, one begins to suspect, is too convenient a way, after explaining a not very sensitive taste, of bringing against Dickens wholly unfair accusations. The facts of his life acquit him of commonness. Indeed, as one considers them and keeps that humble origin in mind the while, one comes more and more to have faith in the " natural goodness of man." For below and above all, and through all, predominate the man's kindliness and courage, his great human heart.

Charles Dickens, the son of John Dickens and Elizabeth Barrow, was born in Portsea on February 12, 1812. His father, to posterity Mr. Wilkins Micawber, lived in grandiloquent poverty. A clerkship in the navy pay office clearly did not support his large family, and after a few years, during which he moved to Chatham and London, he found himself arrested for debt and well settled in the Marshalsea prison. Poor Mrs. Micawber — that is, Mrs. Dickens — had set up her " Boarding Establishment for Young Ladies; " " but I never found," says Dickens, " that any young lady had ever been to school there ; or that any young lady ever came, or professed to come ; or that the least preparation was ever made to receive any young lady. The only visitors I ever saw or heard of were creditors. *They* used to come at all hours, and some of them were quite ferocious." Mrs. Dickens had therefore to abandon the school and join her husband in the Marshalsea, where one can fancy his saying, " for the first time in many revolving years, the overwhelming pressure of pecuniary liabilities was not proclaimed from day to day, by importunate voices declining to vacate the passage."

Charles, aged eleven, was put in a shoe-blacking factory, with the task, on a salary of six shillings a week,

of pasting labels on bottles — a position he considered
degrading and one to which he never referred with
pleasure. During these years of child-labor he subsisted
for the most part on bread, milk, cheese, and stale pas-
try, — sometimes on nothing at all; occasionally there
was a spree on pudding or *à la mode* beef. In his own
words he was a " queer small boy " and he was a sickly
boy; how much he suffered can be understood only by
those who know the pathetic story of little David Copperfield.

In 1824 John Dickens, released from prison, took his
family to the house of a woman who figures as " Mrs.
Pipchin " in *Dombey and Son*, quarreled with Lamert,
his son's employer, and determined, as if by commend-
able though tardy inspiration, actually to send the boy
to school. Charles was forthwith put at Wellington
House Academy, the head master of which, Mr. Jones,
is said to have been "a most ignorant fellow, and a
mere tyrant."

The boy's schooling, however, was a brief and, tech-
nically, a poor one. In three years it was all over, such
as it was, for at fifteen he entered the office of a solicitor, where he stayed till November, 1828. Then, his
father having become a reporter, the son decided to
follow the same calling. In his boyhood, nevertheless,
he did receive a very valuable education — that which
made *Oliver Twist*, *Nicholas Nickleby*, practically all
his novels, possible. He was not merely familiar with
the London streets, as was Macaulay; he was *of* them.
What he wrote down in *David Copperfield* was not
what he had observed, but what he had lived. The
squalor, the pathos, the humor, had entered into his
soul. There was at least one lesson, in the great school

of the world, which Dickens had learned better than
any one else, — as he was soon abundantly to show.

At his trade of reporter the young boy of the streets
worked with zeal. He learned shorthand; he reported
for *The True Sun*, *The Mirror of Parliament*, and
The Morning Chronicle, and was soon considered one
of the quickest reporters in London. Years later he told
graphically of his experiences. " I have often transcribed
for the printer," he said, " from my shorthand notes,
important public speeches, in which the strictest accuracy was required, and a mistake in which would have
been, to a young man, severely compromising, writing
on the palm of my hand, by the light of a dark lantern,
in a post-chaise and four, galloping through a wild country, and through the dead of the night, at the then surprising rate of fifteen miles an hour. . . . Returning home
from excited political meetings in the country to the
waiting press in London, I do verily believe I have been
upset in almost every description of vehicle known in
this country. I have been, in my time, belated in miry
by-roads, towards the small hours, forty or fifty miles
from London, in a wheelless carriage, with exhausted
horses, and drunken post-boys, and have got back in
time for publication, to be received with never-forgot-
ten compliments by the late Mr. Black, coming in the
broadest of Scotch from the broadest of hearts I ever
knew."

Like young David Copperfield, Dickens had his Dora,
in 1829, when he was a lad of seventeen. In 1855 he
thus wrote of his feeling to Forster: " I don't quite
apprehend what you mean by my overrating the strength
of the feeling of five-and-twenty years ago. If you mean
of my own feeling, and will only think what the desper-

ate intensity of my nature is, and that this began when
I was Charley's age; that it excluded every other idea
from my mind for four years, at a time when four years
are equal to four times four; and that I went at it with
a determination to overcome all the difficulties, which
fairly lifted me up into that newspaper life, and floated
me away over a hundred men's heads: then you are
wrong, because nothing can exaggerate that. . . . No
one can imagine in the most distant degree what pain
the recollection gave me in *Copperfield*. And, just as
I can never open that book as I open any other book, I
cannot see the face (even at four-and-forty), or hear
the voice, without going wandering away over the ashes
of all that youth and hope in the wildest manner."

Instead of winning his Dora, Dickens unfortunately
married Catharine Hogarth, the daughter of a fellow
worker on the *Chronicle*. He was then unused to the
society of ladies and would seem to have fallen in love
generally with all the Hogarth daughters and by ill luck
to have married the one whom he later found least suited
to him. He was married in April, 1836, and took his
wife to live in Furnival's Inn, where their first child, a
boy, was born. The following year he moved to 48,
Doughty Street, and in 1839, with improving fortune,
to 1, Devonshire Terrace.

In Dickens's case the journalistic road led to substantial success and early fame. In 1835 he began his humorous *Sketches by Boz*, in the *Monthly Magazine* and
in the *Morning* and the *Evening Chronicle*. These were
continued the following year with such skill that he was
asked by Chapman and Hall to write humorous papers
to illustrate the sporting sketches of Seymour. Dickens,
however, who usually managed to have his own way

with publishers, soon brought it about that the sporting
subject was dropped — except for that gallant sports-
man, Mr. Winkle — and that Seymour illustrated him.
After eight numbers Seymour killed himself, and Hablot
Browne ("Phiz") took up the picture-making. These
papers, which appeared monthly from April, 1836, to
November, 1837, were no less than the *Posthumous
Papers of the Pickwick Club, edited by Boz*.

The young humorist sprang into immediate fame.
As Mr. Chesterton puts it, " Dickens was evidently a
great man ; unless he was a thousand men." More than
this, as he wrote *Pickwick*, as he immortalized Mr.
Tracy Tupman, Sam Weller, and Mr. Samuel Pickwick G. C. M. P. C., Dickens stumbled on the best
sort of subjects for his other novels. Not in ancient
knights, not in country gentlemen, but in the very creatures of the London he knew so well, — creatures fat,
absurd for heroes, unromantic in the usual sense of the
word, was he to find the characters who were to move
the whole world to laughter and tears. While *Pickwick*
was still going through serial form, in 1837, *Oliver
Twist* began to come out in *Bentley's Miscellany*, and
in 1839, from January to October, *Nicholas Nickleby*
followed. Soon after, in 1840–41, *Master Humphrey's
Clock*, which started as a weekly, dropped the *Clock*
and developed into *The Old Curiosity Shop* and *Bar-
naby Rudge*.

The fame of Dickens, although he was not yet thirty,
was now secure. Mr. Pickwick, Sam Weller, Jingle,
Fagin, Charley Bates, Squeers, Dick Swiveller, Little
Nell, and Quilp, to say nothing of many others, were
important persons, known in almost every household.
Men of distinction sought the author out and honored

him. He was well acquainted with Carlyle, Washington
Irving, Ainsworth, Bulwer Lytton, and later with Wilkie
Collins, Mrs. Gaskell, and Thackeray. One of his best
friends was William Macready, the actor; Dickens himself had a strong turn for the stage, thought at one
time of becoming a professional player, and often organ-
ized and acted in excellent amateur theatricals. He had
already written, indeed, a burlesque, *The Strange Gentleman*, and a comic opera, *The Village Coquettes*.
Closest of all his friends was, of course, John Forster,
his best biographer.

Dickens was personally a very striking figure. "He
had a capital forehead," says Forster, "a firm nose with
full wide nostril, eyes wonderfully beaming with intellect and running over with humour and cheerfulness,
and a rather prominent mouth strongly marked with
sensibility. . . . Light and motion flashed from every
part" of his face. "It was as if made of steel," said
Mrs. Carlyle. We to-day are, in fact, too apt to think
of the elderly, bald, bearded Dickens of photography;
the young man, with rich brown hair and clean-shaven
face, kept to the last only one of his youthful features —
what Forster calls "the eager, restless, energetic out-
look." Carlyle gives an interesting picture of him: "He
is a fine little fellow — Boz, I think. Clear, blue, intelligent eyes, eyebrows that he arches amazingly, large
protrusive rather loose mouth, a face of most extreme
mobility, which he shuttles about — eyebrows, eyes,
mouth, and all — in a very singular manner while
speaking. . . . For the rest, a quiet shrewd-looking
little fellow, who seems to guess pretty well what he
is and what others are."

Dickens had long been eager to visit America, the

land of democracy, as he supposed. Urgent invitations
were extended; and so on the 4th of January, 1842,
he set sail with his wife. He was received everywhere
with ovation. Very soon, however, he grew weary of
dinners and calls and speeches, and was disappointed
at not finding the model democracy he expected. His
discontent was no doubt largely due to his absence
from London, the home of his inspiration; but there is
no mistaking this, written to Macready March 22 : " It
is of no use, I *am* disappointed. This is not the republic I came to see; this is not the republic of my imagination. I infinitely prefer a liberal monarchy — even
with its sickening accompaniment of court circulars —
to such a government as this. . . . I see a press more
mean and paltry and silly and disgraceful than any
country I ever knew. . . . In the respects of not being
left alone, and of being horribly disgusted by tobacco-
chewing and tobacco spittle, I have suffered considerably." It is true that Dickens was easily irritated by
insignificant things and that he had not learned that
he who runs for praise may reap adulation; but it is
true, too, that the America of 1842 must have presented to an Englishman the ill-assorted vigor and bad
manners of youth. In those days young Europeans
were still carried on the wave of revolutionary enthusiasm for a Utopia, and they naturally looked to America.
Of course they were disappointed; as they would have
been with any other land had they cherished the same
high expectations of it. The German poet Lenau had
very nearly the same experience as Dickens at very
nearly the same time — without, of course, the ova-
tions, which at first pleased Dickens and which later, by
their iteration, disgusted him. The author of *Pickwick*

was back in London by June and soon published his *American Notes*, full of ungentle sayings, and, beginning with January, 1843, *Martin Chuzzlewit*, with more hits at America.

Much the most important publication of 1843, however, was the *Christmas Carol*, with illustrations by John Leech. It was the first of a number of Christmas stories, the next of which was *The Chimes*, in 1844, followed in 1845 by *The Cricket on the Hearth*. To read *The Chimes* to a choice circle at Forster's house on December 2, 1844, was the reason for Dickens's sudden return from Italy, where he had been during the fall. Maclise, who was of the party, has made the night immortal in his picture: Dickens with his manuscript, and among his friends about him Carlyle, Douglas Jerrold, and Forster. The author went back to Italy the same month and remained there till the following June. In 1846 he began in the *Daily News* his *Pictures from Italy*. Antiquity had pleased him more than the brand-new democracy of America, and Italy hence escapes with better treatment.

Dickens had, in fact, started the *Daily News* in January, 1846, for the purpose of having a medium of expression outside his novels. But after only three weeks he resigned his editorship and returned to novel-writing. Four years later, however, he discovered a more convenient form of periodical in a weekly serial, *Household Words*, which he conducted from 1850 to 1859, and in which appeared, besides Christmas stories, *A Child's History of England* (1851–53) and *Hard Times* (1854). It was succeeded by a similar weekly, *All the Year Round*, begun in April, 1859, and continued by him to his death, 1870, after which his son managed it. In it appeared, besides more Christmas stories, *A Tale of Two Cities* (1859), *Hunted Down* (1860), *The Uncommercial Traveller* (1860), and *Great Expectations* (1860–61).

Nor were these the only fruits of Dickens's inexhaustible power. *The Pictures from Italy* were followed, in 1846, 1847, and 1848 by *Dombey and Son*, in twenty monthly numbers. An old charwoman's remark, told by Forster, reveals the great popularity of Dickens's stories. She lodged at a snuff-shop, where on the first Monday of every month the landlord read *Dombey* aloud. "Lawk, Ma'am!" she said one day to Mrs. Hogarth, "I thought that three or four men must have put together *Dombey!*" The intimacy of the woman with the book is of course the point for remark, but it is not uninteresting that the author's several-handed fertility should have struck her in exactly the same way as *Pickwick* struck Mr. Chesterton; it is indeed hard to believe that Dickens was one man. For fast on the heels of *Dombey* came *David Copperfield*, begun in May, 1849, and finished in serial form in November, 1850. Other great novels followed in rapid succession. Besides what he published in *Household Words* and *All the Year Round*, Dickens wrote *Bleak House* (1852–53), *Little Dorrit* (1855–57), *Our Mutual Friend* (1864–65), and *The Mystery of Edwin Drood* (1870), cut short by the author's death.

Yet through all this success and in spite of his natural cheerfulness, Dickens was not wholly happy at home. He had been for some time unwontedly irritable and depressed, and finally, in 1858, showed by his letters to Forster that the chief trouble, besides failing health, lay in Mrs. Dickens, whom he had married in such a burst of enthusiasm for all the Hogarth daughters. "Why is it," he wrote " that, as with poor David, a sense comes always crushing on me now, when I fall into low spirits, as of one happiness I have missed in life, and one friend and companion I have never made?" Again: "We are strangely ill-assorted for the bond there is between us." In May, 1858, he and his wife agreed to separate, Dickens allowing her £600 a year and nothing in his will.

The weakest thing Dickens did in connection with the whole unfortunate affair was to publish a defense of himself, in answer to some scandal, thus making the matter public; and to write a letter to his secretary, his " violated letter," as he called it, which got into the papers. Dickens was strangely sensitive about some matters, notably this and certain questions of publication, though, oddly enough, he was lacking in the finer sensitiveness which would have made him shrink from petty public wrangling.

Just before his separation from his wife, Dickens bought Gad's Hill Place, on the London road near Rochester. As a boy he had resolved some day to buy the house which stood near the scene of Falstaff's encounter with the men in buckram; and though on his travels he always longed for London, he managed to break the spell of the metropolis for the dream of his boyhood and in 1860 to move permanently to Gad's Hill.

His was nevertheless still the active spirit of earlier years. He walked incessantly, often twenty miles a day, and filled spare moments with planting trees and shrubbery, making the " tunnel " under the London road, and building summer-houses in the " wilderness," a

thicket reached by the tunnel. In 1853, moreover, he
had begun public readings of his works. They were no
doubt remarkable, for Dickens was a dramatic man
with a fine voice; indeed even the old Carlyle would
leave Chelsea to hear them ; but they were no doubt
not indicative of a very modest taste. Certainly the exertion necessary hastened his death. For, once he had
begun them, and once people expected him, in spite of
very poor health, to fulfill his engagements, he was the
indefatigable, active-spirited Dickens of newspaper days.
He read all over England ; he even visited America
again, where he found the people ready, with the quick
recovery of youth, to forget the quarrel of twenty-five
years before. His audiences were everywhere very large,
and his pay was proportionate. But the trip to America
was a great strain on his health ; soon the doctors had
to forbid his public readings. He retired to Gad's Hill
to rest, was in pain and without sleep much of the time,
but outwardly very cheerful and still determined to
work at *Edwin Drood*. Suddenly one day, as he rose
from dinner, he fell by the fireplace, never regained
consciousness, and died the next day, June 9, 1870.
He was buried in Westminster Abbey.

Dickens was only fifty-eight, in full career of middle
life, when he died. Indeed, when his scant education,
the struggle he had to make for mere existence, and
what he did actually achieve are considered, his life is
a phenomenal record — not so much because of the bulk
as because of the quality of the work. Many half-for-
gotten men are buried in the Poets' Corner; but Dickens has joined those who will be remembered when
Westminster is forgotten, who have created a few great
characters more real than living men, — Falstaff, Don

Quixote, Sir Roger, Tristram Shandy. *We* may be "such stuff as dreams are made on;" but no one dare bring such an allegation against the imperishable person of Mr. Pickwick. More than this, wherever kindly optimism, not blatant, cocksure optimism, cheers the faint of heart, wherever Scrooges are transformed and Tiny Tims are loved, the name of Dickens will be an enduring and a blessed name.

WILLIAM MAKEPEACE THACKERAY

"POOR Thackeray, adieu, adieu!" wrote Carlyle when he heard of the novelist's death; "he had many fine qualities, no guile or malice against any mortal, a big mass of a soul, but not strong in proportion; a beautiful vein of genius lay struggling about him." Mr. Leslie Stephen adds that Thackeray's weakness was "the excess of sensibility of a strongly artistic temperament." When this excess of sensibility was thrown back upon itself by the rebuffs of the world, it found expression not, as with Carlyle, in rage and denunciations, but in a humor which moved between the extremes of laughter and tears, and in that form of fiction which exposes the follies and hypocrisy of mankind rather than its great vices and great virtues.

William Makepeace Thackeray was born July 18, 1811, at Calcutta. His great-grandfather was archdeacon of Surrey, while his grandfather, his father, and several of his uncles had been distinguished in the civil service of the East India Company. The father died when Thackeray was five years old, and the latter was sent back to England in 1817, living there with an aunt. His mother was married soon after in India to a Major Smyth, coming, however, to England with her husband in 1821. At the age of eleven Thackeray was sent to the Charterhouse School, and remained there till he was seventeen. His experiences are described with fair accuracy in the story of *Pendennis*, where the school is called Greyfriars, and the place itself is fondly

In 1854. After a drawing by Samuel Laurence

pictured in the latter chapters of *The Newcomes.* Mr.
Merivale prints the recollections of a school-comrade,
who remembered breaking Thackeray's nose in a fight,
and admiring the "little poems and parodies" which
the victim wrote in the latter years of his course. The
broken nose remained as a deformity throughout the
novelist's life, and spoiled an otherwise handsome face.
Joined with his great height (he was well over six feet),
his bulk, and the enormous size of his head, this defect
lent itself easily to caricature, but he was not very
sensitive about it, and loved to tell how he proposed to
a traveling showman who had just lost the giant of the
show, that he should take the giant's place. "You're
nigh tall enough," was the answer, "but I'm afraid
you're too hugly." One of his friends at Charterhouse
was John Leech, afterwards his fellow worker on *Punch.*
After a short residence with his parents in Devonshire,
where he contributed some verses to a local newspaper,
he entered Trinity College, Cambridge, in 1829. One
side of his life here, the dining and wining and expensive side, may be followed between the lines of Pendennis's career at Oxbridge, though the weak and conceited Pen himself is no portrait of the author. As a
matter of fact, he made friends among the best men of
his day, such as Thompson, afterwards Master of Trinity, who was a member of a little essay club which
Thackeray himself formed, Edward FitzGerald, King-
lake, Milnes, Spedding, and Tennyson. The first of
these friends says that though "careless of university
distinction," Thackeray "had a vivid appreciation of
English poetry, and chanted the praises of the old English novelists, especially his model, Fielding. He had
always a flow of humor and pleasantry and was made

much of by his friends." With regard to actual literary effort we hear only of a parody upon Tennyson's prize poem of *Timbuctoo*. He left Cambridge in 1830, taking no degree. He now traveled on the Continent and made some stay at Weimar, where he met the poet Goethe and picked up enough of the language to serve him for his delightful translations and for his still more delightful but harmless satire on the provincial life of that day, especially the pomposities of the little German courts. No one has succeeded better than Thackeray in portraying the continental watering-places with their eternal *rouge-et-noir*, the cosmopolitan crowd of adventurers and gamblers, the petty German aristocracy, and the haughty English tourists, papa stolid and contemptuous, mamma vigilant and censorious, the daughters all innocence and ignorance, and the sons making voyages of discovery in roulette. Next year he was settled in chambers in the Temple reading law, the same quarters where his Pendennis and Warrington wrote " copy " and led their delightful Bohemian life.

The fact of Thackeray's transition from the study of law to the practice of letters is certain ; but the reasons for the change are somewhat obscure. Of course he had a strong impulse towards the vocation of author, and in Germany had sketched out plans for serious literary work. When we find him actually writing, however, it is to earn his bread. He had a fortune from his father, variously stated at from ten to twenty thousand pounds. Some of this he sank in unsuccessful journalism. Two newspapers in which he invested money along with his stepfather came rapidly to grief. Funds, moreover, had been injudiciously invested, and he lost heavily by the failure of an Indian bank, a tragedy which is reflected

to some degree in the ruin of Colonel Newcome's great
project. Worst of all, he had undoubtedly lost large
sums at play. Walking, in his later days, with Sir
Theodore Martin through the playrooms at Spa, and
stopping at the *rouge-et-noir* table, Thackeray pointed
out a seedy broken-down man among the gamblers, and
said, "That was the original of my Deuceace; I have
not seen him since the day he drove me down in his
cabriolet to my brokers in the City, where I sold out
my patrimony and handed it over to him." The patrimony in this instance seems to have been only £1500;
but there may have been other cases of the kind. Like
his own Clive Newcome, he thought to earn his living
by art, and studied hard in Paris. This was in 1834,
but in 1835 he was already known as a journalist, acting as the Paris correspondent of a new Liberal newspaper, *The Constitutional;* and journalist he was to
remain for years in spite of occasional attempts in the
other profession, as when, upon the death of Seymour,
he called on Dickens with two or three drawings in his
hand and asked permission to go on with the illustrations of *Pickwick.* The contrast implied by this interview has been duly noted by Thackeray's biographers.
Dickens was about to spring into the full tide of a popularity which never failed him, while the young man
whom he dismissed was to struggle on for a dozen years
before the public acknowledged his greatness.

With eight guineas a week for his work as correspondent, and with no other fortune, Thackeray now
married, August 20, 1836, a lady of Irish extraction,
Isabella, daughter of Colonel Shawe. For six months
he drew his pay, and then his newspaper failed. For a
while he earned ten francs a day in Paris by writing

for Galignani, but came back the next year to London
and plunged manfully into journalistic work. This work,
of course, was miscellaneous, — reviews in *The Times*
and *The Chronicle*, and stories, the most important of
which were the *Yellowplush Papers* and *Catherine*, in
Fraser's Magazine. The *Shabby-Genteel Story* and *The
Great Hoggarty Diamond* also date from this period.
The name he now assumed, "Michael Angelo Titmarsh,"
shows the combination of artist and literary hack which
he felt himself to be. Unlike Dickens, he was never sure
of himself or of his fame. Still, his daily life, though
full of stress and anxiety, was a happy one. Three
daughters were born, one of whom died in infancy; but
in the spring of 1840 his wife's health began to fail,
and the disease took a distressing turn; mentally de-
ranged, she had to be placed under proper care, and
Thackeray's home was broken up. He took her to Paris,
and afterwards to Germany; but her case became hopeless, she could not see her husband, and by 1843 Thackeray was living alone in London. A letter of FitzGerald's,
in 1841, advises a friend to buy Thackeray's little book,
The Second Funeral of Napoleon, as "each copy sold
puts 7½d. in T.'s pocket; which is not very heavy just
now, I take it." Critics who sneer at the cynicism of
Thackeray, a totally unjust term, by the way, even for
his saddest mood, would do well to recall the manifold
trials of his early manhood, the brave spirit with which
he met them, and the tenderness which made him write,
years afterwards, "though my marriage was a wreck
. . . I would do it over again; for behold Love is the
crown and completion of all earthly good." He lived
for some years without attaining any real reputation
with the public or any substantial returns from his arti-

cles and his books; but it must not be forgotten that he had great powers of enjoyment and was no unwilling citizen of Bohemia in its more respectable quarters. He was an eager and welcome contributor to *Punch* during its earliest years, sending in prose and verse which are now included in his works. Best known are his ballads and songs, like *The Cane-Bottomed Chair* and *The Ballad of Bouillabaisse*. The Snob Papers, too, first appeared in *Punch;* and those "prize novelists" which parody so well the stories of Disraeli, Lever, and others. His connection with *Punch* ended about 1854, and the breach was due to his disapproval of the paper's attitude towards certain questions of the day. In 1842 he made a tour in Ireland to gather materials for his *Irish Sketch-Book*, which appeared the next year. In 1844 *Fraser's Magazine* printed his *Barry Lyndon*, now regarded as a masterpiece, but then little heeded; this was "by Fitz-Boodle," as his *Catherine*, in the same magazine, had been "by Ikey Solomons, Esq. junior," and *The Yellowplush Correspondence, Fashionable Fax and Polite Annygoats*, "by Charles Yellowplush." The same year, 1844, FitzGerald reports him "writing hard for half a dozen reviews and newspapers all the morning."

But this long time of trial and obscurity came at last to an end. By January, 1847, Thackeray was settled in a house of his own in Kensington, and was writing *Vanity Fair*. Refused by the editor of *Colburn's Magazine*, it was published, like Dickens's novels, in monthly parts, the last of which appeared in July, 1848, when its author was thirty-seven years old. At last he had found the public. Mrs. Carlyle, no mild critic, thought that he "beat Dickens out of the world." In December,

1847, Charlotte Brontë dedicated to Thackeray the
second edition of her immensely popular *Jane Eyre*.
Moreover, he was taken up by that very society which
Vanity Fair satirizes with such tireless power; and
some of his old friends complained, unjustly enough,
that he was dangling about noblemen's houses and forgetting the companions of his adversity. Whatever his
change of life, he was now recognized as one of the foremost writers of his day. In eight years he produced his
best work; *Vanity Fair* was followed by *Pendennis*,
which reflects much of his own experience, in 1850,
by *Esmond* in 1852, and by *The Newcomes* in 1855.
Of these, *Esmond*, which is perhaps the best, was
received with the least enthusiasm; even *Pendennis*
met with some depressing criticism, and its publication
was suspended for a while by the author's serious illness in the autumn of 1849. But Thackeray had a
secure hold upon the reading world, and gained a good
income from these books. It is true that his satire made
him both feared and disliked in some quarters, and he
was blackballed on his first attempt to enter the Athenæum Club; moreover, he spent his money lavishly and
probably exceeded his income. But almost within a year
of his rejection he was elected to the Athenæum; and
his finances were repaired by a series of lectures which
he gave in London in 1851, repeating them in other
cities like Oxford and Edinburgh, and, a year later,
in America. These were the lectures on *The English
Humourists*. Though highly nervous, and the very
opposite of a "platform man," Thackeray held his
audiences by the charm of his style and by the simple,
almost colloquial manner of delivery. His biographers
insist on the contrast with Dickens; not only was

the latter dramatic, rhetorical, confident, where Thackeray was tentative and undemonstrative, but a certain florid and insistent style in Dickens sundered him from the aristocratic quietness and repression of his rival. The plain truth is that nowhere did Thackeray's instincts as a gentleman tell more than in his manner as a public speaker; and his manner was invariably perfect in public and private alike. "Very uncertain and chaotic in all points," wrote Carlyle of him, "except his outer breeding, which is fixed enough and perfect according to the modern English style." The same contrast is evident when Thackeray visited America and gave his lectures there. Not a public criticism of any kind upon his hosts was heard, and even his private utterances were kindly and appreciative. Dickens, the born reporter, eager for copy, works everything ludicrous, crude, and outrageous into his *American Notes* and *Martin Chuzzlewit;* Thackeray, in his *Virginians*, a not altogether successful sequel to *Esmond*, completed, in 1859, takes a precisely opposite course. It was in October, 1852, that Thackeray sailed for Boston in the company of his countryman, A. H. Clough, and of James Russell Lowell. After more than a month of lecturing and visiting, he writes to an intimate friend that he likes the people, finds many "pleasant companions" who are "natural and well-read and well-bred too." He notes the rush and restlessness of American life, but is not displeased with it. He made about ten thousand dollars, it would seem, by his lectures, and returned home in the spring of 1853. In October, 1855, he visited America again, extending his tour well into the South and West. Instead of his previous lectures on *The English Humourists*, he now gave his course on

The Four Georges ; and some of his English critics were inclined to sneer at him for truckling to American prejudices by his satire and ridicule of the kings and by his praise of Washington. It must be remembered, however, that he gave the same lectures afterward in England, getting fifty guineas a night and being received, especially at Oxford and Edinburgh, with great enthusiasm.

It was probably the success of these lectures which induced Thackeray in 1857 to stand for Parliament for the city of Oxford. He advocated the Liberal policy of a limited extension of the suffrage; but though he spoke well and made an earnest struggle, he was beaten by the narrow margin of sixty votes, and went back, after a campaign which was highly creditable both to himself and his opponent, to his literary tasks. It must be admitted that his writings, so far as fiction is concerned, never rose to their former level. *The Virginians* showed distinct decline, and the novel, *Lovel the Widower*, which he wrote for the *Cornhill Magazine*, a shilling periodical which now began under his editorship, has very little to recommend it. On the other hand, the essays which he published as editor of this magazine under the title of *Roundabout Papers*, contain some of his most admirable work and have the full charm of his style. But Thackeray had long been in ill health; his late hours and lack of exercise combined, in spite of his pleasant home life, to aggravate an already serious complaint. He often suffered from severe spasms of pain; and his paper on "Dr. Edinburgh" and "Dr. London" may well reflect his own premonitions of a near and sudden death. Though by no means what is called a pious man, he held steadily to the belief of his church and looked cheerfully into the future. "Can't you fancy sailing into the calm?" he wrote to a friend. For him to die was to go "out of our stormy life" and "nearer the Divine light and warmth."

In March, 1862, he practically resigned his task as editor of the *Cornhill Magazine*. Throughout this year and the next he lived in the old way, concluding his *Adventures of Philip* for the *Cornhill*, and working on a promising novel, *Denis Duval*, which, like Dickens's *Edwin Drood*, was left unfinished. Very sensitive to criticism, and holding strictly to his rights as a gentleman, Thackeray had, in 1858, hotly resented an article printed in *Town Talk* by the editor, Edmund Yates, who spoke of the novelist as one who "cut his coat according to the cloth," flattering the aristocracy at home and the democracy abroad. Thackeray forced the Garrick Club to expel Yates, who refused to make "ample apology;" but the latter had the aid and comfort of Dickens in this contest; and the two great writers were estranged for three or four years. It is pleasant to know that big-hearted Thackeray made the advances which led to reconciliation. With all his sensitiveness, he had no petty jealousies; his admiration of Dickens was unfeigned and was communicated freely to his friends. No more charming letters were ever written than those which Thackeray dashed off in the intervals of his work, often with a caricature or other sketch, and often, it must be admitted, with an atrocious pun or so into the bargain. His generosity was lavish, and spared neither his money nor his pen. One of his best essays appeared in the *Times*, to support an exhibition of Cruikshank's drawings and bring relief for a brother artist. His own affairs were in good case; and in the

spring of 1862 he had moved into a new house of unusually ample and luxurious design. Among his close
friends of these latter days were Sir Theodore and Lady
Martin, the latter best known as Helen Faucit, a charming actress who had made the heroines of Shakespeare
her special study. His daughters, too, were all that a
father could desire; and there was no lack of "that
which should accompany old age" in the last scenes
of Thackeray's life. In December, 1863, he seemed in
ordinary health, though confined to bed for a few days
by one of his attacks. Recovering, he spoke cheerfully
to Dickens about the work he had in hand; but on the
23d he went to rest in some pain, was heard moving
about in the night, and must have died, as Trollope
conjectures, between two and three o'clock on the morning of the 24th. He was buried on the 30th in Kensal
Green Cemetery.

GEORGE ELIOT

"THERE'S allays two 'pinions," says Mr. Macey in *Silas Marner;* " there's the 'pinion a man has of himsen, and there's the 'pinion other folks have on him." Just at present the sagacity rather than the humor of this statement is the point for remark. The fairness of Mr. Macey, his desire to give both sides of the question fair play, was highly characteristic of his creator. George Eliot was certainly conspicuous among women for the masculine nature of her thought: its vigor, its philosophic zeal, its eagerness for truth. She sought earnestly, whether in poem, essay, or novel, to discover the moral motives underlying society. Her chief claim to renown, of course, lies in the skill with which she could follow those motives through the lives of characters in her novels.

The charge that her eagerness to teach her moral discoveries got the better of her, especially in her later works, is not wholly unfair. " She was born to please," writes one, " but unhappily persuaded herself, or was persuaded, that her mission was to teach the world, . . . and, in consequence, an agreeable rustic writer . . . found herself gradually uplifted until, about 1875, she sat enthroned on an educational tripod, an almost ludicrous pythoness." Though this estimate may go a little too far, it is nevertheless true that her pedantic manner obscures for many the full lustre of her genius. Still, in extenuation of the position of teacher which to many she seemed unduly to assume, it must be remembered that after the death of Dickens in 1870 she was really the greatest living novelist and that the reading public of England did look to her for instruction.

Yet from all accounts, this heavy manner of writing did not destroy the charm of her personality in conversation. Personally unattractive to strangers, she impressed those who knew her as a woman of extraordinary intellect and high ideals. Though her ways of thinking were vigorously masculine, her quick sensibility and affection were strikingly feminine; and the absolute necessity she felt for a supporting, sympathetic companion was also singularly feminine.

Mary Ann (or Marian) Evans, known to fame as George Eliot, was born at South Farm, Arbury, in Warwickshire, on November 22, 1819. Her father, Robert Evans, who had married Christiana Pearson as his second wife in 1813, was the son of a carpenter and was himself agent of one Francis Newdigate for estates in Derbyshire and Warwickshire. A few months after Mary Ann's birth the family removed to Griff House, on the high road near Nuneaton. About her childhood there was very little remarkable except the signs, to which her chief biographer, Mr. Cross, calls attention, of " the trait that was most marked in her through life — namely, the absolute need of some one person who should be all in all to her, and to whom she should be all in all." The country in which she grew up and the manners of the people there are familiar to readers of *Scenes from Clerical Life*, *Adam Bede*, and *The Mill on the Floss*. When she was five she was sent to Miss Lathom's School at Attleborough, near Nuneaton, and three years later to Miss Wallington's large school in Nuneaton. By this time she had begun to read consid-

erably, such books as *The Pilgrim's Progress*, Defoe's
History of the Devil, *Rasselas*, and the works of Scott
and Lamb. When she was twelve she went to the
Misses Franklin's school at Coventry, only to be called
home at fifteen by the fatal illness of her mother. The
death of Mrs. Evans in 1836 and the marriage of the
eldest daughter, Christiana, in 1837, threw the charge
of the household at Griff on Mary Ann.

Now begins one of the hardest yet perhaps most fruitful chapters of her life. The keeping of household accounts, the purchase of provisions, the making of butter
and jelly and cheese occupied much of her time; but
though she had to give up regular schooling, she did
not, in spite of weak health, abandon her intellectual
pursuits. Besides reading widely in English, she studied
German, Italian, and science, and found time to play
the piano for her father, who was very fond of music.
She herself was already a skillful musician. In 1841,
when her brother Isaac married and succeeded to his
father's position at Griff House, she retired with the
latter to Foleshill, near Coventry, and there formed a
close friendship with the Brays. Mr. Bray, a wealthy
ribbon manufacturer and a man of great culture, who
often had as guests such men as Emerson and Froude,
gave an added stimulus to the intellectual zeal of young
Miss Evans. She took lessons in Greek and Latin,
renewed her modern language studies with her old
Coventry teacher, Signor Brezzi, and worked by herself at Hebrew. " She had no petty egotism, no spirit
of contradiction," said one who knew her. " She never
talked for effect. A happy thought well expressed filled
her with delight : in a moment she would seize the point
and improve upon it — so that common people began

to feel themselves wise in her presence." It was not strange that under the influence of the Brays she should renounce the unthinking, dogmatic faith of her youth and resolve, at the end of 1841, to give up going to church. This brought on trouble with her father, a devout church-goer; Miss Evans went to live with her brother and talked of teaching at Leamington; but after a few months' dispute, she returned to take care of her old father, attended church as before, and was so influenced by the event that she resolved never to say in her books anything to shake the religious faith of her readers.

About this time (1842) her literary labors began. Her earliest published piece was a poem in the *Christian Observer* for January, 1840. Two years later she undertook to finish the translation of Strauss's *Leben Jesu*, and finally published her work in June, 1846. Soon after, though her study continued, she was frequently depressed by the failing health of her father, and after his death, in 1849, save for the friendship with the Brays, she was constantly in the depths of melancholy. Some time was spent abroad, but except in study she was aimless and unhappy, in an intellectual solitude. In 1851 her work in connection with the *Westminster Review* gave her a new interest and indirectly brought about her greatest good fortune. For through Mr. Chapman, the editor, she became intimate with Herbert Spencer, and through the latter met George Henry Lewes. For a short time she continued her work on the *Westminster Review*, she translated Feuerbach's *Essence of Christianity* (1854), and then through Spencer and Lewes was urged to try her hand at fiction.

Of her union in 1854 with Lewes there is now little need for discussion. A legal divorce from his wife, who was living separated from him, was impossible on a technical ground, he having forgiven her a previous offense. Though the benefit of his union with Miss Evans, which in a spiritual sense was a most true marriage, is not to be questioned, of course one cannot condone in general what in this particular case seems almost to have been justified. "No legal marriage," says Leslie Stephen, "could have called forth greater mutual devotion." George Eliot, very much a woman in this respect, was miserable without a sympathetic person to lean upon, and in Lewes she found all that her nature craved — congenial pursuits and a generous spirit.

Urged on by Lewes, George Eliot wrote *Amos Barton*, her first fiction, in the fall of 1856. Lewes sent it to Blackwood, who paid fifty guineas for it and supposed that the author was a clergyman! It was finally published again in the *Scenes from Clerical Life* in 1858. Impelled by the good fortune of these stories, she finished *Adam Bede*, which appeared in February, 1859. The success was so tremendous that in her later work she often despaired of doing so well as in this her first attempt at a long novel. Soon she set to work on *The Mill on the Floss*, half reminiscent of her youth. It appeared early in 1860. Through its composition she was again visited by periods of depression, by torturing self-questionings. " I feel no regret," she says to Mrs. Bray, "that the fame, as such, brings no pleasure; but it *is* a grief to me that I do not constantly feel strong in thankfulness that my past life has vindicated its uses, and given me reason for gladness that such an unpromising woman-child was born into the world."

After their union George Eliot and Lewes lived chiefly in or near London, though much time was spent abroad, usually in Germany, Switzerland, and Italy The trip which was taken in 1860, immediately after the completion of *The Mill on the Floss*, gave the first suggestion of *Romola*, a new kind of novel for George Eliot and one accomplished only with difficulty and depressing labor. She spent much time in Florence accumulating historical matter and putting off the actual writing, so that, before starting it, she found time to write a short novel after her earlier manner. *Silas Marner*, which was published in 1860, has given us Mr. Macey, the personage who along with Mrs. Poyser of *Adam Bede* can safely move in the immortal society of Messrs. Pickwick and Micawber. A few extracts from the author's journal show what trouble *Romola* caused : "Aug. 1 [1861]. Struggling constantly with depression. . . . Aug. 12. Got into a state of so much wretchedness in attempting to concentrate my thoughts on the construction of my story, that I became desperate, and suddenly burst my bonds, saying, I will not think of writing ! . . . Oct. 4. My mind still worried about my plot — and without any confidence in my ability to do what I want. . . . Oct. 31. Still with an incapable head — trying to write, trying to construct, and unable." The novel was at last fairly started on January 1, 1862, and appeared in the *Cornhill Magazine* in 1862–63. Mr. Cross notes that she said, "I began it a young woman, — I finished it an old woman."

By 1859 the identity of George Eliot, which had been remarkably well concealed, was sufficiently known for many to seek her in her London home. Mr. Oscar

Browning thus describes the scene: " Mrs. Lewes generally sat in an armchair at the left of the fireplace. Lewes generally stood or moved about in the back drawing-room. . . . In the early days of my acquaintance the company was small, containing more men than women. Herbert Spencer and Professor Beesly were constant visitors. The guests closed around the fire and the conversation was general. At a later period the company increased, and those who wished to converse with the great authoress whom they had come to visit took their seat in turns at the chair by her side. She always gave us of her best. Her conversation was deeply sympathetic, but grave and solemn, illumined by happy phrases and by thrilling tenderness, but not by humor. Although her features were heavy, and not well proportioned, all was forgotten when that majestic head bent slowly down, and the eyes were lit up with a penetrating and lively gaze. She appeared much greater than her books. Her ability seemed to shrink beside her moral grandeur. She was not only the cleverest, but the best woman you had met. You never dared to speak to her of her works; her personality was so much more impressive than its product."

After *Romola* there was a pause in George Eliot's work. This book seemed to point to a kind of novel differing slightly from the earlier productions, *Adam Bede* and *The Mill on the Floss*, to a new type, at last achieved in *Middlemarch* and *Daniel Deronda*. Meanwhile, in the transition, she wrote *Felix Holt*, published in 1866, a book which in manner though not in success should be classed with *Silas Marner*. At the same time a greater interest in poetic composition was growing upon her and resulted in 1868 in the long dramatic poem, *The Spanish Gypsy*. She had for some time considered and worked on this poem and had chosen Spain as the fittest scene, just as Florence had been suited to *Romola*. It was with the purpose of studying details that she and Mr. Lewes visited Spain early in 1867. These days seem to have been among her happiest; her letters, usually not very interesting reading, take on a brighter, less self-analytic turn. Instead of questions as to her usefulness in this sad world, she is more apt to write such sentences as, " Last night we walked out and saw the towers of the Alhambra, the wide Vega, and the snowy mountains by the brilliant moonlight."

Soon after, however, depression returned. The sad sickness and slow death in 1869 of young Thornton Lewes, whom she nursed, made a strong impression on her sensitive nature. "This death," she wrote, " seems to me the beginning of our own." *Middlemarch*, too, by this time well under way, brought the same travail as *Romola*. " When a subject has begun to grow in me," she said, " I suffer terribly until it has wrought itself out — become a complete organism; and then it seems to take wing and go away from me. *That* thing is not to be done again, — that life has been lived." During the pauses in the writing of *Middlemarch* she composed more poetry, which, including *Jubal* and other poems, was published in 1874. *Middlemarch* began coming out in eight bi-monthly parts on December 1, 1871, under the title *Miss Brooke*, and was finished in September, 1872. It was immensely successful; nearly 20,000 copies sold by the end of 1874.

Though conceived almost as early as *Middlemarch*, *Daniel Deronda*, which is in the estimation of some her greatest work, did not appear till 1876. The composition of it caused her the same anxiety,— the "fear lest I may not be able to complete it so as to make it a contribution to literature, and not a mere addition to the heap of books,"— but she was comforted on looking back to see "that I really was in worse health and suffered equal depression about *Romola ;* and, so far as I have recorded, the same thing seems to be true of *Middlemarch.*" Her interest in the Jews, an interest especially revealed in this book, had been growing for some time and was enough to stimulate her manner of moralizing which so many deplore. People "hardly know," she wrote to Mrs. Stowe, "that Christ was a Jew. And I find men, educated, supposing that Christ spoke Greek. . . . The best that can be said of it is, that it is a sign of the intellectual narrowness — in plain English, the stupidity — which is still the average mark of our culture." The English people were being indeed scourged at all hands ; for the genial Dickens was dead, and if they turned from George Eliot, they were like to encounter Ruskin, now grown shrill, or Carlyle, violent with his anathemas.

On November 28, 1878, George Lewes died, leaving her almost inconsolable. One of the first things she did, on collecting herself, was to arrange for a Cambridge "studentship" endowed in his name. The *Impressions of Theophrastus Such*, her last work, was published the following year. Not long after, May 6, 1880, she married her subsequent biographer, Mr. John Cross. "No one," says Mr. Oscar Browning, "can have studied the character of George Eliot, even superficially, without being convinced how necessary it was for her to have some one to depend upon, and how much her nature yearned for sympathy and support." But she did not live long to enjoy the world which she now found "so intensely interesting." She died, after a short attack of throat trouble, "something like croup," on December 22, 1880, and was buried beside Mr. Lewes in Highgate Cemetery.

ALFRED TENNYSON

As the nineteenth century recedes, and so comes more and more into view as a whole, so much greater seems the likelihood that Tennyson will always be regarded as its representative poet in English literature. He was born in its first decade, and died in its last. He came of age during the agitation for the great Reform Bill, echoed the hopes of ardent Liberals who were fain to press on with the good cause, —

"Till the war-drum throbb'd no longer, and the battle-flags were furl'd
  In the Parliament of Man, the Federation of the World;"

but lived to share a growing distrust in democracy, to sneer at "the suffrage of the plow," and to say —

"Let us hush this cry of 'Forward!' till ten thousand years have gone."

He was precisely fifty years old when Darwin's book on the *Origin of Species* appeared, marking a revolution in man's thought; but he had shared the doubts and dissensions which preceded Darwin's summary, and in his *In Memoriam* grapples hard with the many difficulties which attended the meeting of a new science and an ancient faith. In poetry he could remember Byron as a living voice, and records the grief with which on an April day in 1824, "a day when the whole world seemed to be darkened for me," he went out and carved on a rock the words "Byron is dead." When the world recorded the poet's own death, he had outlived all but

one of the great singers of the century, and left only
Swinburne to hand down the traditions of our nobler
verse. Unlike Browning, he was popular with all classes
of readers, yet he kept intact the dignity and distinction of his own personal art. Unlike Browning, too, he
shunned society ; his love of nature was as genuine as
it was profound ; and all his portraits show the face of
an artist and a dreamer. Clearly, then, he must be accepted as the representative·poet of his nation and of
his time.

Alfred Tennyson was born at Somersby in Lincolnshire, August 6, 1809, the fourth of twelve children.
His father was rector of the parish, and belonged to a
very old family of that country. The mother, born Elizabeth Fytche, was also of ancient descent. His native
country is described in many poems ; we are told that
the stream which flowed through Somersby is addressed
in that charming lyric *Flow down, Cold Rivulet, to the
Sea*. At seven he was sent to school in Louth, and
went through the common experience of that day, —
copious floggings from the master and still more copious
cuffings from the boys. " How I did hate that school !"
was his comment in later life. After four years he returned to Somersby and was taught by his father, a
man of great ability and varied tastes, until he was
ready for Cambridge. Juvenile poems of this period
show uncommon ability compared with most effusions
of the kind ; and when he was but sixteen years of age
he was engaged on verse which was published two years
later along with that of his elder brother Charles, as
Poems by Two Brothers. Some of these *Juvenilia* are
now included in the poet's collected works.

In February, 1828, the two brothers entered Trinity

College, Cambridge, whither their older brother Frederick had preceded them. Alfred is described in these days as striking and distinguished in appearance. His son and biographer quotes the following: "Six feet high, broad-chested, strong-limbed, his face Shakespearean, with deep eyelids, his forehead ample, crowned with dark wavy hair, his head finely poised, his hand the admiration of sculptors, long fingers with square tips, soft as a child's, but of great size and strength. What struck one most about him was the union of strength with refinement." The two brothers lived in lodgings, and so missed the more intimate college life; but they made friends among the best men of the University. Nearest and dearest of these to the poet was Arthur Henry Hallam, a man of great attainments and promise, whose early death called out the *In Memoriam*. Other friends were Monckton Milnes, afterwards Lord Houghton; Trench, afterwards Archbishop of Dublin; Thompson, subsequently Master of Trinity; Maurice, celebrated as a great liberal preacher; Spedding, the editor of Bacon. In the formal debates of their society Tennyson took little part and is said never to have read a paper before them, but his conversation was brilliant enough in that

> "band
> Of youthful friends, on mind and art,
> And labour, and the changing mart,
> And all the framework of the land."

This society went by the name of "The Apostles." In 1829 Tennyson won the prize medal in poetry on the subject of Timbuctoo. He was too shy to declaim the poem at Commencement, and that part of the task was performed by his friend Merivale; but in the presence

of a few friends Tennyson was already famous for his
noble and sympathetic recitation of poetry, declaiming
one of his own poems or a ballad like *Clerk Saunders*.
In 1830, while he was still an undergraduate, was published his first volume, *Poems, Chiefly Lyrical*. The
reviews were fairly encouraging; and though there was
an affectation, a kind of overdone daintiness, in these
early verses, about which Tennyson heard and was yet
to hear much sarcasm from *The Quarterly Review*
and *Blackwood's Magazine*, there were many discrimi-
nating readers who hailed him as the coming poet of
England. Another break in the even course of college
life was Tennyson's departure for Spain with Arthur
Hallam for the purpose of giving financial help to
the revolutionists who had risen against King Ferdi-
nand and the Inquisition. This romantic expedition, in
which the two friends conferred with leaders of the revolt, left a permanent impression on Tennyson's mind
of the splendid scenery of the Pyrenees. He was particularly moved by the beauty of the streams and water-
falls. "Somehow," he said in after life, "water is the
element I love best of all the four." In the valley of
Cauteretz, his son tells us, he then wrote part of his
Œnone, which is full of that wild scenery, and thirty-
two years later the music of its stream still echoed in
the lines beginning "All along the valley," and recalled
the man he loved, the comrade of his wanderings.

He left Cambridge in February, 1831, without taking a degree. Shortly afterward his father died; but
by an arrangement with the new rector the family kept
their home for six years. Meanwhile, Arthur Hallam
had become engaged to Tennyson's sister, and made
frequent visits to the rectory. The poet lived quietly at

home, took long walks, read, studied, and made a few
contributions to magazines and annuals. For two years
his intercourse with Hallam was constant, now in Lincolnshire and now at Hallam's house in London, where
much tobacco was smoked and discussion ranged from
the exciting events of the day — all England was in
the throes of the Reform agitation — to the ideals of
poet and philosopher. The poems of Tennyson's new collection were circulated in manuscript among his friends
and duly appreciated. The volume itself appeared at
the close of the year 1832. Here was the real Tennyson.
The public now could read *The Lady of Shalott, The
Miller's Daughter, Œnone, The Palace of Art, The
May Queen, The Lotos-Eaters,* and the *Dream of Fair
Women.* Here was indeed richness, but the great reviews thought otherwise. The *Quarterly* made a savage
and clumsy attack. Tennyson had laid himself open to
ridicule by the ineffectual and almost fatuous lines to
his " darling room ; " and the reviewer paid his compliments to the supposed " white dimity " of the couches in
the dear little room as "a type of the purity of the
poet's mind." Thirteen years later, when Tennyson received his pension from the government, Bulwer, in a
poem called the *New Timon,* could still mock School-
miss Alfred and —

> " her chaste delight
> In darling little rooms so warm and bright."

Tennyson's reply in *Punch,* in which he called Bulwer
a " bandbox," was a perhaps regrettable but sufficiently
energetic blow in return. But in 1832 all the praise
of his friends could not nerve the poet to brave the
thunders of the mighty *Quarterly,* and his son says
that had it not been for the intervention of these same

friends, Tennyson would have ceased to write, after the death of Arthur Hallam.

That this irreparable loss should deepen the poet's lack of confidence in his literary fortunes was natural. He had hardly received an enthusiastic letter from Hallam about pictures in Vienna when news came of his friend's sudden death in September, 1833. His grief found expression in several poems, none of which is more profoundly affecting than the simple lines beginning "Break, break, break!" But a series of "elegies" composed in a metre little used up to that time, which he began in 1833 in the first flood of sorrow, was continued, elaborated, and revised as the years went on, and finally appeared in May, 1850, in a limited edition, as *In Memoriam*. It was published soon after without the author's name, but was of course attributed at once to Tennyson, who in that year, by the death of Wordsworth, became the foremost living poet of England.

Tennyson's life from 1832 to 1842 is now difficult to follow. He wrote few letters, and his movements are traced chiefly from the notes and recollections of his friends. In 1837 the Tennysons had moved to Epping Forest, and again in 1840 to Tunbridge Wells. In 1835 the poet and Edward FitzGerald were in the Lake Country together with James Spedding, and Tennyson read to his friends such poems as *Morte d'Arthur*, *The Day-Dream*, and *The Gardener's Daughter*. It is a delightful glimpse that FitzGerald gives us of himself and Tennyson resting on their oars in a boat on Windermere while Alfred quotes his lines about the lady of the lake and Excalibur : —

> " Nine years she wrought it, sitting in the deeps
> Upon the hidden bases of the hills."

" Not bad, that, Fitz, is it?" was the poet's comment.
He called on Hartley Coleridge, who wrote a sonnet on
the occasion, and whom Tennyson afterwards described
as " a loveable little fellow;" but the shy young bard
could not be persuaded to visit Wordsworth at Rydal
Mount. In brief, during these years Tennyson was perfecting his art, pondering over the burning political
questions, and over problems of metaphysics and religion now particularly significant to him through the
death of Hallam, communing with his gifted friends,
and corresponding with Miss Emily Sellwood, who was
later to be his wife. Her older sister Louisa was married
in 1836 to Tennyson's brother Charles; and she had
met the poet as early as 1830, " a beautiful girl of seventeen, in her simple gray dress," in a forest walk, getting
from him the somewhat startling question, " Are you
a Dryad or an Oread wandering here?" In 1837 Tennyson began his friendship with Gladstone ; and from this
time on, under the spur of his engagement to Emily
Sellwood, and with an inward assurance of success, he
seems to have put most of his doubts and difficulties and
morbidness behind him, and bent all his energies upon
the completion of his new volume of verse. It is true
that his poverty and meagre prospects caused all correspondence with Miss Sellwood to be forbidden, and
the marriage did not take place until June, 1850; but
the deeper engagement was unbroken, and the consola-
tions of friendship and of his art sustained Tennyson
through this period of struggle. In October, 1841,
John Sterling writes: " Carlyle was here yesterday
evening, growled at having missed you, and said more
in your praise than in anyone's except Cromwell, and
an American backwoodsman who has killed thirty or

forty people with a bowie-knife and since run away to Texas."

The new collection appeared in 1842. Tennyson now lived part of the time in London, dining at the Cock, whose head-waiter he celebrated in the famous verses, and meeting, besides his old friends, Thackeray, Carlyle, Rogers, Dickens, Landor, Leigh Hunt, and Campbell. These social occasions alternated with solitudes; and Carlyle describes him in a letter to Emerson " dwelling in an element of gloom, carrying a bit of chaos about him, in short, which he is manufacturing into cosmos." The description which follows is famous : " One of the finest looking men in the world. A great shock of rough dusky dark hair; bright laughing hazel eyes; massive aquiline face, most massive yet most delicate ; of sallow brown complexion, almost Indian looking, clothes cynically loose, free-and-easy, smokes infinite tobacco. His voice is musical, metallic, fit for loud laughter and piercing wail, and all that may lie between; speech and speculation free and plenteous; I do not meet in these late decades such company over a pipe! We shall see what he will grow to." With the appearance of the poems of 1842, which were brought out by Edward Moxon in two small volumes and were in their fourth edition by 1846, Tennyson's success was assured. There was what his son calls a "chorus of favorable reviews." Many of the poems became like household words on both sides of the ocean, and while *The Lord of Burleigh* appealed to the humblest minds, there were *Ulysses* and *Morte d'Arthur*, *Sir Galahad* and *The Vision of Sin* for a higher mood. It is said that a part of *Ulysses* remained Tennyson's own favorite. At the age of thirty-three, then, Tennyson had really taken by

storm the heart of the public. The new poems and
the old favorites now revised made up a body of verse
individual in character, exquisite in form, and as distinctly human and sincere in their lyric quality as the
best poems of Wordsworth. Indeed, FitzGerald, who
was as jealous a critic as he was an ardent admirer of
the poet's work, always maintained that Tennyson's
best work was done at this time.

The prosperous years, however, had not yet begun.
In 1844 Tennyson's health was seriously impaired. He
had sold his small estate in Lincolnshire, and with the
money thus realized, together with a legacy of £500,
had gone into a scheme of wood-carving by machinery
undertaken by an enthusiastic neighbor. The project
failed utterly; and with Tennyson's own money went
" a portion of the property of his brothers and sisters.
So severe a hypochondria set in upon him," says his
son, " that his friends despaired of his life." He tried
a hydropathic cure, wrote little or nothing to any one
and was at the lowest ebb of fortune and spirits. Meanwhile his friends were not idle. Carlyle, using his
weapon of words, and Milnes, marshaling the more
effective ranks of political influence, persuaded Sir
Robert Peel in 1845 to grant the poet an annual pension of £200. It is said that the minister was balancing
the rival claims of Tennyson and an older and more
obscure poet, Knowles, when Milnes read him *Ulysses*
and decided the question outright. In 1846 Tennyson
went abroad, and the next year was still taking his
hydropathic treatment and neglecting his friends. But
this same year, 1847, saw the publication of *The
Princess*. In the opinion of friends like Carlyle and
FitzGerald it was a grievous lapse. The poem, to be

sure, was what it called itself, a medley; it attacked
the great question of woman's rights, a question which
few Englishmen then took seriously, and solved it with
those famous lines which assert that "woman is not
undeveloped man, but diverse," and define her rights
as based on an equality which is "not like to like, but
like in difference." Along with this moral runs a romantic adventurous tale, and scattered through the
whole are some of Tennyson's most exquisite lyrics,
notably the "Bugle Song," inspired by his visit to the
Lakes of Killarney.

In 1850 Tennyson, who had been living the past four
years at Cheltenham, published *In Memoriam*. Doubt-
fully received at first, this poem, which reflects so faithfully the troubled intellectual condition of the times,
beginning with personal grief, and then passing into a
series of lyrics on life and death, on faith and despair,
and ending with a sort of epithalamium on the marriage
of the poet's sister, found a sympathetic audience in
the best minds of the day. One of the most appreciative
reviews was from the pen of Gladstone, who had been
the intimate school friend of Arthur Hallam. Even the
publisher predicted financial success, and on the strength
of this expectation, along with his pension, Tennyson
and Miss Sellwood were married, June 13, 1850, at
Shiplake on the Thames. Moreover, what the world
would regard as the most important result of this publication was the admiration felt for the poem by Prince
Albert, and the consequent appointment as Poet Laureate. Wordsworth had died a few months before, and
after a formal offer of the post to Rogers, who declined
it on account of his great age, it was bestowed upon Tennyson in November. Apart from the great honor of this

post, the recipient must have appreciated its commercial
importance. He had been a poor and struggling man,
but from this date the sales of his books grew rapidly; his arrangements were shrewdly made, and the
material success of his career is attested by his comfortable home at Farringford in the Isle of Wight,
the stately house which he afterwards built in Surrey,
and the income which permitted him to accept a peerage.

After the death of their first child the Tennysons
made a tour in Italy, and the poet records the impressions of that journey in a poem called *The Daisy*. The
books he took with him were "his usual traveling
companions, Shakespeare, Milton, Homer, Virgil, Horace, Pindar, Theocritus," and probably Dante's *Divine
Comedy*, and the poems of Goethe. In Paris they met
the Brownings. In August, 1852, Hallam Tennyson
was born; the poet's letters breathe a spirit of domestic
happiness, which was to be uninterrupted, save by the
death of their second son, for forty years. The next
year he leased the house at Farringford with the option
of buying it; and here, close to the sea that he loved,
with the great downs near him for his solitary walks,
and groves of elm and chestnut and pine at his very
door, he wrote the most romantic and melodious of his
poems. *Maud*, like *The Princess*, failed at first of
hearty and general applause. Gladstone afterwards admitted that he had misunderstood it, and only caught
the real meaning of the poem when he heard Tennyson read it aloud. But the Brownings were enthusiastic
from the first, and public taste came in time to recognize its merits. The lyrical passages were prime favorites with their author, whose wonderful voice was never

so sympathetic as when he read the passage beginning, " O that 't were possible," or the long, tremulous, exultant lines, "I have led her home, my love, my only friend." But the great public did not take time to discover the beauties of this " monodramatic lyric; " they read rather passages bearing upon the all-absorbing subject of the Crimean War, and blamed the author for attacking John Bright as the man "whose ears are stuffed with cotton and ring even in dreams to the chink of his pence," and worse, as a " huckster who would put down war." One man actually thought that Mr. Layard was the Assyrian Bull of the poem, while Tennyson's own aunt imagined that *Maud* contained a dastardly attack on the owners of coal mines. One Dr. Mann came out with a " vindication," for which he got hearty thanks from the poet. What the public did like, however, unreservedly and permanently, was a poem published in the same volume with *Maud*, but first printed in *The Examiner* for December 9, 1854, *The Charge of the Light Brigade;* and also the memorial ode on the Duke of Wellington, which had been printed separately in 1852. The larger volume appeared not only with the title of Poet Laureate, but with the degree of D. C. L. attached to the author's name. He had received the doctorate at the Oxford commemoration in June. He was nervous before the ordeal, and said that the shouts of the students were like the cry of the Roman crowd to " fling the Christians to the lions." His son and biographer properly records the great ovation which the poet received, — the shouts of " In Memoriam ! " and the applause, but does not tell how students in the gallery called out such questions as " Did they wake and call you early, call you early, Alfred

dear?" and other kindly jests recorded by those who
saw and heard.

Farringford was finally purchased in the spring of
1856, "with the proceeds of the sale of *Maud*." Here
Tennyson worked on his *Idylls of the King*, watched
with careful eye the life and the growth of nature
about him, making many a note, as was his wont, that
afterwards appeared as a striking metaphor or simile
in verse, translated the *Odyssey* aloud to Mrs. Tennyson in the winter evenings, walked and talked with his
children. Visitors sought him out, now Bayard Taylor, who has left a sympathetic account of his visit,
noting particularly Tennyson's minute knowledge of
botany and geology, and now the Prince Consort, who
took back a bunch of cowslips for the Queen. In 1858
the poet records a visit from "young Swinburne," whom
he thought "a very modest and intelligent young fellow." Tyndall and Newman were also pilgrims; while
the Carlyles, the Brownings, Jowett, Ruskin, and
Thackeray were frequent correspondents. To the last-
named he is "my dear old Alfred." In 1859 appeared
the *Idylls of the King*. As the Duke of Argyll wrote
the author, detractors were silenced and applause went
on *crescendo*. Macaulay, Gladstone, Clough, Ruskin, his
tried old friend Aubrey de Vere, who speaks of these
"glorious chivalrous legends," and even that prosaic
person Walter, the proprietor of the *Times*, were full
of enthusiasm. Prince Albert, in an admiring letter,
asked for the poet's name to be written in the royal
copy; in short, the success of the *Idylls* was overwhelming and the poet was requested to continue the epic.
In 1862 Tennyson, who was in high favor at court,
and had dedicated his *Idylls* to the memory of her late

Consort, paid his first visit to the Queen. "There was
a kind of stately innocence about her," he reports; and
she told him that, next to the Bible, *In Memoriam* was
her comfort. In 1863 he writes his official but hearty
welcome to Alexandra, the new Princess of Wales. In
the midst of all this visiting and correspondence with
dukes and princesses and great ladies of the court, it is
pleasant to read the letter in which Tennyson congrat-
ulates Swinburne on his *Atalanta in Calydon;* it is long,
he says, since he has read anything so fine. The poem
has both "strength and splendor," and shows, adds the
elder poet, "a fine metrical invention which I envy
you."

In 1864 appeared *Enoch Arden.* It was deservedly
and immediately popular, and Sir Alfred Lyall says
that it has been dramatized in London and New York,
translated into Latin and into seven modern languages,
seven distinct translations being made in France alone.
In the same volume with *Enoch Arden,* of which sixty
thousand copies were almost immediately sold, was a
poem in dialect, then a rare experiment in English
poetry, which must count among Tennyson's successes.
In *The Northern Farmer* is heard the voice of that
sturdy breed that Tennyson knew so well, combined
with genuine pathos and humor.

Marked mainly by increase of fortune and fame,
Tennyson's life moved on these pleasant lines for many
years. Honors were showered upon him and visitors high
and low sought him out, though his shyness and dislike of conspicuous positions was always asserting itself,
as many an anecdote could testify. A pleasant glimpse
of him is at Marlborough school, whither he had taken
his older son Hallam, reading *Guinevere* to the Upper

Sixth after dinner. *The Holy Grail* was published in 1869, and he continued his *Idylls of the King*. In 1875 the public was surprised by a new phase of the poet's art in *Queen Mary*, the first of his dramas. More than this, he intended his plays to be acted, and whatever may be thought of his dramatic success, there is something admirable in the vigor with which a man of sixty-five turned to labor in a new field. *Queen Mary* was played by Irving and his company, and Browning affirmed the first night to be a complete triumph. *Harold* and *Becket* soon followed. The latter, refused by Irving in 1879, was staged a dozen years later, and the actor in 1893 records the fiftieth performance in the "hey-day of success." In 1882, however, a very disagreeable incident had occurred. *The Promise of May*, a kind of village tragedy, was misunderstood by the public and very roughly handled. " In the middle of one of the performances Lord Queensberry rose, and in the name of Free Thought protested against ' Mr. Tennyson's abominable caricature.' " Even more noteworthy than these dramatic ventures was the vigor of production which Tennyson showed in the ballads and occasional pieces of his old age. Some of his best known poems appeared in the volume dedicated to his grandson by one who had passed his threescore and ten. Here were the swing and noble sentiment of *The Revenge, The Defence of Lucknow, The Voyage of Maeldune*, and the spirited rendering of the Anglo-Saxon *Battle of Brunanburh*. Almost to the end this vigor of production asserted itself. Probably none of his shorter poems will be remembered longer than *Crossing the Bar*, which was written in his eighty-first year and came, as he said to his son, "in a moment;" it is rightly called the crown of the poet's life-work. A few days before his death he requested that *Crossing the Bar* should be put at the end of all editions of his poems.

As early as 1868 he had begun to build his stately house at Aldworth in Surrey, and henceforth had two homes. He was wont to stay at Farringford until the early summer, and then went to Aldworth, where he got relief from his hay fever and enjoyed his country walks. If on these rambles, we are told, " a tourist were seen coming towards him, he would flee." Gladstone had proposed a baronetcy to him, but it was declined. In 1874 Disraeli again pressed this honor upon him, and Tennyson again declined it, but proposed that it should be kept in a kind of storage for his son. This, of course, was impossible. In the fall of 1883, however, Tennyson made a voyage with Gladstone on the Pembroke Castle as far as Norway, getting a particularly warm welcome at Copenhagen, where, in the small smoking-room of the steamer, the poet read his " Bugle Song " and *The Grandmother* to the crowned heads of Russia and Denmark and the Princess of Wales. During the whole journey Gladstone and Tennyson had infinite talk on poetry and philosophy. One day the former proposed to Hallam Tennyson that his father should accept a peerage ; the matter was mentioned to Tennyson, and statesman and poet discussed it without result. The upshot may be given in Tennyson's own words : " By Gladstone's advice I have consented to take the peerage, but for my own part I shall regret my simple name all my life." In 1884 he took his seat in the House of Lords as Baron Tennyson.

Meanwhile he was paying the invariable penalties of old age. His friend FitzGerald had died in the preceding

year, and to the poet life seemed scarce worth living
out, —

> " Remembering all the golden hours
> Now silent, and so many dead,
> And him the last."

In 1886 his second son, Lionel, died on the homeward
voyage from India, and was buried at sea. In 1888 he
suffered a serious attack of illness, but recovered and
was again working on a new volume of poems when he
was shocked by the news of Browning's death, in December, 1889. In 1892 it was noted that for the first
time Tennyson's voice failed while he was reading his
Lotos-Eaters aloud. At the end of June he left Farringford for Aldworth, and for a while was able to take
his regular walks, but soon he was confined to his garden, and rested in a summer-house sheltered from the
wind. In July he visited London for the last time.
Late in September his illness took its fatal turn. As
the end approached he called repeatedly for his Shakespeare. Early on the morning of October the 6th he
passed quietly away. *Cymbeline*, one of his favorite
plays, was placed with him in his coffin; and on the
12th, with stately funeral ceremonies, he was buried
in Westminster Abbey, not far from his friend and
generous rival, Robert Browning.

ROBERT BROWNING

VITALITY, versatility, intellectual curiosity — these were the most obvious characteristics in Browning's life. "Since Chaucer was alive and hale," wrote Landor of him in 1846, —

> " No man has walked along our roads with step
> So active, so enquiring eye, or tongue
> So varied in discourse."

Yet in the external aspects of his life there was nothing sensational. Born in a quiet, conventional atmosphere, he lived and died conventional. In religion a dissenter, he was a conformist in little matters of daily life; he hated eccentricity. The same eager spirit, however, which in another age would have discovered Guiana or caught the fire of the French Revolution inspired him. By his energy and grasp of realities he outran most of his contemporaries in discovering and expressing the catholic, inquiring spirit of his time. His interest in the life about him was unflagging; all through his long experience he pursued untiringly his ideal, and to the end he bore his burden with an exuberant enthusiasm.

Browning's parents were Robert Browning and Sarah Anne Wiedemann. Camberwell, where they lived, was then on the outskirts of London, and surrounded by fairly open country, and there, on May 7, 1812, their first child, Robert, was born. His father had succeeded the grandfather Browning in a respectable position in the Bank of England, but he had, unlike his practical, somewhat stern parent, gone unwillingly into banking, with the result that he never attained the business success of his predecessor. In fact, his interests lay increasingly among his books, for the most part curious old volumes which he had bound with blank leaves at the end to contain the notes he liked to make. He remembered, moreover, the strait jacket of his own youth, and when he saw inclination leading his growing son to other places than the Bank of England, he gave the boy a free rein. To this father, a man full of interesting and accurate information, a man whose reticence and modesty shut him off from the prominence he deserved, Browning owed most of his education. As a non-conformist the father was, of course, unable to give his son the customary public school and university career. Indeed, except for four years (1822–26) in a Mr. Ready's school, occasional lessons from a private tutor, and a few months at London University, all of Browning's youthful training came from his father or from omnivorous reading in his father's library.

In his mother, too, Browning was fortunate. From her he inherited a love of music and a religious inspiration, but, most of all, a spontaneous and striking tenderness. From her also must have come, with the quick sensibilities that awakened the poet in him, what little physical weakness he had. It is common to speak of Browning as robust; intellectually robust he was, and, as men go, he was possessed of more than average physical robustness. He never knew, as did his wife, for instance, what prolonged sickness or great fatigue meant, — he suffered little; but the idea that his good health was remarkable is erroneous and probably the result of his own optimistic retrospect. His early letters to Miss Barrett speak often of headache — a thing

which his scrupulous modesty would have forbidden had
there been no cause. During the first days at Florence
his wife nursed him through sleepless nights, and in
later life he was attacked by severe colds. That he
rarely allowed sickness to interfere with his active life
does not bear witness so much to his good health as to
his unfailingly good spirits, a much more important
thing to remember.

From the first Browning felt an intense interest in
life. As a boy he always kept many pets — mice, snakes,
monkeys, hedgehogs, owls, and an eagle. Among his
earliest pets were two lady-birds, which he brought home,
put in a box lined with cotton, and labeled, " Animals
found surviving in the depths of a severe winter."

In poetry he began early. His sister Sariana remembered him toddling around the dining-room table,
and telling off the scansion of verses with his fingers.
When he was twelve years old he had written enough
verses for a volume. These he showed to the Misses
Flower, the elder of whom thought them so remarkable that she made a copy which she sent to the Rev.
William J. Fox, a Unitarian clergyman of considerable
reputation as a political and critical writer. He thought
the verses too juvenile for publication, but he prophesied
great things of the author. When these verses were
written Browning was entirely under the influence of
Byron, but the next year he passed to a deeper, more
lasting influence, that of Shelley. At that time the
works of Shelley were not widely known, but Browning's mother at last found copies at a shop in Vere
Street; besides the works of Shelley she returned with
three volumes written by a " Mr. John Keats," — all
but *The Cenci* in first editions. Browning devoured

them eagerly, and tells how two nightingales sang, one in a laburnum, the other in a copper beech, the spirit of the poets' verse.

Still under the Shelley influence he produced, at twenty-one, *Pauline*, his first publication. The poem, brought out anonymously, met with almost no success; Browning himself soon grew to consider it as youthful incompetence and would not, until his later fame rendered it a curiosity, suffer it to be included among his works. Yet D. G. Rossetti, twenty years later, thought it of sufficient merit, on running across a copy in the British Museum, to transcribe the whole, and when he met the author of it he told him it might have been written by Browning himself.

By this time, 1833, Browning had definitely chosen the vocation of poet. This interest appears in his friendship with Alfred Domett, to whom, on the latter's setting out for New Zealand, he wrote his poem of *Waring*, and with whom he kept in close correspondence for some years. Soon after the publication of *Pauline*, he spent a short time traveling in Russia and half-seriously considered diplomacy as a calling; but after a stay of some months he was back in London at his poetry. Mr. Fox, who had reviewed *Pauline* favorably in the *Monthly Repository*, got Browning to contribute, in 1834, four lyrics, — "Johannes Agricola in Meditation" and "Porphyria's Lover," later published in *Men and Women*; the song, "A King lived Long Ago," later included in *Pippa Passes*; and the sonnet beginning, "Eyes calm beside thee." The following March (1835) came out Browning's first great achievement, the dramatic poem, *Paracelsus*.

Paracelsus, though it was not any greater success

with the world at large than *Pauline* had been, gained
the poet recognition in literary circles. He met among
others R. H. Horne, Leigh Hunt, Carlyle, Bryan
Waller Procter, Monckton Milnes, and T. N. Talfourd.
Especially eventful was the acquaintance with William
Macready, the actor, and his friend John Forster, the
critic. Macready, who was first met one evening, November 27, 1835, at the Rev. Mr. Fox's, was much
pleased with the slender, handsome poet and noted in his
diary that his "face was full of intelligence." The following New Year's Eve Browning met Forster at Macready's place at Elstree. Forster had written in the *Examiner* one of the few favorable reviews of *Paracelsus*,
and the friendship was cemented at once. The next
spring Browning attended at Talfourd's a dinner more
significant in his life even than the "immortal dinner" Haydon gave to Keats, Lamb, and Wordsworth.
Macready had just risen into fame ; after a long fight
in the law courts with Bunn, the manager of Drury
Lane, and incidentally with the person of Bunn in
that worthy's office, he had been transferred to Covent Garden, where he was first associated with Miss
Helen Faucit, the brilliant actress ; Talfourd's *Ion* had
just been produced with great success; and now on
the author's birthday, May 26, there was celebration
at Talfourd's. Macready sat between Wordsworth and
Landor, with Browning opposite ; others of the company were Forster and Miss Mitford. The host proposed
the toast of the English poets and, in spite of Wordsworth's presence, called on "the youngest of our poets"
for a response ; and Browning, although public speaking even in later life caused him positive dread, answered with "grace and modesty." As the party left the

house, Macready, who was in financial trouble, said to
Browning, " Write me a play and keep me from going
to America." Immediately the poet replied, " What do
you say to *Strafford ?* " By the next March the play
was finished and, thanks to the excellent acting of
Macready and Miss Faucit, was made, in spite of a
"positively nauseous " Pym and "whimpering schoolboy " Vane, a complete success.

Thus was begun Browning's connection with the
stage, to end unfortunately a few years later in a
quarrel over *A Blot in the 'Scutcheon.* By 1842 Macready was still a financial uncertainty. He had developed, however, a feeling that he was necessary to the
success of any piece, yet at the same time an apprehension lest he should accept a play which might not make
a hit. But he did, in the spring of 1842, accept *A Blot
in the 'Scutcheon* for his next season. In the fall, at
Drury Lane, however, he met with considerable loss,
and, hoping that Browning would withdraw the play,
wrote that failure had " smashed his arrangement altogether," but that he was still prepared to bring out
the piece if the author wished. Browning did not take
the hint; whereupon Macready first made the play
ridiculous by giving it to a wooden-legged, red-faced
prompter to read, then, on Browning's remonstrating,
read it himself with better effect, but next declared
himself unable to act owing to pressure of management, and gave the part to one Phelps, who seemed at
first too ill to master it. More than this, Macready attempted to change the title to *The Sisters*, and to re-
write many of the best lines; but he was thwarted in
this by the author's taking the manuscript to Moxon,
the publisher, who in a few hours printed a correct ver-

sion, which was placed in the hands of the actors the day before the performance. The result was that the play was put on the stage without adequate properties or rehearsals. Yet in spite of this it met with success; Phelps outdid himself and Miss Faucit again came to the rescue. But Browning broke finally with Macready and practically with writing for the stage, though *Colombe's Birthday* (published in 1844) was played ten years later at the Haymarket.

During these seven years of intimacy with Macready the active spirit of Browning was producing other work. In 1838 he went alone to Italy, chiefly to study for his long poem, *Sordello*, which was published in 1840. From this poem arose much of the talk of Browning's obscurity. " There were only two lines in it that I understood," said Tennyson, "and they were both lies; they were the opening and closing lines, —

'Who will may hear Sordello's story told,'

and

'Who would has heard Sordello's story told!' "

And Carlyle remarked that his wife after reading it was unable to discover " whether 'Sordello' was a man, or a city, or a book." The trip to Italy gave rise to other pieces, some of his best, such as *How they brought the Good News from Ghent to Aix* and the drama *Pippa Passes*. On his outward voyage as the ship neared Gibraltar he was carried sick on deck, where he wrote the famous little *Home Thoughts from the Sea*.

At the suggestion of Moxon the publisher his poems were brought out in a series of eight publications, which he called *Bells and Pomegranates*. The first of these was *Pippa Passes*, in 1841. The rest in order were: —

King Victor and King Charles, a drama (1842).
Dramatic Lyrics (1842).
The Return of the Druses, a drama (1843).
A Blot in the 'Scutcheon, a drama (1843).
Colombe's Birthday, a drama (1844).
Dramatic Romances and Lyrics (1845).
Luria and *A Soul's Tragedy*, both plays (1846).
In later editions the poems in Nos. III and VII were considerably changed about and some were put under other headings.

In all these publications Browning attained very little fame. One recognition, however, was the beginning of the most interesting experience of his life — an experience which especially reveals his 'character. On returning from a short trip to Italy in 1844 he found that the poems of Miss Elizabeth Barrett had taken both London and New York by storm; and among those poems he read the lines: —

" Or at times a modern volume, Wordsworth's solemn-thoughted
    idyll,
Howitt's ballad verse, or Tennyson's enchanted reverie, —
Or from Browning some ' Pomegranate,' which, if cut deep down
    the middle,
Shows a heart within blood-tinctured, of a veined humanity."

Browning, who was much touched by the reference, one day mentioned his delight to an old friend of the Barretts, — John Kenyon, "the Magnificent." Miss Barrett had been an invalid ever since a riding accident in her youth, but it was still possible to visit her by letter, and so Kenyon replied, "Why don't you write and tell her so?" Browning did write: "I love your verses with all my heart, dear Miss Barrett;" and thence sprang the interesting correspondence of two years culminating in their marriage. It is pleasant to think that this poet's love needs no explanation or apology; the simple story is itself Browning's defense and praise.

On the 25th of May, 1844, the two met face to face. A closer intimacy grew up, and the letters, at first chiefly given over to literary discussion, became more personal. For a moment a slight misunderstanding arose. Browning wrote a letter which he regretted, and Miss Barrett, who felt that her poor health precluded all idea of marriage, feared she had been too " head-long;" she was always so, she said, "precipitously rush-ing forward through all manner of nettles and briars instead of keeping the path; . . . tearing open letters, and never untying a string, — and expecting everything to be done in a minute, and the thunder to be as quick as the lightning." Once, long after their marriage, when he appeared with his beard shaved off, she de-manded that he restore it — " that minute." He did let it grow, and it came out white. But it was impossible, if the correspondence and visits continued, to shut out love between two such persons. There was no doubt, moreover, that Miss Barrett's health had vastly im-proved during the acquaintance. Browning saw it, and once in love, he determined to free her from the pesti-lential, sick-room atmosphere of her home. But she would do nothing without her father's consent, a thing which she knew it was now hopeless to ask.

Mr. Barrett, in fact, was the worst of domestic ty-rants. He fancied he was doing all out of love for his daughter when, as a matter of fact, he was merely satisfying his now incurable passion for the atmosphere of the sick-room. He had grown, as Mr. Chesterton

excellently puts it, to live, "like some detestable deca-
dent poet, upon his daughter's decline." He came, says
the same writer, and "prayed over her with a kind of
melancholy glee, and with the avowed solemnity of a
watcher by a death-bed."

In the autumn of 1845, however, a solution seemed
at hand. The doctors agreed that she should go abroad.
Her brothers favored the scheme, and her sister Arabella was ready to accompany her; but her father, in
his misguided, selfish affection, did just what might
have been expected — he refused. A mild winter was
fortunately survived by Miss Barrett. The following
summer, however, Browning decided that there was
only one course, — to marry secretly and leave for
Italy. The invalid, too, was quite ready for this departure; she now saw that her father was, at least on this
one point, incurably mad. Such a step, however, was
particularly distasteful to a man of Browning's frank
nature and thorough belief in serious respectability.
Nothing disgusted him more than the Bohemian atmosphere so often associated with poets and artists. Yet
in this one instance the highest action was obviously to
break all the principles to which he had so strictly
adhered. Mr. Chesterton again expresses it forcibly:
"He had always had the courage to tell the truth, and
now it was demanded of him to have the greater courage
to tell a lie, and he told it with perfect cheerfulness
and lucidity." It is to his great credit that he did not
go on in unconventionalities, justifying step after step
by the admirable results of the first break. He remained sincerely conventional to the end.

On the 12th of September, 1846, Elizabeth Barrett
slipped quietly from the house and accompanied Brown-

ing to the Church of St. Marylebone, where they were
married. But the strain of marriage and elopement on the
same day would be, he realized, too great for his invalid
wife, so the actual escape was arranged for a week later.
It is highly characteristic of Browning that he would
not see his wife during this week; he could not bring
himself to ask at the door for *Miss* Barrett; it had
been necessary in one great instance to deceive her
father, but it was intolerable, to his frank nature, to
carry the deception into every little possibility. So,
after a week's separation, Mrs. Browning, with her
maid and faithful dog, Flush, who had the tact not to
bark, left for the last time her father's house, joined her
husband, and traveled post-haste to Paris. Mr. Barrett
never even hinted the possibility of reconciliation.

The marriage more than justified itself. Under the
blue skies of Italy Mrs. Browning rapidly recovered
her strength, and for the remainder of her life enjoyed health she had not known since childhood. During
this time Florence was the main place of residence,
though visits to other spots — chiefly Pisa, the Bagni
di Lucca, Venice, Siena, and Rome — were scattered
through the fifteen years. In the summer of 1851 the
Brownings revisited England, spent the following winter in Paris, and returned to England in 1852 and
again in 1855.   Their home in Florence was the Casa
Guidi, an old house jutting with its terrace into the
sunny square opposite the Pitti Palace. Here their
only child, Robert Barrett Browning, was born on the
9th of March, 1849.

In Mrs. Browning's letters to her friends we catch
glimpses of a very happy life; a selection will give the
general atmosphere: "We drive day by day through

the lovely Cascine, just sweeping through the city. Just such a window where Bianca Capello looked out to see the Duke go by — and just such a door where Tasso stood and where Dante drew his chair out to sit. Strange to have all that old world life about us, and the blue sky so bright." All readers of Browning know from many poems how he felt and remember the picture of his wife in *By the Fireside*, —

> " that great brow
> And the spirit-small hand propping it,
> Mutely, my heart knows how !"

In all things, indeed, save a little difference of opinion about Spiritualism, of which Browning was stoutly incredulous, the poet and his wife were surpassingly happy. "Nobody," wrote Mrs. Browning, "exactly understands him except me, who am in the inside of him and hear him breathe." Through her last illness Browning nursed her with a touching tenderness. On the 29th of June, 1861, she died quietly in his arms, with the word "Beautiful" upon her lips. Her memory was consecrated the next fall in *Prospice*, with Browning's vision of his after-life : —

> "Then a light, then thy breast,
> O thou soul of my soul ! I shall clasp thee again,
> And with God be the rest ! "

During his married life Browning was intimate with several whose names, even in so short an account, must at least be noted. At Florence he and his wife were well acquainted with Margaret Fuller Ossoli, the remarkable New England woman. In Paris they met, among others, George Sand the novelist, then at the height of her reputation, presiding among her " young

men" à *genoux bas* in her dingy salon.   There, too,
they renewed the acquaintance with Carlyle.   Others
were Dante Gabriel Rossetti, who painted Browning's
portrait; Mr. and Mrs. William Story, the Americans;
Fanny Kemble, the actress, who, as well as Thackeray
and his sister, frequented Mrs. Sartoris's salon in Rome;
Lockhart, the biographer of Scott; Tennyson and
Ruskin; and Landor with his "carnivorous laughter."

At this time, with his attention given on the one hand
to his wife and son and on the other to a new interest
in modeling, Browning had produced proportionately
little poetry. *Christmas Eve and Easter Day* (1850);
an *Essay on Shelley* (1852), his only prose work; *The
Statue and the Bust* (1855); and *Men and Women*
(1855) were the only new productions between 1846
and 1864, but in 1848 he had collected and revised
his earlier work for publication in two volumes.

Browning, with characteristic delicacy, repressed any
outward show of dejection over his wife's death.   He
refused to haunt sentimentally her grave; he would
never indeed revisit Florence.   He threw himself into
the education of his son and into his work — more especially his great work, "the Roman Murder Story."
He moved first to 19, Warwick Crescent, London,
where he was joined by his sister Sariana after their
father's death in 1866.   Browning's words to Miss
Blagden give a charming picture of himself, his father,
and his wife, and of their common affection.   "So
passed away," he says, "this good, unworldly, kind-
hearted, religious man, whose powers natural and acquired would easily have made him a notable man, had
he known what vanity or ambition or the love of money
or social influence meant. . . . He was worthy of

being Ba's [1] father — out of the whole world, only he, so far as my experience goes. She loved him — and *he* said, very recently, while gazing at her portrait, that only that picture had put into his head that there might be such a thing as the worship of the images of saints.

After this, for the most part, Browning's winters were spent in London, his summers usually along the coast of France or in Switzerland. Little by little he began to go again into society. His fame had at last become considerable, and his delightful conversation and quiet, courtly manners made him everywhere a desirable guest. A brilliant dinner party it must have been on February 12, 1864, at the house of Francis Palgrave, editor of the *Golden Treasury*, when, besides the three Palgraves, there were present Tennyson, Browning, and Gladstone. As time went on honors were heaped upon Browning. He was given honorary degrees by Oxford, Cambridge, and Edinburgh; in 1871 he was elected life governor of London University, and he was offered the rectorship of Glasgow and St. Andrew's universities and the presidency of the Wordsworth Society. In 1881 the Browning Society, more than anything else a testimony of the fame he lived to enjoy, was started by Dr. F. J. Furnivall. The effect of all this adulation, although Browning was for the most part amused, was an increase in the grotesque mannerisms which had already struck his readers. Like most men, the poet lost by over-much praise.

More than half of Browning's work was done in these last years, but only part takes rank with his earlier work; much is marked by his increasing mannerism. Among the best known are *Dramatis Personæ* (1864);

---

[1] Elizabeth Barrett.

The Ring and the Book (1868); *Balaustion's Adventure* and *Prince Hohenstiel-Schwangau* (1871); translation of the *Agamemnon* of Æschylus (1877); *Dramatic Idyls* (1879 and 1880). In 1887 he moved to 29, DeVere Gardens, Kensington Gore, where he started to arrange his father's large library and to decorate with some of his Italian treasures. The same year he published *Parleyings with Certain People*, and the day of his death, December 12, 1889, *Asolando*.

Of all these works, *The Ring and the Book* is incontestably the greatest in character as well as bulk. A short consideration of this poem, quite aside from any literary discussion, is almost necessary to an understanding of Browning's many-sided genius. Out of a little yellow Latin book, containing the evidence for the execution in 1598 of one Count Guido Franceschini, Browning received the impulse for the " Roman murder story." So much for the *Book*. But Browning saw more in the case than the mere facts; he saw the facts as presented through every conceivable witness — first the One Half-Rome, the popular rabble, with its ready sentiment; then the Other Half-Rome, the aristocracy, with its prejudices; next the *Tertium Quid*, the finical and pedantic few not in either half, the persons whose refinements reach no solution. After that the principal actors in the tragic story, then the advocates, then the Pope with his judgment, and finally the convicted with his last plea, have their say; and each makes so reasonable a case that it is only at the end that the reader finds both his reason and his best sympathy siding with Pompilia, the murdered wife. Thus out of some falsehood and much fiction Browning arrives, after taking every conceivable point of view, at the final truth of the matter. Here is the figure of the *Ring*: pure gold, truth, is unmalleable, but when mixed with alloy, the falsehood and fiction of different personalities, it can be fashioned to a ring, from which the artificer now extracts the alloy and produces "the rondure brave" of pure gold —

"Gold as it was, is, shall be evermore."

Now the great point about *The Ring and the Book*, in studying Browning's life, is the attitude of mind. This willingness — nay, this necessity — to see every side, even to champion the worst side, for the golden truth that lurks somewhere in the alloy of falsehood, characterizes most of Browning's work — except his purely lyrical or dramatic pieces. Accordingly, he speaks for Fra Lippo Lippi, for Andrea del Sarto, for Bishop Blougram, for Rabbi Ben Ezra, for Abt Vogler, even for the scoundrels, Mr. Sludge and Prince Hohenstiel-Schwangau. After all, says Rabbi Ben Ezra, "that rage was right i' the main." It would be ridiculous to hold that Browning hence agrees with all. It is rather that he believes that the greatest truths of life in its complexity exist, entangled with fiction and falsehood, in every conceivable sort of person; indeed, that it is only with fiction and falsehood that truth is given to us, and that it is the duty of the artist thus to present it, not as an unreal, dissociated ideal.

Towards the end of his life Browning turned more and more to Italy. As early as 1878 he began regularly to spend each autumn there, usually at Asolo or Venice. In the winter of 1887 he suffered from severe, recurring colds, but the next year he returned to England for the winter, and seemed to thrive on the damp cli-

mate. The summer of 1889 was particularly happy at
Asolo, where he renewed the associations of *Pippa
Passes*, first enjoyed over forty years before. In the
following winter, however, he rapidly declined — with
age rather than with sickness — and died at his son's
home, the Palazzo Rezzonico, in Venice. Westminster
Abbey claimed his body, but the loyal Venetians put
an inscription on the wall of his son's house, with the
lines from *De Gustibus* : —

> "Open my heart and you will see
> Graved inside of it 'Italy.'"

Throughout his life Browning was —

> "One who never turned his back but marched breast-forward,
>   Never doubted clouds would break,
> Never dreamed, though right were worsted, wrong would tri-
>   umph,
> Held we fall to rise, are baffled to fight better,
>   Sleep to wake."

These lines are in the last poem he wrote. "It almost
looks like bragging to say this," he is reported to have
remarked, "and as if I ought to cancel it; but it's the
simple truth; and as it's true, it shall stand." For his
was a fundamental optimism, not the careless joy that
is dashed the minute health or projects fail. His spirit
was as dauntless as that of the traveler in his *Childe
Roland ;* he himself, in this last poem, "put the slug-
horn to his lips and blew : " —

> "No, at noonday in the bustle of man's work-time
>   Greet the unseen with a cheer !
> Bid him forward, breast and back as either should be,
> 'Strive and thrive !' cry 'Speed, — fight on, fare ever
>   There as here !' "

APPENDIX

CHRONOLOGICAL TABLE

The following table attempts to give merely the chief English authors in connection with the outstanding events of their times. The period of a writer's activity, rather than the date of his birth, determines his position in the list. Those whose lives are given in the text are printed in heavy type.

AUTHORS

FOURTEENTH CENTURY

Geoffrey Chaucer, 1340–1400.
John Gower, about 1330–1408.
William Langland, about 1332 to about 1400.
John Wiclif, 1324–1384.

FIFTEENTH CENTURY

Chaucer's School : —
　Occleve, about 1370–1450.
　Lydgate, about 1370–1451.
　James I of Scotland, 1394–1437.
　Henryson, about 1430–1506.
Sir Thomas Malory, about 1430– ?.
William Dunbar, about 1450–1513.

HISTORY

EDWARD III, 1327–1377.
　Battle of Crécy, 1346.
　Battle of Poitiers, 1356.
RICHARD II, 1377–1399.
　Wat Tyler's Insurrection, 1381.
　Battle of Chevy Chase (Otterburne), 1388.

HENRY IV, 1399–1413.
　Battle of Shrewsbury, 1403.
HENRY V, 1413–1422.
　Battle of Agincourt, 1415.
　Treaty of Troyes, 1420
HENRY VI, 1422–1461.
　Jeanne d'Arc, 1429.
　Jack Cade's Rebellion, 1450.
　Constantinople taken by the Turks, 1453.
　Wars of the Roses, 1455–1485.
EDWARD IV, 1461–1483.
　Battles of Barnet and Tewkesbury, 1471.
　First printing in England, 1474.
　Lorenzo de Medici rules in Florence, 1469–1492.
RICHARD III, 1483–1485.
HENRY VII, 1485–1509.
　Discovery of America, 1492.
　Erasmus comes to England, 1498.

EARLY SIXTEENTH CENTURY

John Skelton, 1460–1529.
Sir Thomas More, 1478–1535.
William Tyndale, 1485(?)–1536.
Sir Thomas Wyatt, 1503–1542.
Henry Howard, Earl of Surrey, 1517–1547.
John Heywood, 1506(?)–1565.
Roger Ascham, 1515–1568.

ELIZABETHAN AGE

John Foxe, 1516–1587.
Raphael Holinshed, ?–1580.
Sir Thomas North, 1535(?)–1601(?).
Richard Hakluyt, 1553–1616.
Edmund Spenser, 1552–1599.
Sir Walter Ralegh, 1552(?)–1618.
Sir Philip Sidney, 1554–1586.
Richard Hooker, 1553–1600.
John Lyly, 1553(?)–1606.
Thomas Lodge, 1558(?)–1625.
Robert Greene, 1560–1592.
George Peele, 1558(?)–1598(?).
Thomas Kyd, end of 16th century.
Thomas Nash, 1567–1600(?).
Christopher Marlowe, 1564–1593.
William Shakespeare, 1564–1616.
George Chapman 1559(?)–1634.
Samuel Daniel, 1562–1619.

HENRY VIII, 1509–1547.
Battle of Flodden, 1513.
Charles V, Emperor, 1519–1556.
Diet of Worms, 1521.
Act of Supremacy, 1534.
Society of Jesuits founded, 1540.
Council of Trent, 1545.
EDWARD VI, 1547–1553.
Book of Common Prayer, 1548.
MARY, 1553–1558.
Latimer and Ridley burnt, 1555.

ELIZABETH, 1558–1603.
Acts of Supremacy and Uniformity, 1558.
Massacre of St. Bartholomew, 1572.
"The Theatre," the first English playhouse, 1576.
Drake sails round the world, 1577–1580.
Execution of Mary, Queen of Scots, 1587.
The Spanish Armada, 1588.
Battle of Ivry, 1590.
Tyrone's Rebellion, 1597.
East India Company incorporated, 1600.
Bodleian Library founded, 1602.

HISTORY

JAMES I, 1603-1625.
Gunpowder Plot, 1605.
Virginia settlement, 1607.
The Thirty Years' War, 1618-1648.
Puritan Emigration to America, 1620.
CHARLES I, 1625-1649.
Petition of Right, 1628.
Parliament dismissed, 1629.
Hampden's Trial, 1637.
Scottish Covenant, 1638.
Bishops' War, 1639.
Long Parliament called, 1640.
Theatres closed, 1642.
The Great Rebellion, 1642-1646.
Battle of Marston Moor, 1644.
Battle of Naseby, 1645.
Battle of Preston, 1648.
Execution of Charles I, 1649.
THE COMMONWEALTH, 1649-1660.
Battle of Dunbar, 1650.
Battle of Worcester, 1651.
OLIVER CROMWELL, LORD PROTECTOR, 1653-1658.
RICHARD CROMWELL, LORD PROTECTOR, 1658-1660.

AUTHORS

Michael Drayton, 1563-1631.
Francis Bacon, 1561-1626.
Ben Jonson, 1573-1637.
Thomas Dekker, early 17th century.
John Webster, early 17th century.
John Fletcher, 1579-1625.
Francis Beaumont, 1584-1616.

EARLY AND MIDDLE SEVENTEENTH CENTURY

John Donne, 1573-1631.
Robert Burton, 1577-1640.
George Herbert, 1593-1633.
Robert Herrick, 1591-1674.
Thomas Carew, 1598(?)-1639(?).
Sir John Suckling, 1609-1642.
Richard Lovelace, 1618-1658.
John Milton, 1608-1674.
Isaac Walton, 1593-1683.
Jeremy Taylor, 1613-1667.
Edmund Waller, 1606-1687.
Abraham Cowley, 1618-1667.
Samuel Butler, 1612-1680.
John Bunyan, 1628-1688.

RESTORATION

John Evelyn, 1620-1706.
Samuel Pepys, 1633-1703.
John Dryden, 1631-1700.
John Locke, 1632-1704.
Thomas Otway, 1651-1685.
William Wycherley, 1640-1715.

EIGHTEENTH CENTURY

Daniel Defoe, 1661(?)-1731.
Matthew Prior, 1664-1721.
Jonathan Swift, 1667-1745.
William Congreve, 1671-1729.
Colley Cibber, 1671-1757.
Richard Steele, 1672-1729.
Joseph Addison, 1672-1719.
Alexander Pope, 1688-1744.
John Gay, 1685-1732.
Edward Young, 1681-1765.
James Thomson, 1700-1748.
Samuel Richardson, 1689-1761.
Henry Fielding, 1707-1754.
Samuel Johnson, 1709-1784.
Lawrence Sterne, 1713-1768.

CHARLES II, 1660-1685.
Louis XIV, King of France, 1643-1715.
Plague in London, 1665.
Great Fire in London, 1666.
Triple Alliance, England, Holland, and Sweden, 1668.
Test Act, 1673.
Titus Oates — Popish Plot, 1678.
Rye House Plot, 1683.
JAMES II, 1685-1688.
Insurrection of Monmouth, 1685.
Revolution, 1688.
WILLIAM III, 1689-1702.
Battle of the Boyne, 1690.
Peter the Great, 1689-1725.

ANNE, 1702-1714.
Battle of Blenheim, 1704.
Battle of Oudenarde, 1708.
Battle of Malplaquet, 1708.
Charles XII of Sweden, 1697-1718.
Treaty of Utrecht, 1713.
GEORGE I, 1714-1727.
Jacobite Rebellion, 1715-1716.
Walpole, Prime Minister, 1721-1742.
GEORGE II, 1727-1760.
Jacobite Rebellion, 1745-1746.
Frederick the Great, 1740-1786.
Seven Years' War, 1756-1763.

HISTORY

GEORGE III, 1760–1820.
Peace of Paris, 1763.
War of American Independence, 1775–1783.
No-Popery Riots — Lord George Gordon, 1780.
Storming of the Bastille, 1789.
September Massacres in Paris, 1792.
France declared a Republic, 1792.
Execution of Louis XVI, 1793.
War of the French Republic against England, Holland, and Spain, 1793.
Reign of Terror in France, 1793–1794.
Fall of Robespierre, 1794.
Battle of the Nile, 1798.
The French Consulate, 1799–1804.
Napoleon, Emperor of France, 1804–1814.
Battle of Trafalgar, 1805.
Battle of Austerlitz, 1805.
End of the Holy Roman Empire, 1806.
Battle of Jena, 1806.
Battle of Corunna, 1809.
War between England and the United States, 1812–1814.
Napoleon's Invasion of Russia, 1812.
Battle of Leipzig, 1813.
Congress of Vienna, 1814–1815.
Battle of Waterloo, 1815.
The Holy Alliance, 1815.
Second Peace of Paris, 1815.

AUTHORS

Tobias George Smollett, 1721–1771.
David Garrick, 1717–1779.
Thomas Gray, 1716–1771.
Oliver Goldsmith, 1728–1774.
Philip Stanhope, Earl of Chesterfield, 1694–1773.
Horace Walpole, 1717–1797.
Thomas Percy, 1729–1811.
Edmund Burke, 1729–1797.
Edward Gibbon, 1737–1794.
James Boswell, 1740–1795.
Richard Brinsley Sheridan, 1751–1816.
Frances D'Arblay (née Burney), 1752–1840.
William Cowper, 1731–1800.
Thomas Chatterton, 1752–1770.
William Blake, 1757–1827.
Robert Burns, 1759–1796.

EARLY NINETEENTH CENTURY

Walter Scott, 1771–1832.
William Wordsworth, 1770–1850.
Samuel Taylor Coleridge, 1772–1834.
Robert Southey, 1774–1843.
Charles Lamb, 1775–1834.
Jane Austen, 1775–1817.
Thomas Campbell, 1777–1844.
Thomas Moore, 1779–1852.
Leigh Hunt, 1784–1859.
Walter Savage Landor, 1775–1864.
William Hazlitt, 1778–1830.
Samuel Rogers, 1763–1855.

George Gordon Noel Byron, 1788-1824.
Percy Bysshe Shelley, 1792-1822.
John Keats, 1795-1821.
Thomas De Quincey, 1785-1859.
Thomas Hood, 1798-1845.

MIDDLE AND LATE NINETEENTH CENTURY

Thomas Babington Macaulay, 1800-1859.
Bulwer Lytton, 1803-1873.
Benjamin Disraeli, 1804-1881.
Elizabeth Barrett (Browning), 1806-1861.
Charles Dickens, 1812-1870.
Thomas Carlyle, 1795-1881.
John Ruskin, 1819-1900.
John Henry Newman, 1801-1890.
Alfred Tennyson, 1809-1892.
Robert Browning, 1812-1889.
William Makepeace Thackeray, 1811-1863.
Charlotte Brontë, 1816-1855.
Charles Kingsley, 1819-1875.
Matthew Arnold, 1822-1888.
Arthur Hugh Clough, 1819-1861.
Edward Fitzgerald, 1809-1883.
Dante Gabriel Rossetti, 1828-1882.
William Morris, 1834-1896.
George Eliot (Marian Evans), 1819-1880.
Anthony Trollope, 1815-1882.
Charles Darwin, 1809-1882.
William Ewart Gladstone, 1809-1898.
Herbert Spencer, 1820-1903.
Walter Pater, 1839-1894.

GEORGE IV, 1820-1830.
War of Grecian Independence, 1821-1829.
Catholic Relief Act, 1829.
Revolution in France, 1830.

WILLIAM IV, 1830-1837.
First Steam Railroad in England, 1830.
Reform Bill passed, 1832.
Abolition of Slavery in the British West Indies, 1833.
VICTORIA, 1837-1901.
Revolution in France: Abdication of Louis Philippe, 1848.
Crimean War, 1854-1856.
Indian Mutiny of the Sepoys, 1857.
Liberation of Italy, 1860.
American Civil War, 1861-1865.
Telegraphic Communication between Great Britain and the United States, 1866.
Vatican Council, 1869.
Franco-Prussian War, 1870-1871.
Battle of Sedan, 1870.
Third French Republic established, 1871.
German Empire established, 1871.
Turco-Russian War, 1877-1878.
War in the Soudan, 1885.
Gladstone's Home Rule Bill, 1886.
Jameson Raid in South Africa, 1895.
Spanish-American War, 1898.
First Hague Peace Conference, 1898.
Boer War, 1899-1902.
Boxer Rising, 1900.

AUTHORS

George Meredith, 1828———.
Thomas Hardy, 1840———.
Algernon Charles Swinburne, 1837———.
Austin Dobson, 1840———.
Andrew Lang, 1844———.
Robert Louis Stevenson, 1845–1894.
Leslie Stephen, 1832–1904.
Rudyard Kipling, 1865———.

HISTORY

Edward VII, 1901———.
Russo-Japanese War, 1904–1905.
First Wireless Telegraph between England and America, 1907.

BIBLIOGRAPHY

BOTH for facts and for lists of the best biographies the *Dictionary of National Biography* is the most useful source. For the assistance of readers, however, to whom so comprehensive a work is not accessible there are given in the following accounts: (1) the chief biography of each man; (2) when this may be found too long, the most useful shorter biographies (not exceeding one volume each).

1. For CHAUCER the "Life" by A. W. Ward, in the *English Men of Letters Series* (1 vol.), is the most useful. It is based, of course, on the Life Records of Chaucer printed in various numbers of the Chaucer Society publications. Valuable for further reading are: "Chaucer and Some of his Friends," by G. L. Kittredge, in *Modern Philology*, i, 1; "English Wayfaring Life in the XIV Century," by Jusserand; "Fifteenth Century Prose and Verse," by A. W. Pollard.

2. For RALEGH the "Life" (2 vols.) by Edward Edwards is valuable chiefly for the letters it contains; a better and shorter life is that (1 vol.) by W. Stebbing; a careful though highly colored life is that by M. A. S. Hume. Other references: "Letters by Eminent Persons and Lives of Eminent Men," by John Aubrey; "The Life of Sir Walter Ralegh," by J. Buchan; "The Temper of the XVII Century in English Literature," by B. Wendell.

3. For SPENSER the best life is that (1 vol.) by R. W. Church, in the *English Men of Letters Series*. Other reference: "Some Landmarks in the History of English Grammar," by G. L. Kittredge.

4. For BACON the authority is "Francis Bacon and his Times" (2 vols.), by J. Spedding; briefer is the "Life" by R. W. Church, in the *English Men of Letters Series*.

5. For SHAKESPEARE the fullest life is by Sidney Lee; a shorter, excellent biography is that by Walter Raleigh. Readers are also referred to "The Development of Shakespeare as a Dramatist," by G. P. Baker.

6. For MILTON the "Life in Connexion with the History of his

Times " (6 vols.), by David Masson, is the standard ; " Autobiographical Selections," by H. Corson, is useful and interesting ; the best shorter life is by R. Garnett in the *Great Writers Series.*

7. For BUNYAN the best full account is that by John Brown ; the best short life is by Canon E. Venables in the *Great Writers Series;* and much material is furnished by Bunyan's " Grace Abounding."

8. For DRYDEN Sir Walter Scott's long account is still one of the best ; a shorter life is by G. Saintsbury in the *English Men of Letters Series.*

9. For DEFOE the " Life " by William Lee is the best ; that by William Minto in the *English Men of Letters Series* is short and excellent.

10. For SWIFT the " Life " (2 vols.) by Sir Walter Scott is still one of the best ; shorter good biographies are those by Leslie Stephen (*English Men of Letters Series*) and by John Forster ; an essay by A. S. Hill in the *North American Review* for 1868 will be found valuable.

11. For ADDISON the most comprehensive account is that (2 vols.) by Lucy Aiken. More valuable will be found the shorter lives by Dr. Johnson, Macaulay, and Thackeray, and the volume on Addison by W. J. Courthope in the *English Men of Letters Series.*

12. For POPE the best life is that by W. J. Courthope (1 vol.). A good shorter life is by Leslie Stephen in the *English Men of Letters Series.* Other references: "Pope," by De Quincey; "Pope," in the "Lives of the Poets," by Dr. Johnson ; " Pope," in the "English Humourists," by Thackeray ; and the life by A. W. Ward in the Macmillan edition of Pope's works.

13. For JOHNSON the authority is Boswell's " Life " (ed. by G. Birkbeck Hill). Shorter valuable biographies are by Leslie Stephen in the *English Men of Letters Series*, and by Macaulay in his " Essays."

14. For GOLDSMITH the best account is Washington Irving's in his " Life of Goldsmith." The " Life " by Austin Dobson, in the *Great Writers Series*, is briefer, and Macaulay's vivid little essay must not be forgotten.

15. For BURKE the fullest " Life " is that by Sir James Prior. Briefer and more valuable is that by John Morley in the *English Men of Letters Series.* An essay by Augustine Birrell in " Obiter Dicta " will be found interesting.

16. For BURNS the fullest life is that by Robert Chambers. An excellent account is that by Allan Cunningham. Good shorter biographies are to be found in the *Great Writers Series* (J. S. Blackie) and the *English Men of Letters Series* (J. C. Shairp). Better known than any of these is Carlyle's "Essay on Burns;" and almost equally valuable as an interpretation is Stevenson's "Some Aspects of Robert Burns."

17. For SCOTT the "Memoirs of the Life of Sir Walter Scott" (5 vols.), by J. G. Lockhart, is indisputably the authority — one of the greatest biographies. A shorter life by R. H. Hutton, in the *English Men of Letters Series*, is good, and the "Life" by Andrew Lang, in *Literary Lives*, is sympathetic.

For most of the writers of the early nineteenth century, especially for Wordsworth, Coleridge, Lamb, and De Quincey, the following are full of matter : H. C. Robinson's "Diary," Dorothy Wordsworth's "Journal," De Quincey's "Literary Reminiscences," and Leigh Hunt's "Autobiography." Other references are : —

18. For WORDSWORTH : "Life" (3 vols.) by W. Knight; "Memoirs of W. Wordsworth" (2 vols.), by Christopher Wordsworth; and the volume by F. W. H. Meyers in the *English Men of Letters Series.*

19. For COLERIDGE : "Life" (1 vol.) by J. Dykes Campbell; "Life" by Alois Brandl, translated by Lady Eastlake ; "Life of Sterling," by Carlyle ; "Biographia Literaria," by Coleridge himself; and the volume by H. D. Traill in the *English Men of Letters Series.*

20. For LAMB : "Life" (2 vols.) by E. V. Lucas ; the "Essays of Elia," by Lamb himself; and the volume by Canon Ainger in the *English Men of Letters Series.*

21. For DE QUINCEY : "Life and Writings" (2 vols.), by H. A. Page ; the volume by David Masson in the *English Men of Letters Series;* and "Confessions of an English Opium-Eater " and " Autobiographic Sketches," by De Quincey himself.

22. For BYRON the fullest life is that in six volumes by Thomas Moore, but it is not without serious defects. Much the best life is that (1 vol.) by the Hon. Roden Noel, in the *Great Writers Series.* Other good lives are "Lord Byron," by Karl Elze (translated by A. Napier), and "The Real Lord Byron," by J. C. Jeaffreson.

23. For SHELLEY the "Life" (2 vols.) by Edward Dowden is

the fullest and best. An interesting account is that in two volumes by Shelley's friend, T. J. Hogg. One of the best is the brief biography by W. M. Rossetti. The most useful, on the whole, is that by J. A. Symonds in the *English Men of Letters Series*.

24. For KEATS there is no exhaustive biography. The best results can probably be got from the brief account by H. Buxton Forman, in his edition of Keats's works, and from the "Letters of Keats" (published with the works). The short life of Keats by Lord Houghton must always be interesting ; and an essay by Lowell ("Literary Essays," ii) is very suggestive. The most convenient, if not wholly satisfactory, biography is that in one volume by Sidney Colvin, in the *English Men of Letters Series*.

25. For MACAULAY, as for Scott, there is an indisputable standard, the "Life and Letters" (2 vols.), by his nephew, G. O. Trevelyan. A good one-volume life is that by J. Cotter Morrison, in the *English Men of Letters Series*.

26. For CARLYLE much the most valuable matter is to be found in the voluminous correspondence of him and his wife and in the "Reminiscences" (ed. by C. E. Norton, 1887). The "Life" (2 vols.) by J. A. Froude, though not wholly trustworthy, is the fullest, and must always be depended on for much. A better, shorter life is that by R. Garnett in the *Great Writers Series;* an excellent brief account is by David Masson, in "Carlyle : Personally and in his Writings." Readers will of course note the partial autobiography in Carlyle's "Sartor Resartus."

27. For RUSKIN the authoritative life is that (in two volumes) by W. G. Collingwood, but except for the letters contained in it, it is not nearly so valuable as Ruskin's own "Præterita" (3 vols.) or the excellent one-volume account by Frederic Harrison in the *English Men of Letters Series*.

28. For ARNOLD the best references are the "Life" by G. W. E. Russell and the "Letters" (ed. by G. W. E. Russell).

29. For DICKENS John Forster has done almost as well as Lockhart for Scott and Trevelyan for Macaulay. Those for whom his "Life" (2 vols.) is too long will find excellent accounts (one volume each) by F. T. Marzials (*Great Writers Series*) and by A. W. Ward (*English Men of Letters Series*). A brilliant book is G. K. Chesterton's "Charles Dickens," and one of the most understanding is "The Childhood and Youth of Charles Dickens," by Robert Langton.

30. For THACKERAY the best lives are by H. Merivale and F.

T. Marzials (*Great Writers Series*) and by A. Trollope, in the *English Men of Letters Series*.

31. For GEORGE ELIOT the "Life and Letters" (3 vols.) by her husband, J. W. Cross, is the authoritative account, but too unqualified in its praise. Better and shorter lives are by Oscar Browning (*Great Writers Series*) and by Leslie Stephen (*English Men of Letters Series*).

32. For TENNYSON the authority is "Alfred Lord Tennyson — A Memoir by his Son" (2 vols.). A shorter life is that by Sir Alfred Lyall, in the *English Men of Letters Series*.

33. For BROWNING the "Life and Letters" by Mrs. Sutherland Orr is the fullest, but more useful and less misleading for those who have only a short time to spend on Browning are the accounts by W. Sharp (in the *Great Writers Series*) and by G. K. Chesterton (in the *English Men of Letters Series*).

BIBLIOGRAPHY

INDEX